Postwar Vietnam

Asian Voices
Series Editor: Mark Selden

ABOUT ISEAS

The Institute of Southeast Asian Studies (ISEAS) in Singapore was established as an autonomous organization in 1968. It is a regional research center for scholars and other specialists concerned with modern Southeast Asia, particularly the many-faceted problems of stability and security, economic development, and political and social change. The Institute's research programs are Regional Economic Studies (RES, including ASEAN and APEC), Regional Strategic and Political Studies (RSPS), and Regional Social and Cultural Studies (RSCS).

Postwar Vietnam

Dynamics of a Transforming Society

Edited by
Hy V. Luong

INSTITUTE OF SOUTHEAST ASIAN STUDIES, SINGAPORE
and
ROWMAN & LITTLEFIELD PUBLISHERS, INC.
Lanham • Boulder • New York • Oxford

ROWMAN & LITTLEFIELD PUBLISHERS, INC.

Published in the United States of America
by Rowman & Littlefield Publishers, Inc.
A Member of the Rowman & Littlefield Publishing Group
4501 Forbes Boulevard, Suite 200, Lanham, Maryland 20706
www.rowmanlittlefield.com

PO Box 317, Oxford OX2 9RU, United Kingdom

Copyright © 2003 by Rowman & Littlefield Publishers, Inc.

First published in Singapore in 2003 by
Institute of Southeast Asian Studies
30 Heng Mui Keng Terrace
Pasir Panjang, Singapore 119614
www.iseas.edu.sg/pub.html
ISBN 981-230-207-7
For distribution in Southeast Asia,
Australia, Japan, and India

British Library Cataloguing in Publication Information Available

Library of Congress Cataloging-in-Publication Data

Postwar Vietnam : dynamics of a transforming society / edited by Hy V.
Luong.
    p. cm.— (Asian voices)
Includes bibliographical references and index.
  ISBN 0-8476-9864-5 (cloth : alk. paper) — ISBN 0-8476-9865-3 (paper :
alk. paper)
  1. Vietnam—Social policy. 2. Vietnam—Social conditions. 3.
Vietnam—Economic policy. 4. Vietnam—Economic conditions. 5.
Vietnam—Politics and government—1945–1975. 6. Vietnam—Politics and
government—1975– I. Luong, Hy V. II. Series.
  HN700.5.A8 P67 2003
  306'.09597—dc21

                                                    2002014891

Printed in the United States of America

♾™ The paper used in this publication meets the minimum requirements of American
National Standard for Information Sciences—Permanence of Paper for Printed Library
Materials, ANSI/NISO Z39.48-1992.

Contents

Acknowledgments

I would like to thank Mark Selden for suggesting a volume on contemporary Vietnamese society and for his thoughtful comments on the entire book manuscript. I would also like to thank Susan McEachern, editor at Rowman & Littlefield, for her advice and sustained interest, Jane McGarry for her careful copyediting, and Jehanne Schweitzer for overseeing the production of the book.

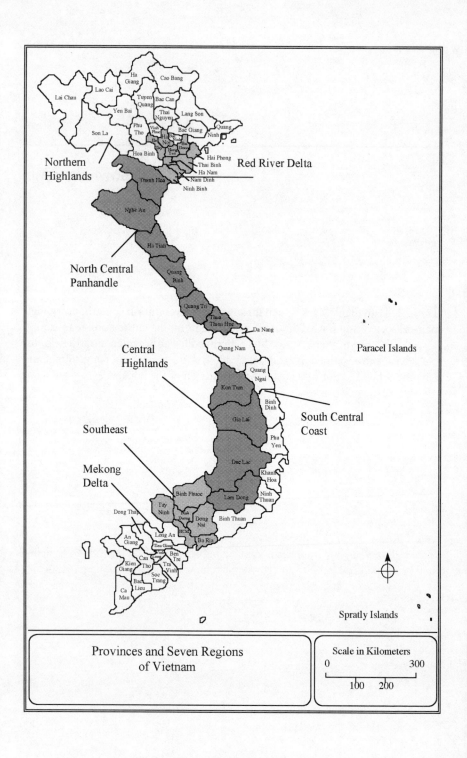

Ha Giang

Cao Bang

Lao Cai

Lai Chau

Tuyen
Quang

Bac Can

Yen Bai

Thai
Nguyen

Lang Son

Phu
Tho

Vinh
Phuc

Bac Giang

Son La

Ha
Noi

Quang
Ninh

Hoa Binh

Hai Phong

Thai Binh

Ha Nam

Thanh Hoa

Nam Dinh

Ninh Binh

**Northern
Highlands**

Red River Delta

Nghe An

Ha Tinh

**North Central
Panhandle**

Quang
Binh

Quang Tri

Thua
Thien Hue

Da Nang

Quang Nam

**Central
Highlands**

Quang
Ngai

Kon Tum

Binh
Dinh

Gia Lai

**South Central
Coast**

Phu
Yen

Paracel Islands

Dac Lac

Khanh
Hoa

Lam Dong

Ninh
Thuan

Southeast

Binh Phuoc

Tay
Ninh

Binh
Duong

Dong
Nai

Binh Thuan

**Mekong
Delta**

Dong Thap

HCM

Ba Ria

An
Giang

Long An

Tien Giang

Vinh
Long

Ben
Tre

Kien
Giang

Can
Tho

Tra
Vinh

Soc
Trang

Bac
Lieu

Ca
Mau

Spratly Islands

| Provinces and Seven Regions
of Vietnam | Scale in Kilometers
0   300
100   200 |

Introduction

Postwar Vietnamese Society: An Overview of Transformational Dynamics

Hy V. Luong

For more than half a century, in popular Western images, Vietnam has been seen as a war-ravaged and poverty-stricken country. War-ravaged, Vietnam has undoubtedly been, as two generations of Vietnamese successively fought French, American, and Chinese forces on Vietnamese soil from 1946 to 1979, and as Vietnamese troops were sent to Cambodia from 1978 to 1989. Poor, Vietnam has also been. In 1990, the gross domestic product (GDP) per capita in Vietnam was only U.S. $114. Even when we take into account the considerably lower costs of living in Vietnam, the purchasing power parity of the GDP per capita in Vietnam was less than U.S. $700 at the time.

However, in the 1990s, the Vietnamese economy grew at an average annual rate of 7.5 percent. This was achieved despite the impact of the Asian economic crisis toward the end of this decade. As a result, despite an 18 percent population growth in the 1990s, the Vietnamese GDP per capita increased from U.S. $114 in 1990 to U.S. $397 in 2000 and U.S. $414 in 2001.[1] According to the World Bank's analysis of two living standard survey data sets in Vietnam, the poverty rate declined from 58 percent in 1992–1993 to 37 percent in 1997–1998 (Vietnam and World Bank 1999: 4). These achievements are impressive in many respects. On one level, they were facilitated by the political stability and economic renovation policy (*doi moi*) adopted at the Sixth Congress of the Vietnamese Communist Party in 1986. On another, the political stability and economic reform policy are deeply embedded in the dynamics of state-society relations, which have undergone transformation themselves in the past quarter-century. In the 1970s and 1980s, resistance to the command economy took the form of foot dragging, moonlighting, greater attention to household economic activities, and refusal to sell agricultural products to the state at low state procurement prices. Resistance was considerably stronger in the southern third of Vietnam, which had been well incorporated into the world capitalist system since the days of French colonialism (see Luong 1994). This everyday resistance undermined the command economy. It triggered a major economic crisis in the late

1970s, which the Vietnamese state attempted to solve through piecemeal reforms. In the 1990s, in the context of a market economy, resistance surfaced more often in the form of open grievances and protests. Local voices and action have led the state to change its policies in various domains. It is the dynamic and dialogical relationship between Vietnamese state and society that has shaped not only the economy but also other domains of life in Vietnam in the past few decades.

HISTORICAL BACKGROUND: WAR, SOCIETY, AND POLITICAL ECONOMY

From 1946 to 1989, Vietnam suffered repeatedly from warfare, either on its own soil or in neighboring Cambodia. From 1946 to 1954, a war of national liberation from the eight-decades-long French colonialism ended in the temporary division of Vietnam into two parts, with the north allying with China and the Soviet Union, and the south coming under a strong American influence.[2] Within a decade of French military withdrawal in 1954, as unrest intensified in South Vietnam, the United States began sending combat troops to support the Saigon government against southern guerillas armed by the north. The following decade witnessed probably the most violent war in Vietnamese history, as the United States undertook massive bombing of North Vietnam, and of the parts of South Vietnam and neighboring Laos and Cambodia under the control of Vietnamese Communist forces and/or their Laotian and Cambodian allies. From 1965 to 1973, U.S. planes dropped over 7.5 million tons of bombs on Vietnam, Laos, and Cambodia. It was equal to the explosive force of over 700 Hiroshima-type atomic bombs (Harrison 1982: 3).

The reduction of U.S. support for its ally in South Vietnam after the 1973 Paris peace agreement precipitated the collapse of the Saigon government in 1975, leading to the unification of Vietnam in 1976. However, peace was shortlived as a former ally of North Vietnam, the Khmer Rouge (Communists), took control of Cambodia and resorted to military means to solve border disputes with Vietnam and Thailand. Vietnam sent troops to Cambodia in December 1978, overthrew the Khmer Rouge government, and maintained a military presence in Cambodia to support a Vietnamese-installed government (see Chanda 1986). China launched a brief invasion of Vietnam in 1979 in response to the Vietnamese overthrow of its protégé Communist government in Cambodia, highlighting the powerful force of nationalism in modern international politics and exposing the fallacy of the concept of monolithic Communism underlying the original U.S. involvement in Vietnam. The United States and China subsequently supported an armed coalition of Marxist guerillas and King Sihanouk's anticommunist supporters against Vietnamese forces and the Vietnam-supported Cambodian government. The United States also led a trade embargo on Vietnam until 1994. In contrast to the end of the war in Japan and many parts of Southeast Asia in 1945, in China in 1949, and in Korea in 1953, Vietnam's war footing did not really end until its troop withdrawal from Cambodia in 1989. And in contrast to the significant aid that assisted in the postwar reconstruction of many war-torn Asian countries, including Japan and Korea, Vietnam had to rebuild from decades of ruinous wars from 1975 to the early 1990s in the context of the end of Chinese aid, a significant reduction in Soviet and East European aid, and under the impact of a U.S.-led trade embargo.

The prolonged warfare in Vietnam had major impacts on the Vietnamese environment, society, culture, and economy. In terms of environmental impact, in South Vietnam alone, according to one estimate, 10 million hectares of cultivated land and five million hectares of forests were damaged, many defoliated with the highly toxic Agent Orange, while in the north, all the railways, bridges, industrial centers, main roads, and sea and river ports were destroyed or seriously damaged during the U.S. bombing (Gough 1990: 3–4, see also Lewallen 1971).

Prolonged warfare also had diverse and at times contradictory impacts on Vietnamese society. On one level, it inflicted major casualties and caused demographic imbalance in all parts of Vietnam. For the 1965–1975 period alone, it is estimated that 800,000 to 1,200,000 Vietnamese died in the war (Hirschman, Preston, and Vu Manh Loi 1995).[3] The higher number of war deaths among men contributed to a demographic imbalance. According to the Vietnamese 1979 census data, for five-year interval cohorts born between 1915 and 1954 and reaching adulthood during the Franco-Vietnamese and American war periods, there were only between seventy-eight and ninety men for every one hundred women (Banister 1993: 9).

Protracted wars led many Vietnamese to accept the state's call for personal sacrifice and many state-imposed measures to transform the economy and society. With the overwhelming majority of Vietnamese living in the countryside during the various wars from 1946 to 1989, land reform was the most important. In the Franco-Vietnamese war, for example, the Vietnamese Communist Party and the Communist-led government under Ho Chi Minh issued a number of resolutions and decrees between 1948 and 1952, including resolutions to:

- lower land rent and loan interest, as well as to abolish secondary rents (gifts to landlords at New Year's and other occasions);
- abolish pre-1945 loans and loans whose interest payments had doubled the principal;
- distribute French, French collaborators', landlord-abandoned, and communal land to poor peasants (Lam Quang Huyen 1985: 24–25; Hoang Uoc 1968: 58ff).

In the northern half of the country, 302,739 hectares of cultivable land had been distributed by April 1953 (Hoang Uoc 1968: 70–71). In the southern half of the country, Ho Chi Minh's government redistributed over 750,000 hectares of land during the Franco-Vietnamese war. Of this amount, 564,547 hectares of land that belonged to large landowners seeking refuge in French-controlled urban areas were redistributed to poor peasants in the southern third of Vietnam, where land ownership was heavily concentrated and where two-thirds of rural households were estimated to be landless (Lam Quang Huyen 1985: 25).[4] These measures helped to consolidate the support of poorer peasants for the war. As the redistributed land belonged to French or absentee Vietnamese landowners (including those seeking refuge in French-controlled areas), the land redistribution did not impose heavy political costs on the anti-French national liberation movement.

Nor was land reform limited to the areas under the control of a Communist-led government. In response to the land policy of the Vietnamese Communist Party, the Saigon government subsequently launched two major land reform campaigns to reduce socioeconomic inequality in South Vietnam: the 1956 reform limiting holdings of rice land to 100 hectares, and the 1970 reform reducing them further to 15 hectares in the more fertile southern third, and to 5 hectares in the more densely populated central coast. Between 1956 and 1972, 1,884,037 hectares of rice fields were distributed to almost 1.3 million households in South Vietnam (Lam Thanh Liem 1995: 70, 78–79; Nguyen Thu Sa 1990: 144).

Other factors associated with war contributed to different patterns of population dislocation and socioeconomic stratification throughout the country. In the southern part of Vietnam, rural-to-urban migration increased dramatically, especially during the American war, as war raged on in rural and mountainous areas and as cities were under firmer U.S. and Saigon-government control and relatively less affected by warfare. It is estimated that the urban population of South Vietnam increased from 2.8 million (20 percent of the South Vietnamese population) in 1958 to 8 million (43 percent of the population) in 1971 (Thrift and Forbes 1986: 125). The urban population in the Saigon area correspondingly increased from 2.3 million to 3.5 million (125). In contrast, in North Vietnam, as U.S. bombing intensified from 1965 onward and targeted particularly urban and industrial centers (96), the urban population of North Vietnam dropped from 2.1 million (11 percent of the North Vietnamese population) in 1965 to 1.8 million (8.4 percent of the population) in 1970 (89). Corresponding figures are not available for Hanoi for the same period, but according to one estimate, the population of Hanoi dropped from .9 million in 1961 to .71 million in 1970 (89).

In the southern part of Vietnam, the war-related massive rural-to-urban flow led to uncontrolled urbanization, with an estimated 1.5 million Saigon residents living in slums (153). At the opposite end of the socioeconomic spectrum, many elite and middle-class members in areas under the control of the Saigon government benefited from massive foreign aid and troop presence to maintain comfortable or even luxurious living conditions for themselves. Socioeconomic gaps became glaring in Saigon and many other southern cities under the control of the Saigon government. Consequently, despite the aforementioned land reform campaigns in 1956 and 1970 under the Saigon government, socioeconomic inequality across the rural-urban divide and within rural and urban areas in the south was still considerably greater than that in the north.

In North Vietnam, ideologically, war footing facilitated at least a temporary acceptance of a shared poverty and the ideological emphasis on relative equality in both rural and urban communities and in the North Vietnamese population at large. Across the rural-urban divide, as more urban intellectuals and cadres or their children went to the countryside to avoid U.S. bombing and depended more on rural populations at the height of the U.S. bombing campaign, this fostered a greater rural-urban solidarity and reduced the urban-rural gap during the war. War hardships provided an additional rationale, besides that of economic construction needs, for the North Vietnamese state to push for a simplification of such rites of passage as weddings and funerals (see Malarney, this volume and 2002, and Luong 1993b and 1994). The mobilization of millions of men into armed services also facilitated women's greater access to public power behind the front line. For example, the percentage of woman deputies in the North Vietnamese National Assembly increased from 2.5 percent in 1946 to 32.3 percent in 1976.

Warfare also had differential effects on South and North Vietnamese politics. Governments in both parts of Vietnam used the war as a major reason to clamp down on public dissent and to exercise a heavy censorship of the press. However, in the areas under the control of the United States and the Saigon government, the need to maintain an appearance of democracy as a U.S. ally left a small space for moderate and alternative voices, most notably those of the third force as distinct from both the Saigon government and the Communist-controlled National Liberation Front of South Vietnam (later called the Provisional Revolutionary Government of South Vietnam). In the north, as Marr discusses in depth in his chapter in this volume, all the private print shops and publishing houses had been nationalized by 1960. The outrage in North Vietnam at U.S. bombing and the heavy dependence of most members of the population on state-controlled employment and other resources also led to the absence of noticeable public dissent between 1957 and 1975.

More generally and on a broader comparative scale within the Asian regional context, the mobilization efforts and the emphasis on solidarity during wartime in North Vietnam rendered impractical any state plan for a radical and divisive transformation of society as in China in the 1950s and 1960s. Class warfare against former landlords and capitalists did not last as long in Vietnam, and intellectuals were not denounced or persecuted as during China's Cultural Revolution in the 1960s (Chan, Kerkvliet, and Unger 1999: 9). Of the two major political purges within the Marxist-Leninist political system in North Vietnam, that of cadres from well-off families during the land reform in the mid-1950s was shortlived, as the top Communist Party leadership acknowledged land reform errors in 1956. The second and less well-known purge involved the imprisonment, starting in 1964 and reaching its peak in 1967, of a small number of senior officials suspected of being pro-Soviet in the aftermath of the Sino-Soviet split (Vu Thu Hien 1996, Thanh Tin 1994: 189–91, 371–88, Boudarel 2002: 136–40). None of the pro-Soviet suspects among ranking party officials was killed, while some were rehabilitated in the aftermath of the Sino-Vietnamese war in 1979 and Vietnam's closer alliance with the Soviet Union in the second half of the 1970s and in the 1980s.[5]

The most intense period of warfare, when the United States was involved, also had differential direct economic impacts on different parts of Vietnam. In the south, war had the strongest adverse impact on agriculture. The raging war in the countryside led to land abandonment and the decline in paddy output from over 5 million tons in 1962–1964 to the nadir of 4.3 million tons in 1968 (Tran van Tho et al. 2000: 247).[6] In the north where industries were more heavily concentrated, as the massive U.S. bombing focused more on the transportation system and industrial-urban centers, industrial production was heavily damaged. Cement production, for example, dropped from an average of 594,500 tons in 1964–1965 to the nadir of 70,000 tons in 1968, and never got above 400,000 tons before 1975 (257–58). At the height of U.S. bombing, industrial production facilities and equipment were significantly dispersed, leading to more local adaptations and probably greater decentralization than in China at the time (Thrift and Forbes 1986: 77–79). War had lesser effects on agricultural production in the north as the northern dyke system was not systematically targeted by U.S. bombing. The aid from China, the Soviet Union, and other socialist countries amounted to 20–50 percent of the annual gross national product (GNP) of North Vietnam in the 1965–1975 period (Tran van Tho et al. 2000: 119). It helped to mitigate the economic impact of U.S. bombing and to sustain the flow of materials to anti-U.S. forces in the south.

Despite the diverse impacts of wars on different regions of Vietnam, the victory of the Communist-led cause at the end of the American war in 1975 reinforced the Vietnamese Communist leadership's confidence in their ideology and command-economy model of development, which had been applied to the northern half of Vietnam from 1954 to 1975. It was a model that sought to achieve rapid industrialization and economic development through state control of key resources (raw materials, labor, and capital) and marketing of output (through the state's trading network) (de Vylder and Fforde 1988: 10, 26, 61; Fforde and Paine 1987: 1). The economy had three main sectors: state, cooperative, and household. In the state's ideological vision, the state sector was to play the leading role in the economy, especially in industries and services. The cooperative sector dominated agriculture: the percentage of households belonging to cooperatives increased from 86 percent in 1960 to 96 percent in the 1970–1975 period (Vu Tuan Anh and Tran thi Van Anh 1997: 75). If in 1960, almost 90 percent of the cooperatives were still low-level ones where members' incomes depended partly on their labor input and partly on their land and farm equipment contributions, by 1975, the percentage of low-level cooperatives had dropped to less than 10 percent. The percentage of high-level cooperatives where members' incomes depended solely on their labor input had increased to over 90 percent (75). In rural northern Vietnam, the household sector survived in the form of household handicraft production and household garden plots. The total acreage of garden plots exceeded the official limit of 5 percent of a cooperative's land in many localities (Kerkvliet and Selden 1999: 105). These plots accounted for approximately 30 percent of rural households' incomes (79).[7]

In the north, after 1975, the government pushed for larger agricultural cooperatives and for the district as a basic agro-industrial unit (Werner 1988). The size of agricultural cooperatives in the north increased from an average of 199 households and 113 hectares in 1975 to that of 368 households and 201 hectares in 1980 (Chu van Lam 1990: 104). In the south, the government tightened its control of the economy by nationalizing large private industrial enterprises, clamping down on compradors, and pushing for agricultural collectivization. When the wage-and-price control of the wartime period was imposed on the southern economy, with the state price for rice dropping as low as 10 percent of the black market price in 1979, peasants in the Mekong delta withheld rice from the state commercial system. The government's food procurement steadily dropped from 950,000 metric tons in 1976 to 398,800 metric tons in 1979, not because of any significantly lower paddy or food production in 1979, but because of the declining purchasing prices for foods and the shortage of desirable consumer goods from the government available to agricultural producers (Ngo Vinh Long 1988: 170–71; Fforde 1999: 56).[8] The failure of a procurement system based on wage-and-price controls aggravated the food and paddy shortage and led to the partial replacement of rice by other cereals in urban areas in the late 1970s, which numerous urban residents of the period can still vividly recall after two decades. As another sign of deep-seated difficulties of the command economy, the majority of cooperatives formed in the south after 1975 had collapsed by 1980 (Kerkvliet and Selden 1999: 109; Lam Quang Huyen 1985: 191–92). If by the end of 1979, the government had formed 1,286 cooperatives and 15,309 labor exchange teams, by the end of 1980, there remained only 137 cooperatives and 3,739 labor exchange teams, mostly in the parts of the central Vietnamese coast where there had existed a long tradition of communal land before the twentieth century and where the Vietnamese Communist Party enjoyed relatively strong support during the French and American wars.

The command economy model encountered difficulties not merely in agriculture and not only in the southern third of Vietnam. In many northern agricultural cooperatives, after 1975, there was a vicious cycle of enlarged cooperative membership due to population growth, lower returns on cooperative labor input, members' greater attention to their household garden plots, and declining or essentially stagnating agricultural productivity from cooperative land (Luong 1992: 204). In certain localities, officials reexperimented with the household contract system that had been introduced in Vinh Phu province in 1968, at the height of the American war (202–3). The system provided incentives for households as contractors to invest more labor and other input into the contracted land by allowing them to keep a part of the surplus above specified production targets.

The local and officially unsanctioned experiments with the household contract system in agriculture in the late 1970s paralleled similar experiments in handicraft production. In the well-known northern ceramic center of Bat Trang, for example, as early as 1969, the state firm contracted out to 100 workers and their families two specific tasks (moulding and trimming) in order to allow workers to supplement their incomes and to meet the state's production targets. The range of contracted tasks and the number of contracting households increased over the years. By 1977, the contract system had evolved to the point that the firm delivered raw materials, provided bricks for the construction of household kilns, received final products, and paid contractors for their labor. The number of family kilns had increased to at least 218 by 1978. The number of contracted products increased steadily from 200,000 semi-products in 1969 to 8.5 million products in 1978, accounting for more than 25 percent of the state firm's total and official output (Luong 1993a: 124–25). More importantly, in both the agricultural and industrial sectors, an increasing percentage of products ended up in the open market as state procurement prices were kept artificially low. The resulting shortage of foods and industrial goods in the state commercial system and their availability on the open market at considerably higher prices contributed to the erosion of the purchasing power of cadres' and state workers' salaries on the one hand and de facto inflation in the economy on the other. Between 1976 and 1980, the purchasing power of state employees' salaries declined by 49 percent (Tran van Tho et al. 2000: 242). This decline in living standards took place on top of the decline of approximately 25 percent in the purchasing power of state salaries in the 1960–75 period (Fforde and Paine 1987: 93–95). While in order to supplement their incomes, a number of state workers could obtain contracts from their firms for work outside official factory hours, or engaged in other sideline production activities, many others and urban civil servants could not. Hanoi residents can still vividly recall numerous state employees raising chickens or even pigs in open-air apartment building hallways or even in the overcrowded apartments themselves in order to compensate for the declining purchasing power of their state salaries. As salaries steadily lost purchasing power, the microeconomic incentives for workers accordingly declined, contributing to a 4 percent decline in industrial output in 1979 and an additional 19 percent decline in 1980 (Tran van Tho et al. 2000: 293). De facto annual inflation rate varied between 18 percent and 25 percent in the 1976–1980 period (273).

Agricultural production achieved only 68.5 percent of the production target set in the rosy five-year economic plan of 1976–1980. Output in specific industries achieved only 37–80 percent of the production targets set out in this plan. GNP increased annually by an average of .4 percent, in comparison to the target of 13–14 percent annual increase (Tran van Tho et al. 2000: 140). The 1976–1980 economic plan was in tatters, and by the end of the 1970s, the Vietnamese command economy was in a major crisis. Many local units or individuals adapted by fence breakings and a greater reliance on the informal market, further undermining the state and cooperative sectors of the economy.

SOCIOCULTURAL DYNAMICS AND ECONOMIC RENOVATION

The Process and Results of Economic Renovation

The Vietnamese state adapted to the economic crisis in the late 1970s by providing more material incentives for local units and producers, while still adhering to the command economy vision for the country. In agriculture, starting in 1981, cooperatives could enter into 2-to-5-year contracts with households for the tasks of rice planting, crop tending, and harvest, which accounted for 70 percent of labor input in agricultural production. The cooperative still provided for plowing, irrigation and drainage work, the spreading of fertilizer and seeds, and the spraying of insecticide. Cultivators could retain the surpluses above specified production targets. The state also increased its purchase price for paddy to a level only slightly below the local market price.

Similarly in industries, in 1981 the state allowed state enterprises to procure raw materials on the open market; to use surplus labor, materials, and equipment to produce beyond the state's specified targets; and to sell their products directly to other parties at mutually agreed prices. These prices were considerably higher than state-set prices. According to the three-plan production system, in plan A, a state enterprise utilized the materials supplied by the state to meet the state's production target. Fifty percent of the profits were retained by the enterprise, and 50 percent delivered to the state. In plan B, the enterprise obtained materials from sources other than the supervising agency in order to manufacture products in its main lines, and it marketed them at mutually agreed prices. The percentage of profit retained by the enterprise from plan B increased to 60 percent. In plan C, the enterprise might produce other items and sell them to other parties at negotiated prices. It could keep 90 percent of the profit from these secondary lines of products. As long as a state firm fulfilled its obligations toward the state under plan A, it could engage in plan-B and plan-C production without having to obtain permission from the supervising agency (Luong 1993a: 127–28).

As a result of greater material incentives for producers, agricultural production increased by an annual average of 6 percent in the 1981–1985 period, while the annual rates of industrial growth exceeded 8 percent. Annual GDP growth averaged more than 6 percent from 1981 to 1985 (Tran van Tho et al. 2000: 293). However, the state still adhered to a command model of the economy. It still pushed for collectivization and for a dominant role of the state sector in the economy. In the southern half of Vietnam, the number of labor exchange teams and cooperatives increased respectively from 3,732 and 173 in 1980 to 35,853 and 622 by the end of 1985 (Chu van Lam et al. 1992: 48; Lam Thanh Liem 1995: 136–37). As late as November 1984, in the southern center of ceramic production in Bien Hoa, the municipal government exerted intense pressure on the remaining private firms to form cooperatives (Luong 1993a: 119).

However, as the state increased its procurement prices, and as agricultural and industrial producers could sell any output above state- or cooperative-specified quotas at mutually agreed prices, annual inflation rates crept into the 50–92 percent range in the 1981–1985 period. Despite salary adjustments, the purchasing power of state employees' salaries declined by more than 50 percent between 1981 and the third quarter of 1985 (Tran van Tho et al. 2000: 242, 273). The state's increase of salaries and money supply, in conjunction with price reforms and currency exchange in September 1995, reduced confidence in the value of new currency and led to the galloping inflation rate of 775 percent in 1986. The command economy faced a profound crisis. The U.S.-led trade embargo on Vietnam and the loss of Chinese aid since the late 1970s exacerbated the crisis but did not play determining roles.

In response to the deep economic crisis in the mid-1980s, the Vietnamese Communist Party endorsed the policy of economic renovation (*doi moi*) at its Sixth Party Congress in December 1986, shifting away from the command economy model toward a market system. As widely recognized in scholarly circles, the policy shift took place in the context of an ongoing market formation process within Vietnam since the late 1970s (Beresford, this volume; Fforde and de Vylder 1996; Ljunggren 1993; Dang Phong and Beresford 1998). Fforde and de Vylder have cogently argued that, while influenced by foreign aid cuts in 1978–1979 and 1989–1990 (following the conflict with China and the difficulties in the Soviet Union), economic policy reforms in Vietnam were mainly determined by internal factors (15).[9]

By 1989, a number of fundamental reforms had been implemented. First was the elimination of the two-priced system (state prices, associated with the rationing system, and market prices), with the exception of services under a handful of government monopolies.[10] Second was the sanctioning of private and joint state-private firms, including 100 percent foreign-owned ones as specified in the foreign investment law of 1987. The Vietnamese economy has since officially included five sectors: state, cooperative, household, private, and joint state-private.[11]

The balance among those five economic sectors has shifted significantly since the onset of economic reforms. In agriculture, the reforms in 1988 allowed households to decide on their own production and product distribution within the context of market prices for input such as fertilizers and for crop output. Agricultural cooperatives, to the extent that they remain, have provided only selected services (such as irrigation, plowing) to cultivators. In industries, in 1989, real positive interest rates (above the rate of inflation) were introduced. While this was temporarily reversed in 1990–1991 due to the increase in inflation, it constituted a part of the larger trend of reducing capital, material, and food price subsidies to state enterprises and allowing them more autonomy in production and product distribution. The number of industrial state enterprises dropped from 3,092 in 1988, to 2,030 in 1993, and to 1,821 in 1998 (table I.1).[12] The number of industrial cooperatives suffered a sharper decline, from 32,034 in 1988 to 949 in 1998. The number of state industrial workers correspondingly dropped from 843,800 in 1988 to 745,028 in 1998, while industrial cooperative employment declined from 1,177,800 to 76,274 in the same period. In contrast, the number of private domestic enterprises increased from 318 in 1988 to 5,714 in 1998; those with foreign capital, from 1 to 830; and handicraft households, from 318,557 to 553,043 in the same period. In 1998, the combined number of private industrial workers (including those in foreign enterprises) and household handicraft workers stood at 1,847,777, in comparison to 923,000 in 1988 (table I.1; see also Do Hoai Nam 1994: 105, 107). The state sector, playing a major role mainly in manufacturing and selected services such as utilities, telecommunication, and petroleum distribution, accounted for only 38–40 percent of the GDP for most of the 1990s (table I.2).

Table I.1.   Relative Strength of State, Cooperative, Private, and Household Sectors in
Industrial Production in Vietnam, 1988–1998

	1988	1993	1998
State industrial enterprises	3,092	2,030	1,821
Industrial cooperatives	32,034	5,287	949
Private domestic enterprises	318	3,322	5,714
Enterprises with foreign capital	1	n/a	830
Handicraft households	318,557	452,866	553,043
State industrial workers	843,800	706,200	745,028
Industrial cooperative members	1,117,800	287,000	76,274
Workers in private/household enterprises	923,000	n/a	1,847,777

Sources: Tran Hoang Kim and Le Thu 1992: 33; Vietnam-General Statistical Office 1995: 31, 212, 216, 219, 223;
Vietnam-General Statistical Office 1992: 13; Vietnam-General Statistical Office 1999b: 49, 53, 58, 99, 104.

In the 1990s, markets strongly developed for land, labor, and capital in Vietnam. Despite the legal requirement that land remain under state and collective ownership, a land market had developed in urban areas and in the southern third of rural Vietnam by 1990. Even in the agricultural village of Khanh Hau in the upper Mekong delta in southern Vietnam (one of my field sites for longitudinal study), in late 1991, a hectare of land along the national highway was sold for U.S. $25,000–$33,000, given its nonagricultural use potential, in contrast to the price of approximately U.S. $4,100 for a hectare of paddy field with little nonagricultural potential. Ten years later, the price for a hectare of paddy field along the national highway rose to U.S. $81,000–$130,000. Land right transfer has been recognized by local governments. Since 1990, labor has freely migrated in search of better wages and employment conditions. While an informal capital market had long existed in Vietnam in the form of credit associations, a formal capital market, including a small stock market established in July 2000, has developed.

Since the implementation of the major components of the 1986 economic reform policy by 1989 and in the context of relatively stable political conditions in comparison to the Soviet Union and Eastern Europe, Vietnam has achieved generally remarkable successes on the economic front:

1. Economic growth averaged 8 percent annually in the 1990–1997 period. Even during the Asian economic crisis, the Vietnamese economy still grew at the average annual rate of 5.8 percent. This growth was partly fueled by the increase in export, from 2.4 billion U.S. dollars in 1990 to 14.3 billion in 2000 and 15 billion in 2001. Vietnam not only increased the export of primary products (oil, coal, seafoods, rice, coffee, rubber), but it also kept labor costs low to attract foreign direct investments (FDI) and began exporting labor-intensive industrial products such as garments and footwear (see table I.2). These two industrial products made up 23 percent of the Vietnamese export in 2001.[13]

The economic growth helped to raise the GDP per capita from U.S. $114 in 1990 to U.S. $397 in 2000 and U.S. $414 in 2001 (Vietnam-General Statistical Office 2001a: 105; Thoi Bao Kinh Te Viet Nam 2002: 48–52). It contributed to the reduction in the poverty rate from 58 percent in 1992–1993 to 37 percent in 1997–1998. It has been heralded by international economic institutions as a remarkable success in poverty reduction.

2. Economic growth in Vietnam was based on the steady increase in investments from 1986 to 1996, and the relative stability in absolute investments in the 1997–2000 period (table I.2). As nonstate domestic investments leveled off in the second half of the 1990s, and since FDI declined after 1997, the state played a more important role in stimulating the economy toward the end of the 1990s. Its share of total investments increased from 38 percent in 1995 to 62 percent in 2000.

The growth in nonstate domestic and foreign direct investments was facilitated by: the shift to a market economy more conducive to the participation by nonstate domestic and international businesses; relative macroeconomic and political stability; and the loosening and eventual end of U.S.-led trade sanctions against Vietnam in 1994 and Vietnam's generally stronger relations with other countries in the region and the world. As a reflection of macroeconomic stability, the annual rate of inflation declined from 775 percent in 1986 to 67 percent in 1990–1991, to an average of 12.4 percent in the 1992–1995 period, and an average of 3.4 percent from 1996 to 2000. And in contrast to some other Association of Southeast Asian Nations (ASEAN) countries such as Indonesia and the Philippines, Vietnam was politically stable in the 1990s. In the international political arena, after Vietnam withdrew its troops from Cambodia in 1989, its political relations with other countries in the Asia-Pacific region and the world generally improved, facilitating trade, foreign direct investments, and development assistance. The U.S. trade embargo against Vietnam ended in 1994. Vietnam joined the Association of Southeast Asian Nations in 1995 and the Asia-Pacific Economic Council (APEC) in 1998. The annual disbursement of overseas development assistance (ODA) steadily grew from 413 million U.S. dollars in 1993 to 1.7 billion dollars in 2000 and 2001, facilitating a greater investment by the Vietnamese state in the economy, as domestic and international private investments either leveled off or even declined from 1995 onward. The ODA flow and the investment by the Vietnamese state helped to reduce the impact of FDI decline and to sustain economic growth at an annual average rate of 6.5 percent in the 1997–2001 period in the face of the Asian economic crisis.

The relatively strong economic growth with the shift toward the market economy and in the context of relative political stability in Vietnam bears fundamental similarities to the Chinese reform experiences and diverges from the paths of transformation in the former Soviet Union and Eastern Europe. However, Vietnamese economic reforms seem to have been shaped to a greater extent by historically conditioned bottom-up societal pressures than those in China. As a result of the division of the country between 1954 and 1975, almost half of the Vietnamese population had had very limited experiences with the command economy model of North Vietnam by the time the economic reform policy was adopted. In the fertile Mekong delta of the south, which had been well incorporated into the world capitalist system since the days of French capitalism, the strong resistance of cultivators to collectivization and to the command economy model considerably deepened the procurement crisis faced by the state and aggravated the food shortages in urban areas in the late 1970s.

Not unlike its Chinese counterpart, the Vietnamese state adopted initial reform measures in a piecemeal fashion (Perry and Wong 1985: 14; Fforde and de Vylder 1996). However, the Vietnamese state moved more slowly in sanctioning market mechanisms and implementing measures of transition toward a market system. In agriculture, for example, while China sanctioned the experiment with the household responsibility system in 1978 and moved quickly to return land cultivation rights to households by 1982, the Vietnamese state did not sanction the experiment until 1981 and did not return land cultivation rights to households until 1988 (Kerkvliet and Selden 1999: 110).

However, once the economic renovation policy was adopted, the move toward market mechanisms seemed more complete in Vietnam. In the 1990s, the cooperative sector had virtually collapsed, and the Vietnamese economy faced fewer state constraints in agriculture, industries, and services than its Chinese counterpart (Fforde 1999). The relatively stronger pressure on the command economy and the more complete move to a market system probably result from a shorter period of command economy at least in half of Vietnam and the stronger presence of an informal market economy in northern Vietnam than in China. The reasons for China's faster economic growth in the 1990s deserve a more systematic investigation, but the greater flow of investment capital from overseas Chinese and from Hong Kong, and these investors' knowledge of global business practices, might have played an important role. Certain differences notwithstanding, in both China and Vietnam, the move toward a market economy, economic growth, the stronger integration into the global market, and a reduced role of the state have had major impacts on society and state-society relations.

Society, the State, and Economic Renovation

In Vietnam, economic growth, the strong integration of the Vietnamese economy into the global market system, and the more selective role of the state have imposed many costs on the environment, increased the vulnerability of producers to the wide fluctuation in global market prices, and significantly exacerbated inequalities along the urban-rural axis, and along regional, class, and ethnic lines. They have also made more complicated the move toward gender equality.

Digregorio, Rambo, and Yanagisawa (this volume) discuss the increasing environmental problems rooted in the Vietnamese trajectory of economic growth in

Table I.2. Growth in Vietnamese GDP Per Capita, Export, and Investments, 1990–2001

	1990	1991	1992	1993	1994	1995	1996	1997	1998	1999	2000	2001
GDP per capita (in U.S. $)	114	117	143	190	237	291	337	360	355	374	397	414
State share of GDP (%)	32	31	34	38	40	40	40	40	40	39	39	39
Export												
Value (Billion U.S. $)	2.4	2.1	2.6	3	4.1	5.4	7.3	9.2	9.4	11.6	14.3	15.1
Oil (Million tons)	2.6	3.9	5.4	6.2	6.9	7.7	8.7	9.6	12.1	14.9	15.5	17
Coal (Million tons)	.8	1.2	1.6	1.4	2.1	2.8	3.6	3.5	3.2	3.3	3.3	4.3
Seafoods (Million U.S. $)	239	285	308	427	551	621	697	782	858	974	1475	1778
Rice (Million tons)	1.6	1	1.9	1.7	2	2	3	3.6	3.7	4.5	3.5	3.6
Coffee (1000 tons)	90	94	116	123	176	248	284	392	382	482	734	931
Rubber (1000 tons)	76	63	82	97	135	138	194	194	191	265	280	308
Garments (Million U.S. $)	214	117	190	239	476	850	1160	1503	1450	1747	1892	1975
Footwear (Million U.S. $)	8.3	0	5	68	122	296	530	978	1031	1387	1472	1560
Electronics (Million U.S. $)	0	0	0	0	0	0	0	0	0	585	790	605

	1990	1991	1992	1993	1994	1995	1996	1997	1998	1999	2000	2001
% Agriculture & Forestry (including seafoods)	47.8	52.2	49.5	48.4	48.1	46.2	42.3	35.3	35.5	32.7	30.1	33.4
Minerals & Heavy industry	25.7	33.4	37	34	28.8	25.3	28.7	28	27.9	31	35.6	30.6
Manufactured goods	26.4	14.4	13.5	17.6	23.1	28.5	29	36.7	36.6	26.3	34.3	36
Investment												
Annual total (Billion U.S. $)	1.4	1.4	2.2	4	5.1	6.6	7.9	9.2	8.7	9.4	10.2	11
% of GDP	18.1	17.6	22.4	30.1	30.4	31.6	32.1	34.6	32.4	32.8	32.9	33.7
Sources (in %):												
• State	40	38	35	44	38	42	49	49	56	59	58	58
• Non-state-domestic	47	48	44	31	31	28	25	23	24	24	24	24
• FDI	13	14	21	25	30	30	26	28	21	17	19	18

Source: Thoi Bao kinh te Viet Nam 2001: 52-54; Thoi Bao Kinh te Viet Nam 2002: 48-52; Vietnam-General Statistical Office 2001a: 97, 106, 105, 172, 201, 204, 206; 2002: 55, 319, 370, 378–79.

the 1990s: deforestation, loss of biological diversity, and land degradation; the pollution of air and water sources due to urbanization, the increasing consumption of fuel, the increasing amount of untreated household wastewater as well as industrial wastes dumped into rivers and canals; the increase in health risks for those reasons and due to the rather indiscriminate use of agricultural chemicals on crops and fruits; and the threat to the long-term sustainability of economic growth. Ho Chi Minh City, for example, daily generates between 800,000 and 1 million cubic meters of wastewater, 80 percent of which is from household sources, and which is flushed into rivers and canals without treatment.

Despite many successes, the Vietnamese economy remains beset by problems associated with the global market. As Vietnam is linked more closely to the world capitalist system, the widely fluctuating prices of many export commodities such as rice, coffee, coal, and oil have dealt heavy blows to producers. As coffee production in Vietnam increased dramatically from 92,000 tons in 1990 to 218,000 tons in 1995 and 698,000 tons in 2000, the coffee acreage correspondingly increased from 119,300 hectares, to 186,400 hectares, to 516,700 hectares, coffee export prices suffered a dramatic decline from 4,000 dollars a ton in 1994 and 2,300 dollars a ton in 1995, to 870 U.S. dollars a ton in January 2000, 430 dollars a ton in December 2000, and 320 dollars a ton in December 2001 (Thoi Bao Kinh te Viet Nam 1996: 39; 2001: 47; *Thoi Bao Kinh te Viet Nam* December 25, 2000: 5; 2002: 43). In the summer of 2001, the price of 300 dollars a ton in the Central Highlands obtained by coffee growers reportedly covered only half of the production costs (*Thoi Bao Kinh te Viet Nam* August 13, 2001: 1). Similarly, the price of rice, another key agricultural export commodity, rose from 189 dollars a ton in 1990 to 315 dollars a ton in 1995, but then dropped to 174 dollars for a ton of high-quality rice in 2000 (Thoi Bao Kinh te Viet Nam 1996: 18–19; 2001: 46). The Central Highlands as the major coffee-producing region and the Mekong delta as the major rice basket are highly vulnerable to these price fluctuations on the global market.

In the 1993–1998 period, among the seven socioeconomic regions of Vietnam, the Mekong delta had the slowest rate of growth, which stood at 46 percent cumulatively in comparison to the national cumulative rate of 64 percent. Among the provinces, the coal-producing center of Quang Ninh in the north had an even more modest cumulative growth rate of 32.5 percent. The slower growth in the Mekong delta and in Quang Ninh province resulted from the drop in the prices of rice and coal in the global market by 1998. The Central Highlands were similarly and severely affected by the drop in the coffee price in 1999–2001.

The increase in risks and vulnerabilities as well as the benefits of economic growth have been spread unevenly along the urban-rural axis, among different socioeconomic regions, as well as among different classes and ethnic groups. Using different sources of data, two recent economic studies have suggested a widening rural-urban gap in Vietnam. Using provincial GDP figures, Melanie Beresford (this volume) suggests that the gap between industrial and more heavily urbanized provinces on the one hand and agricultural ones on the other increased between

1993 and 1997, while the gap within each group declined. (In Beresford's study, the industrial centers are Hanoi, Haiphong, and Quang Ninh in the designated northern growth triangle, and Ho Chi Minh City, Dong Nai, Vung Tau–Ba Ria, and Binh Duong in the designated southern growth triangle [see map].) Using per capita expenditure data from two large household surveys, the World Bank also suggests that the growth in inequality between urban and rural areas accounts for 96 percent of the increase in inequality between 1992–1993 and 1997–1998 (Vietnam and World Bank 1999: 72–73).

A similar gap also exists among different regions of Vietnam. Using provincial GDP figures, I calculate that in the 1993–1998 period, the cumulative economic growth rates in the Red River delta, the south central coast, the Central Highlands, and the southeast clearly exceeded the national average of 64 percent (table I.3). The southeast region around Ho Chi Minh City led the country in the rate of economic growth, with Ho Chi Minh City serving as the most dynamic part of the country. The cumulative economic growth in Ho Chi Minh City was the highest

Table I.3.   Economic Growth in Seven Vietnamese Socioeconomic Regions, by Percentage, 1993–1998

	1993		1998		1993–98
	Pop.	GDP	Pop.	GDP	GDP growth
Northern Uplands	**17.3**	**12.1**	**17.2**	**11.5**	**55.9**
Quang Ninh	1.3	1.6	1.3	.9	32.5
Red River Delta	**19.7**	**18.5**	**19.4**	**18.8**	**66.7**
Ha Noi	3.1	6.2	3.5	6.8	79.1
Hai Phong	2.3	2.6	2.2	2.8	57.1
Northern Central Panhandle	**13.6**	**8.0**	**13.2**	**7.7**	**60**
South Central Coast	**10.5**	**7.1**	**10.6**	**7.5**	**67.9**
Quang Nam-Da Nang	2.7	2.1	2.7	2.2	74
Khanh Hoa	1.3	1.6	1.4	1.4	43.8
Central Highlands	**4.1**	**3.3**	**5.2**	**3.5**	**73.8**
Southeast	**12.4**	**29**	**13.2**	**31.5**	**77.9**
Ho Chi Minh City	7.0	17.1	6.6	18.7	79.1
Dong Nai	1.4	3.3	2.6	3.5	73.2
Ba Ria-Vung Tau	0.9	6.2	1.0	6.5	71.2
Binh Duong	n/a	n/a	0.9	1.2	n/a
Mekong Delta	**22.2**	**21.9**	**21.2**	**19.5**	**46**

Sources: World Bank 1995: 160; Vietnam-General Statistical Office 1999c: 19–20, 157–731.

in the country, reaching 79.1 percent in the 1993–1998 period. Although having only about 13 percent of the population, the southeast accounted for 29 percent of the GDP in 1993 and 31.5 percent in 1998 (table I.3). In the aforementioned World Bank study, the growth in inequality among seven socioeconomic regions accounts for 83 percent of the increase in per capita expenditure inequality in the country between 1992–1993 and 1997–1998 (Vietnam and World Bank 1999: 72–73). In that context, in the 1989–1999 period, approximately one million migrants from other regions settled in Ho Chi Minh City, accounting for almost one-fifth of its population by 1999 (Luong 2001a). The other region with a net in-migration is the Central Highlands. As Hardy points out (this volume), much of this migration is not under the state's control. The full impact of this migration process on regional economic development, including that of migrant-receiving and -sending areas, is still to be analyzed systematically.

Inequality also grew rapidly along class lines in the context of a weakened state-sponsored social safety net despite the state's official commitment to socialism. For example, health care became a two-tiered system in which anything beyond the most cursory or basic diagnoses cost extra money. The state financed only 16 percent of the total health care costs in 1992–1993 and 21 percent in 1997–1998. A major illness or medical operation would cost the equivalent of one year of income for a relatively poor rural family. In South Vietnam, where social networks were not as strong as in the center and the north, it was not uncommon for a relatively poor rural family with a member in prolonged illness to sell off land in order to cover medical expenses.

As discussed in Luong's chapter on wealth and poverty in this volume, the commodification of land in the Mekong delta in the context of a weakened state-sponsored social safety net and the globally rooted increase in producers' vulner-abilities had rendered 22 percent of the rural households there landless by 1997–1998 (Vietnam and World Bank 1999: 27). In the village of Khanh Hau in the upper Mekong delta where I have conducted research in the past decade, land-less households increased from 14.6 percent in 1992 to 37.6 percent in 2000. The costs of agricultural production in Khanh Hau in particular and in the Mekong delta in general were higher than in the north due to the heavy reliance on chem-ical fertilizers and hired labor in the south. Southern agriculture was also strongly export-oriented. A farming household who could not repay a short-term loan to the state bank of agriculture due to the low export or domestic prices for agricul-tural products lost its eligibility for bank credit. It normally resorted to buying fer-tilizers on credit and at high interest rates from private shop owners. If the prices for agricultural products remained depressed for three to five crop seasons, many farmers would resort to selling their land. They became landless laborers, or in rare cases, industrial workers at nearby factories. (Four factories, each of which employed between one hundred and four hundred workers in 2001, were built in the village of Khanh Hau between 1991 and 2001 thanks to its location along a na-tional highway.) Many of the households losing their land also sent young family members to the southeast region around Ho Chi Minh City to seek work.

In industrial contexts, the relatively lax enforcement of labor laws led to many problems for workers. For example, in the peak export production season in the second half of the calendar year, garment workers might work fourteen hours a day, for six or even seven days a week, and without overtime pay in many cases (cf. Kolko 1997: 110–18). My research into Vietnamese textile and garment firms in 1995–1996 reveals that many private Vietnamese firms officially declared the majority of their workers seasonal employees in order to avoid making social insurance contributions, which would add 15 percent to the labor costs and reduce their global competitiveness. Labor unions were not always effective in representing workers' interests. Not only did a high percentage of enterprises not have unions, but also union representatives were paid by owners and managers (Tran 2002, Chan and Norlund 1999).

While aggregate incomes clearly rose in Vietnam in the 1990s, and while the poverty rate declined from 57 percent in 1992–1993 to 38 percent in 1997–1998 (Vietnam and World Bank 1999), a good number of those officially above the poverty line were still dangerously close to this line and highly vulnerable to poverty: it may take only a natural calamity, a drop in the prices of agricultural commodities, or a sickness in the family in the context of the state's lesser coverage of health care costs, for a family to fall back into poverty (Vietnam and World Bank 1999: iv, 17). While national tax revenues recovered well in the 1990s, the Vietnamese government decided to give a high priority to long-term infrastructure investments. The increase in the government's educational and social expenditures did not keep up with the actual increase in costs: the state financed only 51 percent of the total educational expenditures and 16 percent of the total health care ones in 1992–1993, and 48 percent of the former and 21 percent of the latter in 1997–1998 (World Bank 1995: 86, 99–100; Vietnam-International Donor II: 98–99, 128; Vietnam-General Statistical Office 2000b: 267, 274).

Inequality also seems to take on an ethnic dimension, as the expansion of coffee production in the Central Highlands, spearheaded by ethnic Vietnamese, has significantly infringed on the indigenous land use rights of ethnic minorities and reduced the land available for these minorities. The population in the Central Highlands increased from 1 million in 1975 to 2.7 million in 1990 and at least 4.2 million in 2000 (Vu Dinh Loi et al. 2000: 10; Vietnam-General Statistical Office 2001b: 37–39).[14] The Vietnamese government organized migration to the Central Highlands in the 1975–1985 period, but much of the migration from the late 1980s onward was spontaneous. As a result, migrants, mostly ethnic Vietnamese, made up three-quarters of the Central Highlands population by 1998. In the Central Highlands provinces of Daklak and GiaLai-Kontum, by 1985, the state plantations had taken over 3,150,000 hectares or 70 percent of the provincial territories (Vu Dinh Loi et al. 2000: 77–79). The forest acreage in the Central Highlands was also reduced from 3.3 million hectares in 1975 to 2.5 million hectares in 1988. Since the onset of economic renovation, the acreage under the control of state plantations in those three provinces has been reduced to 1.95 million hectares (44 percent of the provincial territories); however, in the same years, private plantation owners have entered in large numbers (103, 124). Land conflict with indigenous ethnic minorities has intensified, since their traditional access to land and forest resources has been severely curtailed (103–8, 151ff.). A study in 1997 revealed that 22 of 29 studied indigenous communes in Daklak province did not have enough land to sustain their livelihood (163). The poverty rate among ethnic minorities stood at 86 percent in 1992–1993 (28 percent above the national average) and declined only to 75 percent in 1997–1998 (38 percent above the national average) (Luong Hong Quang et al. 2001: 86). Twenty-five thousand cases of land conflict went to higher authorities in Central Highlands provinces for mediation and resolution between 1990 and 1998. Three-quarters of the sixty sampled cases involved disputes between indigenous people and state plantations (157–59). As early as 1995, in a land dispute, the ethnic Giarai in three communes felled thousands of rubber and coffee trees in a plantation under the control of the 15th Army (157).[15] Added to those problems is a process of economic, social, and cultural marginalization of ethnic minorities, as Rambo and Jamieson point out in their chapter in this volume.

At the opposite end of the spectrum, a new monied class has emerged, involving an alliance between enterpreneurs and many corrupt bureaucrats. The vice chair of the Budget and Economic Committee of the Vietnamese National Assembly recently estimated that 20–30 percent of the state's investment funds were wasted due to corruption and other reasons (*Dau Tu*, 9 June 2001; see also *Saigon Giai Phong*, June 25, 2001) (see also Luong's chapter on wealth and poverty in this volume).

On the gender dimension, while the income and education gaps between men and women were reduced in the 1990s, and while the decline in women's political representation between 1975 and 1987 has been slowly reversed, the commodification of women's bodies has become widespread with the resurgence of prostitution throughout the country. In the kinship domain, patrilineages have been strongly revitalized throughout northern and northern central Vietnam, rendering kinship and domestic relations more male-centered. In the era of economic renovation and globalization, gender relations in Vietnam have been at the intersection of major crosscurrents (see Luong's chapter on gender relations in this volume; Werner and Belanger 2002).

From a comparative perspective, growing environmental problems, greater vulnerability of producers to the vicissitudes in the global economy, and growing inequalities in Vietnam parallel those in China (see Perry and Selden 2000). However, producers' vulnerability to global price fluctuation seems greater in Vietnam, as agricultural exports constitute an important part of the Vietnamese economy. As earlier discussed, this has led to increasing landlessness in the southern third of Vietnam where land has long been treated as a commodity. The problem of landlessness in the southern third of Vietnam and its class implications are unparalleled in the Chinese context.

With varying degrees of effectiveness, the Vietnamese government has attempted to address those problems. The Law on Environmental Protection was passed in

1994. However, as pointed out by Digregorio, Rambo, and Yanagisawa (this volume), enforcement has been hampered by concern about its impact on production, by the ambiguity in regulations, as well as by the conflicts between environmental regulators and the home ministries of state enterprises, among other factors.

The Vietnamese government has also attempted to reduce the impact of global price fluctuation on Vietnamese rice growers by offering a price floor for paddy. In March 2001, it ordered state export companies to stockpile 1 million tons of rice and provided over 10 million U.S. dollars in interest subsidy on the bank loans to these companies, in order to boost the domestic price of paddy to 1,300 dongs a kilogram (above the estimated production costs of 1,000–1,100 dongs a kilogram in the Mekong delta). However, growers received only 900–1,100 dongs per kilogram since export companies and their layers of middlemen needed to cover their transportation costs and sought to maintain their profit margins (*Saigon Giai Phong* July 17, 2001: 6; *Nguoi Lao Dong* May 10, 2001: 5).

In order to address the issue of poverty, the Vietnamese government has targeted 1,715 communes, largely in the highlands, for infrastructure investments (Program 135) and encouraged provincial authorities to provide low-interest small business loans and free health insurance cards to the poor. In the first year of governmental fund disbursements under Program 135, 1,200 communes in 30 provinces received on the average 423 million dong each (about U.S. $30,000) (World Bank et al. 2000: 73). The infrastructure investments in the highlands, however, were not free from corruption, if the aforementioned analysis of a ranking member of the Vietnamese National Assembly is reliable. Similarly, only about 25 percent of the poor targeted for free health insurance had received health insurance cards by the summer of 2001. There have also been reports of the not-so-poor given free health insurance and low-interest business loans (*Tuoi Tre* April 6, 2001: 12; *Nguoi Lao Dong* October 13, 2000: 6).

It is not surprising that there has been increasing tension within the Vietnamese social fabric. Most dramatic is the rural unrest in the northern province of Thai Binh in 1997 and in the Central Highlands in February 2001. In An Ninh commune (Quynh Phu district) of Thai Binh, in late June 1997, villagers smashed flowerpots, chinawares, and furniture in the commune's administrative building, which had been constructed and furnished at the cost of 800 million dong (almost U.S. $70,000). The bust of Ho Chi Minh was smashed in the pandemonium. Villagers also caused damages in the houses of eight commune officials. In Quynh Hoa commune in the same district, in the same period, at one point the local population placed twenty policemen coming from outside under house arrest for five days. In the district of Quynh Phu where these two communes are located, on May 11, 1997, about two thousand peasants from thirty-six of the thirty-eight communes in the district rode their bicycles to the district and provincial capitals. At the district capital, the gathering of protestors at one point was estimated to increase to ten thousand people. When the district leadership used police with gas grenades, dogs, and three fire trucks to spray water on the demonstrators, violence broke out.

Nine to ten policemen got wounded. At the peak of the unrest in June 1997, according to the Vietnamese president Tran Duc Luong, in many localities, party and local government apparatuses were paralyzed, leading to the situation of "no government" (*Saigon Giai Phong* March 4, 1998, p. 5). Even by June 1998, according to the provincial party secretary, of the 285 administrative units in the province, high tension remained in 30 communes, and the situation was still described as quite complicated in 207 others (*Thoi Bao* No. 443, June 25, 1998, p. 75).

The Thai Binh unrest caught the national leadership by surprise because Thai Binh was the cradle of the Vietnamese Communist Party in the Red River delta. In the province, Quynh Phu district was considered a model district, and in this district, the commune of An Ninh had been considered exemplary for decades by the provincial leadership (see also Kerkvliet's chapter in this volume). In early February 2001, unrest also erupted in the provinces of Daklak and Gia Lai in the Central Highlands, where thousands of ethnic minorities demonstrated in provincial capitals as well as in some district towns and communes, over land and religious issues (*Agence France Presse* Feb. 7, 2001, *Nhan Dan* Feb. 8, 2001). President Tran Duc Luong attributed the unrest in Thai Binh to onerous local taxes on the poor, corruption and inefficiency in the use of local resources, and local authorities' unresponsiveness to grievances (*Saigon Giai Phong*, March 4, 1998, p. 5). The Vietnamese media attributed the highlands unrest to agitation and misunderstandings (*Nhan Dan* Feb. 8, 2001), an analysis that overlooks the deeper currents of changes adversely affecting ethnic minorities in the highlands.

In urban and industrial contexts, labor unrest rose quickly in the first half of the 1990s and has still erupted regularly since 1996. A hundred strikes reportedly took place from 1989 to mid-1994, forty-eight in 1995, and at least seventy-three in 1996. The majority took place in the south, and 70 percent, in enterprises with foreign capital (Chan and Norlund 1999: 211–12). Those strikes were seldom sanctioned by the government-supported trade union. The striking workers demanded, among other issues, better treatment by foreign supervisors, and the payment of wages on time. The pattern of industrial labor unrest in Vietnam exhibits similarities to that in China (Chan and Norlund 1999, Lee 1999); but the confrontation between rural populations and the state, as in the northern Vietnamese province of Thai Binh or in the Central Vietnamese Highlands, is on a scale unparalleled in the Chinese context.

A DIALOGIC RELATION OF THE STATE AND SOCIETY?

I would like to suggest that the aforementioned large-scale and open protests reflect a fundamental transformation in the Vietnamese economic and sociocultural landscape and a subtle shift in the relation between the state and society in Vietnam.

As discussed by Ben Kerkvliet (this volume, and Kerkvliet 1995c), there have been three main interpretations of state-society relations in Vietnam: "dominating state," mobilizational authoritarianism, and dialogical relations. While the state attempted to retain tight control of society, especially in the pre-reform era (1954–1986), Shaun Malarney's discussion of rituals and religion, Hardy's analysis of migration, and Hy V. Luong's examination of gender relations (all in this volume) suggest that at least in the past decade, the state no longer tightly controlled many aspects of the public sphere, except in the event of a threat to the monopoly of power by the Communist Party. Luong's and Malarney's chapters discuss how rituals (both family rites and public rituals) and nongovernmental local organizations such as patrilineages have been revitalized in the past decade. While the state has condoned in this period an emphasis on tradition as a safeguard against globalization, it would be simplistic to consider the reemergence of selected traditional forms or greater autonomy to society strictly as a result of state policies. Patrilineage resurrection is not compatible with the state's ideological emphasis on gender equality. Neither are spirit mediumship and elaborate ritual meals compatible with the modernist scientist vision of the Vietnamese state. These sociocultural changes do not reflect the policies of a dominating state or its mobilizational efforts. Similarly, although the state still seeks to control the media tightly, many books from the precommunist era have been reprinted, and many previously banned songs have been performed again. Hardy (this volume) also suggests that spontaneous migration in Vietnam has been as much a cause as an effect of the state's loss of control.

Even the sensitive domestic political arena has gradually been transformed as a result of direct and indirect "dialogues" of the state with society. If in the 1980s, the National Assembly met briefly for three to six days each year to rubber-stamp governmental and party decisions, it nowadays meets two times a year for four to five weeks during each session. Its deputies routinely raise critical questions to ministers and even veto the government's cabinet nominations, as in the case of the state bank governor in 1998. Similarly, at a local level, in the commune of Son Duong where I have conducted field research over the years, the local population refused the payment of local levies and irrigation fees, and critically questioned local leadership, leading to a quick succession of four Communist Party secretaries and five presidents of the commune administration in the five-year period between 1993 and 1998. Leading the protest were a president of the state-sponsored veterans association and a female neighborhood leader. The mobilization of local populations for collective action and overt confrontation with the state in rural northern Vietnam and the Central Highlands, I would suggest, is facilitated by tight rural social networks based on kinship, religious, communal or ethnic ties. In rural northern Vietnam, voluntary associations have dramatically proliferated as the domain under state control has contracted in the past decade and a half. In the commune of Son Duong, only two of those associations, the veteran and elderly associations, receive some support from the state (cf. Frolic 1997). The rest (same-age associations, alumni associations, etc.) are not even recognized by the state. While none of those new associations are political or tolerated to be political in their orientation, the ties formed through them have been mobilized for collective action and for a concerted voice for better local governance (cf. Brook 1997: 41–42). They are at least as effective in strengthening the voices of local populations as bourgeois-dominated voluntary associations constitutive of civil society are in communities with a greater market penetration. Spontaneous local associations based on kinship, religious, and communal ties, constitutive of "alternative civilities" in rural northern Vietnam, can serve as a strong foundation for the mobilization for collective action in the face of growing local socioeconomic inequality (cf. Weller 1999).

In Vietnam, local voices and action have led the state to change its policies in various domains. The Thai Binh unrest led to the grassroots democracy decree (Decree 29) that requires local governments to consult closely with elected representatives or local populations on local finances and levies (Vietnam 1999). Producers' foot-dragging in both agriculture and industry led to declining productivity in the formal economy under the state's control in the 1970s and triggered off economic reforms (Kerkvliet's chapter, this volume; Luong 1994; Fforde and de Vylder 1996). Even in the tightly controlled domains of publications, the performing arts, and the mass media, the state has gradually and selectively changed its view in response to the voices and action of many intellectuals and other members of society. A number of once-banned books have been reprinted and are available in bookstores. Among them are the novels of the Tu Luc van doan (Self-Reliance Literary Group) from the 1930s and the former Prime Minister Tran Trong Kim's *Viet Nam su luoc* (A summary history of Vietnam).[16] Since the late 1980s, there has also been an increasing official acceptance of many composers and romantic songs from the 1946–1954 period and from the area under the control of the pre-1975 Saigon government, as a large number of people in both the north and the south ignored the ban on those songs in the late 1970s and 1980s (Ebbeson 1997). Many of those songs have been officially reprinted and sung on CDs released by state companies for over a decade.

On the other hand, it would be simplistic to take the emergence of certain ritual or social organizational forms or economic activities or political protest as indicative of a total resistance to state power. While the state's capacity to compel compliance has diminished in the past decade with the advance of globalization, including people's access to the electronic media, and while its control capacity has never been absolute, many rituals, certain aspects of gender relations (such as northern women's rights to inherit agricultural land), or the highly egalitarian distribution of land in the north and many parts of the center in 1993–1994, have been influenced by the state's Marxist and egalitarian ideology (see Luong's chapter on wealth and poverty in this volume).

As long as we understand *dialogue* in a broad sense of the word to include indirect and nonverbal communication, and do not assume dialogue partners to have equal power vis-à-vis each other, state-society relations in Vietnam, at least since the local experiment with household contracts in agriculture in the 1960s, may be described as dialogic. It can be argued that this extended back to 1956 when the state had to admit excesses in the land reform campaign and to rectify its errors. The state sought to expand public space under its control from 1954 to at least 1981 (the beginning of nationwide household contracts in agriculture), but the control was never absolute and totally insensitive to local pressures. The transformation of Vietnamese society and the changes in state policies cannot be fully understood without a full consideration of societal dynamics and the dialogical nature of state-society relations in contemporary Vietnam.

NOTES

I am grateful to Mark Selden and Terry Rambo for their comments on an earlier version of this chapter, and to Michael Digregorio for providing a map of Vietnamese provinces.

1. The conversion of GDP per capita from Vietnamese dong into U.S. currency is based on open-market exchange rates.

2. French colonialism was established in half of Cochinchina (the southern third of Vietnam) by 1862, in the rest of Cochinchina by 1867, and in central and north Vietnam by 1884.

3. Other estimates of Vietnamese war dead during the American war are in the range of one million to two million (Lewy 1978: 450; Harrison 1982: 3–4). For the earlier Franco-Vietnamese war, one estimate puts the number of Vietnamese war dead at up to half a million (Harrison 1982: 124).

4. For the southern third of Vietnam in the French colonial period, two-thirds of rural households were estimated to be landless. 2.5 percent of the landowners (less than 1 percent of rural households) who owned more than 50 hectares of land owned 45 percent of the cultivable surface (Gourou 1940: 273; Henry 1932: 152ff.).

5. War probably had the same impact on North Vietnamese politics in the 1954–1975 period as it had had on Chinese politics during the Chinese resistance to Japanese occupation before World War Two. However, in this chapter, my comparison of Vietnam and China focuses on political, economic, and sociocultural conditions before and during economic reforms.

6. The introduction of high-yield rice varieties helped to restore the output to over five million tons for 1969–1970 and to raise it to over six million tons in the 1971–1974 period (Tran van Tho et al. 2000: 247).

7. It is frequently reported that household economic activities accounted for over 50 percent of rural household incomes in the 1966–1975 period and 60 percent in 1976–1980 (Nguyen Sinh Cuc 1990: 48; Dao The Tuan 1993: 10; Kerkvliet and Selden 1999: 105). Vu Tuan Anh and Tran thi Van Anh (1997: 79) argue that the products from the cooperatives were calculated at low state prices (e.g., .25–.35 dong for a kilogram of paddy in 1965–1975), while those from the household economy were calculated in free market prices (mainly over one dong for one kilogram of paddy). They suggest that if we adjust for price differences, the share of the household sector in the rural agrarian economy dropped to about 30 percent for the 1960s and early 1970s.

8. Paddy production was 11.8 million tons in 1976 and 11.4 million tons in 1979 (Tran van Tho et al. 2000: 248).

9. It remains an open question to what extent Vietnam's sanctioning of the household contract system in agriculture was influenced by China's household responsibility system.

However, in Vietnam, local cooperatives had experimented with household contracts on their own as early as in the 1960s. Politically, in the aftermath of the Chinese invasion of Vietnam in 1979, Sino-Vietnamese political relations remained very tense for over a decade. Although there has been a political rapprochement since the early 1990s, the two countries still have territorial disputes over the Spratly and Paracel chains of islands.

10. The two-price system was eliminated also for foreign currency exchange.

11. Household enterprises differ from private ones in that the former utilize primarily family labor while the latter rely primarily on hired labor.

12. In the 1999–2001 period, 611 state enterprises were equitized, while 34 were sold off and 47 were transferred to other sectors of the economy (Thoi Bao Kinh te Viet Nam 2002: 29).

13. If the percentage of exported manufactured goods to the total export value dropped in 1991 due to the collapse of the Soviet and East European markets, it rebounded steadily up to 1997–1998. It dropped in 1999 only due to the rising oil price and oil production, which accounted for a higher percentage of exported mineral products from Vietnam toward the end of the 1990s.

14. Official Vietnamese statistics do not include seasonal migrants or migrants who reside in a locality for less than six months. Therefore, they underestimate the flow of migration in Vietnam.

15. An analysis of living standard survey data in 1992–1993 reveals that the average annual per capita expenditure reached 3.13 million dong among the mostly urban ethnic Chinese, 1.52 million dong among the Vietnamese ethnic majority, dropped to 1.07 among the ethnic Khmer in the Mekong delta, and declined further to the .4 million–1 million dong range for ethnic minorities in the highlands (Wong 1994: 11). These data already converted subsistence goods produced by ethnic minority households for their own use to their market value.

16. Tran Trong Kim served as Prime Minister for less than half a year in 1945, under King Bao Dai and during the Japanese occupation of Vietnam.

1

Authorities and the People: An Analysis of State-Society Relations in Vietnam

Benedict J. Tria Kerkvliet

Vietnam's leaders say the government is "of the people, for the people, and by the people." Yet the country's political system has only one political party, the Communist Party. Elections typically have only candidates approved by that party. Tight restrictions make very difficult the formation of any organization or the establishment of any publication that criticizes the Communist Party's domination of the political system. In such a system, what is the relationship between the rulers and the ruled, the authorities and "the people"? Second, what is being said and debated in the country about what those relationships should be?

This chapter offers an approach to analyzing such questions, using three interpretations in the scholarly literature to examine specific political arenas. It finds that each interpretation contributes to an understanding of the political system but is incomplete. This approach also reveals contending notions in Vietnam about appropriate relations between state and society.

CONCEPTUALIZING RELATIONS BETWEEN *STATE* AND *SOCIETY*

State and *society* are important concepts in everyday life as well as in political analysis, but these concepts are elusive and hard to define. One of the most perplexing problems is distinguishing between the two. Where does the state "end" and society "begin," and vice versa? State and society are different, yet they are not entirely separate. For example, in a country like Australia or the United States, is a government-funded university part of "the state" or is it part of "society"? People working in such a university are on the government payroll; they are often part of a state employee health care or retirement system; they are probably bound by certain restrictions applicable to all government workers. The highest governing body of such a university typically is often a board or council that includes representatives from the state. Yet most people in a university would probably not think of themselves as being part of "the state." They would not see themselves as being responsible to the government's chief executive or the state agency "in charge" of higher education. Students at the university, even those on state scholarships, would not likely say they are part of the state. Instead, students and faculty are likely to think of themselves as independent scholars, free to pursue their own course of study and teach and take the courses they want within the bounds of university-designed—not state-designed— requirements. Periodically, issues do arise that highlight the complexities of a university's position. For instance, when a state official or agency tries to tell a faculty member how or what to teach or threatens to withhold funding from a university or an academic program until it does as the government says or when faculty members and students who criticize the government are threatened with expulsion, then debates are likely to erupt over the role of the university and its obligations to state authorities, to "the community," and to scholarship. Boiled down, such discussions are about the state in the affairs of society, specifically, the relations between the state and the university.

This is but one of many examples in which boundaries between *state* and *society* are murky and in which trying to locate and draw them is important yet highly contentious. This situation is true in many countries, including Vietnam.

It brings me to an important point about how to conceptualize and talk about relations between the state and society. Rather than trying to say that one entity is part of the state and another entity is part of society, a more fruitful approach is to think of arenas in which boundaries, rights, jurisdictions, and power distribution between state and societal agencies are debated, contested, and resolved (at least temporarily).[1] These arenas can be within physical institutions, including those that, structurally speaking, clearly belong to the state, for example, government ministries and militaries. The arenas can also be other institutions, like a government-funded university, whose locations in the state structure are ambiguous. Arenas can be groups and organizations not part of a state structure yet in one degree or another penetrated by state rules and regulations, such as families, villages, and religious groups. Arenas may also be problems and controversies that are not confined to a particular institution. An example in the United States today would be the issue of abortion, which is swirling with questions about the proper role of state agencies and individuals and organizations in society. In Vietnam, a current contentious state-society issue is corruption, which I examine later in this chapter.

Society, as used here, is a summary term for people in a country, including their institutions and customs, who share political and economic circumstances and environment.[2] *State* refers to officials and institutions that make, implement, and enforce rules intended to apply across the entire society and its various parts.[3] No society, however, is thoroughly uniform. Rarely does it have a single set of institutions, customs, and circumstances. To be a society, however, it must have in common some significant features, certain practices, or particular conditions. Rules and regulations of the state are among the circumstances that people in a society share, that influence the way they live, and that people, in turn, can shape. In other words, a society has many organizations, activities, and institutions. One of them is the state. The state, therefore, is in society. The state, however, claims to be, and in fact may be, the ultimate agency setting and arbitrating the rules and regulations that frame what other institutions, groups, and so on in society do, including how they interact with the state. In this sense, the state, although in society, may also be the chief agent defining and delimiting society. This conceptualization does not presume, however, complete, societywide acceptance of the state or the form of a particular state. A society may well have individuals, groups, and communities struggling against the state and rejecting the state's attempts to constrain or set terms for how and where they live. At the same time, society may, and usually does, have groups and other actors seeking protection, support, and intervention from the state. Nor does this conceptualization presume that the state is capable of ruling and regulating all sectors of society, or that it acts alone in attempting to do so. Such matters require investigation and analysis in order to know how people in society see the state or how able the state is to set parameters for society.

Society, I hasten to add, is not the same as *civil society*. Not all societies possess civil society's qualities or features. Civil society, as I think of it, refers to individuals and groups on their own—without the state's instigation and manipulation—speaking, writing, teaching, acting, and organizing around various interests and issues and doing so in public places.[4] It requires considerable civility—the give and take of contending ideas and claims but with controlled passions and restrained exuberance. It requires tolerating differences in opinion, organization, and practices. It also requires the willingness to work and interact with the state. Resorting to killing one's political opponents or to violent revolution against the state amounts to abandoning civil society. Civil society also requires an accommodating state—one that not only tolerates differences and criticisms but helps to maintain institutions, laws, and practices that make public debate possible without violent or silencing repercussions. Of course, the degree to which civil society exists varies over time within the same society and from one society to another.

Many questions can be raised about relations between state and society. A single chapter cannot explore them all. I concentrate here on relations between government authorities and people living within the jurisdiction of that government. In particular, I ask two kinds of questions. The first concerns how the political system works. How, if at all, does the state allow or encourage citizens to be involved in the process of setting and implementing rules and policies of the country; how, if at all, do people in society affect or try to affect what state authorities do; and to what extent do people abide by what authorities say? The second are normative questions. What should be the relations between state authorities and people in society? What involvement should the state have in people's economic, social, cultural, and political affairs; and what involvement should groups and individuals in society have in state affairs?

THREE INTERPRETATIONS OF THE POLITICAL SYSTEM

Tentative answers to some of these questions appear in the scholarship on Vietnam's political system and state-society relations. Few analysts would say their findings are adequate. Too much remains unknown. Research is sparse and generalizations often rest on slender evidence. Nevertheless, efforts have been made to analyze how the system works. They can be synthesized into three interpretations.[5]

The first, which I call the "dominating state" interpretation, says that rules and programs governing Vietnam are done by and within the state, in which the Communist Party is the most powerful and pervasive institution. One such formulation argues that Vietnam is a "vast and coordinated party-state which pre-empts alternative and autonomous societal organizations from the national center down to the grassroots of the village and the workplace" (Womack 1992: 180). "Vietnam's system is mono-organizational socialism," writes Carl Thayer (1992a: 111–12), in which "there is little scope for the organisation of activity independent of the party-led command structures." Although the Communist Party relaxed its grip following reforms in the mid-1980s, Thayer says, its control was reasserted after 1988, hence "civil society [is] awaiting the erosion of mono-organizational socialism before developing further."

With regard to policy making and implementation, according to this dominating state interpretation, society has no significant impact. Gareth Porter (1993: 101) is clearest on this:

> The model of the *bureaucratic polity*, in which major decisions are made entirely *within* the bureaucracy and are influenced by it rather than by extra-bureaucratic forces in society—whether parliamentary parties, interest groups, or mass movements—aptly describes how the Vietnamese policy system works. Not only the determination of major policies but the power over the selection of political and governmental leadership is confined to a small group of party officials. (emphasis in the original)

Differences within the state do arise. Scholars analyze internal debates and factions within the Communist Party and other components of the state.[6] The only important influences outside the state, however, that the dominating state interpretation acknowledges are international ones. For instance, events in communist countries in Eastern Europe and the Soviet Union in the 1980s are said to have had a profound impact on Vietnam's political leadership (Porter 1993: 96; Kolko 1997: 29–30, 133–37).

A second interpretation modifies the first by saying that forces in society can influence policy through organizations that the state itself dominates. Some analysts talk about this phenomenon as "mobilizational authoritarianism"; others call it "state corporatism." Setting aside fine distinctions between them, I refer to both as "mobilizational corporatism." It draws attention to the importance of various organizations, typically one for each major social sector, that the state, particularly the party, has established and runs. Using these organizations, the state can mobilize people to support its programs and policies, maintain channels of communication between authorities and each sector of society, and manage social and economic groups that otherwise might become unruly. William Turley (1993a: 269–70, 1993b: 330–31) argues that because other organizations independent of the state are few, indeed are usually prohibited, and because the Communist Party retains considerable legitimacy, "the power elite has been able to invite popular involvement under its supervision without much fear that things will get out of control. . . ." At the same time, people's concerns expressed through these authorized channels can influence policy debate among national leaders.[7] This interaction between leadership and citizens through state-instigated and managed organizations also helps to perpetuate the political system.

The first and second interpretations focus on formal institutions of politics. Both also emphasize national-level politics, paying little attention to local political dynamics. They also concentrate primarily on policy and policy making; they say little about discrepancies between what state leaders have decided and what people in society actually do.

According to a third interpretation, the above conceptualizations attribute too much power to state and too little to society. In the first place, due to insufficient resources and other inadequacies, the state's capacity to coordinate programs and implement policies is considerably less than what a dominating state or mobilizing corporatist interpretation would lead one to believe (Woodside 1979; Thrift and Forbes 1986: 81–83, 101–104). The state, concludes Melanie Beresford (1995b: 10), has long been "highly decentralized," making it difficult for the central authorities' policies and programs to actually be implemented and involving considerable negotiation between local and central authorities.[8] Furthermore, social groups and processes not under state control have remained afoot, shaping Vietnam's economy and society as much as or more than state policy and administration. Such factors in society together with weak administrative machinery help to explain discrepancies between what the state claims and what actually occurs (Thrift and Forbes 1986: 82–83). Another part of this interpretation is that social forces outside of the state and official organizations have affected national policies. Beresford (1989: 116–18), for instance, indicates that the Communist Party has been responsive to pressures from below and recognizes the "existence of independent sources of political power." Other analysts have linked significant policy changes to pressures from various quarters of society (White 1985; Fforde 1989: esp. 203–5; Chu Van Lam et al. 1992: esp. 78–79; Kerkvliet 1995c). The main message running through studies highlighting these features of Vietnam's political system is that there can be negotiation between various components of the state and interests in society. This phenomenon can be summarized, however imperfectly, as "dialogue" in the broad sense of the word, which incorporates communication of contentious ideas and preferences in ways that,

in Vietnam, are often indirect and nonverbal.[9] (Also see Hy Van Luong's introduction to this volume.)

With these three interpretations of Vietnam's political system in mind, let us
now look at four arenas to investigate the two kinds of questions on state-society
relations raised above.

GOVERNING INSTITUTIONS AND PROCESSES

This arena includes how the state makes and implements policies and rules for
society. Much that we know about how Vietnam is governed fits within the dominating state and mobilizational corporatism interpretations. Not only is the
Communist Party the only political party in the country, but authorities reject any
suggestions of a multiparty system and squash any potential rival political organizations. Vietnam's state is even more rigid in this regard than neighboring China,
where at least a few tiny opposition political parties are allowed. Vietnam's Communist Party has about 2.1 million members (Kolko 1997: 72). Although they
constitute only about 3 percent of the nation's total population, party members
compose a large percentage of government officials, from the smallest unit of administration, called subdistricts (*xa*) in the countryside (generally composed of
two to five villages) and precincts (*phuong*) in the cities, to the district and wards
(*huyen, quan*) and the provinces and to the national ministries, courts, and National Assembly. Elections are regularly held to select the representatives to run all
these levels of government. The nomination system organized by local units of the
Fatherland Front (Mat Tran To Quoc), which is dominated by the Communist
Party, almost always produces candidates who meet the approval of party leaders
in the locality and, for higher offices, the approval of the party's Central Committee (about 150 people), Political Bureau (about a dozen members), and the Executive Committee (usually thirteen people).[10] Most candidates, especially for
provincial and national level offices, are party members, and the overwhelming
majority of those elected are party members. In the National Assembly, for example, about 90 percent of the nearly 400 delegates during the late 1990s were members of Vietnam's Communist Party.

Most policies and laws are made in a process that is hard to follow. Much of it
seems to occur within the Communist Party and government offices behind
closed doors. Rarely are deliberations open to the public. Access to decision makers at the national and provincial levels is very restricted. Although the average
person probably knows more about how district and subdistrict authorities make
decisions, even there the process is rarely accessible to most citizens. A national
bureaucracy, charged with implementing policies and enforcing rules, has
branches extending down to district and often subdistrict levels. It includes a national police and domestic security system whose work monitors people thought
to be disenchanted with the political system or engaged in activities potentially

damaging to the regime. Alongside the nationwide bureaucracy is the Communist Party's own elaborate hierarchy that extends down to villages.

Helping to generate support for the state and to channel citizens' concerns and criticisms in a nonthreatening manner to the leaders are numerous organizations of the party or other institutions of the state. Some two dozen are affiliates of the official overarching association, the Fatherland Front. The organizations are supposed to represent various sectors of Vietnamese society: e.g., the Peasants' Association (Hoi Nong Dan) for agricultural producers, the General Confederation of Labor (Tong Lien Doan Lao Dong) for workers, the Women's Association (Hoi Phu Nu), the Ho Chi Minh Communist Youth League (Doan Thanh Nien Cong San Ho Chi Minh), and so on. One that has become prominent in recent years is the Chamber of Commerce and Industry of Vietnam (Phong Thuong Mai va Cong Nghiep), which was established by the Ministry of Foreign Trade.[11] Communist Party leaders head these organizations and typically occupy key positions in their local branches.

Just as the mobilizational corporatist interpretation says, authorities use these state organizations to carry out government programs and policies. In North Vietnam during the 1950s, for example, the official peasant organization of the day (then called Nong Hoi, a predecessor of today's Peasants' Association), helped local officials and party leaders to carry out a sweeping land redistribution and then to persuade, encourage, and coerce villagers to join agricultural collectives. In recent years, government and party authorities have called upon the Women's Association, Peasants' Association, Youth League, and Confederation of Labor to drum up support in neighborhoods and villages for national campaigns against illegal drugs, prostitution, gambling, and other "social evils." Statements from the Peasants' Association make clear that the organization is a "prop [*cho dua*] of the [Communist] Party and State, a crucial force of the peasants' movement to implement the policies and undertakings of the party and the state."[12] The largest and longest mobilizational role of these groups and the party itself was keeping up citizens' determination to join the war to fight the Americans and reunite the country (1960–1975). Many Vietnamese no doubt would have sacrificed a lot for this cause even without these organizations circulating information, holding meetings, singing patriotic songs, and putting on performances depicting the heroics of their countrymen. Nevertheless, those activities were ubiquitous and probably helped the war effort significantly.[13]

Although often boosters for whatever the government and party leadership want, these state organizations also promote their members' interests. The Chamber of Commerce and Industry lobbied on behalf of businesses during debates and deliberations over investment laws and helped to shape the 1994 legislation. In national policy-making circles during 1993–1994, the Confederation of Labor pressed for minimum wage laws, the right to strike, and other measures supported by large numbers of workers (Stromseth 1998: chaps. 4 and 6). Officers of the Peasants' Association have faulted state authorities for mistreating peasants. They have also urged the state to subsidize farm-gate prices for rice, increase the volume of low-interest loans for peasants, and put in place other programs beneficial to rural people's needs. The Peasants' Association also claims to have influenced, on behalf of its members, the content of the 1993 land law, especially sections allowing villagers to transfer their land use rights to others.[14]

What has been said thus far synthesizes a great deal about state-society relations in governing processes. However, additional evidence about how the government works that does not fit within the dominating state and mobilizational corporatist interpretations also needs to be taken into consideration. For one thing, many activities affecting government operations are unauthorized or fall outside official channels. Informal arrangements between officials and ordinary citizens constitute one cluster of such activities. Personal connections can figure prominently in how decisions are made and rules are implemented. Family ties, friendships, and relationships carrying over from when people were classmates or in the army together or hailing from the same province or village can influence how officials behave. Having "connections" makes it possible, at least in some cases, for a citizen to get a favorable decision from a government office even if otherwise not merited or to have that office ignore an infraction that the person has committed.

A second cluster of evidence is the dispersed, unorganized, yet extensive actions that violate what state agencies stipulate. One such phenomenon, discussed in Andrew Hardy's chapter in this book, is that many people moved from place to place within the country and even left Vietnam altogether irrespective of laws and regulations against it. Another, covered in Shaun Malarney's chapter, is the persistence of various rituals and religious activities despite official prohibitions. That such practices continued even during times of greatest restrictions arguably contributed to state agencies eventually taking a more relaxed stance and reducing the regulations against them while at the same time continuing to impose restrictions. Housing practices is another area that has been researched (Thrift and Forbes 1986; Koh 2000: chap. 5). In the 1980s, tens of thousands of urban residents in Vietnam ignored and sometimes blatantly defied state rules and regulations about building and renovating dwellings. For a combination of reasons, among them limited resources for state law enforcement in the face of widespread violations and many local officials turning a blind eye or actually helping people to skirt the law, residents frequently did as they wanted yet avoided fines and other punishments.[15] At several junctures during the 1980s and 1990s, the widespread violations compelled national authorities to make new laws that were more in line with what people were actually doing. In other words, unorganized societal pressure outside official channels had helped to shape the state's rules. This conforms to the dialogical interpretation of government.

So does a third cluster of evidence: organized activities beyond official channels to voice citizens' concerns and demands. Workers in numerous state-owned and private companies went on strike in the early 1990s before such actions were legal. Besides seeking better pay and working conditions, the strikers also often demanded "democracy in the workplace." By 1994, these and other public demonstrations by workers had pressured Confederation of Labor leaders to champion the right to strike and contributed to the National Assembly's decision to legalize strikes that conformed to certain guidelines (Greenfield 1994: 226–28; Kerkvliet 1995a: 17–19). Placard-holding citizens periodically step outside authorized channels to demonstrate in front of government offices and in the streets in order to draw attention to their grievances against golf courses being built on their rice fields, excessive government taxes, government confiscation of land, abusive authorities, flawed elections, corruption, and other conditions. In May 1998, for instance, over five hundred angry villagers surrounded the provincial government offices in Nam Dinh province; a year later one hundred peasants staged a silent demonstration in front of the National Assembly in Hanoi. Sometimes, such as in parts of Thanh Hoa province in 1989 and Dong Nai province in 1997, demonstrators become more aggressive, throwing stones through office windows, shouting abuses at officials, and taking policemen hostage until they extract some concessions from authorities.[16] Government responses are typically a combination of sending in the police to make arrests and attending to some of the protesters' complaints.

During the 1990s, a couple of dozen organizations emerged that helped drug addicts, unemployed people, homeless children, minority groups, and others. These "nongovernment organizations" (NGOs) have also launched modest campaigns to draw attention to social and economic problems and solicit help from government and international aid agencies (Beaulieu 1994; Gray 1997; Ljunggren 1994: 27–33). While these organizations have to comply with certain state regulations, many have avoided becoming handmaidens of state officials. Across Vietnam, hundreds, probably thousands of other small organizations have no legal standing but are active in furthering their interests. There are, for example, groups of vegetable growers, associations for the repair and maintenance of religious temples, and organizations among vendors and pedicab drivers.

There is one large organization wholly outside the state. It is the Unified Buddhist Church of Vietnam (UBCV, Giao Hoi Phat Giao Viet Nam Thong Nhat). Formed in 1951 in south Vietnam, its spokespersons claim that it represents the majority of Buddhists in the country. In 1981, the state sought to bring all Buddhists under a single organization, called the Buddhist Church of Vietnam (Giao Hoi Phat Giao Viet Nam), but many monks and lay Buddhists refused to join. They remained instead in the UBCV, defying the state. From time to time leading monks in the UBCV demand that the government stop meddling in religious affairs. Some have written scathing critiques of the government's violations of human rights and have advocated a multiparty political system. Authorities' reactions have included clamping down on UBCV activities, detaining several UBCV monks for such offenses as causing public disorder and undermining national unity, sentencing prominent monks to years in prison, and harassing UBCV activists. So far such reactions have not expunged the organization. State authorities have refrained, however, from launching a determined frontal assault against the organization, probably for fear that such an extensive repression would arouse widespread anger and unrest.[17] Shaun Malarney's chapter in this book has more to say about this and about other religious groups' ongoing struggles with state agencies.

Another aspect of governing processes pertinent to state-society relations is debate over state-society boundaries that occurs within state institutions. In recent years an important dynamic within the Confederation of Labor, the only authorized national organization for workers, has been an ongoing discussion, punctuated occasionally by heated outbursts, about its purpose. Many workers and local confederation leaders have criticized the organization for behaving primarily in a top-down manner, conveying to workers what the Communist Party and government leaders want rather than pressuring state authorities to address workers' needs (Greenfield 1994: 220–23). In more general terms, members have insisted on a distinction between what they want and what the state wants. Elections have been another site of struggle for a clearer distinction between people's interests and the state's. For instance, twice in recent years, voters in a subdistrict on the outskirts of Hanoi have dumped candidates favored by party officialdom. To a significant degree the reasons came down to this: most voters' conception of a good public official was at odds with what authorities were insisting on (Malarney 1997). Equally significant, the majority of voters there had managed to turn elections their way rather than leave them controlled by local representatives of the state. Letters to the editors of some newspapers and articles by some journalists have conveyed discontent with the electoral system because it allows voters too little choice and has but one political party. Some of these writings insinuate, contrary to the official line, that the system is not democratic. In many urban electorates in Hanoi, officials countenance proxy voting, even though it is illegal, in part to assuage many residents' discontent with being compelled to go through the motions of voting when they see the process as largely meaningless (Koh 2000: chap. 3).

One does not need, however, to look at local politics to find debate within state institutions about where the boundaries between state and society should be. Beginning at least as early as the mid-1970s, leaders in the national government and the Communist Party itself were arguing about whether, and if so how, the state should cease trying to plan and control the country's economy. Gradually, those advocating greater scope for free markets, removing price controls, allowing private enterprises, returning farm land to individual households, and the like, brought about significant changes.[18] Debates on these issues continue to this day, with some in the party arguing that the state has ceded too much to free markets, domestic entrepreneurs, and foreign investors. The result thus far, officially summarized as "renovation" (*doi moi*) has been much more space in the economy for individuals, households, private enterprises—in short, society—and far less for the state. Debates within national offices about allowing more space in the political system for autonomous organizations, possibly even other political parties, have also flickered from time to time, although with only modest changes thus far.

MEDIA

Another arena for observing state-society relations and contested views about what the boundaries should be is the mass media. Much that we know about how it is organized and used by the state conforms to the dominating state and mobilizational corporatist interpretations of the country's political system. All television, radio, and telephone systems; filmmaking; and Internet service providers in Vietnam are owned and operated by state agencies. All newspapers, publishing houses, and printing presses are owned and operated by government ministries, the Communist Party, and official organizations. Authorities in the Ministry of Culture and Information and the Communist Party's Department for Culture and Ideology scrutinize and often intervene to determine the content of publications and of radio and television broadcasts. The state uses these media outlets not only to inform and educate citizens but also to inundate them with official positions on a wide range of domestic and international issues and to mobilize people to do what government, party, and mass organization leaders require.[19]

Individuals and groups trying to publish and disseminate a publication, make a radio or TV broadcast, or produce a film outside the state's system encounter virtually insurmountable obstacles. Compared to rules regarding housing, traffic, and residency requirements, which people in many parts of the country often ignore with near impunity, rules against unauthorized outlets of media are rarely breached and when they are, the law enforcement agencies respond quickly to stop the infraction and often punish the violators.

State authorities made their position clear in the mid-1950s. At that stage the Communist Party government was still young, and many of its policies and rules were still being formed. Although the state ran the radio stations and telegraph offices and produced newspapers and other publications, private publishing houses and printing presses also existed. By 1958, however, those private outlets had been shut down following a heated struggle over a range of issues regarding the extent to which the state should control what writers, artists, scholars, and other people could say, publish, and create. I say more about the content of that struggle below. Since 1958 other efforts to produce and distribute publications outside the state's media network have been quickly snuffed out. In early 1989, for example, several members of the Club of Former Resistance Fighters (Cau Lac Bo Nhung Nguoi Khang Chien Cu) in Ho Chi Minh City managed to publish a magazine and some letters in defiance of the authorities' prohibitions. Their efforts to continue doing so and establish, in effect, a private publication, collapsed as national and local authorities blocked the club members' efforts to find printing presses or use mimeograph machines to reproduce their texts. By early 1990, police had detained these club members and placed the most prominent one, Nguyen Ho, under house arrest (Heng 1999: chap. 7). That same year authorities arrested Doan Viet Hoat, a critic of the regime, for writing and circulating unauthorized material. Since then few Vietnamese have managed to distribute letters and short essays critical of particular policies or of the political system before being arrested and, usually, imprisoned or confined to house arrest.

Technological changes have made it somewhat easier for people who are determined to circulate contraband publications and other printed materials. Photocopy machines, previously as scarce as meat in a vegetarian restaurant, have become ubiquitous since the early 1990s. Convenient for people of all kinds, this machine is also a handy tool for critics wanting to produce quickly copies of materials that the state would not approve. Being caught possessing such forbidden material, however, can mean grave consequences, which of course continues to make people nervous and reluctant to keep it. Fax machines and the Internet are new ways to distribute unauthorized materials. Despite state authorities' efforts to monitor what is zipping electronically into and out of the country, they have not yet figured out how to stop all communication they dislike. Previously, writings by such critics as Ha Si Phu, Duong Thu Huong, Lu Phuong, and Nguyen Thanh Giang that could not be published in Vietnam might eventually appear in newspapers and magazines published in Paris, Toronto, San Jose, Melbourne, or other foreign places with Vietnamese communities. Since the late 1990s, such material is instantaneously flashed to email lists around the world. Numerous websites, most of them established by anticommunist Vietnamese organizations outside the country, feature writings and statements by people in Vietnam who have criticized policies or the party-state itself. Since about 1996, a few newsletters and magazines said to be by people in Vietnam and crammed with unflattering accounts about the regime and particular authorities have also circulated via the Internet.[20]

Although the state's grip on the mass media is firm, there is an undercurrent of debate about what the proper line should be between state and society regarding media operations and content. This debate is not only between authorities and dissidents but within the state's media system itself.

According to Vietnam's constitution, citizens have the freedom to speak, publish, create, and form associations. In the mid-1950s, shortly after the Communist Party government was established in the north following the defeat of the French army and the division of Vietnam into two parts, numerous Vietnamese writers and scholars in Hanoi began to exercise these constitutional rights. In independent publications they wrote short stories, poems, and essays on a range of topics, including the importance of research, speech, writing, and publications separate from the state. Articles also criticized efforts by the party and other state authorities to control all media. Few attacked the regime per se. Indeed, many of these intellectuals had fought in the revolution against French colonialism on the side of the Communist Party. They supported the new government. One line of argument in their publications was that open debate, free from state prohibitions, was in the party's own best interest. Such freedom, writers said, would help to prevent authorities from becoming dogmatic and authoritarian. Advocates of an independent media quickly collided with national authorities who held very different ideas. The clash became known as the *Nhan Van – Giai Pham* affair, referring to two of the independent journals published in 1956 that promoted free expression.[21] (For more background, see David Marr's chapter in this book.) National authorities argued that in order to press ahead with revolutionary change on all fronts—including culture, technology, and education—the state, led by the Communist Party, must have a firm hand on the mass media. Intellectual work unconnected to advancing the socialist revolution and preserving national independence, officials argued, would undermine the regime and the nation and help to revive capitalism and all its oppression. Excessive freedom and "unconstructive criticism," they said, also would play into the hands of those in south Vietnam and the United States who opposed the socialist regime and the country's reunification.

Similar justifications for restrictions on what citizens can say, do, and publish persisted into the 1990s. The expansion of a market economy and other reforms since the 1980s have led to much greater variety of content in mass media, including frequent accounts of improper behavior among officials. Officials repeatedly emphasize, especially to foreigners, that people in Vietnam have considerable freedom to say and do what they like. They also argue that the state has a right and a duty to guard the nation against hostile domestic and international forces that hide behind a pretense of "human rights" and "democracy" to threaten peace and order and the country's hard-won independence and its social and economic improvements since the end of colonial rule and war.[22] Drastic changes in the political system, they contend, such as allowing several political parties and independent media outlets, will result in chaos, similar to what happened to the Soviet Union. Numerous people within the country strenuously disagree. They advocate freedom to speak, assemble, and organize as well as freedom from state domination in the media, arts, and research. To support their views, they often invoke Vietnam's constitution and other official documents. Some cite Ho Chi Minh's writings decades ago that lambasted the French for depriving Vietnamese of these very freedoms.[23] Like *Nhan Van – Giai Pham* contributors and publishers in the 1950s, such Vietnamese today are essentially saying that the state's grip on the expression and circulation of ideas is wrong. Citizens should be able to speak and publish independently of the state.

Sites of these ongoing debates and struggles over how much or how little the state should regulate the mass media include some of the state's own institutions, even those in charge of media outlets.[24] In 1957, for example, members in the state-organized Vietnam Writers' Association (VWA, Hoi Nha Van) produced the magazine *Van* (Literature) that resonated the concerns of those independent publications that had been banned in 1956. Writers in *Van* frequently criticized the intensifying pressure on artists to conform to what officials wanted said. Many poems and short stories published there flew in the face of the party leadership's insistence that literature should adhere to "socialist realism." Even after higher officials had forced the publication to close, many writers within the association refused to join the state leadership's campaign against those who had produced and contributed to the magazine. Other struggles have erupted over censorship when newspaper editors and reporters try, sometimes successfully, to publish things that their superiors or party-state agencies regulating the media object to. In 1986, two newspapers persisted, despite pressures to stop from regulatory agencies and high-ranking party officials, to expose corruption and other nefarious activities of the party secretary and other officials in Thanh Hoa province. Although a complicated matter, a struggle over censorship was a central dynamic in this episode.

Another dispute surfaced in 1988. Tran Do, head of the party's Commission on Culture and the Arts, together with Nguyen Ngoc, editor of the state's main literary magazine, *Van Nghe*, clashed with superiors and media regulatory bodies over the publication's content. (For elaboration, see David Marr's chapter in this volume.) Ultimately they lost their jobs. They had wanted to publish more creative and lively work as well as essays that debated important issues of the day. Like many other intellectuals, Tran Do and Nguyen Ngoc were weary of doctrinaire articles that filled newspapers and magazines. Not that these men and their many supporters within party-state media circles were necessarily pressing for liberal democracy or complete separation between state and media; their views on these issues are not clear from the material at hand. What is clear is that they wanted journalists and writers to have a much freer hand to publish and write and greater distance from state intervention and supervision.[25]

AGRICULTURAL COLLECTIVES

Beginning in the mid-1950s, the Communist Party state in North Vietnam established collectivized farming, a centerpiece for its radical reorganization of agricultural production.[26] Collectives were crucial to the state leadership's overall program to make Vietnam a socialist country with state-controlled markets, state-owned companies, an equitable distribution of wealth, and other features of a centrally planned economy. After the country was reunified in 1975–1976, the state extended this program to the south. Collectivized agriculture required farming households to pool their lands, draught animals, and labor and then work together to raise crops and livestock. Villagers were organized into teams. Several teams made up a collective, which was directed by a committee typically headed by Communist Party members. Initially, each collective encompassed only households in the same village or part of a village, but fairly quickly the size grew to incorporate households in several villages.[27] Collective members were paid, usually in rice and other produce, according to complicated formulas that took into consideration how much work each person did, the quality of that work, the need to assure everyone enough to eat, and the imperative to prevent large inequalities in living conditions.

National officials used the state bureaucracy, various organizations under the Fatherland Front, and the Communist Party to form and run the collective farms. Agencies of the state organized wave after wave of educational, training, and political campaigns to get villagers to join the collectives, become model collective workers, believe in the superiority of collective farming over individual or household farming, and embrace socialism. During the war against the United States and to reunite the country (1965–1975), authorities from central to local levels stressed that the collectives were vital for providing food and other supplies to soldiers at the front and to those soldiers' families back in the villages. Indeed, one responsibility of the collectives' leaders was to recruit young villagers to join the army.

Officials frequently debated various aspects of how collectives were organized and administered. In the early years, some officials argued against plans to increase the pace at which collectives were being established. In the 1960s, officials debated about ways to improve the efficiency and productivity of collective farming. Some favored smaller sizes; others insisted on large collectives; some wanted to allow more latitude for household-based farming and other production, while others disagreed. Some input to such debates had percolated up through mass organizations of the state and other official channels. During meetings with local officials, for instance, villagers complained about how work points were counted, favoritism in work assignments, low prices for the commodities they produced, and other problems with how collectives operated. Periodically, a small percentage of members even requested permission to leave the collectives. Such concerns did reach the central offices of the Communist Party and its government. Although collectivized production remained the official policy, discussions and debates did result in modifications to specific rules and regulations regarding how it was supposed to be done and how produce should be distributed. In the mid-1970s, officials also disagreed over how rapidly or extensively collectivized farming and other aspects of the centrally planned economy should be imposed on the south following reunification. By the late 1970s, there were deep divisions within the party and various government ministries about how to reorganize collectives in order to prevent production from falling further and further behind what the nation needed. In 1979 such disagreements contributed to modest shifts away from collectivized production toward individual household farming. The swing in that direction became larger during the 1980s, and by the early 1990s nearly all farming was done by individual households. Collectivized farming was no longer the official policy.

As synthesized thus far, the evidence regarding the rise and demise of collectivized farming corresponds well to the dominating state and mobilizational corporatist interpretations of Vietnam. There is more to the story, however, which corresponds to the dialogical school. One significant influence on the debate within official circles was what was happening in the villages and fields where collectives were supposed to be operating. From the outset, few villagers had been enthusiastic about the state's collectivization policy. Most had joined reluctantly, realizing that, because authorities were determined to collectivize farming, they had no viable alternatives. Others joined on the condition that living conditions would improve, which is what authorities had assured them would happen. Initially life did get better. But by the early 1960s, improvements stalled, and by the middle of that decade through the 1970s living conditions deteriorated for a large proportion of villagers. The collectives were not the only reason, but many villagers believed that the collective system stood in the way of having more to eat, better housing, and other improvements. For evidence, many simply pointed to the fact that productivity was at least twice as high on the tiny plots of land that authorities allowed households to farm individually than on the collectively farmed land. To many villagers, one basic problem was that collective farming did not reward diligent work. Whether one worked hard or not, one still did not have enough to eat. Moreover, individuals doing the same task received virtually the same amount of payment regardless of how well or poorly each person had labored. Often villagers were also disgusted with local leaders who abused their authority and embezzled money and other resources belonging to the collective. (Melanie Beresford's chapter in this volume outlines some of these and other problems within the collectives, or what she calls cooperatives.)

Rarely did villagers openly demonstrate against collectivization. Known cases of such opposition were in southern Vietnam in the late 1970s when villagers in several areas marched to protest against being forced to turn over their lands to the collectives. There are several reasons for so little public opposition. One is that people were intimidated. Because collectivization was a major policy of the state, challenging it meant challenging the state. A second major reason applies to northern Vietnam during the war. Because officials repeatedly emphasized the importance of collective farming to defend the country, open opposition to the collective could be misinterpreted as being opposed to the war and unpatriotic. Another aspect is that many villagers, despite their reservations about and even dislike for collectivized farming, suppressed as much as possible their discontent for the good of the country and the war for national reunification.

Although public opposition to collectivization outside authorized channels was rare, widespread discontent was expressed in subtle, nonconfrontational ways that continuously worried local and central authorities. In many parts of the country, villagers went about their duties on the collectivized farms in a halfhearted manner. Leaders of production teams complained in the 1960s and 1970s that members worked lackadaisically, showed up late and made all kinds of excuses to go home early, and "dragged their feet" (*lan cong*). For instance, transplanters, who earned work points according to how many bunches of seedlings they planted, would make their bunches smaller than was stipulated, thus getting by with less work. Harvesters often "worked as though they were playing," cutting each stalk one by one rather than taking a handful at a time. Disinterest and disgust toward collectivized farming was so serious in some areas that land went unplanted. By the late 1970s, at least 150,000 hectares of the nation's collectivized land lay fallow because farmers were not "enthusiastic about production."[28]

In many places, families took bolder steps. They encroached on collective land to increase the area for private farming, enlarge their gardens, and build their houses. Such encroachment during the 1960s and 1970s, wrote one researcher, was "widespread and had been going on for many years" (Dinh Thu Cuc 1977: 40). In

Ha Bac province, for instance, the improper use of collective land and especially the unauthorized enlargement of private plots in many villages angered provincial leaders who implored local officials to recover those lands and vigilantly enforce the rules. By the mid or late 1970s, the percentage of land farmed as household plots may actually have been 7–13 percent of the land nominally under the jurisdiction of cooperatives, significantly greater than the authorized 5 percent.

By the mid to late 1960s and through the 1970s, several villages in northern and central Vietnam were quietly tinkering with production arrangements, seeing how much they could get away with without attracting unwanted attention from officials, especially beyond the village. These alternative arrangements were often called "sneaky contracts" (*khoan chui*). In some villages where pig raising was supposed to be done by cooperative teams, it was instead contracted to households, who were allowed to keep a high percentage of net earnings (Luong 1992: 202–203). In others, land used in the winter months for growing vegetables or land that could not be irrigated during the dry season was allocated to interested households who paid a certain amount to the collective and could do as they pleased with the rest of what they grew. Encouraged by the results of these modifications, some collective officials in several areas gave in to villagers' pressure to contract rice production to individual households. Provinces in which such "sneaky contracts" intermittently occurred included Ha Bac, Ha Nam Ninh, Ha Son Binh, Hai Hung, Hai Phong, Nghe Tinh, Phu Tho, and Vinh Phuc (Tran Duc 1991: 25, 29; Vietnam, Ministry of Agriculture 1981: 66–67). Authorities in some districts with "sneaky contracts" turned a blind eye. Others even encouraged these modifications so long as production improved. Vinh Phuc provincial authorities, knowing that villagers were often disgusted with collective farming, began in 1966 to support limited contractual arrangements so long as the spirit of collective farming was maintained. Soon, however, villagers were exceeding those limits. They farmed fields as their own, turning over only a fraction of their harvests to collective officials. Some surrendered none of their crops. To prevent further unraveling of the collective system, national authorities stepped in, reprimanded the provincial authorities, and insisted that the family contract system stop. That was effective for a while, but gradually "sneaky" arrangements reappeared.

The persistent and extensive problems of getting villagers to behave as good collective members gradually influenced officials who were deliberating how to revive the flagging agricultural economy in the 1970s. Wave after wave of campaigns to improve productivity, restructure the size and administration of collective organizations, introduce new agricultural technologies, and convince villagers to embrace collectivized farming had done little to improve the economy or make collectives stronger. A Ministry of Agriculture report in 1984 summarized the situation in the late 1970s:

> while some advanced cooperatives still maintained and protected production achievements, many cooperatives had come to a halt and some had fallen into ruins.

The masses had little enthusiasm to labor and produce energetically. In many places production was at a standstill and deteriorating. This reality was an obstacle for enhancing agricultural output and building a new socialist countryside.[29]

In effect, the reality was bearing down on authorities. It was also strengthening those in official circles who were questioning the wisdom of collectivized production and contributed significantly to policy makers discarding collectivized farming and making new policies that authorized family-based farming.

Some analysts have suggested that, because agricultural collectives were supposed to be the lowest rung on state apparatus, villagers' foot dragging, sneaky contracts, and other resistance against them were all within the state (Vasavakul 1999: 166–67). The implication is that such struggles had nothing to do with state-society relations, but whether collectives were part of the state is unclear. Like public universities in North America, their location was mixed. Certainly, they were creations of the state, and they were part of the state's overall effort to centrally control the nation's economy—but did members see themselves as part of the state? Like students and faculty in many universities in the example used at the beginning of this chapter, few villagers probably did. They were not on the state's payroll. Not even collective officials received a salary from the state; they were paid from what the collective itself produced. Meanwhile, collectives had to pay the state a certain portion of their produce.[30]

More important for state-society relations than determining whether collectives were inside or outside the state is to query what the struggles were about. One of the main issues was the preferred role of the state in agricultural production and other rural activities. Vietnam's state authorities had sought to control farming, the distribution of produce, and many other aspects of village society in order to socialize agriculture and village life. This meant minimizing as far as possible what individuals and households could do on their own, especially regarding production and distribution. Authorities expended enormous time and other resources to bring about these changes. Although most villagers in the north by the early 1960s had joined the collectives, few shared the socialist vision of collectivized farming. Most preferred instead to farm individually, as members of households and families, not as members of collectives. Later, after the war and the country had been reunited, many rural producers in the south indicated similar sentiments. For the most part, villagers expressed their preferences more through what they did than what they said. Through their actions, they were engaged in an extended dialogue with state authorities about how much agricultural production and other facets of village life should be given to state institutions and how much to societal ones. Eventually, those Vietnamese pressing for much more space for societal institutions gained ground while those insisting on state institutions lost it.

Seeking an end to collectivized farming did not mean villagers wanted the state to abandon entirely agriculture or the countryside. Since the end of collectivized farming in the late 1980s and the revival of household-based farming, small rural producers have asked for state assistance. Many villagers have wanted the state to protect land from being accumulated by a few at the expense of the majority (Scott 2000: 77–78; Kerkvliet 1995b: 84–85). This was an important concern in debates, manifested in various fora within and beyond official channels, leading to a new land law in 1993. Villagers have frequently asked the state to subsidize prices for fertilizer and other inputs, provide low interest agricultural loans, crack down on smuggling, and protect villages against criminals. In short, the state, villagers are saying, has roles to play in rural society but one of them is not to compel villagers to farm collectively.

CORRUPTION

One prominent claim in the three arenas discussed so far is that people should have more autonomy from state authorities and that the distance between the state and society should be greater than it has been. A prominent claim regarding corruption, however, is the opposite: less autonomy from the state for organizations, groups, and individuals and less room for nonstate activities. Corruption in Vietnam within the Communist Party, government ministries, and other agencies of the state has many forms and methods. Often it involves, as one prominent party leader explained, someone in authority taking advantage of his or her position for personal or family gain through such activities as smuggling, accepting or demanding bribes, embezzlement, and other forms of stealing, graft, and kickbacks.[31] Another side of corruption is citizens who manage to obtain—through personal connections, monetary enticements, and illicit arrangements—resources from the state or be allowed privileges by state agencies to which they are not legally entitled. The various forms boil down to individuals and groups personally benefiting, usually materially (money, land, or other property), from illicit uses of state resources, authority, and privileges. Corruption, therefore, amounts to appropriating for the benefit of oneself or others in society that which is supposed to remain in the public domain or be used by state agencies in order to govern. Preventing and stopping corruption requires maintaining strict boundaries between what belongs to or should be protected by the state for the public good and what people in society, as individuals and groups, can use as their own.

Specifying those boundaries are anticorruption laws and regulations in Vietnam. These rules, however, are not well monitored and enforced. However, unlike the widespread violations of rules and regulations about housing, for which citizens seem only infrequently to want strict enforcement, violations of laws and regulations against corruption have frequently aroused people to demand better law enforcement—better maintenance of the separation between what belongs to or should be used by state authorities for public benefit and what individuals can use or appropriate for their own personal benefit.

Corruption has been a problem for the Communist Party state since at least the early 1960s when it afflicted some agricultural collectives. In those days, typical incidents involved officials taking for themselves small amounts of rice or money that belonged to the state or taking for their own use cement or other construction materials that were supposed to be used for public buildings. Although serious, considering that those years were times of great scarcity, the amounts were tiny compared to what occurred in the 1990s when corruption appeared to be far more widespread and represented much more money. Figures from police reports show that, on average, each known case of corruption in 1999 amounted to about $86,000 going into officials' pockets.[32] According to sources cited in Hy Van Luong's chapter on wealth and power in this volume, corrupt officials frequently steal between 10 to 40 percent of the funds allocated for building roads and other projects.

In ways consistent with the dominating state view of Vietnam's political system, party and government officials have deliberated the corruption problem many times in recent years. National Assembly sessions and Communist Party congresses have passed resolutions and expressed concern. Rank-and-file party members have written to higher leaders detailing corrupt behavior of various officials.[33] Ministries have issued instructions and injunctions against corruption. Police have arrested officials for corruption and associated crimes (e.g., smuggling and selling contraband products like heroin). Courts have convicted many, including some prominent officials. The former minister for energy, Vu Ngoc Hai, for example, was fired from his post in 1992, expelled from the Communist Party in 1994, and was tried and convicted that same year for masterminding a scam during the construction of the country's north-south electrical power lines that caused losses to the state of nearly U.S. $300,000.[34] The highest official to date known to have been dismissed from office for corruption is Ngo Xuan Loc. The National Assembly dismissed him from his post as deputy prime minister in December 1999. Reportedly known as "Mr. Cement" because of his leverage over construction projects, he had used his various government positions during the 1990s to become extremely wealthy.[35]

There is evidence, too, supporting the mobilizational corporatist interpretation. The Peasants' Association, Confederation of Labor, Women's Association, and other state organizations have campaigned against corruption, urged members to report cases, and in other ways been mobilized by the state to fight corruption. Journalists of these organizations' official publications have exposed corrupt police, tax collectors, local government officials, and bureaucrats.[36] Average citizens have used official channels to complain against authorities who use their government or party positions to steal tax revenues, give lucrative favors to relatives, and demand bribes for public services. Each year, when the National Assembly tallies citizens' written submissions regarding various problems, corruption and related misbehavior generally rank among the most common complaints. Allegations of wrongdoing reported through these official channels have helped to prompt authorities to investigate and enforce anticorruption laws.

Pressure on authorities also comes from beyond official channels and the state's mass organizations. In 1988, angry peasants marched in Ho Chi Minh City protesting against "local mandarins" who abused their authority and used their positions to benefit themselves. This event was an early warning that prompted central authorities to pay more attention to corruption (Thayer 1992b: 354). Since then, many more protests against corrupt and loathsome local officials have occurred in the country and have helped turn these matters into national issues. Some poignant examples from Ha Tay and Phu Tho provinces are presented by Hy Van Luong in his chapter on wealth and power in this book. In nearby Thanh Hoa province, a principal cause of 120 incidents of "major or even fierce struggles" between November 1988 and November 1993 was that "some of the local leaders had engaged in corruption, violating the ownership rights of the people," making them "detested" by a majority of ordinary residents and party members. After failing to get satisfactory results from higher authorities to whom villagers had sent petitions and complaints, some residents resorted to public demonstrations and heated confrontations with officials (Nhi Le 1994: 49–50).

In recent years, the most vivid and influential expression of ordinary people's views about corrupt officials was the outburst in Thai Binh, a province at the southeastern end of the Red River delta.[37] Beginning in 1994 and increasing during 1995–1996, villagers sent through normal channels petitions and letters complaining about local authorities. The statements alleged that these authorities were pocketing proceeds from selling land that did not belong to them, misallocating land in ways that made money for themselves, using local tax revenues for their own private purposes, claiming public expenditures were higher than they actually were and then keeping the difference for themselves and their families, and misusing their authority in other ways in order to benefit personally. Adding insult to injury, these authorities flaunted their illicit wealth. They built large houses, filled the homes with nice furniture and appliances, bought expensive motorcycles, and wore fine clothing. The petitioners and letter writers wanted higher authorities to step in, investigate, and punish the culprits. In effect, they wanted higher authorities to maintain the boundaries in these matters between the state and society.

The petitioners received no or only perfunctory responses. Unsatisfied and now more angry, several stepped outside the formal channels and into the streets to voice publicly their discontent. Between late 1996 and the early months of 1997, nearly half of the province's 260 subdistricts had peasant demonstrations; at least forty more occurred in the provincial capital as well. In October 1996, for instance, two groups, the first with 700 and the second with 1,500 people, both from the same subdistrict, went in succession to the provincial capital to present petitions and demand investigations into local officials' improper use of public land and funds. These various demonstrations produced no satisfactory response. This was the situation in May 1997 when thousands of villagers gathered in the district town of Quynh Phu and then made their way on foot and bicycle to the provincial capital. As word spread, villagers from elsewhere also converged on the capital, bringing the total to about 10,000 demonstrators.

Up to this point, all the demonstrations in Thai Binh had reportedly been peaceful, consisting mostly of people sitting or walking in front of government offices pleading for proper investigations into abuses. But the May protest resulted in violence. How it started is not clear. It included police throwing tear gas canisters at the crowds and clubbing and chasing protesters; meanwhile demonstrators threw bricks and stones, smashed office windows, and wrecked a fire truck that had been sent to the scene. Although this clash soon subsided, it proved to be a turning point, leading to more violent clashes during May and June between villagers and authorities in many places across the province. In some areas, villagers overwhelmed policemen, held several of them hostage, and set fire to some local officials' homes (understandable targets given the villagers' complaints), and damaged other property.

The scale and nature of the unrest in Thai Binh provoked national authorities to act. They did not, however, send in the army. National officials, according to available accounts, used limited force to restore order. Their approach emphasized instead dialogue with the demonstrators. They also took measures to minimize publicity and press coverage about the unrest until conditions had been restored to normal. Meanwhile, party and government officials in Hanoi organized investigations into what had happened and why. From such studies they reached basically three conclusions. Many of the villagers' allegations of corruption and other abuses by local authorities were well founded. Second, provincial and other local authorities were negligent for not responding more promptly and thoroughly when villagers first began to complain about the problems. Third, some villagers were provocateurs who took advantage of the discontent to make matters worse. As of September 1999, nearly 2,000 officials in the province had been disciplined.[38] Among them were the provincial secretary of the Communist Party and the chairperson of the provincial council (the two highest officials in Thai Binh), who were removed from office. Further details about disciplinary measures are not reported other than to indicate that about thirty officials were imprisoned. At the same time, some protesters were also charged with crimes having to do with destruction of property, disturbing the peace, and provoking unrest. Between forty and sixty-two protesters were convicted. Most apparently were given short or suspended prison sentences. Some, however, were still in prison more than two years after the event.

The Thai Binh protests sent a strong message to national leaders that corruption is political dynamite. Numerous party and government offices have been studying what happened and drawing lessons about how to avoid similar or worse situations in the future. The message from many top leaders, such as from the nation's president in February 1998, is that firmer, more persistent and determined measures must be taken to defuse the situation by curbing corruption and taking more seriously villagers' complaints about authorities.[39] Whether state authorities are capable of this is debatable. Critics within Vietnam, some of them current and former party members, argue that significant change is impossible so long as the state's leadership refuses to tolerate open and candid criticism and to permit other political organizations to rival the Communist Party. In any event, the demonstrations in Thai Binh and elsewhere are proof that political struggles regarding state-society relations are not confined to official channels and state-dominated organizations.

This chapter suggests an approach for analyzing state-society relations in Vietnam that eschews trying to distinguish between what is in the state and what is in society. Instead, the approach emphasizes arenas in which relations between state and society are problematic. The arenas can be specific places but may also include organizations, groups, policies, and controversies. The four arenas examined here are governing institutions and processes, mass media, agricultural collectives, and corruption. Each is analyzed by using three prominent interpretations in the scholarly literature regarding politics and state-society relations in Vietnam and focusing on two matters: how the political system works and discussions about appropriate state-society relations.

Each arena has considerable evidence to support the "dominating state" interpretation of Vietnam's political system. The Communist Party, government ministries, police, and other agencies of the state have tremendous powers not only over policy making and implementation but over the media, religion, and organizations for various sectors of society. There is also evidence for the "mobilizational corporatist" interpretation, which highlights the role of official organizations in both mobilizing support for the state and being a channel through which people's concerns can influence what state agencies do. However, individuals, groups, and social forces outside official channels can also affect the political system. This is what the "dialogical" interpretation is pointing out. State agencies do not completely control policy making and implementation. People can ignore the state's rules on some matters. They can also go beyond official channels to make their views and concerns known. Groups and forces in society beyond the reach of the state not only exist but their activities from time to time influence what authorities decide.

In each arena, this chapter also finds ongoing deliberations regarding proper relations between the state and the rest of society. Discussion on these matters occurs in many forms and in numerous places, including inside state institutions themselves. The tendency during the last twenty years, resulting in part from societal forces and activities, has been to reduce and change the scope of what the state should do in the economy and other aspects of society. The outcome thus far has been more space in which people can live without directly interacting with agencies of the state. At the same time, the state remains in control of the media. State institutions still, despite pressures from within and outside them, allow citizens only a little room to establish their own organizations in order to speak and act publicly on important issues. Hence, Vietnamese nongovernment organizations and other signs of civil society have only recently begun to emerge.

NOTES

For their helpful and challenging comments on drafts of this essay, I am grateful to Kit Collier, Adam Fforde, Andrew Hardy, Melinda Tria Kerkvliet, David Koh, David Marr, and Kim Ninh. I also thank Pham Thu Thuy for assisting with the research for this study and Bev Fraser for helping to prepare the manuscript.

An earlier version of "Authorities and the People: An Analysis of State-Society Relations in Vietnam" by Benedict J. Tria Kerkvliet appeared as "An Approach for Analysing State-Society Relations in Vietnam" in *SOJOURN: Journal of Social Issues in Southeast Asia*, Vol. 16, No. 2 (October 2001), pp. 238–78. It is reproduced here with the kind permission of the publisher, Institute of Southeast Asian Studies, Singapore.

1. Helping me to come to this position are Migdal 1994 and Mitchell 1991. For earlier analyses of Vietnam using a similar approach, see Fforde and Porter 1994: 8–9, 27; and Kerkvliet 1995a: 40–43.

2. My discussion of society and state corresponds broadly to how the two are used in Migdal 1994 and in Kohli and Shue 1994.

3. I am trying to include here both the physical and structural aspects of state (buildings, offices, army, bureaucrats, government officials, roadways, etc.) and the ideological dimension and psychological impact of a state. The state includes agencies that keep the wheels of government turning (issue passports, police cities, create new laws, punish violators, mobilize armies, collect taxes, build new buildings); but the state also has purposes, plans, and objectives. How extensive and elaborate those are varies over time within the same state and from one state to another.

4. "Civil society," as several well-read scholars have explained, has meant many, often contradictory, things in "western" political thought and practice. My usage draws on Keane 1988; Krygier 1996; and Kumar 1993.

5. In order to elaborate and illustrate each, I refer to some publications written in English. By no means do the mentioned ones exhaust the literature. A comprehensive synthesis of pertinent literature is another project entirely. Also, a reference to a particular scholar's work does not mean that everything that person has written about Vietnam fits within one interpretation and one only. Given that this field of study is relatively young and new information appears frequently, an individual scholar can come to one tentative conclusion at one stage but arrive at a different one later on.

6. See, for example, Thai Quang Trung 1985 and Stern 1993. Also see Kolko 1997: 119–25, 130–32. While arguing that the party runs the country, Kolko says it is riddled by factions competing over "wealth and power," not ideological issues, and united only by the desire that the party retain "total power" (125, 130).

7. For state corporatist arguments, see Jeong 1997 and Stromseth 1998.

8. Also see Vasavakul 1996, which highlights disarray in the Vietnam state's administrative capacity and efforts by national authorities in the mid-1990s to regain the upper hand over local officials.

9. Such usage applied to Vietnam appears in Post 1989: 14, 212; Pelzer 1993; Luong 1994; and Kerkvliet 1999.

10. For studies of election processes, see Thayer 1993; Koh 2000: chap. 3; and Porter 1993: 153–57.

11. For details of the chamber's growth and its relationship to the state, see Stromseth 1998: chaps. 3 and 4. Presumably the chamber is now under the Fatherland Front, although Stromseth's discussion does not make that clear.

12. Hoi Nong Dan Viet Nam, Ban Chap Hanh Trung Uong, "Bao Cao cua Ban Chap Hanh Trung Uong Hoi Nong Dan Viet Nam (Khoa 1) tai Dai Hoi Dai Bieu Toan Quoc Lan Thu 2, 15–19/11/1993" [Vietnam Peasants' Association, Central executive committee, "Report of the central executive committee, Vietnam Peasants' Association (1st session), at the second national congress, 15–19 November 1993"], p. 12.

13. A short history of the Peasants' Association has pages listing war-related efforts of its predecessor organizations in south and north Vietnam. Ban Chap Hanh Trung Uong Hoi Nong Dan Viet Nam – Vien Lich Su Dang, "De Cuong Chi Tiet Lich Su Phong Trao Nong Dan va Hoi Nong Dan Viet Nam, 1930–1992" [Central executive committee of the Vietnam Peasant Association and the Bureau for (Communist) Party history, "Detailed guidelines for a history of Vietnam's peasant movement and Peasants' Association, 1930–1992"], Hanoi, 1992. I thank Jonathan Stromseth for providing me a copy of this unpublished report.

14. Interview with Nguyen Van Chinh, President, Vietnam Peasants' Association, Hanoi, 21 September 1995. Also see Kerkvliet 1995b: 87–88.

15. Local authorities sometimes assisted residents out of compassion and empathy for people who had no other options but to ignore the building codes; other times they helped because the residents were relatives; still other times they helped in exchange for payments and other remuneration from residents. See Koh 2000: chap. 5.

16. Several news reports about Dong Nai appear in Reuters News Service between November 1997 and 15 January 1998. References for other cases include Deutsche-Presse-Agentur, 21 October 1998, Reuters News Service, 20 May 1999; and Kerkvliet 1995b: 76–79; Vasavakul 1998: 317–18.

17. For illustrative writing and reports about UBCV and its encounters with Vietnamese authorities see Denny 1992: 3–7, and Amor 1998. For views of a prominent UBCV leader, see Thich Quang Do 1995.

18. For a splendid analysis, see Fforde and de Vylder 1996.

19. For an informative account of how the media is organized in Vietnam under the Communist Party, see Heng 1998.

20. Examples are "Nguoi Sai Gon: Tieng Noi cua Nhan Dan Them Tu Do Ngon Luan" [Saigoner: voice of the people craving free speech], which began in early 1996 (as of mid-1999, issues appeared in the following website but when I checked again in early 2000, they were not there: www.lmvntd.org/dossier/ngsaigon); and "Thao Thuc: To Bao cua Gioi Tre Viet Nam trong Nuoc" [On alert: newspaper of young Vietnamese in the country], beginning in March 1998 (for several issues, see www.lmvntd.org/dossier/thaothuc).

21. For recent analyses of this episode, see Boudarel 1990: 154–74; Boudarel 1991; Nguyen Hung Quoc 1991: chap. 2; Ninh 1996: chap. 4; and Heng 1999: chap. 3.

22. See articles in *Nhan Dan*, the daily newspaper of the Communist Party (e.g., a series on human rights, 2, 3, 28 June 1993; 1 and 16 May 1998); and statements to international fora, such as Deputy Minister of Justice Ha Hung Cuong's message to the United Nations Commission for Human Rights, Geneva, 28 March 2000 (BBC Summary of World Broadcasts, 3 April 2000).

23. "Nha Van Hoang Tien Phan Doi Ha Noi Dan Ap Tu Do Ngon Luan" [The writer Hoang Tien opposes Hanoi for suppressing free speech], *Tivi Tuan San*, 16 September 1998, 56. *Tivi Tuan San* [TV Weekly], published in Melbourne, frequently carries articles about and by people in Vietnam who criticize the government.

24. This paragraph draws on Russell Heng's perceptive analysis of the print media (1999: chaps. 3, 5, 6).

25. Years later, after retiring from the military, General Tran Do expressed his views more fully in letters addressed to the highest party officials. The letters were subsequently circulated around the world through Internet and foreign publications. These writings, which upset top officials so much that they expelled him from the Communist Party in January 1999, have made him a well-known "dissident" who seeks a more open and competitive political system. Tran Do, "Tinh Hinh Dat Nuoc va Vai Tro cua Dang Cong San" [The state of the nation and role of the Communist Party; an undated (circa December 1997) letter to Communist Party leaders], serialized in *Tivi Tuan San* (Melbourne), 11, 18, 25 February 1998. (An English translation was put on the Internet in early January 1998: www.fva.org/document/dissident/trando.htm.). This long letter was followed in 1998 and 1999 by several more missives, which also appeared in Vietnamese language publications outside the country. His letters, so far as I am aware, have yet to be published in Vietnam.

26. Unless otherwise noted, my discussion of agricultural collectives leans on Vickerman 1986; Quang Truong 1987; Fforde 1989; and Kerkvliet 1998 and 1999.

27. Indicative is that the average collective in 1960 had 59 households but a decade later had 156 and in 1980 had 387. Vietnam, General Statistical Office 1973: 557, 559; Vietnam, General Statistical Office and Ministry of Agriculture and Food Industries 1991: 73.

28. *Nhan Dan*, 25 April 1984, quoted in Quang Truong 1987: 263.

29. Vietnam, Ministry of Agriculture, "Bao Cao Tong Ket Nong Nghiep Nam 1983 va Ba Nam 1981–1983 va Nghiem Vu Chu Yeu Cua Nganh Nam 1984" [Ministry of Agriculture, Summary report on agriculture in 1983 and the three years 1981–1983 and particular tasks for 1984], February 1984, p.14 (Phong Bo Nong Nghiep, ho so 548, vinh vien, National Archives number 3, Hanoi).

30. Asked whether the collective was part of the state, a villager gave me a puzzled face as if to say "what kind of question is that?" He then answered with a wry smile that if it were, he should have been getting a state salary, and if he had that salary, he would not have lived so miserably as he did during the height of collectivization. (Interview in Nghiem Xuyen, Thuong Tin, Ha Tay, 2 May 1996.)

31. Nguyen Van Linh, former Communist Party secretary general (1986–1991), Reuter News Service, 10 May 1993. Similar usage appears in many publications in Vietnam. See, for instance, Dao Tri Uc 1997, an article by the head of Vietnam's Institute on State and Law.

32. The 1,115 known cases of corruption in 1999 involved 1.35 trillion *dong* going illicitly to authorities. (*Kyodo News*, 21 January 2000, through Reuters Limited.) At 14,000 *dong* per U.S. dollar, the average is U.S. $86,482 per case. No doubt the extent of actual corruption is far greater than the number of known cases.

33. For an example, see "Huyet Tam Thu To Cao Tham Nhung cua 11 Dang Vien Dang CSVN" [A painful letter denouncing corruption from eleven members of the Communist Party of Vietnam], *Tivi Tuan San*, 5 August 1988, pp. 68, 100.

34. Accounts by Reuter News Service, 17–23 February 1994.

35. Accounts by Reuter News Service, 12 November and 6 December 1999 and 15 January 2000.

36. For examples, see Heng 1999: chap. 5; Sidel 1998.

37. Unless otherwise indicated, the following account relies primarily on a report commissioned by the prime minister and written by Tuong Lai, head of the Sociology Institute of the National Center for Social Sciences and Humanities, entitled "Bao Cao So Bo ve Cuoc Khao Sat Xa Hoi tai Thai Binh cuoi Thang Sau, dau Thang Bay Nam 1997" [Prelim-

inary report of a sociological investigation in Thai Binh in late June and early July 1997], 8 August 1997; a serialized story published in *Tien Phong* 2, 4, 7, and 9 October 1997; and an article in *Dai Doan Ket*, 23 February 1998, p. 6.

38. This and the following information about punishments come from news reports from Associated Press, 11 November 1997; AFP, 25 August 1998; *Vietnam Economic News*, 23 September 1999; *South China Morning Post*, 25 September 1999; *San Jose Mercury News*, 31 October 1999.

39. President Tran Duc Luong's February 1998 speech in Thai Binh appears in *Sai Gon Giai Phong*, 4 and 5 March 1998, p. 5.

2

Economic Transition, Uneven Development, and the Impact of Reform on Regional Inequality

Melanie Beresford

From the outset in the Soviet Union during the first half of the twentieth century, one of the main reasons for introduction of the socialist economic model was to eliminate the uneven development characteristic of capitalism. This unevenness can be seen in the constant pursuit of profit which causes capital to move to new industries and regions, abandoning old ones and leading to a pattern of boom in one sphere together with decline in another. The very competitiveness of capitalism, while it provides enormous benefits through technological progress, leads to insecurity for the poor, for workers in declining industries, and for those living in regions left behind in the otherwise dynamic search for profit. Uneven development can be manifested in income inequality between and within social classes, between regions, between cities and countryside, between genders, and between ethnic groups, depending on how this dynamic growth affects the distribution of investment and employment. Socialism as implemented (in the Soviet Union and other countries) through central planning and state ownership of productive assets was, at least initially, seen as a way of overcoming uneven development and creating a more egalitarian economic system.

Even within the most advanced market economies state intervention, whether at the national or local level, has historically been a tool for attempting to reverse the pattern of uneven development. Moreover, while differentials are to a certain extent inevitable due to varying resource endowments, there is broad agreement among economists of all persuasions that growth with equity provides the best possibility for long-term sustainable growth. There is now abundant evidence, especially from East Asia, that more equitable growth, by maintaining a strong domestic demand, reducing bottlenecks in the supply of skilled labor and domestic savings, and creating dynamic linkages between urban and rural areas, can speed up the growth process. Greater equality can also reduce class tensions and the potential for regional fragmentation of the national polity. For the less developed regions of the globe, the issue is thus a very important one.

For Vietnam, this issue has been complicated by the process of transition from a socialist planned economy to a market economy. Two decades of implementing the socialist model brought neither the expected rapid growth nor, as argued below, growth with equity. At the end of the 1970s the country embarked on a process of economic reform, while a decade later saw it transformed into a market economy, albeit not overtly capitalist. In Communist Party ideology the new system is described as a "market mechanism with State management and a socialist orientation" (Vietnam, Communist Party 1996: 15). In the new context "socialism" is taken to mean continuation of public ownership of key economic assets, state intervention to guide resources into politically desired avenues, and the creation of an "equitable and civilised society" (37). During the 1990s, the reforms were largely successful in producing rapid growth, to the extent that many commentators spoke of a new Asian "tiger" economy. Some progress was made, therefore, toward entering the virtuous circle of growth at the national level. However, there is also a widespread perception that the high growth has been distributed very unevenly and has led to an increase in both social and regional inequality.

The objective of this chapter is to examine regional aspects of the economic transformation that has taken place over the last two decades in Vietnam. In order to achieve this aim, part 1 first examines the socialist planned economy and the factors contributing to the adoption of reform measures. It suggests that while the threat to the growth project entailed in the series of economic crises that hit Vietnam in the second half of the 1970s was the major reason for embarking on reform, the issue of equity and a perception of unfairness in the actual operation of the planned economy was also present among the political pressures leading to change. Part 2 focuses more narrowly on regional issues, particularly the impact of the transition process on interprovincial inequality. It gives some empirical foundation to the widespread perception that inequality has increased as a result of the transition and shows that state intervention currently is, at best, only partially directed toward reversing the trend. Unless a more even development process is achieved in the future, there are dangers of tensions reemerging. This is especially likely to occur if, in the post–Asian crisis era, growth and poverty reduction are slower.

A word of caution is in order before we proceed, however. Data on which to base an empirical examination of regional inequality have been, and remain, extremely scarce. Few statistics on province-level economies have been published that would permit an examination of changes over time. The most detailed information is available for the 1990s, but it is still fragmentary and reliability is reduced by frequent boundary changes and lack of consistency due to the transition from socialist methods of accounting to the UN system of national accounts. Tracking changes through time has been possible by using data on gross value of industrial output (GVIO) which provides only a partial indicator of the relative performance of local economies. GVIO does have the advantage that it provides a good reflection of the relative wealth of provinces: the level of industrialization has long been a primary indicator of economic development.[1] The results presented below may, however, provide only a broad indication of trends during the transition from central planning and, due to the limitations of statistical data collection during this period, it seems unlikely that more adequate data will become available in the future.

THE PLANNED ECONOMY AND THE TRANSITION PROCESS

A Developing Crisis in the Planned Economy 1976–1986

Under the Geneva Accords of 1954, the Democratic Republic of Vietnam (DRV) established undisputed control over the northern half of the country and was able, in the ensuing years, to achieve a partial rehabilitation of its war-torn economy. In view of the increasingly hostile attitude of the United States and its supporters in the South, the DRV turned to China and the Soviet Union for support and began, during 1958–1960, to establish a Soviet-style socialist economy. Nationalization of French-owned assets had taken place as soon as the French army departed and the process was now extended to Vietnamese and ethnic Chinese capitalists, while petty traders and artisans were propelled into cooperatives. Collectivization of agriculture was also stepped up, especially during 1959, with the widespread application of a cooperative model borrowed from China. Finally, in late 1960, at the Third Party Congress, the introduction of mandatory central planning was announced together with the First Five Year Plan (1961–1965). Within the space of a few years, private sector activity became illegal, except on the so-called "five percent plots" which farm households were permitted to retain, and markets were supposedly eliminated.

The reality of the DRV economy during the ensuing two decades, however, was more complicated than suggested by the model the party attempted to impose. Throughout the period of central planning, a tension existed between the desire of the Communist Party to tighten and expand the influence of planning, and the activities of cadres and ordinary citizens that tended to undermine the plan. Like other socialist countries, Vietnam developed an "outside" (in the Vietnamese terminology) or second economy.

In the sphere of agriculture, for example, the process of collectivization did not proceed smoothly. During 1960–1963 the number of peasant households belonging to cooperatives actually fell, while there was apparent lack of interest from upper middle and rich peasants,[2] despite their domination of both party membership and cooperative management boards (Gordon 1981: 30–35). The move toward establishing higher-level cooperatives was renewed in 1964, but Fforde's detailed study of the cooperative management system during the 1970s shows that few actually functioned as the government intended (Fforde 1989). Instead, a wide variety of arrangements existed, including extension of household plots beyond the 5 percent of land officially permitted (often in favor of cadres and their families and friends) and refusal to issue plan targets by cooperative managers. In the celebrated case of Vinh Phuc province, the local Party Committee passed a resolution in 1966 permitting subcontracting of land to individual households, a move that was quashed by the center two years later. However, as several authors have shown, such fundamental modifications of the official model for cooperatives showed a tendency to recur, although it was not until 1981 that they were legalized.

The basic problem with cooperatives, not only in the north but in the south after reunification in 1976, lay in the lack of incentives for increased output and productivity. At the root of this problem was the official pricing system, which offered low procurement prices to cooperatives in order to maintain low wages in the urban sector and boost industrial profits of state-owned enterprises. Market prices for both agricultural produce and industrial goods, on the other hand, tended to be above the official prices, encouraging the diversion of state-supplied goods onto black markets and leading farmers to devote more time and effort to production on their household plots, the output from which could be legally sold on the free market. Estimates of peasant income earned from these plots rose from about 40 percent in the 1960s to 60–70 percent by the late 1970s. Since those with priority access to state-supplied goods were generally party members and officials, the system created opportunities for capital accumulation and new class divisions within the countryside. It is important to note here that it was their position within the cooperative structures that gave cadres such opportunities to profit from outside activities and this is one of the key factors leading to widespread perception of the unfairness of the system.

Distribution of income within the cooperatives also created problems for increasing output and productivity. It was, in a formal sense, highly egalitarian since minimum supplies of food and security of land tenure were guaranteed while health, education, and other welfare facilities (such as child care) were also provided to all members. These benefits came at a high cost, however, as cooperative production stagnated in the long term and egalitarianism became a case of "shared poverty" rather than rising overall living standards. Moreover, as demands from the government for procurement to feed urban cadres and industry rose, the residual output available for distribution to cooperative members declined, creating further incentives to reduce labor in cooperative fields and increase that applied to household plots and to commercial activities outside the plan (Beresford 1989; Fforde 1989).

A further element that led to growing popular dissatisfaction with the cooperative model arose from the socialist objective itself. Cooperatives were actually rather successful in providing social benefits. Schools, for example, were established in every village, as were health clinics, child care centers, and other social services. Those who could no longer lead active productive lives received assistance from the cooperative. During the anti-American war, with the absence from home of large numbers of able-bodied males at the front, such facilities took some of the burden off the remaining workforce (especially women) and, given wide popular support for the war effort, were generally supported. They were a major factor leading to Vietnam's high ranking on social indicators like life expectancy, infant mortality, and literacy compared with other countries of similar or even considerably higher national incomes (Beresford 1995a). After the war, however, the need to support large numbers of teachers, health workers, and other cadres on a low production base made them unpopular. Standards of service also began to drop when Chinese and Soviet aid cuts bit into the state budget in the late 1970s and further reduced resources available to sustain welfare and education.

Conflict of interest was therefore very apparent in the actual functioning of the cooperative system in Vietnamese agriculture. The needs of the poorest families for a more equal distribution and those of households most able to benefit from outside activities differed, as did those of cooperative farmers as a whole and of the government. Pressure on lower- and middle-level cadres tended to increase as, on one side, farmers' demands to reform the cooperative system grew and, on the other side, the center's procurement requirements also rose.[3] These contradictions only sharpened after reunification, particularly in the Mekong delta–Ho Chi Minh City region, where the market economy was firmly entrenched. The so-called "middle" peasants, the chief beneficiaries of land reforms in the 1960s and 1970s, stood to lose substantially through the collectivization campaign of 1977–1978. Their passive resistance meant that available surpluses dropped sharply (Beresford 1989: 113–15) and black market activities intensified, despite the massive government clampdown on mainly ethnic Chinese businesses during 1978.

As Vietnam entered the 1980s, the scope of "outside" economic activity in the rural areas continued to increase and a powerful coalition of rural interests in favor of system reform began to emerge. Southern provincial politicians in particular, fearing the loss of their peasant support base, became vocal spokespersons for change within the party and government apparatus. They found allies among the generation who had earlier thought that collectivization in the north had gone too far.

A similar state of affairs existed within the state-owned industrial enterprise system. This had expanded rapidly following implementation of the First Five Year Plan (FYP) (1961–1965), but problems were already emerging (Fforde and Paine 1987) before American wartime bombing operations destroyed much of the capacity created. High investment rates in industrial capacity, particularly in heavy industry projects with long lead times, created a demand for resources that could not be met from the existing stream of output (Beresford 1989). While the resulting shortages were to some extent alleviated by foreign aid, they were never eliminated altogether and the Vietnamese economy, like other socialist economies, became characterized by chronic disequilibrium between supply and demand. Moreover, shortages within the planned sector were aggravated by the difference between official and market prices, which diverted resources to the outside economy (Fforde and Paine 1987). They were further exacerbated by the very large investment program entailed in the Second Five Year Plan (1976–1980), undertaken in a context of aid cuts. Reduced levels of foreign aid meant that supplies of raw materials and consumer goods were further restricted as long as the program of construction was maintained. Total aid availability fell from an average of U.S. $25 per head (including U.S. aid to the south) during 1970–1974 to only half that amount in 1976–1980 (Beresford and Dang Phong 2000).[4] While imports of investment goods were maintained at or above planned levels, those of raw materials for domestic production declined. Between 1976 and 1980, domestic availability per capita of iron and steel more than halved, fertilizer supplies fell by 65 percent, and petroleum products fell by a third. Per capita imports of rice and other cereals, on the other hand, had to be more than doubled up to 1979 as the combination of natural disaster, reduced fertilizer supplies, and failing collectivization in the south cut the availability of food for urban workers (Beresford and Dang Phong 2000).

Faced with a serious crisis situation, which was scarcely alleviated by renewed warfare (with Pol Pot's Kampuchea and with China in 1979), and under pressure from multiple sources within Vietnam, the party leadership opted for a process of gradual reform. During 1979–1981 a number of key reforms were pushed through, essentially legalizing some outside activity by individuals and production units. The earliest reforms, in the second half of 1979, allowed limited autonomy to farmers and enterprises. More important were:

- the partial decentralization of foreign trade in early 1980, which allowed local authorities to trade on their own behalf and effectively began the process of Vietnam's integration into the Asian regional economy;
- the introduction in 1981 of output contracts in agriculture, permitting allocation of cooperative land to individual households and sale of surplus product on the free market;
- the so-called "Three Plan System" in industry which, from 1981, for the first time sanctioned some production for the market by state enterprises (SEs);
- a price reform in late 1981 that brought official prices and wages closer to market prices and removed all but a handful of consumer goods from the centralized rationing system.

By early 1982, a recovery was underway and party fears of the reemergence of capitalism were renewed, causing it to take measures against further private sector development, including a renewed attempt to collectivize southern agriculture. However, the structural changes taking place since the second half of the 1970s meant that these were only partially successful, if at all. The outside economy continued to expand while the difficulties of the planned sector continued, not least because in reality the bulk of state investment still flowed into large-scale heavy industry projects. Shortages in the latter sector were exacerbated by the attempted recentralization, leading to high inflation in the increasingly monetized outside economy (176 percent in 1984 [World Bank 1994: 131]). Moreover, the necessity to subsidize unprofitable SEs contributed to high budget deficits, an inability to finance the external debt, and renewed stagnation in the agricultural sector.

In the face of the new crisis the government, in September 1985, introduced a further round of reforms aimed at price liberalization, ending the ration system, and monetization of wages for state employees. By that time almost all the southern and central provinces plus a number in the north were refusing to implement plan directives and/or pressuring the government for wider reform. However, the impact of this reform was blunted by several different political pressures on the government at this time (see Beresford and Fforde 1997 for a more detailed discussion). The southern provinces were already at a more advanced stage of commercialization, with a correspondingly higher cost of living, and demanded big wage increases for government workers that resulted in large budget deficits. SE directors, especially those in the older, less efficient northern sector, demanded retention of the two-price system for industrial inputs.[5] Within three months of the reform's implementation Vietnam had galloping inflation,[6] and the reform was partially reversed. Nevertheless, a further substantial shift toward commercialization of the economy had been achieved.

Doi Moi (Renovation)

By 1986 the Vietnamese socialist economy had already undergone major structural and institutional changes toward the formation of a market economy. Official statistics on this period do not reflect these changes as they continued to measure only the planned economic sector. However, other evidence indicates strongly that transactions taking place outside the scope of the plan were of increasing importance (Fforde and de Vylder 1996). Not only was a large proportion of agricultural output being marketed, but there were also signs of a rudimentary capital market as SEs sought ways to utilize capital accumulated through nonplan activities. Under the impact of these developments and also the fact that the rationing system had virtually disappeared after the 1985 reform, political pressure for further changes to the system increased.

At the Sixth Party Congress in December 1986, membership changed in favor of a younger generation more versed in the problems of the local level economy. There was also increased representation in the highest positions of those with long experience in the south (Beresford 1988: 113), a change that seems to reflect recognition of the relative success of the more commercialized southern region in overcoming the constraints of the planning system. The emergence of these and other reformers at the top in turn opened the way for many more junior cadres to express their views freely. The 1986 Congress thus became a turning point for the reform process in the sense that it took a conscious decision to build a market economy in Vietnam, rather than attempt further adjustment and reform of the planned economy.

By the late 1980s the planned economy had disintegrated to the extent that there was no longer sufficient strength of interest in attempting to make it work. Even within the SE sector, which had strongly resisted the proposal to implement market prices in 1985, there was no longer any interest in maintaining the old system. The upsurge of inflation during 1986 forced state sector workers, unable to survive on their official wages, to devote more and more time and effort to outside activities.

Productivity in the SEs declined, requiring higher levels of subsidy and generating yet more inflation through rising budget deficits. While Soviet aid continued to be available in the late 1980s, the rise of Gorbachev to power and the introduction of Perestroika (restructuring) in the Soviet Union in 1986 meant that aid would no longer be provided on the same generous terms as before (it was finally cut in 1991). The Vietnamese state was therefore faced with a looming fiscal crisis that convinced even the highest levels that further reform was their only option.

The reforms of the late 1980s are widely regarded in the Western literature as the only ones of importance. Indeed a number of authors have described the reform package of 1989, in particular, as constituting a "Big Bang" or "shock therapy" type of reform that introduced the market economy for the first time in Vietnam. What we have seen above, however, is that the market economy had been in the process of forming in Vietnam since the late 1970s. If we want to understand the relative success of these reforms in Vietnam (as compared, for example, to the results of "shock therapy" in some East European countries or the Soviet Union), then it is important to understand that to all intents and purposes the Vietnamese economy by the late 1980s was already a market economy. Policies designed for a market economy are more likely to work in a market economy than in a planned economy.

The first major reform of Doi Moi was the Foreign Investment Law, passed in December 1987 and implemented in the following year. By Southeast Asian standards, this was a very liberal law, allowing for 100 percent foreign ownership and profit repatriation, significant tax holidays, and concessions for enterprises investing in a number of priority areas (including exports, consumer goods, technology transfer, and processing of local raw materials). The resulting inflow was small at first, but by 1994 it amounted to $U.S. 1.5 billion per annum and constituted nearly a third of Vietnam's total investment effort. The majority was in joint ventures with Vietnamese partners, mostly SEs. Moreover, in the 1990s Western aid to Vietnam began to increase rapidly and this brought with it a stream of foreign contractors. Foreign companies and aid donors now constitute an important interest group applying pressure for further market-oriented reforms and for changes to the legal system to bring it into line with Western norms.

In March 1988 Resolution 10 of the Politburo effectively led to decollectivization in the Vietnamese countryside. Although many cooperatives continued to exist, their functions were severely curtailed and, most importantly, they were no longer given a role in production. Instead land was distributed for a period of fifteen years (or fifty years in cases of perennial crops) to households who were put in charge of all decisions relating to production and investment. Government procurement contracts were abolished and all output could be sold at market prices. This reform had very positive effects on agricultural output and in 1989 Vietnam shifted from being a net importer of rice to being the world's third largest exporter (although the immediate increase in supply was also related to the success of anti-inflation measures in that year). However, a number of the more useful functions provided by the cooperatives were adversely affected. In particular, householders were reluctant to make contributions to cooperative health and welfare facilities, and the cooperative maintenance of irrigation schemes also tended to suffer. Responsibility for provision of these, as well as other local infrastructure, has shifted to the commune (village) and district levels of government, yet these also suffered severe cuts in revenue after 1989. The impact of these changes has inevitably fallen hardest on the poor. However, as overall living standards have risen, the potential for rural class conflict has been blunted at the same time.

During 1989 the government abolished official prices (except for a handful of government monopolies), floated the exchange rate, and introduced positive real interest rates in the banking system. The first two of these mean that all prices, including the exchange rate against foreign currencies, are now basically market prices, although the State Bank does control the exchange rate through its market operations. Direct subsidies from the state budget to SEs were effectively ended—a clear necessity in the face of the impending termination of Soviet aid. Positive real interest rates[7] (temporarily reversed in 1990–1991) were used to encourage savings, halt the dollarization of the economy,[8] reduce indirect subsidies to SEs via cheap credit provision, halt the growth of the budget deficit, and bring inflation under control.

The impact of this package on the economy was dramatic. Inflation was reduced from 308 percent per annum in 1988 to only 36 percent in 1990 (World Bank 1994: 131) and the domestic savings ratio improved. With the reduction in inflation, much of the incentive to hoard goods for speculative purposes disappeared and there was an increase in supply (particularly of rice) so that shortages were eliminated and inflation was able to be brought further under control. Industrial output has also risen rapidly since the reform. At the same time, many of the least profitable SEs closed their doors—the number of still operating enterprises had been halved by 1993—and in industry there was a significant reduction in employment as formerly subsidized SEs sought to become profitable. Within the state sector, the total number of employees was reduced from 3.86 million in 1985 (about 15 percent of the total labor force) to 2.92 million in 1993 (or 9 percent). Employment in the cooperative industrial sector declined even more precipitously, from 1.2 million in 1988 to 287,600 in 1992 (Vietnam, General Statistical Office 1995). Women workers were the majority of those affected. Unemployment rose to some 13 percent of the workforce, but many of those laid off were able to find work in the burgeoning household sector or in the informal sector, particularly in farming, trade, and services. There was therefore a substantial shift in the employment structure.

Control over inflation has seen a significant return of confidence in the Vietnamese currency, an increased savings ratio and a rapid growth of GDP (at over 8 percent per annum in 1992–1997). These sustained high growth rates in a labor-intensive economy mean that unemployment began to diminish, although given the irregular character of much informal sector employment, underemployment remains a serious problem affecting farmers and women most of all.

Following on the heels of forced restructuring during 1989–1991, the high growth rates of the early 1990s were brought about chiefly through improvements in efficiency. The elimination of hyperinflation reduced speculation and the waste of resources, abolition of subsidies to SEs provided incentives for improved productivity and a shift of resources into more profitable areas of production, while labor shedding tended to increase output per worker. Later in the decade, as foreign investment increased, chiefly in joint ventures with SEs, and the rate of domestic saving and investment continued to improve, growth moved on to a more sustainable footing. The large budget deficits of the 1980s were eliminated, exports increased dramatically, and Western aid flowed in to fund infrastructure improvements and restore financing for education and health. Overall living standards improved and the number of people living in extreme poverty declined dramatically. However, there remain a number of clouds on the horizon—notably a precipitous decline in foreign investment during the Asian crisis since 1997, a lack of capacity to raise revenue from the burgeoning private sector, and the difficulty of achieving further structural reform of the SEs and of the state-run banking system. Moreover, there are clear indications that while uneven development was by no means absent in the old system, the market economy of the 1990s has brought with it greater inequities than existed before.

UNEVEN DEVELOPMENT: THE REGIONAL IMPACT OF REFORM

Uneven Development in the Planned Economy

Planned economies did not succeed in eliminating uneven development. Indeed, in most countries, investment patterns were deliberately biased toward urban-based industry rather than agriculture or rural industries, and toward heavy rather than light industry. However, they did succeed in bringing about reductions in social inequalities, especially those between classes.

In the case of northern Vietnam, there is evidence that while social inequalities were greatly reduced under central planning, regional inequalities in output and accumulation were large and persistent. In the case of social inequality, despite the existence of the nomenclature system which gave privileged access in consumption to those in the higher echelons, the differentials were by no means as high as those prevailing in the capitalist world. Apart from the relative equality of individual incomes, social consumption was also more widespread than in similarly less developed capitalist countries. Women, farmers, and ethnic minorities had more equal access to education, health care, and other social benefits than their counterparts in some regional countries with much higher per capita incomes. Nor is there much to indicate that the social inequality that did exist contained a strong spatial dimension (Beresford and McFarlane 1995: 57); in other words, such social divisions were spread uniformly across the country.

Regional variations in output and accumulation, however, were much larger. Gross value of industrial output (GVIO) in 1974 was 46 times higher in Hanoi (the richest province) than in Lai Chau (the poorest) (Beresford and McFarlane

1995: 56). The three richest provinces (Hanoi, Hai Phong and Quang Ninh), containing 15 percent of the population, produced half of all industrial output. Capital accumulation and growth were thus very much concentrated in a handful of more industrialized cities and provinces. Planned investment expenditures favored the three industrialized cities/provinces, despite some redistribution toward the five poorest provinces (Vietnam, General Statistical Office 1976). While social redistribution could be achieved by allocating subsidized consumer goods and services to the rural population, these had little effect on the skewed pattern of accumulation and growth set in motion by state investments. Once the transition to a market economy began, however, the legacy of this pattern was an economy that lacked many of the prerequisites for an equitable regional distribution of growth.

Regional inequality in production and investment was further skewed by reunification of the country in 1976. Data are not available until 1981, at the outset of the transition, and indicate that the 14 percent of the population living in the eight poorest provinces produced just 3 percent of industrial output, while the same proportion living in the five richest provinces (the industrial centers of Ho Chi Minh City, Hanoi, Vung Tau, Haiphong, and Quang Ninh) produced 58 percent of output (Vietnam, General Statistical Office 1982).

While we have no data on interprovincial income distribution for the southern region prior to reunification, it seems safe to assume that these figures reflect greater inequality in the south.[9] The data presented below in table 2.1 show higher inequality in the south than in the north in 1981. Improved interprovincial equality in the former DRV during 1974–1981, shown in this table, also suggests that the higher inequality was not the result of introducing the socialist model across the whole country after 1976.

Spatial Inequality during the Transition from Plan to Market

If central planning was characterized by persistent regional inequalities, the transition to market shows a more variable trend. In the initial stages of reform spatial equality improved, but as the full force of the reforms came into effect around 1990 there was a sharp deterioration. By the second half of the 1990s a pattern of rising inequality was clearly emerging along the urban-rural divide.

As noted in the introduction, provincial data are most consistently available for gross value of industrial output (GVIO), from which table 2.1 is derived. The table presents coefficients of variation, a relatively simple measure of changes in inequality between provinces over a period covering twenty-four years from 1974 to 1997. Coefficients of variation are based on standard deviations from the mean which, in this case, measure the average amount by which GVIO of provinces deviate from the average for all provinces in the sample. Since GVIO at different periods is measured at different prices, however, it is necessary to reduce these to ratios that will make the numbers comparable over time.[10] The higher the coefficient, the greater the degree of inequality.

Table 2.1. Coefficients of Variation in Per Capita GVIO Between Provinces, 1974–1997

Year	Whole country	Agricultural provinces	Industrial provinces	North (former DRV)	South (former RVN)
1974				1.186	
1981	1.212	0.629	0.623	1.092	1.424
1987	0.939	0.440	0.617	0.993	0.904
1990	1.826	0.582	1.024	1.658	1.839
1993	2.559	0.745	1.440	1.385	2.367
1997	2.086	0.631	1.032	1.226	2.013

Source: Vietnam, General Statistical Office, *Statistical Yearbook,* various issues.

For the year 1974 data are available only for the eighteen provinces of the former DRV, but for later years figures are given for thirty-nine provinces of the reunified country. Since there have been several province divisions during the period under consideration (there are now sixty-one provinces), data for new provinces have been aggregated into the earlier ones for consistency.

Table 2.1 indicates that some convergence in provincial incomes occurred during the earlier stages of transition in the 1980s, but that this convergence was dramatically reversed after the major reforms of 1988–1989. This pattern is replicated for the mainly agricultural provinces, and for the more industrialized regions comprising two of the government's designated "growth-pole" regions, around Ho Chi Minh City and the Hanoi–Hai Phong–Quang Ninh triangle. Since 1993, however, the pattern is less clear. The data on per capita GVIO show a renewed tendency toward interprovincial equality, although inequality remained very high. For these years, however, data have also become available for per capita GDP (table 2.2) and these show an opposing tendency, toward continued divergence, suggesting that convergence in industrial output has been offset by increasing inequality in other sources of income such as agriculture, construction, or services. Since GDP provides a more reliable measure of income than GVIO alone, it is fairly safe to conclude that the trend to greater interprovincial inequality continued during 1993–1997. However, if agricultural and industrial provinces are treated separately, both sets of data show convergence. The latter finding suggests that increases in inequality since 1993 have been along the urban-rural divide.

Table 2.2. Interprovincial Coefficients of Variation in Per Capita GDP, 1993 and 1997

Year	Whole country	Agricultural provinces	Industrial provinces
1993	0.972	0.336	0.917
1997	1.000	0.293	0.836

Source: Vietnam, General Statistical Office 1999c; Vietnam, General Statistical Office 1998.

Convergence of Provincial Incomes during the Early Reform Period 1981–1987

A number of possible explanations exist for this variable pattern of increasing and decreasing equality. One possibility is that the convergence pattern during the 1980s was largely driven by growth in agricultural production leading to increased demand for outputs of local industries. We know that agricultural output grew rapidly after the introduction of output contracts in January 1981 until 1986, permitting increased surplus retention at the local level.[11] Higher prices paid to farmers also reduced the element of surplus extraction from agriculture, allowing greater retention of resources in agricultural provinces and promoting higher growth in those regions. Decree 25-CP (also in January 1981) allowed increased commercial activity of state enterprises (SEs), although the centrally managed enterprises remained more constrained by central allocation and a series of policy reversals. By 1987, output from locally managed industrial enterprises was almost double its 1980 level, while that from centrally managed enterprises had risen by only 64 percent (Vietnam, General Statistical Office 1989). Rapid local growth during this period may also be accounted for by the partial liberalization of foreign trade in 1980, allowing provinces to establish trading companies and directly exchange agricultural output for key agricultural and other inputs that were in short supply through the central apparatus (Beresford and Dang Phong 2000). Indeed, in all spheres, shortages in the centrally planned sector were increasingly exacerbated by diversion of resources to local, often illegal, uses (Fforde and de Vylder 1996).

Fiscal deconcentration, or an increase in the share of total revenues available to localities, is a further possible explanation for the convergence of interprovincial incomes during the 1980s.[12] Actual budget figures are not available, but the deconcentration can be seen in the rise in provincial investment outlays from an average of 24.2 percent of the total during 1980–1982 to 41.4 percent during 1983–1987 (Vietnam, General Statistical Office 1996b, 1998). Part of this increase can be explained by budget transfers from the center and part by increased retention by localities of revenues raised through their foreign trade activities and other enterprises. There was also widespread use of illegal interprovincial and interdistrict tax barriers in the 1980s as local authorities increased their efforts to retain resources within their areas.[13]

There seems little doubt that the shift of resources to the more rural provinces prior to 1988 came about as a result of the political pressures that had built up during the 1970s. As the Vietnamese state sought to preserve its legitimacy in the face of severe economic crises and political pressure for reform, from within and without the state apparatus, it ceded more and more of its allocation powers to local authorities and farmers.

The Sharp Rise in Inequality, 1988–1993

Between 1988 and 1993 interprovincial inequality began to rise again very rapidly, such that in the north it was considerably worse than it had been in 1974 and, for

both halves of the country, inequality became markedly worse than at the commencement of the reform process. Previous convergence among the agricultural
provinces also went into reverse. Part of the explanation for this sharp reversal lies
in the collapse of parts of the budget-dependent state and collective sectors and part
lies in the market-driven patterns of urban-based domestic and foreign investors.

Restructuring of industry was necessitated by the ending of budget subsidies and
liberalization of all industrial prices in 1989. On the one hand, centrally managed industries were, and are, heavily concentrated in only a handful of cities and provinces.
They were much more protected during the restructuring process, chiefly through
privileged access to credit, and more than doubled their output between 1987 and
1993. Locally run state enterprises, cooperatives, and the private sector are, on the
other hand, more evenly distributed among the provinces and the restructuring affected them much more strongly. Local state-owned industry suffered negative
growth in 1989–1990 and was still only 21 percent above its 1987 level by 1993. Industrial cooperatives went into a precipitous decline: output in 1993 was only 17.5
percent of the 1987 level. The private sector, although it more than trebled its output
over these six years, had not yet grown sufficiently large to compensate for the losses
of output from these other two areas (Vietnam, General Statistical Office 1996b).

A further explanation for the increased inequality after 1987 may be related to the
rapid increase in foreign direct investment that took place after the passage of
the Foreign Investment Law in December 1988. Between 1988 and 1996, foreign invested projects increased their share of GVIO from zero to 27 percent (Vietnam,
General Statistical Office 1998). At the end of 1993, 57 percent of the capital was invested in Ho Chi Minh City and three neighboring provinces, while a further 30
percent was in Hanoi and Haiphong (Vietnam, General Statistical Office 1995).
Thus 87 percent of total foreign capital was located in just six provinces.

During this period, the degree of inequality among the southern provinces became much more extreme than that within the north. This result is somewhat surprising since the period was one of renewed reform in the agricultural sector. The
combined effects of Resolution 10 and price liberalization were to encourage a
more sustained burst of growth in farm output across the country. A mixture of ge-
ographical and demographic conditions meant that the southern provinces were in
a better position to take advantage of the changes than those in the north. Consequently, nearly the entire export surplus of rice was produced in the Mekong River
delta of the south. On the face of it, one would therefore expect the southern agricultural provinces to increase their incomes, at least partially offsetting the
tendency to greater inequality brought about by the collapse of local industry.
However, we can also surmise that the emergence of large-scale rice exports led to
the resumption of surplus extraction from the rural areas. There is little hard evidence, but a number of international agencies expressed concern that rice export
quotas were highly concentrated in the hands of urban firms able to take advantage of the gap between low farm-gate prices and higher world market prices.

Further investigation reveals that most of the increase in southern inequality is
accounted for by an industrial boom in and around Ho Chi Minh City, notably

crude oil production in Vung Tau. Whereas in 1987 average per capita industrial output from these four cities/provinces was less than three times higher than that from the predominantly agricultural provinces, by 1993 it was eleven times higher. For the northern region the ratio only increased from five times to six times higher over the same period.

Provincial shares of state investment fell only slightly during 1988–1992, indicating that there was no great reversal of the previous fiscal deconcentration. In 1991, however, in the face of Soviet aid termination and in order to bring inflation under control, the absolute size of budget spending was severely reduced—to about two-thirds of its previous level—with a corresponding reduction in the size of the deficit. Given the massive size of the cut in total spending, the capacity of government at all levels to influence economic development was greatly reduced. It would seem, then, that government was in no position during these years to influence interprovincial inequalities in either direction.

We can conclude, therefore, that the huge increase in interprovincial inequality between 1987 and 1993 was brought about by a combination of local industries collapsing under the pressure of withdrawn subsidies, a heavy concentration of foreign direct investment (FDI) in a small number of provinces, and a large widening of the urban-rural gap in the southern half of the country. The last two factors are possibly closely linked since FDI was so heavily concentrated in the southern cities. It is also likely that surpluses extraction from the rural provinces, through rice exports for example,[14] resumed and the surpluses were reinvested in the cities rather than in diversifying rural economies.

Regional Distribution of Income and Growth after 1993

If the widening of income inequality was produced by the forced restructuring brought about by the end of Soviet aid and planning, mainstream economic theory nevertheless predicts that in a more normal market economy, the gap would start to close again. As we see in table 2.1, convergence in provincial industrial output did indeed reappear after 1993. However, the GDP data, which became available for the 1990s (table 2.2) and give a more reliable picture of provincial incomes, showed a continued divergence at the national level. Moreover, both tables show a pattern of convergence within the two groups of industrial and agricultural provinces, suggesting that the gap continues to widen along urban-rural lines.

This pattern of increasing inequality at the national level and decreasing inequality within the two urban and rural sectors can be further illuminated by looking at the relative dynamism of provinces within the two groups. There will be a tendency for incomes to converge to the extent that poor provinces can grow fast enough to catch up to the average per capita income and/or richer provinces grow more slowly. However, what we see in reality (table 2.3) is that the wealthier provinces have shown a more consistent pattern of high growth. Throughout the 1990s, the majority grew at above-average rates and they were also the least agriculture-dependent provinces in the country. All except one were in the designated "growth poles" (Hanoi–Haiphong–Quang Ninh, Da Nang City, and the Ho Chi Minh City region) and all had relatively high levels of urbanization, industrialization, and services. Among the wealthier provinces, the only slow-growing ones were predominantly rural.

Poor provinces, on the other hand, showed much less consistent dynamism. During the early 1990s, while the restructuring process discussed in the previous section was going on, a large majority performed poorly. During 1995–1997, however, the pattern was reversed, with a majority growing at above-average rates, as shown in table 2.3. Unfortunately, the economic slowdown produced since 1998 by the Asian crisis means that the shift to a higher growth trajectory of many poor provinces in the mid-1990s may have been shortlived. In the case of these provinces, agriculture accounted for more than 30 percent of GDP (average 53 percent). The poorest among them were concentrated in the northern highlands and along the central coast north of Quang Tri, the wealthiest were concentrated in the Mekong delta.

Table 2.3. Regional Differences in Per Capita GDP and Average Growth Rates

Poor—high growth	Poor—low growth	Rich—high growth	Rich—low growth
16 northern mountains and uplands provinces			
8	7	1	
6 north central coast provinces			
2	4		
9 Red River delta provinces			
4	3	2	
7 south central coast provinces			
4	1	2	
4 central highlands provinces			
3	1		
7 south eastern provinces			
3		4	
12 Mekong River delta provinces			
3	6		3
Total			
27	22	9	3

Source: Vietnam, General Statistical Office 1999c; Vietnam, General Statistical Office 1998.
Note: Based on sixty-one provinces. Poor provinces are defined as those with below-average per capita GDP, and slow-growth provinces are defined as those with below-average rates of growth. Conversely, rich provinces have above-average GDP and high-growth provinces have above-average growth rates.

In relation to the distribution of growth, both low and high rates were found in most regions, with perhaps a concentration of slow-growing provinces in the richer Mekong River delta and the poor north central coast region, while faster growth was more likely to be found along the south central coast and in the Central Highlands. In the southeastern region around Ho Chi Minh City only high rates are found. Note, however, that Long An, which lies immediately to the west of the city, has experienced persistently low growth rates throughout the 1990s. The "trickle down" effects one might expect from proximity to other urban growth centers are also unevenly distributed. Such patterns are difficult to explain without a more detailed examination of such factors as spatial growth of cities, industrial structures, degree of agricultural diversification, and attitudes and policies of local authorities, and this is not yet feasible. Nevertheless, the acceleration in relative growth rates of many poor provinces during the later part of the 1990s, but prior to the onset of the Asian crisis, no doubt contributed to the pattern of declining inequality among the agricultural provinces observed in tables 2.1 and 2.2.

Factors Contributing to Spatial Inequality

Changes in population do not seem to have played a role. Some provinces with high population growth rates have experienced high economic growth rates, while others have grown rather slowly. It is possible that these differences reflect variation between provinces whose population growth is chiefly due to immigration by able-bodied workers, and those with high natural population growth, and consequent high dependency ratios. At the same time, provinces with abnormally low population growth (possibly due to out-migration or boundary changes), have also shown highly differentiated growth rates. Unfortunately, little information is available on the impact of out-migration on source province economies. Li Tana, in her study of migration to Hanoi, found that there was an expectation among local authorities that remittances would be beneficial to the source economy (Li Tana 1996: 32), although the quantity of migrants may as yet be too small and localized to make any real difference at the provincial level.[15]

The continued concentration of foreign investment is one possible explanation of the continued increase in interprovincial inequality after 1993. Compared with 1993, concentration of capital around Ho Chi Minh City and Hanoi-Haiphong had diminished only slightly, from 87 to 80 percent by 1997, while the government's third designated "growth pole" around Da Nang and Hue cities had shown no tendency to emerge as a major center (Vietnam, General Statistical Office 1995; 1998). The high concentration of FDI shows up even more clearly in the figures on gross output of FDI industries in table 2.4.

Since productivity in industry is generally higher than that in agriculture and services, a spurt in growth of the industrial sector in poorer provinces is, prima facie,

Table 2.4.   Gross Output of Foreign Invested Industries in Three "Growth Poles" and Rest of Country

Year	Ho Chi Minh City and 3 surrounding provinces	Hanoi and Hai Phong	Da Nang and Thua Thien-Hue	Rest of country
1995	80.5	10.5	1.7	7.3
1996	80.0	11.6	1.4	7.0
1997	78.7	12.2	1.3	7.8

Source: Vietnam, General Statistical Office 1998.

likely to make a large contribution to higher growth rates and in the provinces' capacity to catch up. Raiser, for example, has noted that for the Chinese coastal provinces where light industry has recently expanded rapidly outside the main cities, there is a strong relationship between this growth of light industry and interprovincial convergence (Raiser 1998: 15). In fact, simple regression showed that industry and construction taken together provided a much better explanation of the variation in growth rates than industry alone,[16] indicating that a combination of local construction booms and growth in industrial output, especially the former, was the main contributor to variability in GDP growth. The same is true for the agricultural and industrial province groups taken separately. However, the relationship is much stronger for the wealthier provinces than for the poor, least industrialized ones. It seems likely that the absolute levels of industry and construction are so low in the poor agricultural provinces that even a rapid increase is likely to make little difference to overall GDP growth in the short run. There is also a stronger correlation in high-growth compared to the low-growth provinces, suggesting that in the low-growth provinces, even where growth of industry and construction was sometimes high, other local factors intervened to slow down the overall rate of growth.

The mainstream economists' hypothesis of increased capital mobility between provinces leading to greater regional equality in a market economy is not given much support by these findings. On the one hand, foreign investment has continued to be highly concentrated in a handful of provinces and, despite the rapid recovery of local industry following the forced structural adjustment of the late 1980s and early 1990s, interprovincial income inequality has continued to grow. On the other hand, some domestic (state or private) capital did flow to a rather large number of poor provinces enabling them to move to higher growth rates, fueled by industrial production and/or construction, and significantly reduced inequality among rural provinces. Nevertheless, the equally high growth rates of the few wealthy, industrialized provinces have widened the rural-urban gap. The results suggest that nonmainstream theories that predict uneven development due to a cumulative capital flow toward the wealthier regions contain a better explanation of reality.

The question that remains to be asked is to what extent the pattern of convergence within the rural areas with divergence between rural and industrial provinces is the result of deliberate redistributive policies pursued by the government. In other words, to what extent has deliberate state action contributed to ameliorating the widening inequalities? Fiscal transfers to poor provinces could potentially play an important role in increasing incomes and investment in both the state and nonstate sectors and in boosting their growth rates. Moreover, in the absence of such transfers, it seems likely that with the general decline in growth rates and investment retrenchment since the onset of the Asian crisis in 1997, the poor provinces might slide back into relative stagnation.

Capital Mobility via Fiscal Redistribution

As noted above, fiscal deconcentration had halted or even partially reversed by 1993, but it was only after that date that revenues acquired sufficient buoyancy for central government to resume positively influencing growth and accumulation. Given the apparent tendency of transfers from the central budget to favor accumulation in wealthier provinces and cities under the central planning system, it is interesting to ask whether the renewed capacity of the center in the 1990s has followed the same tendency. This question can be examined on the basis of data on provincial revenues and expenditures, available only for the year 1994 in the period that concerns us here (World Bank 1996).

Vietnam has a centralized budget system in which local autonomy in revenue raising and spending decisions is highly restricted. Under both the 1989 and 1996 budget laws, provinces were entitled to retain revenues from certain taxes, while others (chiefly turnover and profit taxes) were shared between center and provinces according to a formula decided by the center. All other tax revenue belonged to the center.[17] The capacity of individual provinces to raise expenditure above the amount retained thus depended largely on subsidies from the central budget, particularly in the case of poor provinces. In this case, the *actual* budget revenue of the province is not that which it collects on behalf of the center, but equals retained revenue plus any subsidy.

Table 2.5 shows, in summary form, the extent to which provinces depended on supplementation from the center to maintain their actual revenue and expenditure

Table 2.5. Per Capita Expenditure and Central Subsidy of Provinces in 1994

Province	Expenditure (in 1,000 dong/head)	Subsidy (in 1,000 dong/head)	Subsidy as % of expenditure
Group 1	350	0.6	0.3
Group 2	264	168	64
Group 3a	177	1	0.6
Group 3b	150	54	36
Average	221	44	20

Source: World Bank 1996: 158, 179–80, 183–84.

levels. The redistribution is unevenly spread, but a pattern emerges that enables us to group the provinces under three major headings:

1. 8 major industrial centers and provinces linked to "growth poles" that received zero or insignificant subsidies;[18]
2. 14 mountainous and remote provinces with significant ethnic minorities that received large subsidies ranging from 21 to 84 percent of total expenditure;[19]
3. 31 densely populated, predominantly agricultural provinces in which per capita expenditure levels were significantly lower than for the above two groups.

Group 3 can be further divided into:

3a. 9 provinces that received zero or insignificant subsidies[20]
3b. 22 provinces that received subsidies ranging from 5 to 63 percent of total expenditure.[21]

In the case of the provinces (group 1) that form part of the government's planned "growth poles," per capita spending was well above average. These high expenditures may be partly explained by spending on infrastructure and other programs not subject to population norms and partly by the higher per capita allocations for such current expenditure items as education and health in the major cities. Among these eight provinces are some of the wealthiest in the country.[22] Government expenditure thus continued to favor the wealthier, more urbanized and industrialized provinces.

One might also consider that a redistributive fiscal policy would aim to provide a kick start for areas with low growth rates. In reality, however, the wealthy provinces also had high growth rates during the period leading up to 1994 and only Quang Nam–Da Nang was relatively stagnant, with a growth rate of 4.1 percent per annum. This group of generally wealthy and high-growth provinces, containing 20 percent of the total population, accounted for 40 percent of all provincial expenditures. Thus it is apparent that revenue allocations to these more industrialized and generally high-growth provinces tended to aggravate rather than ameliorate rural-urban inequality.

The second group of mountainous and remote provinces also had high per capita expenditure levels. However, unlike the first group, their low revenue collections meant that expenditure was substantially enabled by central supplementation. Together these fourteen provinces, which raised a mere 3 percent of tax revenues, accounted for 16 percent of total expenditures. They received 45 percent of all subsidies from the central government. In some cases, the proportion of subsidies was extremely high (over 70 percent of expenditures), suggesting that significant efforts were being made by the center to redistribute resources to these provinces, several of which were indeed very poor. However, within the group, the pattern of higher subsidies to lower income provinces, although significant, was not strong, suggesting that other factors intervened in the allocation of central resources. When we look at the relative dynamism of these provinces, we find a similarly diverse pattern. There is nothing to suggest that fiscal supplementation was being used to kick start the more stagnant economies.

The third group of provinces are the mainly agricultural, lowland provinces of the Red River and Mekong deltas (and surrounding regions) and the central coastal provinces. All of the thirty-one provinces in this group spent considerably less per capita than those in the first two groups. The lack of dynamism in this group is outstanding: 84 percent had experienced below-average rates of growth in the period leading up to 1994. Moreover, most of them were poor to very poor: only six had average or above-average per capita GDP.

Within group 3, the subgroup 3a provinces were significantly wealthier than those in either of groups 2 or 3b, and central subsidies to this group were insignificant. They received only 0.5 percent of the total, although they had 21 percent of the population and carried out 14 percent of all provincial expenditures. Group 3b provinces showed similarly low levels of per capita spending. However, their revenue collections were also generally much lower and they relied more heavily on central subsidies to maintain expenditure levels. As a group, they received 54 percent of all subsidies, contained 40 percent of the population, and undertook 30 percent of all expenditures.

These figures do suggest a strong spatial element in central government policy favoring the two groups of remoter mountainous provinces (group 2), of which several are among the poorest areas of the country, and the poor, densely populated provinces in the lowlands of the two major deltas and along the central coast (group 3b). A comparison of these two groups shows that per capita expenditures of the group 2 provinces were over 75 percent above those of group 3b and their per capita subsidies were three times higher. Thus the element of redistribution to the mountain provinces was somewhat stronger than to the poor lowland provinces. It would seem that in the case of the mountain provinces, the government's redistributive objectives are much broader than poverty alleviation and possibly relate to defense considerations and policy toward better integration of ethnic minorities into the national polity.

Nevertheless, insofar as they are poverty-related, central subsidies are clearly not able to offset the high actual revenues and expenditures of the "growth pole" regions and achieve equalization of per capita expenditures across provinces. Under an equalization policy, one might expect expenditures to be higher in poor provinces, but this is not the case (World Bank 1996: 53). However, *within the two groups of remote and poor lowland provinces that received subsidies*, there was a significant relationship between per capita GDP and the level of central subsidy. In part, the lower level of subsidies to the group 3b provinces can be explained by the fact that their average per capita GDP was about 9 percent higher than that for the remote mountain provinces. Artificial capital mobility via central fiscal subsidies may, therefore, go some way toward offsetting interprovincial income differentials among the predominantly agricultural provinces.

Strongly redistributive policies would tend to target not only provinces with lower per capita GDP, but those with relatively stagnant economies. However, there was no statistically significant relationship between growth rates prior to 1994 and the level of subsidies received in that year. Moreover, only 60 percent of the groups 2 and 3b provinces receiving subsidies in 1994 were able to maintain or switch to a higher growth path during 1995–1997. On the basis of existing evidence we can only speculate as to whether this uneven pattern was due to local differences in the effectiveness with which state spending programs were implemented or was the result of factors independent of state intervention.

We have no data on fiscal transfers after 1994. However, the Vietnamese government's public investment program for 1996–2000 pursued the same redistributive strategy. Priorities established in the plan included capital intensive investments in national highways, airports, ports, and electric power generation, which would have favored the growth pole regions, but also included large expenditures on rural infrastructure to assist the development of poor regions (Vietnam, Ministry of Planning and Investment 1996). The UNDP public expenditure review conducted in 1996 expressed concerns that the program was underfunded (United Nations Development Program 1996), leading to worries about which priorities would be dropped in the event that funding failed to eventuate. In the wake of the Asian crisis, however, the government has expressed the view that development of the domestic market is a key concern in order to minimize the impact of external shocks like that experienced in 1998–1999 and has emphasized rural development as part of its strategy.

Intraregional Inequality

It is worth noting here that interprovincial differentials are only one aspect of uneven regional development. Intraprovincial spatial differentials are another element hidden by the province-level data and for which little evidence is available. Interprovincial income distribution is not necessarily the best way to measure uneven regional development since provincial boundaries are administrative constructs that economic development does not generally respect. This fact was brought into focus after a number of provincial units used in this analysis were divided, usually along pre-1976 lines, during the 1990s. The division of Song Be, Quang Nam–Da Nang, and Bac Thai provinces, for example, in each case left the poorer of the two new provinces with a per capita GDP approximately half that of the richer one. One Vietnamese researcher suggested to me that, among the merged provincial administrations, jealousy during the transition from central planning over preferential resource allocation to the economically dominant part of the province was indeed a major factor in the decision to split. Even within the new provincial boundaries, one would expect spatial differences to be high, depending on factors such as proximity to urban centers or major transport routes, attitudes and fiscal capacities of local administrations, and local variations in the distribution of land use rights and control over other assets such as fish ponds. Intraprovincial inequality may ultimately be more important than interprovincial inequality.

If, as suggested above, interprovincial fiscal distribution has played some role in ameliorating inequality among the rural provinces in the 1990s, the evidence on intraprovincial distribution is sparse and ambivalent. Studies of eight different provinces have shown widely varying tendencies: some provinces allocate proportionately more to wealthier districts and communes, while others attempt to equalize (World Bank 1996: 55; Adger 1999: 115; Porter 1995: 243). It would appear that factors at the province level largely determine intraprovincial distribution, whatever the central government intention. However, the World Bank study found that delivery of basic services by local authorities tended to be better in wealthier provinces, so that it was "better to be a poor district in a rich province than a rich district in a poor province" (World Bank 1996: 55). Thus the most important determinant of district expenditures was the size of the provincial budget.

During the 1980s, the increasing marketization of Vietnam's economy appears to have led to decreasing income differentials among provinces. The most likely cause is the increased local retention of resources enabled by reforms in agriculture, industry, and trade. At the same time, the central budget and central industry remained constrained by shortages that were indeed exacerbated by diversion of resources to local, often illegal, uses. However, the forced restructuring of the economy brought about by the complete liberalization of prices in 1989 and the termination of Soviet aid in 1991 generated a crisis for local industries and, together with a surge of foreign direct investment in only two major regions during the early 1990s, led to increased divergence of provincial incomes. Continued fiscal deconcentration in this period failed to offset the tendency toward divergence because budget compression reduced the capacity of government authorities to use fiscal spending to stimulate growth. By 1993, the distribution of provincial incomes was considerably worse than it had been at the start of the reform period.

After the major restructuring, very high growth rates in a relatively large number of poor agricultural provinces enabled them to close the gap on their wealthier counterparts, even while the majority of industrialized provinces continued to forge ahead. While the concentration of foreign investment was slightly dispersed during this period, the effect seems too small to have offset the unequalizing tendency it showed earlier. The gap between industrial and rural provinces has continued to widen. At the same time, growth rates were strongly related to expansion of GDP in industry and construction, suggesting that, in contrast to the early reform period of the 1980s, convergence among rural provinces has been driven by a switch from agriculture to industry and/or construction activity. One of the worries here is that as the Asian crisis developed in the late 1990s, the

Vietnamese construction boom came to a halt and industrial growth slowed significantly. The vulnerability of poor regions to fluctuations in market-driven investment and output levels was illustrated by the massive increase in provincial income differentials in 1988–1993 at a time when government intervention through fiscal subsidies played comparatively little role either to promote or to offset the divergence.

Evidence on the use of central fiscal distribution to achieve greater equalization of provincial incomes during 1993–1997 remains ambiguous. On the one hand, the wealthy "growth pole" provinces and cities were able to maintain considerably higher per capita expenditures than other provinces. Central budget expenditures on large infrastructure such as ports, national highways, and power generation may also have favored these wealthy areas. On the other hand, an average of 20 percent of all provincial expenditures was provided through subsidies from the center to local budgets, enabling two groups of relatively poor provinces to increase expenditures substantially above what would have been possible on the basis of local revenue-raising power alone. Within these two groups, the poorest provinces received significantly higher levels of subsidy and also relied more heavily on subsidies to maintain expenditure. Nevertheless, in comparing these two groups, a systematic difference was found between the mountainous, remote provinces and other poor agricultural provinces, suggesting that other factors besides redistribution objectives influenced central allocations to these provinces. The fact that only 60 percent of provinces so assisted were able to move to a high growth path by 1995–1997 may be due to local factors such as poorly targeted provincial allocations, the necessity to sacrifice capital expenditure to essential current expenditures, or corruption. This is a question that requires further research. Given that we only have data on fiscal transfers for one year, it is also possible that the analysis was affected by special conditions applying in that year. Despite these reservations, it would seem that "capital mobility" into the poorer provinces was significantly enhanced by government intervention, enabling them to achieve higher output levels than would otherwise have been possible.

My analysis suggests that in the mid-1990s the government pursued a dual policy of promoting rapid advancement of the growth pole regions while simultaneously assisting a number of the poorest provinces to reduce their poverty levels. The danger of such a strategy is that continued widening of the urban-rural gap can ultimately restrict the longer-term sustainability of rapid growth, particularly if it impacts negatively on social stability. This danger can become a reality if poverty alleviation measures do not contribute to increased dynamism and a closing of interprovincial inequalities. Since, in market economies, it is the poor who inevitably bear the main burden of crisis adjustment, it is particularly important in light of the slower growth rates induced by the Asian crisis that those regions experiencing the most unstable and vulnerable growth are shifted to a more stable growth path. The willingness and ability of both central and provincial authorities to use their available budget resources to offset this impact could be a key factor, not only for renewing the process of regional convergence, but also for longer-term development.

NOTES

1. Rates of productivity growth are commonly higher in industry than in other sectors such as agriculture and services. High levels of industrial growth in less developed regions are thus a good indicator of their ability to sustain high growth and catch up to more advanced regions.

2. The category of middle peasants, defined as those producing "on average" sufficient for household subsistence and not requiring hired labor, is problematical as it includes many above-average farms that produced a marketable surplus.

3. In the late 1970s, for example, there were reports that procurement officials were sometimes arrested by cooperative members and their own bicycles were appropriated because the center was unable to supply the contracted amounts of industrial goods in exchange for procurement quotas.

4. Although Soviet aid was increased during 1976–1980, the increase was insufficient to offset the cancellation of American aid to the south and Chinese aid to the north in 1975. The Chinese did maintain technical assistance to some projects that had already been started by that date, but these too were terminated in 1978.

5. The system of subsidized input prices continued at around 60–70 percent of the market price, while the government's wages bill rose by 220 percent. The budget deficit rose from 24 percent of expenditure in 1984 to 31 percent in 1986 and 39 percent in 1988 (Spoor 1988: 125; World Bank 1994: 126).

6. Inflation during 1986 was 487 percent per annum (World Bank 1994: 131).

7. Meaning that the rate was pegged a few points above the inflation rate.

8. One of the characteristics of high inflation in all the former socialist countries has been increasing use by the population of the U.S. dollar as the preferred currency for domestic transactions, since it holds its value better than the local currency.

9. We know, for example, that due to wartime conditions, wealth was heavily concentrated in the urban areas of Saigon and Da Nang and that there was almost no industry at all outside those two cities. While there was a resurgence of agricultural production during the early 1970s under the impact of land reform in the Mekong River delta, the region to the north of Saigon was largely unaffected. See Beresford (1989) for details.

10. The coefficient of variation is the ratio of the standard deviation (S) to the mean (X), or S/X.

11. Having grown at only 2 percent per annum during 1976–1980 (below the population growth rate), growth in real value of agricultural output accelerated to an average of 4.2 percent per annum during 1981–1986 (Vietnam, General Statistical Office 1989: 42).

12. *Deconcentration* is used here rather than *decentralization* since Vietnam has a unified central budget from which allocations to local authorities are made by the center. In the period under consideration, local authorities had neither legal independent revenue-raising capabilities nor capacity to decide expenditure allocations. A degree of decentralization was possible, however, to the extent that local authorities could raise and retain extrabudgetary revenues. The latter have since been partly legalized under the guise of fees and "voluntary contributions" by the population.

13. Evidence for the existence of these tax collection points is mainly found in the repeated issue throughout the 1980s of central government decrees attempting to abolish them (see various issues of *Cong Bao*, the official gazette).

14. Prior to 1989 Vietnam was a net importer of rice. Large-scale exports by urban-based firms began in 1989.

15. Note, however, that in his 1995–1996 study of two districts in Nam Dinh and Quang Ninh provinces, Adger (1999: 107) found that the combination of wages, transfers, and remittances contributed 11 and 36 percent, respectively, to income inequality in those districts.

16. For all Vietnamese provinces only 19 percent of the variation in growth rate of GDP was explained by growth rates of industrial output alone, compared with 62 percent for *both* industry *and* construction.

17. In addition there were extrabudgetary collections at the local level, which may have been a high proportion of total revenues in the early 1990s, during the period of severe compression of central revenues. One senior Vietnamese economist, interviewed during early 1992, claimed that in 1991 about one-third of all revenues were illegally collected by local authorities for their own use. Such extrabudgetary revenues would be more easily available to wealthier provinces.

18. Hanoi, Ho Chi Minh City, Hai Phong, Quang Nam–Da Nang, Quang Ninh, Ba Ria–Vung Tau, Dong Nai, Song Be.

19. Lao Cai, Ha Giang, Cao Bang, Tuyen Quang, Yen Bai, Bac Thai, Lang Son, Lai Chau, Son La, Hoa Binh, Kon Tum, Gia Lai, Dac Lac, Lam Dong.

20. Khanh Hoa, Kien Giang, Tien Giang, Can Tho, Long An, Dong Thap, An Giang, Minh Hai, Hai Hung.

21. Quang Tri, Thua Thien–Hue, Tay Ninh, Binh Dinh, Vinh Long, Binh Thuan, Thanh Hoa, Ben Tre, Ninh Thuan, Phu Yen, Ha Tinh, Soc Trang, Vinh Phu, Quang Binh, Nghe An, Ha Bac, Tra Vinh, Thai Binh, Quang Ngai, Ha Tay, Ninh Binh, Nam Ha.

22. Song Be and Quang Nam–Da Nang had both industrial concentrations and large rural hinterlands, which pulled down their average GDP.

3

Wealth, Power, and Inequality: Global Market, the State, and Local Sociocultural Dynamics

Hy V. Luong

In 1983, in the famous ceramics center of Bat Trang near Hanoi, officials questioned a local entrepreneur about the source of wealth for the construction of his two-storey house, the first one in the commune. They confiscated the house and turned it into a commune health center, as they accused the owner of accumulating wealth illegally. This confiscation constituted a part of the provincewide campaign to crack down on "ostentatious" private residences and presumably the illicit wealth financing their construction.

A decade later, Hanoi began witnessing conspicuous private wealth, in the forms of large private residences and private mini-hotels, accommodating the flow of tourists, aid officials, and international investors. By the end of the 1990s, more than a few wealthy Hanoi residents owned three-star hotels in the city and four-star tourist resorts in other parts of Vietnam. Conspicuous consumption had also emerged in the form of private automobiles, among other things. Hanoi had eventually caught up with the more freewheeling Ho Chi Minh City, where by the end of the 1980s, private wealth had been more freely displayed in the form of newly constructed private villas behind high walls. By the late 1990s, a small Vietnamese urban elite had accumulated sufficient wealth to be able to finance their children's overseas education in the West while the annual per capita income in 1999 Vietnam remained around U.S. $374. At the other end of the spectrum were beggars and slum dwellers along blackened and highly polluted city canals, the growing landless peasantry in the Mekong delta, and the disenfranchised ethnic minority cultivators in the highlands. Many of the slum dwellers came from the poorer regions of Vietnam, reflecting heightened inequality not only within a city but also along regional lines across the country.

Concurrent with the greater socioeconomic inequality was a general reduction in poverty in the country. The annual per capita income rose from an estimated $110 in 1989 to $374 a decade later. The poverty rate calculated on the basis of the

World Bank poverty line also declined from 58 percent in 1992–1993 to 37 percent in 1997–1998. Vietnam undoubtedly underwent a major transformation in socioeconomic differentiation and standards of living within a decade from 1989 to 1999. This chapter focuses on the process of socioeconomic differentiation in Vietnam in this period of major transformation. It pays attention to the interplay of market forces, governmental policies, and local sociocultural dynamics in the inter- and intra-community differentiation process.

SOCIOECONOMIC DIFFERENTIATION IN THE PREREFORM PERIOD: A HISTORICAL OVERVIEW

Wealth differences in twentieth-century Vietnam before the onset of economic reforms were profoundly shaped not only by government policies but also by historically conditioned and regional socioeconomic differences.

Being a frontier of Vietnam and already well incorporated into the Asian regional economy through its rice export by the eighteenth century, Nam Bo as the fertile rice basket in the southern third of Vietnam witnessed, throughout its history, a considerably greater socioeconomic inequality than the northern and central parts of the country (Bac Bo and Trung Bo) did. Some figures on the magnitude of this inequality became available during the French colonial period: in the 1930s, in Pierre Gourou's estimate, approximately two-thirds of the agricultural households in central and western Nam Bo (Cochinchina) did not have any land, while less than 1 percent of the rural households (2.5 percent of the landowners) owned 45 percent of the land in estates of 50 hectares or more (Gourou 1940: 272). If we include those owning more than 5 hectares of land, over 9 percent of the rural households (28 percent of the landowners) owned 87.5 percent of the agricultural land in those parts of Nam Bo (272). In contrast, in the Red River delta of Bac Bo, for the same period, Gourou estimated 12 percent of the rural households were landless, and that 8.5 percent of the landowners (or 7.5 percent of the rural households) owned 54 percent of the private land (Henry 1932: 109; cf. Gourou 1940: 229). While statistical data are not available on central Vietnam (Trung Bo) and on urban-rural wealth differences, the urban population was relatively small in the colonial period, standing at only 5 to 7 percent of the Vietnamese population of 19 million in 1937 (Marr 1981: 24–25).

When Vietnam was temporarily divided into two parts from 1954 to 1975, regional differences became accentuated due to different governmental policies in the two parts and the impact of the war. In the southern half of Vietnam, primarily under the control of the U.S.-allied Saigon government, socioeconomic differences were clearly greater than in the northern part of the country, despite the two major land reform campaigns in 1958 and 1970–1972 there. A government survey in 1976–1977 in eight southern provinces (7 in the Mekong delta, plus Dong Nai province near Saigon) reported that 5–7 percent of the households did not have any land; 15.7–17.7 percent owned less than .5 hectare of land; 57 percent owned between .5 and 3 hectares; 15 percent owned between 3 and 5 hectares; and 3 percent owned more than 5 hectares (Nguyen Thu Sa 1990: 147–48; Lam Thanh Liem 1995: 79). The first two groups owned approximately 10 percent of the land; the next two (called middle peasants), approximately 80 percent; and the last, approximately 10 percent (Lam Thanh Liem 1995: 79).

The degree of socioeconomic inequality in rural Nam Bo in the mid-1970s was a precipitous decline from half a century earlier. The decline over half a century resulted partly from the socioculturally constituted rule of partible inheritance, leading to the fragmentation of larger holdings among a large number of households, as well as from the land reforms of 1958 and 1970 by the U.S.-allied Saigon government. In the 1956–1969 period, 850,712 hectares of land were appropriated from landlords for distribution to over 400,000 tenants (Lam Thanh Liem 1995: 70). In the 1970 reform, the Saigon government restricted owner-cultivated agricultural landholdings to 15 hectares in the southern third of Vietnam (Nam Bo) and to 5 hectares in the more heavily populated Central Vietnam (Trung Bo). Except for ancestor worship and religious land, land not directly cultivated by its owner and above the regionally specified limit was appropriated. In the 1970–1972 land reform under the Saigon government, 858,821 tenants received slightly over 1 million hectares of land (75–79). With those two land reform campaigns, about 1.3 million tenants received almost 1.9 hectares of land appropriated from landlords. Many of these landlords sought refuge in the cities and invested more in the urban economy fueled by massive U.S. spending, as the war intensified in the 1960s and early 1970s. As many poorer rural dwellers also tried to escape the war in the countryside and to search for higher-paid jobs, the urban population exploded: the population of the larger Saigon area increased from 1 million in 1945 to 3.5 million in 1975 (Lam Thanh Liem and Meillon 1990: 8, 68–80; Quach-Langlet 1991). And as rural socioeconomic differentiation was reduced due to two land reforms and a war-ravaged economy, urban Saigon became a landscape of dramatic socioeconomic contrast: on the one hand were wealthy Vietnamese living behind high-walled villas, and on the other were the poor migrants settling in sprawling slums, many along blackened and polluted canals. Of the approximately 3.5 million long-term residents of Ho Chi Minh City by 1975, approximately 1.5 million lived in slums (Thrift and Forbes 1986: 153).

The degree of socioeconomic differentiation in the southern half of Vietnam under the control of the Saigon government, while greatly reduced by the two land reforms, was still significantly greater than in the northern half of the country, which had undergone a more radical land redistribution in the mid-1950s and the collectivization campaign starting in the late 1950s. By the end of 1955, the government in Hanoi had redistributed 810,000 hectares of land to 2.1 million peasant households (Chu van Lam 1990: 99). The average holding of less than .4 hectare per household in the rural north reflects the overpopulation in the earlier-settled Red River delta and the northern central panhandle (Bac Trung Bo). In the late 1950s, the Hanoi government launched a collectivization campaign that led to the formation of 414,000 cooperatives with 2.4 million households by the end of 1960, incorporating

76 percent of cultivable surface and 86 percent of peasant households at the time (Chu van Lam 1990: 100). By 1975, 97 percent of peasant households had joined cooperatives, and 80 percent of the cooperatives had been transformed into high-level ones where members' earnings depended on their labor contribution and no longer on their original contributions of the means of production (land, draft animals) (101). Fifteen percent of the cooperatives in the lowlands and midlands encompassed entire communes which involved the merger of traditional villages (*lang*) (101). By the late 1970s, the size of a cooperative had mostly coincided with a commune, with an average of 900 households [approximately 4,500 inhabitants] in the Red River delta, approximately 400 households [2,000 persons] in northern central Vietnam, and almost 100 households in the highlands (Vietnam-General Statistical Office and Ministry of Agriculture and Food Industries 1991: 73).[1]

In northern Vietnam under the cooperatives, income differences within the same village were relatively small. Farmers accumulated labor points for their specific task performances, and the value of each labor point increased with higher crop yields in the cooperative. Before Vietnam officially introduced the first household contract system in 1981, one main source of differentiation between neighbors derived from the differing numbers of laboring hands each family possessed and the number of their dependents, which altered cyclically as children became a part of the workforce, and the elderly retired and eventually passed away. Intravillage income differences also resulted from the differing yields from household garden plots (amounting to about 5 percent of the total cultivated surface) and the relatively meager incomes earned by craft specialists and traders in the informal economy. Local cadres gained some economic advantages for themselves and, on the other side of the fence, the former rich peasants and landlords and their descendants faced discrimination. However, political power and class background were not as important in rural Vietnam as in China as a basis for socioeconomic differentiation due to the wartime conditions in northern Vietnam (the war with the United States, the Sino-Vietnamese conflict, and the Cambodia war) and the state's emphasis on political unity during this period. Vietnamese official statistics suggest that the percentage of peasant incomes derived from the household and informal economy increased from 42 percent in 1959 to 53.6 percent in the 1966–1975 period, and 60.8 percent in 1976–1980, although a re-analysis of the same data suggests that this percentage might be only about 30 percent in the 1960s and early 1970s (Nguyen Sinh Cuc 1990: 48; see also Dao The Tuan 1993: 10; Vu Tuan Anh and Tran thi Van Anh 1997: 79).

In contrast to the north, the 1978–1980 collectivization campaign in the southern half of Vietnam encountered a considerably stronger resistance. By the end of 1979, the government had formed 1,286 cooperatives and 15,309 labor exchange teams, whose members comprised respectively 21 percent and 22 percent of rural households. However, the resistance of farmers, most noticeably in Nam Bo (the southern third of Vietnam), led to the collapse of the majority of those units, leaving only 137 cooperatives and 3,739 labor exchange teams, mostly in the southern part of central Vietnam (Nam Trung Bo) (Chu van Lam 1990: 106). By 1985, the percentage of rural households in agricultural cooperatives, many merely nominal, remained only 3.7 percent in the Mekong delta, 15 percent in the southeast (the provinces around Ho Chi Minh City), and 42 percent in the Central Highlands (Vietnam-General Statistical Office and Ministry of Agriculture and Food Industries 1991: 39; cf. Ngo Vinh Long 1993: 184). In other words, in the traditionally export-oriented Nam Bo, the process of agricultural collectivization was never completed (see Luong 1994: 90–91; Chu van Lam et al. 1992: 47–48; and Le Minh Ngoc 1992: 31). Even in those southern communities where collectivization did get enacted, villagers could still retain ownership of other means of agricultural production, such as water pumps and small tractors, on the basis of which they provided services on contract with agricultural cooperatives. In all these respects, the situation in the southern half of Vietnam differed considerably from the north, and it is not surprising that before Vietnam officially introduced a return to family farming, rural socioeconomic differentiation was considerably greater in the southern third of Vietnam. If the statistical data on socioeconomic differentiation are reliable, toward the end of the collective era, the Gini coefficient (measuring inequality of incomes) for the Red River delta in the north stood at .25, compared to .35 in the Mekong delta in the south (Dao The Tuan 1993: 16).

The northern-southern differences extended to the urban context. The economies of northern cities, many of which sent parts of their populations to the countryside at the peak of the U.S. bombing in the late 1960s, remained mostly under the control of an officially equality-oriented state. The majority of urban families lived in small one- or two-room apartments and relied mostly on state rations of foods and consumer products through their work units. Small differences existed primarily due to the rank and privilege differences within the state bureaucratic system, and to the remittances from Vietnamese workers in the former Soviet Union and Eastern Europe. High-ranking cadres had larger apartments, more foods, more commodities of higher quality, and more opportunities to send their children to school in the Soviet Union and Eastern Europe. However, differences remained not highly visible. On the streets of Hanoi, as late as 1988, I saw mostly bicycles. The conspicuous signs of wealth at this time were mainly motorbikes and black-and-white televisions, which only a very small number of households could own.

In Ho Chi Minh City (Saigon), by contrast, wealth differences remained considerably larger. By 1978, the government in Hanoi had launched two campaigns to strike at large entrepreneurs, sending over 30,000 larger trading families to the agricultural economic zones (Lam Thanh Liem 1995: 94ff.) There remained hidden wealth accumulated from a variety of sources, including from industrial and commercial investments as well as from the former Saigon government's compensation for agricultural land appropriation from the pre-1975 period. It was with the hidden wealth that many Saigonese and other urban residents purchased their boats and planned their escape from the country at the peak of refugee flow from Vietnam in 1978–1980. In the 1980s, as many refugees reestablished their lives in the West, they also began sending remittances to their relatives back home, mainly in urban areas in the south. In both rural and urban contexts, on the eve of economic reforms in 1986, wealth differences remained more marked in Nam Bo than in the northern half of Vietnam.

WEALTH AND POVERTY: THE PROCESS OF SOCIOECONOMIC DIFFERENTIATION AMIDST ECONOMIC TRANSFORMATION

Regional and Urban-Rural Inequalities

As market-oriented economic reforms were implemented in the 1987–1989 period, regional and urban-rural differences became more noticeable in Vietnam.

In Nam Bo, by the late 1980s, even in those southern communities that had carried out a socialist land reform in the late 1970s as a way station on the road to collectivization, much of the agricultural land had been returned to its pre-1978 owners, and many of those who had received shares of land had in turn been dispossessed. A sizeable class of rural landless has reemerged there. According to the World Bank living standard surveys, the percentages of landless rural households increased from 16.9 percent in 1992–1993 to 21.3 percent in 1998 in the Mekong delta, and from 21.3 percent to 28.7 percent in the same period in the southeast (around Ho Chi Minh City) (Vietnam and World Bank 1999: 27).[2] In the village of Khanh Hau in the Mekong delta where I conducted field research in 1992 and in 2000–2002, the percentage of landless households increased from 14.6 percent in 1992 to 37.6 percent in 2000.[3]

The pattern of marked land ownership differentiation in Nam Bo also spread to the Central Highlands in the 1990s, where many ethnic Vietnamese entrepreneurs, including government cadres, set up private coffee plantations, intruding into the land under traditional swidden cultivation by ethnic minorities and accounting for the dramatic rise in Vietnamese coffee export from 12,300 tons in 1985 to 89,600 tons in 1990, 248,000 tons in 1995, 694,000 tons in 2000, and 910,000 tons in 2001 (Vietnam-General Statistical Office 1996a: 238, *Thoi Bao*

Table 3.1. Landless Rural Households, by Percentage

	1993	*1998*
Northern Highlands	2.0	3.7
Red River Delta	3.2	4.5
North Central Panhandle	3.8	7.7
South Central Coast	10.7	5.1
Central Highlands	3.9	2.6
South East	21.3	28.7
Mekong Delta	16.9	21.3
Vietnam	**8.2**	**10.1**

Source: Vietnam and World Bank 1999: 27.

Kinh te Viet Nam, 25 Dec. 2000: 5; Thoi Bao Kinh te Viet Nam 2001: 51). The coffee acreage, mostly in the Central Highlands, increased from 44,700 hectares in 1985, to 119,300 hectares in 1990, 186,400 hectares in 1995, and 516,700 hectares in 2000 (Vietnam-General Statistical Office 2001c: 184–85, 407). Plantations of 50–100 hectares of land had emerged in the Mekong delta by the early 1990s (Dang Phong 1995: 167–68) and had become more common in the Central Highlands and the southern third of Vietnam by the end of this decade (Tran Trac 1999; Chu Huu Quy 2001). While the percentage of landless households in the Central Highlands remained at less than 3 percent in 1997–1998 due to the low population density, ethnic minorities practicing swidden agriculture moved to more marginal mountain land and seemed to have led a more precarious existence (see Jamieson and Rambo's chapter in this volume). In rural Nam Bo and the Central Highlands, with their marked differentiations in land ownership, the main basis for socioeconomic differentiation today lies in the initial amount of land owned by each family, in particular the amount and quality of farm acreage.[4]

In contrast, in the central coast (formerly of South Vietnam), the percentage of landless rural households declined from 10.7 percent in 1992–1993 to 5.1 percent in 1998, partly because of the egalitarian land redistribution in 1993–1994. In the three main socioeconomic regions of North Vietnam (Red River delta, northern central panhandle, and the northern highlands), the percentages of landless rural households stood modestly at 2.0–3.8 percent in 1992–1993 and 3.7–7.7 percent in 1998 (Vietnam and World Bank 1999: 27).

It is not surprising in that context that in 1997–1998, of the seven socioeconomic regions of Vietnam, the per capita income of the population in the Mekong delta, the southeast, and the Central Highlands who fell into the national bottom quintile was clearly lower than that elsewhere (table 3.2). Income differentials were also greater in those three regions than in the remaining four regions: my reanalysis of the Vietnam Living Standard Survey data in 1997–98 reveals that the top income quintile earned 14 times more than the bottom one in the Central Highlands, 10.6 times more in the southeast, 10 times more in the Mekong delta. In contrast, this ratio was only 9.1 in the southern central coast, 8.6 in the Red River delta, 8.4 in the northern highlands, and 7.9 in the north central region (cf. Vietnam-General Statistical Office 2000b: 318).[5]

The World Bank's quantitative analysis of living standard survey data in the 1990s also confirms that the increase in urban-rural and regional inequality accounted for a considerably larger part of the total increase in inequality from 1992–1993 to 1997–1998 than the increase within regions or within urban-rural areas did (table 3.3). The increase in the inequality between regions in this 5-year period accounts for 83 percent of the total increase in inequality, while that within regions accounts for only 17 percent. Similarly, the increase in rural-urban inequality accounts for 96 percent of the total increase in inequality, while that within urban-rural areas accounts only for 4 percent.

Table 3.2.   1997–1998 Per Capita Income by Region (in 1,000 of current dong)

Region	Quintile					
	1	2	3	4	5	Average
Northern Highlands	762	1,391	2,096	3,152	6,551	2,036
Red River Delta	777	1,436	2,086	3,152	8,243	3,099
North Central Panhandle	829	1,400	2,107	3,183	6,736	2,317
South Central Coast	814	1,414	2,111	3,141	6,370	2,577
Central Highlands	658	1,431	2,050	3,199	7,244	2,535
Southeast	561	1,431	2,134	3,311	9,261	6,017
Mekong Delta	692	1,433	2,078	3,206	6,685	2,834
Rural/Urban						
Rural	754	1,414	2,090	3,176	6,553	2,409
Urban	855	1,465	2,160	3,294	9,509	7,105
Total	755	1,416	2,094	3,194	7,905	3,073

Source: Vietnam-General Statistical Office 2000b: 318.

Table 3.3.   Decomposition of Expenditure Inequality in Vietnam

	1993	1998	Absolute change 1993–1998
Theil L index of inequality in Vietnam	.177	.201	+.024
Inequality between urban-rural areas	.037	.060	+.023 (96%)
Inequality within urban-rural areas	.140	.141	+.001 (4%)
Inequality between regions	.026	.046	+.020 (83%)
Inequality within regions	.151	.155	+.004 (17%)

Source: Vietnam and World Bank 1999: 72–73.

In the following analysis, I focus more on the factors leading to the variations in wealth and poverty both at the regional and household levels.

MECHANISMS OF SOCIOECONOMIC DIFFERENTIATION: LOCAL SOCIOCULTURAL DYNAMICS AND THE POLITICAL ECONOMY OF DEVELOPMENT

I would like to suggest that the final outcomes, both in the microscopic terms of household wealth and poverty, and the macroscopic terms of community and regional inequality, are shaped by the interplay of the political economy of development on the one hand and the socioculturally and historically embedded local processes on the other. These forces have at times contradictory effects. I would suggest that this interplay of the political economy of development and local processes accounts for the variations in wealth, poverty, and inequality not only among households within a community, but also among communities and regions as discussed above.

Market Forces

In the early years of Vietnam's market-oriented reforms, its image as one of the last frontiers of capitalism in a high-growth region helped to attract foreign direct investments (FDI), especially into the southeast region around Ho Chi Minh City. By the end of the 1990s, the southeast had attracted more than half of the approved foreign direct investment into Vietnam, despite having only 13.2 percent of the national population. This region benefited from its concentration of human resources and socioeconomic networks, especially from the remaining knowledge and entrepreneurial spirit of the local population from earlier decades in the capitalist system, the sizeable ethnic Chinese population and its social network, Ho Chi Minh City's position as the economic capital of Vietnam, and possibly a stronger linkage to overseas Vietnamese in the West. The Red River delta centering on Hanoi also benefited to some extent from the FDI flow due to the traditionally heavy concentration of industries in northern Vietnam, the political leverage associated with being the seat of the national government, and a well-educated labor force. As the southeast became somewhat congested, as its labor costs began rising, and as infrastructure improved in surrounding areas, FDI moved to some extent to neighboring regions, including the central coast, the Central Highlands, and the Mekong delta.[6]

The spread of FDI notwithstanding, the southeast and, to a lesser extent, the Red River delta had attracted disproportionate shares of FDIs, which played major roles in stimulating growth in those two poles. In contrast, the Mekong delta, the Central Highlands, the northern highlands, and the north central panhandle still had disproportionately low shares of FDIs by 2000 despite some improvement in three of those four regions between 1995 and 2000.

Outside the two aforementioned growth poles, of the five remaining regions, the Mekong delta and the Central Highlands actively participated in the global economy through the export of agricultural commodities (most importantly, rice and coffee). What they lacked in FDI-generated industrial and service incomes, they partly made up for through the export of agricultural products. Within a decade from 1989 to 1999, Vietnam's rice export, mostly from the Mekong delta, grew from 1.4 million tons to 4.5 million tons, accounting for the emergence of Vietnam as the second largest exporter of rice in the world. Similarly, coffee export, mostly from the Central Highlands, grew from a modest 89,600 tons in 1990 to 694,000 tons in 2000 and an estimated 910,000 tons in 2001, making Vietnam the second largest coffee exporter in the world (Vietnam-General Statistical Office 1996a: 257; Vietnam-General Statistical Office 2001c: 407; Thoi Bao Kinh Te Viet Nam 2002: 52). However, this

90 Hy V. Luong

Table 3.4. Distribution of Foreign Direct Investments by Region, by Percentage

	Population 1995	FDI by 12/95	FDI by 12/00
N. Highlands	17.3	3.2	4.6
Red River Delta	19.7	29.4	29
N. Central Panhandle	13.3	3.4	2.4
South Central Coast	10.6	4.9	7.9
Central Highlands	4.7	0.7	2.6
Southeast	12.9	55	51.2
Mekong Delta	21.6	0.7	2.4

Sources: Vietnam-General Statistical Office 1996: 53–54; Vietnam-General Statistical Office 2001c: 38-39, 368-69.

linkage to the global economy made the Mekong delta and the Central Highlands highly vulnerable to the wide fluctuation in agricultural commodity prices on the world market. For example, robusta coffee export price was 4,000 dollars a ton in 1994 and 2,300 dollars a ton in 1995, widely fluctuated in the next few years, and dropped to 870 dollars a ton in January 2000, 430 dollars in December 2000, and 380 dollars in July 2001 (Thoi Bao Kinh Te Viet Nam 1996: 39; Thoi Bao Kinh Te Viet Nam 2001: 47; *Thoi Bao Kinh Te Viet Nam* December 25, 2000: 5; *Vietnam News* July 17, 2001). In the summer of 2001, the price of 300 dollars a ton in the Central Highlands obtained by coffee growers reportedly covered only half the production costs (*Thoi Bao Kinh Te Viet Nam* August 13, 2001: 1). Similarly, the price of rice rose from 189 dollars a ton in 1990 to 315 dollars a ton in 1995, and dropped to 174 dollars for a ton of high-quality rice in 2000 (Thoi Bao Kinh Te Viet Nam 1996: 18–19; Thoi Bao Kinh Te Viet Nam 2001: 46).

It is hardly surprising in the aforementioned context that in the 1993–1998 period, the per capita expenditure growth was slowest in the Mekong delta and the Central Highlands, standing respectively at 18 percent and 25 percent, in comparison to 55 percent in the Red River delta and 78 percent in the southeast. Correspondingly, the poverty rate in the Mekong delta declined by only 10 percent between 1993 and 1998, in comparison to 25 percent in the southeast and 34 percent in the Red River delta (see table 3.5). (In the same period, the poverty rate in the Central Highlands declined by 18 percent, above that in the central coast and close to that in the northern highlands, but this was before the dramatic drop in coffee prices in 1999–2001.)

Besides their role in the regional development imbalance, global market forces also contributed to the growing urban-rural gap for three reasons. First of all, FDIs were heavily concentrated in the industry and service sectors. Fifty-three percent of the approved FDI by 2000 were in industries and construction; 42.6 percent, in services; and 4.4 percent in agriculture, forestry, and fisheries. Vietnamese urban areas benefited significantly from this concentration of FDIs in industries and services, which tended to be either in large cities or in close proximity to them. They also benefited from the higher growth rates in industries and services: in the 1990s,

Table 3.5. Changes in Poverty Rate and Per Capita Expenditure by Region

	Poverty rate		% Per capita Expenditure growth		
	1993	1998	Average	Urban	Rural
Northern Highlands	79	59	31	65.8	26.9
Red River Delta	63	29	55	47.2	51.4
North Central Panhandle	75	48	46	86.4	37.2
S. Central Coast	50	35	29	39.1	25.5
Central Highlands	70	52	25	n/a	24.8
Southeast	33	8	78	78.1	59.1
Mekong Delta	47	37	18	35.7	10.6
Vietnam	57	38		60.5	30.4

Source: Vietnam and World Bank 1999: 15, 73–75.

the value of Vietnamese industrial production and services increased at the respective and annual average rates of 11.3 percent and 7.2 percent, in comparison to 4.2 percent in agriculture, forestry, and fisheries (Vietnam-General Statistical Office 2001a: 7). Second, as Ho Chi Minh City, Hanoi, and to a lesser extent, other urban areas occupy central places in a rapidly growing and export-oriented economy, their land prices have increased rapidly. The price of prime commercial land in Ho Chi Minh City and Hanoi reached or even exceeded U.S. $3,000 per square meter in 2001. The generally greater increase in the value of urban land as compared to rural land enriches many urban residents and provides many of them with capital windfalls for investments and consequently for higher incomes and improved standards of living. Third, the wide fluctuation in the prices of agricultural commodities in the global market (of rice by 1998 and coffee by 2000) had a strong adverse impact on rural incomes in the mainly mono-crop areas of the Mekong delta and the Central Highlands, while the lesser fluctuations in the prices of industrial products had a smaller impact on urban incomes.

The State

Within the general framework of a greater emphasis on infrastructure construction (roads and utilities) for long-term development and redressing regional and urban-rural imbalances, the national Vietnamese government adopted a number of measures: direct and indirect income transfers among regions, targeted public spending, and market intervention through decrees and incentive schemes. They have had limited impacts to date.

The government-mediated income transfer among regions accelerated over time in the 1990s. In 1992, the two main growth regions (Red River delta and southeast) collected 60.7 percent of the revenues and accounted for 46.2 percent of the GDP, but their provincial and local budgets accounted only for 41.8 percent of all provincial budgets. In 1998, 76.5 percent of the revenues were collected in those two regions, whose shares of the GDP increased to 50.3 percent, while the aggregate provincial expenditures in those two regions declined to 36.8 percent of all provincial expenditures (see table 3.6). Of these two regions, the southeast suffered the most over the years as its contribution to national revenues exceeded its share of provincial expenditures by only 13.9 percent in 1992 and by a whopping 35.8 percent in 1998; and its contribution to the Vietnamese GDP exceeded its share of provincial expenditures by 3.6 percent in 1992 and a significant 12.5 percent in 1998. The local revenueexpenditure share gap in the Red River delta stood more modestly at 4.9 percent in 1992 and 3.9 percent in 1998; while the GDP-expenditure share gap was only 0.4 percent in 1992 and 1 percent in 1998. (The presence of the national bureaucracy in Hanoi and the city's disproportionate share of the national budget also compensated for those relatively small gaps in the Red River delta.)

In the income-transfer process, the northern highlands were the biggest beneficiary as their share of the provincial expenditures exceeded their contribution to national revenues by 7.8 percent in 1992 and 12.8 percent in 1998, and their share of expenditures exceeded their contribution to national GDP by 4.2 percent in 1992 and 6.9 percent in 1998. The increase in budget share allocation to the northern highlands between 1992 and 1998 (from 16.9 percent to 18.4 percent), like that to the Central Highlands (from 4.3 percent in 1992 to 5.8 percent in 1998), reflects a national program to target the 1,715 poorest communes, all in the countryside and mostly in the highlands, for special infrastructure development assistance.

While not designed to compensate for the regional growth imbalance, the state's increase in social spending also benefited rural northern Vietnam, which was poorer than the southeast and the Mekong delta in the early 1990s. Social spending was mostly for pension and disability benefits for retired or disabled civil servants and state industrial workers (82.4 percent), and payments to war veterans and the families of war dead (16 percent). These categories covered 98.4 percent of the incomes received by households in the VLSS sample from the government's social spending (Vietnam and World Bank 1999: 124–25). This strongly favored the northern parts of the country, especially the Red River delta and the North Central panhandle, which had sent a large number of sons to numerous wars and had bigger shares of the national bureaucratic workforce.[7]

The national Vietnamese government also attempted to redress the market-based imbalance in regional growth by decrees or market incentives. For example, the government attempted to intervene in the market by decree in 1994 by requiring that the first Vietnamese oil refinery be built in the poor central coastal province of Quang Ngai instead of in the center of the oil industry in the southeast. The top government leadership hoped that the oil refinery would serve as the starting point for an industrial corridor from Da Nang to Dung Quat (in Quang Ngai), despite the fact that additional economic costs would be incurred in the transportation of crude oil at a greater distance from offshore oil wells in the south, as well as the transportation of refined petroleum products to the biggest consumption market in the south. Western and Southeast Asian firms subsequently

Table 3.6. Regional Contributions to National GDP and Revenues, and Regional Shares of Provincial Expenditures, by Percentages

	1992				1998			
	Population	GDP	National revenues collected	Provincial expenditures	Population	GDP	National revenues collected	Provincial expenditures
Northern Highlands	17.3	12.7	9.1	16.9	17.2	11.5	5.6	18.4
Red River Delta	19.8	19.1	23.2	18.3	19.4	18.8	21.7	17.8
North Central	13.6	8.3	5.8	9.8	13.2	7.7	3.6	10.3
S. Central Coast	10.5	7.4	7.1	9.8	10.6	7.5	5.0	10
Central Highlands	4.1	3.2	2.2	4.3	5.2	3.5	1.6	5.8
Southeast	12.3	27.1	37.4	23.5	13.2	31.5	54.8	19
Mekong Delta	22.3	22.2	15.2	17.5	21.2	19.5	7.7	18.7

Source: World Bank 1995: 160, 165; and Vietnam-General Statistical Office 1999c.

withdrew from this oil refinery project. They were eventually replaced by a Russian-Vietnamese joint venture by the end of the 1990s, but the oil refinery had not operated by mid-2002, limiting the impact of state intervention.

The government's efforts to redress regional growth imbalance by market incentives were not highly effective either. The policy of lower taxes or tax exemption to foreign capital in mountainous areas did not have any major impact, since the shares of FDIs by the northern and Central Highlands remained disproportionately low in the 1990s. Similarly, the governmental intervention through a price floor support for paddy also had very limited impact, if at all. In March 2001, the government ordered state export companies to stockpile 1 million tons of rice and provided over 10 million U.S. dollars in interest subsidy on the bank loans to these companies, in order to boost the domestic price of paddy to 1,300 dong a kilogram (above the estimated production costs of 1,000–1,100 dong a kilogram in the Mekong delta). However, rice growers received only 900–1,100 dong per kilogram since export companies and their multiple layers of middlemen sought to cover their transportation costs and to maintain their profit margins (*Saigon Giai Phong* July 17, 2001: 6; *Nguoi Lao Dong* May 10, 2001: 5).

Along the same line, the Vietnamese Communist Party made rural development a major policy thrust at its Eighth Party Congress in 1996 in order to limit the growth of rural-urban inequality. The government's investment in strengthening the rural infrastructures (electricity, transportation, and irrigation systems), while clearly beneficial to the majority of rural dwellers, did not have immediate and major impacts on rural income growth in the 1990s. The state's efforts to reduce the urban-rural gap also ran into implementation difficulties since many members of the urban-based bureaucracy sought to trim off the funds through a variety of corrupt practices (see boxes 3.1 and 3.2). This took place partly in the context of the unprecedented pressures on the population to race ahead in the education of their children as a major strategy for socioeconomic advances. Even the program to target poor communes was not immune from the corruption by many urban-based bureaucrats. For example, senior urban bureaucrats in Hanoi made fake receipts to appropriate two-thirds of the 200 million dong funds (U.S. $15,000) allocated to a poor ethnic minority commune for the replacement of its opium crop with an alternative. Yet, the two leading corrupt officials received only 24–30-month sentences (*Tuoi Tre* October 12, 2000: 1, 15). In magnitude, this case paled in comparison to the Muong Te road construction project (in the northern highlands province of Lai Chau). In that project, the officials of two construction companies, one of which was affiliated with the national committee on ethnic groups and mountainous regions of the Vietnamese government, manufactured receipts for 7 billion dong (about half a million U.S. dollars) in the 1997–1999 period out of 72 billion dong disbursed. Of this amount, about 5 billion dong were used for gifts to 117 government officials (*Tuoi Tre* October 26, 2000: 5; and *Tuoi Tre* October 27, 2000: 5). Elsewhere, in the central Vietnamese province of Quang Nam–Da Nang, the director of a construction company under investigation reported spending 32–40 billion dong (8–10 percent of the 400 billion dong for 46 projects) to cover the gifts, commissions, and public relations expenses for government officials (*Nguoi Lao Dong* November 10, 2000: 6). Needless to say, many members of the Vietnamese bureaucracy are not corrupt. Many of their decisions may be made as favors, couched in the idiom of *tinh cam* (sentiment), to people, agencies, and firms in their social networks.[8] The Vietnamese government has also given a high priority to its anticorruption campaign, officially requiring senior officials to file information on their wealth. The Vietnamese press has exposed many cases of questionable behavior on the part of bureaucrats. But the anticorruption campaign and press exposures have had only a limited impact to date.

On a national scale, the Vietnamese government attempted to limit the process of socioeconomic polarization by launching hunger eradication and poverty alleviation programs, by increasing health and educational expenditures, and by restructuring them so as to favor the well-off to a lesser extent. The government sought to reduce the differential access to market opportunities by offering small, low-interest loans to facilitate the poor's participation in the market, partial or full tuition exemptions for the poor in primary and secondary education, as well as health insurance cards to the poor. State educational expenditure increased from 10.9 percent of public expenditure and 2.2 percent of GDP in 1992 to 17.4 percent of public expenditure and 3.5 percent of GDP in 1998 (Vietnam and International Donor Group 2000, vol. 2: 128). Health expenditure correspondingly increased from 5.8 percent of public expenditure and 1.2 percent of GDP in 1992 to 8.5 percent of public expenditure and 1.7 percent of GDP in 1998 (98–99). These expenditures were also shifted away from a pro-rich pattern. Given the highly restricted access of the poor to upper secondary and postsecondary education, the state's coverage of primary education expenses increased from 45 percent in 1993 to 61 percent in 1998; of lower secondary education, from 34 percent to 42 percent in the same period; while its coverage of upper secondary education declined from 40 percent in 1993 to 33 percent in 1998, and of higher and vocational education, from 71 percent to 46 percent in the same period (144).

However, the small credit program as a component of the poverty alleviation program was contingent upon jobs available in the informal sector and on the larger economy as well as on local governments' perspectives on the informal economy. In Ho Chi Minh City, for example, with a maximum loan of 10 million dong (about U.S. $660), a poor household could normally start a small vending business or operate a pedicab. Yet, the provincial government also prohibited street vending on sidewalks and pedicab operations in the city center in the name of a more orderly city and made it more difficult for the poor to earn their livelihoods. Provincial governments also restricted the access to local schools, poverty alleviation loans, and health insurance cards to the official residents of their provinces. Recent migrants were disenfranchised in this process (Vietnam and World Bank 1999: 35–36). Furthermore, educational and health care cost exemptions did not always reach the right targets: 9.5 percent of the households in the top income quintile still received partial or full school charge exemptions, in comparison to 17–20.5 percent among households in

Box 3.1.   Construction Projects and Moneymaking among Officials

According to the experts in governmental fund arrangements, it is necessary to use three techniques in order to ensure success: first, through relations, second, through power, and third, through using the right names (*nhat quen, nhi the, ba la gioi biet van dung su nhan danh*). . . .

Relations here include kin ties, native village or commune ties, and classmate or age-mate relations. . . . Those relations with influential people in government funding agencies are fully used. They facilitate frank discussion, the discourse of sentiment (*tinh cam*), and mutual agreement . . . [including the mutual agreement on commission (*trich lai qua phan tram*) on government funds]. . . .

There are two main methods for paying commissions: as gifts privately presented at home; as additional land, real estate [to the signing officials], or employment opportunities to the relatives of influential officials; or more crudely, in the bags of money brought to the residences of the signing officials. According to affairs specialists [middlemen in governmental fund arrangements], the average commission amounts to 20 percent of the [government] funds. . . . Cruel officials would take up to 30–40 percent of project funds [as commission]. However, some [grant-receiving] people also burn bridges, ignoring the fund-granting officials. . . . [T]here are several solutions among officials in fund-approving agencies [to this problem]. The most common method is to divide the funds into several installments over many years. The disbursement in one year depends on the commission on the previously disbursed installment. . . . This is one of the reasons why many construction projects are stretched out over many years, even over 10 years: the completion of one part may go hand in hand with the request for additional funds to maintain the previous parts and to prevent their deterioration. . . .

There are now many fund-raising middlemen taking care of everything. The agency receiving the funds just signs and puts its seal on the paper. The middlemen construct the rationale for a project, estimate the costs, and implement the project. The agency with the project just receives the final product. (Pham Viet Dao 1996: 77–81).

Construction projects have many loopholes, allowing people to do fake accounting. . . . This is one of the main reasons leading to the phenomenon of state-funded projects costing 50 percent or 100 percent more than justifiable (Pham Viet Dao 1996: 94). . . . Contractors or bidders list more expensive materials but use less expensive ones . . . (84).

One of the main points of this decree [92, issued in 1994] is that the agency with a construction project has to invite bids [from B, or contractors]. . . . When a project has been approved for a large amount of money, the large construction companies which can bid for the project meet to work out an agreement. . . . They agree on which B [contractor] will be the successful bidder, which parts of the project will be subcontracted to other contractors, or to be "sold" to other contractors with a commission. Once an agreement is worked out, the bidding is just a theatrical performance. . . . At present, many As [implementing agencies] use the bidding process . . . to find out which B can offer the highest commission, not to find out who can offer a lower price or a solution to improve the esthetics or quality [of the final product] (64–65).

Box 3.2. How Commune Officials Managed to Get Project Funds

As the President of Xuan Khanh commune (Tho Xuan district, Thanh Hoa province), Mr. Nguyen Thanh Minh requested funds from the provincial Department of Transportation to improve rural roads [in his commune]. But because the bureaucratic system seemed intractable, the commune President tried to find another way. A middleman agreed to help on the condition of a 30 percent commission [on the fund]. It was a throat-cutting commission, but Mr. Minh agreed. Xuan Khanh commune was then granted 100 million dong for its rural road project; and Mr. Minh gave the middleman 30 million dong. But things were not smooth in real life. The provincial Department of Transportation disbursed only 50 million dong. And President Minh "dropped" 15 million dong along the way, and handed in only 5 million dong to the commune treasury. When asked about 15 million dong by inspectors, Mr. Minh lamented: "They were spent on trips [to meet higher authorities] and on public relations [with the latter]" (!). Released from his President position, Mr. Minh faced the possibility of a criminal trial because he did not hand in the mis-spent fund and because he was also involved in another case in which officials forgot to hand in a part of an irrigation project fund. . . (*Tuoi Tre* September 26, 2000: 3).

the bottom three quintiles (Vietnam and International Donor Group 2000: 145). Well-off households in Ho Chi Minh City reportedly received poverty-reduction loans and free health insurance cards, while a desperately poor household was denied a loan due to an outstanding debt of 600,000 dong to another program and, in desperation, had to accept a tubal ligation in exchange for 300,000 dong (U.S. $21) (*Tuoi Tre* April 4, 2000: 12; *Nguoi Lao Dong* October 13, 2000). In general, households still paid approximately 79 percent of health care costs in 1998, which declined only slightly from the 84 percent burden in 1993. Households still absorbed 52 percent of the total educational expenditures in 1998, in comparison to 49 percent in 1992–1993 (World Bank 1995: 86, 99–100; Vietnam and International Donor Group 2000, vol. 2: 98–99, 128; Vietnam-General Statistical Office 2000b: 267, 274).

In the aforementioned circumstances, it is no coincidence that despite the overall reduction in the poverty rate, the degree of inequality in Vietnam, the urban-rural gap, and regional inequality all increased in the 1990s. While the per capita expenditure in the top expenditure quintile was only 4.6 times that in the bottom one in 1992–1993, it increased to 5.5 times in 1997–1998 (Vietnam-General Statistical Office 2000b: 269). Furthermore, rural expenditures rose only 30 percent from 1992–1993 to 1997–1998, while urban expenditures rose by 60.5 percent in the same period. With the exception of the Red River delta, urban expenditures rose more rapidly than rural ones in Vietnam from 1992–1993 to 1997–1998.[9] As previously reported, the increase in urban-rural inequality accounted for 96 percent of the total increase in inequality in this period, while that within urban and rural areas accounted only for 4 percent.

Similarly, among the seven socioeconomic regions of Vietnam, the increase in interregional inequality, measured in per capita household expenditure, accounted for 83 percent of the total increase in inequality between 1992–1993 and 1997–1998, while intraregional ones accounted only for 17 percent. The expenditure growth in this five-year period reached 78 percent in the southeast and 55 percent in the Red River delta thanks to the impact of both market forces and state policies, while it reached 46 percent in the north central panhandle thanks to the income transfer through the state's social spending. The expenditure growth was lowest in the Mekong delta, standing at 18 percent, due to the impact of global price fluctuation. It remained below 31 percent in the other 4 regions due to the lack of global capital and the very limited effectiveness of governmental intervention. It is not surprising that the poverty rate declined by 25 percent in the southeast (from 33 percent in 1992–1993 to 8 percent in 1997–1998), by 34 percent in the Red River delta (from 63 percent to 29 percent), and 27 percent in the north central panhandle (from 75 percent to 48 percent), while it dropped by less than 20 percent in other regions and dropped by only 10 percent (from 47 percent to 37 percent) in the Mekong delta of South Vietnam.

The uneven growth in favor of urban areas, as well as the southeast and the Red River delta, led to the considerable migration from rural to urban areas (especially Ho Chi Minh City and Hanoi), and from many parts of the country to the southeast.[10] The impact of this migration on rural development (through the deprivation of the active young labor force and through remittances to rural areas) still needs to be examined more systematically.

Local Dynamics

While the political economy of development in Vietnam of the 1990s played an important role in accounting for the socioeconomic differentiation process among regions, along the urban-rural axis, as well as among households, our understanding of this process would remain incomplete without an analysis of the historically conditioned and local sociocultural dynamics on regional and community as well as household levels.

It was mentioned above that among the seven socioeconomic regions of Vietnam, the per capita income of people in the national bottom quintile was lowest in the southeast, the Mekong delta, and the Central Highlands, despite the fact that the average per capita income was highest in the southeast, third highest in the Mekong delta, and fifth highest in the Central Highlands. It was also in the southeast and the Mekong delta that the percentages of landless rural households exceeded 21 percent in 1997–1998, far above those in five other regions. As mentioned in the introduction to this volume, in the village of Khanh Hau in the upper Mekong delta where I have conducted research since 1992, the percentage of landless households increased from 14.6 percent in 1992 to 37.2 percent in 2000. I would suggest that the proletarianization of the peasantry and the lower incomes of the bottom 20 percent in the Mekong delta and the southeast are rooted in historically conditioned and local sociocultural frameworks.

As mentioned above, in southern Vietnam, at the time of complete decollectivization in 1988, many peasants who had received land in the preceding decade were dispossessed, and many landowners were able to regain fully or partially their land in the 1975–1978 period, up to ten hectares of land. While a number of the dispossessed peasants were given land in the reclaimed Plain of Reeds, many gave up after a few crops due to rodent infestation and the loss of their seed, fertilizer, and crop investments. They became landless again. Although the Vietnamese constitution and land laws specified that all land remained under state and collective ownership, in the 1990s, in Nam Bo and the Central Highlands, land became an actively bought and sold commodity that many households accumulated and many others lost due to the dispossession in the late 1980s or to cope with their vulnerabilities. By 1992–1993, the percentages of landless rural households in the Vietnam Living Standard Survey had reached 16.9 percent in the Mekong delta and 21.3 percent in the southeast. A 1998 study of 5,025 poor and landless households in 144 hamlets in 12 Mekong delta provinces reveals that, of the 3,079 landless households in this sample, the rural proletarianization process had accelerated over time. A total of 1,020 households became landless before 1988; 1,092, in the 1988–1994 period (averaging 156 a year); and 967, in the 1995–mid-1998 period (averaging 276 households a year) (Nguyen Dinh Huong 1999: 68). If we take into account the 1,946 poorer households with less than 2,000 square meters of agricultural land, 19 percent of the 5,025 households in the sample had long been in this condition; 21 percent fell into the landless and poor categories due to the household division process; 8 percent lost land due to the local-government-supported return of land to former owners; 33 percent sold their land due to sicknesses in their families and due to the lack of capital for production; and 18 percent became landless for other reasons (125).

At the other end of the spectrum, by 1993, a number of farms in the Plain of Reeds of the Mekong delta had already exceeded one hundred hectares in size (Dang Phong 1995: 167–68; Nguyen Dinh Huong 1999: 425, 562). In the Central Highlands, the number of private coffee and tea plantations that exceeded ten hectares numbered in the hundreds, if not in the thousands. The substantial differences in landholdings in the south played a very significant role in the socioeconomic differentiation among households. A World Bank-sponsored study in 1992–1993 concludes on the basis of large-scale survey data that "in the south, the poorest households rely more on off-farm income sources, whereas the wealthiest households are mostly concentrated on the farm" (World Bank 1995: 66). I suggest that the wealth polarization in Nam Bo was rooted in the century-old commercialization of agriculture and the widely accepted premise of land as a commodity. This ideological premise and the practice of agricultural commercialization were imposed on the Central Highlands by the Vietnamese ethnic majority, leading to the economic marginalization of indigenous ethnic minorities.

In contrast, in other parts of Vietnam, land was distributed in a relatively egalitarian fashion, primarily because of community pressures underlain by an egalitarian ideology and tightly knit village networks. Vietnam's agricultural guidelines in

1988, at the time of complete decollectivization, had initially proposed that in order to increase agricultural efficiency, the better cultivators should be given the opportunity to contract for more fertile land with higher production quotas. However, many villagers reportedly complained about the auction of village land to the highest bidders and about its supposed effects in enriching the better-off (see also Dang Canh Khanh 1991: 348). In many communities, these complaints hindered the implementation of the pro-rich 1988 policy. As a result of these widespread and continuing complaints and the desire of the national leadership to maintain sociopolitical stability, by 1994 few northern communities still retained the most fertile fields for annual bidding. Most villages had divided most of the fields among their members on a strictly egalitarian and long-term basis. In the northern Vietnamese villages where I have conducted field research, there were no informal complaints by villagers about the village leadership's favoritism in land allocation. In light of the varying quality of village fields, to ensure equity, a household usually received its land in three to twelve small pieces in different locations. The same egalitarian practice of land division was also adopted in 1994 in two communes in Son Tinh district of the central coastal province of Quang Ngai that I visited in 2000. It was for this reason that the percentage of landless rural households in the central coast even dropped from 10.7 percent in 1992–1993 to 5.1 percent in 1997–1998. It remained under 8 percent in the northern half of Vietnam (table 3.1). The egalitarian land reform in north Vietnam and parts of central Vietnam in 1993–1994, which left in its wake communities of small independent farmers, was strongly rooted in local sociocultural dynamics. While nonagricultural incomes have played an important role in the socioeconomic differentiation process in the north and in certain parts of the central coast in contrast to the situation in south Vietnam (World Bank 1995: 66), the relatively egalitarian land distribution and local pressures against land sales have helped to reduce socioeconomic inequality in northern and many central Vietnamese agricultural communities (see Luong and Unger 1999).

Local sociocultural dynamics in their regional variations also powerfully shaped the intracommunity differentiation process in other ways. Tighter community networks and the stronger egalitarian ideology in rural northern and central Vietnam underlay the greater vigilance and assertiveness of local populations on cadres' corruption. More specifically, the social networks within northern and the majority of central coastal Vietnamese villages were tightened by a high degree of village endogamy. In the northern village of Hoai Thi (pop. 762 in 1990), for example, the rate of village endogamy was around 50 percent for the entire population, while rising to 75 percent among the marriages in the 1986–1990 period. In the village of Son Duong in Vinh Phu province where I have conducted field research, it reached 82 percent for the three-year period of 1989–1991 (see also Luong 1989). In the village of Ta Thanh Oai near Hanoi, 65 percent of the marriages in a sample of 338 households were endogamous (Krowolski 2002: 85). Local social networks in the north were also tightened by the proliferation of local and nongovernmental organizations such as same-age associations and alumni associations, among others. This feature of northern and many central coastal Vietnamese village structures stood in contrast to that in Nam Bo, where community exogamy was preferred and where nongovernmental associations were not as prevalent. Operating in conjunction with a stronger egalitarian ideology, tighter local social networks in the north and the center helped to constrain the self-enriching activities of local cadres. For example, in Yen Son commune of Quoc Oai district in the northern province of Ha Tay, parents refused to send their children to a local elementary school and went to Hanoi to file a grievance against the school principal for his inappropriate use of the fund of 53 million dong (about U.S. $3,700) raised for school construction. They rejected the solution of dismissing the principal from his position and demanded a court trial before sending their children back to school (*Nguoi Lao Dong* October 9, 2000). Similarly, in Son Duong commune in the northern province of Phu Tho where I have conducted field research over the years, villagers accused commune officials of embezzling forty-two tons of paddy (less than U.S. $4,000) in tax collection in 1994–1996. The relation between the local population and the commune administration reached a boiling point during my 1998 visit: local families had reportedly refused to pay not only irrigation fees but also commune taxes. These arrears totaled U.S. $18,000 for half a year. For half a year, commune cadres had not received their salaries because of this politically rooted financial crisis. From 1993 to 1998, under strong local social pressures, four Communist Party secretaries and five presidents of the People's Committee quickly succeeded one another. Public confrontations with local officials were not isolated cases in Yen So or Son Duong. They happened in numerous other northern localities, while virtually absent in Nam Bo despite the fact that corruption was far from absent in the south. They point toward the effectiveness of tight local social networks in allowing local populations to exercise strong control over the potential abuse of power by local officials in the north and the center (see Luong 2000). Regional and urban-rural differences in wealth and poverty in Vietnam are underlain not only by market forces and state policies but also by historically conditioned and local dynamics (see also Sikor 1999).

Sociocultural dynamics became even more salient in the microcosm of Vietnamese household wealth and poverty in the 1990s. They shaped not only a household's access to land as a natural capital, but also its human and social capital, on the basis of which it took advantage of new opportunities and dealt with its crises and vulnerabilities. The vulnerabilities can be individual (affecting single households, like accidents, thefts), or nonindividual (affecting entire communities) (Van de Walle 1999). They can also be either proximate (short-term illnesses, pregnancy, death of a laborer), or structural (gender, ethnicity, high dependency ratio, especially in a certain stage of household development cycle, or the global fluctuation in the prices of agricultural commodities) (Davies 1996).

A household's human capital, both in terms of quantity and quality, was strongly shaped by sociocultural dynamics, either communitywide or household-specific. More specifically, the number of household members contributing to household income was influenced by the socioculturally conditioned household developmental cycle. This number tended to peak when the main couple in the household was in the 45–55-year-old age range, and when their children joined the labor force, still lived at home, and contributed to the household income. A study in Ho Chi Minh City in 1998 well illustrates this pattern. Nuclear family households in a sample of 1,050 in Ho Chi Minh City had the highest probability of reaching the peak of per capita incomes when household heads and their spouses were in the 45–54 years age range (table 3.7). Some members of the second generation were ready to enter the workforce at this time and to contribute to their households' budgets, while most in the first generation no longer had childcare burden and could still participate in the labor force. The average dependency index for nuclear family households with heads and spouses in the 45–54 years age range stood at .38, significantly lower than that of .5 for households with heads and spouses in the 35–44 years age range (cf. Chayanov 1986: 53ff.; World Bank 1999: 24).[11] When household heads and their spouses moved into the next age range (55–64), most in the formal economic sector had to retire. Those not working for the state sector did not have pensions, and for those in the state sector, state pensions were significantly lower than incomes before retirements.[12]

The statistical pattern among joint family households (two or more related nuclear families living together) is not as clearcut due to such intervening variables as whether the main couple's parents were still both alive, and whether they had pensions as retired state employees. Nonetheless, the following case provides a good illustration of the socioculturally mediated relation between household welfare and household developmental cycle:

Household 308 in the ward of Cau Kho [District 1, Ho Chi Minh City] was a joint family household with nine members in 1998–1999. It was composed of the senior couple (aged 61 and 56 in 1998) and all of their five children (three sons,

Table 3.7. Dependency Index and Per Capita Household Income in Nuclear Family Households, Ho Chi Minh City, 1998–1999

	Dependency index		Per-capita household Income (in 1,000 dong/month)	
	Mean	Standard Deviation	Mean	Standard Deviation
Nuclear family	.44	.23	527	463
Average age of household head & spouse				
+ < 25 (n = 10)	.33	.27	524	452
+ 25–34 (n = 116)	.45	.23	489	365
+ 35–44 (n = 243)	.50	.20	525	373
+ 45–54 (n = 121)	.38	.23	672	731
+ 55–64 (n = 58)	.34	.24	464	340
+ > 64 (n = 60)	.44	.26	375	268

Source: Luong 2001b: 325.

aged 33, 30, 18; and two daughters aged 27 and 24). One of the two daughters was married, with her husband and child (respectively 34 and 7 years old) living in the same household. Of the senior couple, the husband was born in Ho Chi Minh City, while his wife moved to the city from Long An province in her childhood. At the time of the study, three of the five children worked; one was unemployed; and one was a student, as was the senior couple's son-in-law. The reported per capita income for the household was 353,000 dong a month, which puts the household in the third income quintile in the 1,050-household sample. This household, however, had suffered severe economic hardships until the mid-1990s, when most of the children began joining the labor force. For almost two decades between 1975 and the early 1990s, the household's income was derived mainly from the wife's job in a state electricity company and her sideline trading activities. The husband had been in a reeducation camp in 1975 and had difficulties in finding a job after reeducation. The couple decided to invest heavily in their children's education as the strategy for upward socioeconomic mobility, instead of terminating their children's education early. The eldest son attended university and had worked as an engineer for an international company before his recent layoff. The second, third, and fourth children all finished high school, while the youngest child was a university student in 1998–1999. When asked about the most difficult and better-off economic periods of the household in the past ten years, the husband replied:

> There were years [before the late 1980s] when on the eve of the New Year, none of my children had got any new clothes, and the family had not been able to buy anything for the New Year. [For daily meals,] we scraped by with whatever we could afford to buy. To be frank, at many meals, we had nothing but rice, a plate of rau muong (Vietnamese spinach), and soy sauce. What else did we have to eat? . . . From 1988 to the mid-1990s, the situation became better, but not much better. . . . More recently, most [of my children] have jobs. Instead of struggling all the time to make ends meet, our load has been lightened by 70 percent. . . . Instead of having to find money to support the children's schooling, we now see that [most of them] have incomes. (interview, Ho Chi Minh City)

When asked about the household's prospect in the next five to ten years, the two daughters in the family expressed a strong confidence that their household welfare would improve once their youngest brother, a first-year university student at the time, graduated from university and entered the labor force. As the senior couple's children remained in the same household, and contributed to the common pot, and as the senior couple got into their late fifties, the household's living conditions improved steadily. It moved probably from the bottom income quintile in the 1975–1988 period into the third quintile in 1998–1999. Had four of the elder children moved off, with nine people from household 308, there would have been five households instead of one household: the senior couple with the youngest son in one household, the eldest son and his two unmarried siblings in three others, and the married daughter with her nuclear family in the fifth. Three of those five households would have been in the top and second income quintiles for Ho Chi Minh City households, while the senior couple's and their married daughter's households would have been in the bottom quintile. With the joint family arrangement, the members of Household 308 all ended up in the third income quintile in the sample of 1,050 households in Ho Chi Minh City.

However, differences in human resource quality also powerfully shaped households' abilities to seize market opportunities and to deal with crises and vulnerabilities. Human resources include not only formal education but also family backgrounds and experiences. The success of some households as opposed to their neighbors appears to be due partly to a combination of drive and skills acquired through formal education as well as through previous work and family experiences. In the northern Vietnamese village of Hoai Thi, for example, 46 percent of the sampled households in 1990 with at least middle-peasant backgrounds produced an agricultural surplus, while only 14 percent of those with poor peasant and landless backgrounds fell into this category. At the opposite end of the spectrum, 36 percent of the households with poor peasant and landless backgrounds had trouble making ends meet, while none of those with at least middle peasant backgrounds fell into this category (Luong and Unger 1999; cf. Truong Huyen Chi 2001: chap. 5; and Szelenyi 1988).

Sociocultural processes in their regional variations also powerfully shaped community structure and households' social capital, on the basis of which households dealt with their vulnerabilities as well as with the emerging inequality within the community. In-depth interviews in four areas of poverty reveal a number of common coping strategies as well as region-specific ones: informal and formal assistance within the community; reduction in consumption and expenditures; interest-free borrowings; loans with interest (as low as 1 percent for nonbusiness loans from formal financial institutions, and as high as 30 percent a month from loan sharks); living with ill health; having family members (including children) find (additional) work (including through migration and pulling children out of school); selling assets; selling blood or accepting a government-sponsored vasectomy for a reward of a dozen dollars (in urban areas); selling babies for adoption or daughters for marriages to Taiwanese (in the south) (World Bank and UK Department for International Development 1999: 44–52).

I would suggest that social capital was higher in northern and central Vietnam due to the high rate of village endogamy and the proliferation of nongovernmental organizations (including patrilineages). The effectiveness of this stronger social capital is reflected in the strong networks of migrants from particular northern and central villages in Hanoi and Ho Chi Minh City: these migrants tended to cluster together residentially and occupationally and formed their same-village associations for mutual assistance and for helping fellow villagers still in the countryside in the migration process or other matters. The Bay Hien area in Ho Chi Minh City, for example, is full of migrants from the central Vietnamese province of Quang Nam who specialized in weaving (Quach Thu Cuc 1997). Migrants from Xuan Thuy district of Nam Dinh province, for another example, made up 70 percent of the non-Hanoi scavengers and junk buyers in

Hanoi and were heavily concentrated in the O Cho Dua neighborhood of the city (Digregorio 1994: chap. 3; see also Li 1996: 34–36). I would suggest that a household's social capital and the characteristics of a local social network played an important role in a household's strategy to cope with different kinds of shocks and with local inequality. The importance of social capital, social networks, and community structure in mitigating the impact of households' vulnerabilities needs to be studied more systematically on a regional and class comparative basis.

The rapid transformation of regional and household wealth and poverty in Vietnam under economic reforms in the 1990s, together with the antipoverty programs of the Vietnamese government and international donors, led to many important large-scale household surveys in that decade (Nguyen van Tiem 1993; World Bank 1995; Vietnam and World Bank 1999; Dollar et al. 1998; Vietnam-General Statistical Office 1999a and 2000b; Haughton et al. 1999; Rondinelli and Litvack 1999). As a part of the 1997–1998 Vietnam Living Standard Survey, complementary qualitative research was also conducted in a number of communities in four Vietnamese provinces, providing preliminary and crucial information on the local parameters of socioeconomic differentiation (World Bank and UK Department of International Development 1999).

In this chapter, I suggest that a full understanding of wealth, poverty, and socioeconomic inequality in Vietnam requires attention not only to market forces and government policies but also to local sociocultural dynamics. The relative importance of those factors, and more importantly, the microscopic processes of households' socioeconomic mobility in different regions of Vietnam, including among different ethnic groups, require more systematic and in-depth research. The large-scale quantitative studies conducted by the Vietnamese General Statistical office, with the technical support of the World Bank and other international donors, have provided important information on regional and urban-rural differentiation, as well as some major insights on the roles of market forces and government policies in the period of economic reforms. These are important beginnings that need to be followed up with in-depth microscopic studies.

NOTES

1. In two of the nine cooperatives that Adam Fforde examines in some depth, members' crop shares were determined not at the cooperative level (commune), but at the production brigade level (Fforde 1989: 123–27).

2. Official Vietnamese statistics from provincial governments put the percentage of landless rural households at 5.7 percent in the Mekong delta in the late 1990s (Nguyen Dinh Huong 1999: 66). However, Nguyen Dinh Huong's survey in 144 hamlets in 1998 revealed that the percentages in those hamlets were considerably higher than official statistics for the entire Mekong delta. The official statistics was probably deflated in order to minimize the attention of the national government in Hanoi.

3. The percentage of landless households in Khanh Hau was below that of 15.8 percent in a hamlet of Thoi Long village (Hau Giang province) but above that of 4.2 percent in Long Hoa village in the municipality of Can Tho in the same province (Nguyen Thu Sa 1992: 45). For comparative purposes, the percentage of landless rural households stood at 5–7 percent in 1978, before the state launched its collectivization campaign (Nguyen Thu Sa 1990: 141–54).

4. A World Bank–sponsored study in 1992–1993 has also concluded on the basis of large-scale survey data that "in the south, the poorest households rely more on off-farm income sources, whereas the wealthiest households are mostly concentrated on the farm" (World Bank 1995: 66). The situation in northern Vietnam was the reverse.

5. No comparative data had been released for 1992–1993.

6. It is not known whether there was a similar concentration of private domestic capital in the southeast region in the 1990s, since no reliable data are available.

7. Incidentally, social spending also favored urban and richer households more than rural and poorer ones: approximately 18.3 percent of urban households, in contrast to 9.4 percent of rural households, received pensions and disability benefits; and 17.5 percent of households in the top expenditure quintiles, in contrast to 8.1 percent in the second lowest quintile and 3.5 percent in the lowest one, received them.

8. A systematic study on the idiom of "sentiment," social relations, and social networks has not yet been conducted in Vietnam (cf. Yang 1994, Yan 1996).

9. The urban poverty rate declined from 25 percent to 9 percent, while that in the Vietnamese countryside dropped from 66 percent to 45 percent (Vietnam-General Statistical Office 2000b: 289). The 15 percent decline in the urban poverty rate in comparison to the 19 percent drop in the rural one despite the more rapid rise in average urban expenditure suggests a greater increase in urban inequality than in the rural one.

10. Rural dwellers in the upper part of the Mekong delta could find work more easily in the southeast without migrating due to the proximity to the latter region. For example, in many villages in Can Giuoc district of Long An province, officially a part of the Mekong delta, hundreds of villagers daily commuted from their home villages to work in Ho Chi Minh City. The landless rural households in the southeast also found numerous nonfarm employment opportunities in the rapidly growing industrial and service sectors in this region.

11. The household dependency index is calculated by dividing the number of dependents by the number of household members earning enough to feed themselves. In Ho Chi Minh City, this earning was set at 80,000 dong a month in 1998.

12. The majority of households (58 percent) in the sample of 1,050 in Ho Chi Minh City were nuclear family households. 11.8 percent of the households involved singles, or singles with relatives other than spouses or children, or unrelated singles. 12.8 percent were extended family households, with one or more relatives on the husband's or wife's side living with the core nuclear family, as long as those relatives did not constitute another full or partially disintegrated nuclear family. 17.4 percent of the households were joint in that two or more related nuclear families had a joint consumption arrangement. 58 percent of the population below the age of 25 in the Ho Chi Minh City sample lived in nuclear households, while 13 percent lived in extended family households, and 24.7 percent, in joint family ones. The percentage of individuals who lived with relatives reached 97.9 percent in Ho Chi Minh City in 1998–1999, if we include the individuals in households without nuclear family bases who lived with their siblings, nieces, nephews, and grandchildren, among others. In a further breakdown, 42.7 percent lived in extended or joint family households; 53.5 percent in nuclear family ones; and 1.7 percent, with other relatives outside their immediate nuclear families.

4

State Visions, Migrant Decisions: Population Movements since the End of the Vietnam War

Andrew Hardy

The story of migration in late twentieth century Vietnam reflects the sort of nation the government aimed to create after the war ended in 1975. It is also the story of the limits to that vision. During the 1980s, these led to a process of reform, Doi Moi (renovation), undoing much of the previous program of socialist construction. The postreunification vision aimed to extend the command economy to the whole country, affecting almost every aspect of people's daily existence. The limits to it, in turn, were defined by numerous decisions and actions of ordinary people. Many of these involved migration, reflecting people's own visions for their future. Migrations became a key interface in the state's relationship with the people. The mobility of the population may be used to measure the effectiveness of the state's vision not simply of economic development but of governance in general.

Sites of this interface may be found throughout Vietnam. Among these are the street junctions of the capital. In a normal city scene, there is nothing remarkable about yellow uniformed policemen attempting to control unruly city traffic, directing vehicles when the lights fail, and hailing and fining lawbreakers. An even more common feature, however, of Hanoi's urban landscape, visible on every corner, are the men in military-style green fatigues, squatting on motorbikes, calling to passing pedestrians. These are the *xe om*, motorbike taxi drivers, who provide an important transportation service to the city's population. A few of them were born in the city, but most come from other parts of Vietnam. Their experiences offer an urban image of mobility, one image among many, an image of the population's aspirations and achievements and the extent to which these influenced the state's vision of the future.

VISION

What was this vision? Speaking of the Doi Moi economic reforms, Pham Van Dong used an image of mobility to stress that it was not a monolithic policy: "we are going along a road without a map . . . every day and every hour resolving practical issues, problems full of complexities and unknowns" (Pham Van Dong 1994, cited in Tuong Lai 1998: 8–9). The direction Vietnam's leaders took reflected developments in the Soviet Union and China, and while this was also true in earlier periods, it would be equally wrong to see policy making before 1986 as entirely unified, especially given the transitional way the reforms emerged in the 1980s (Dang Phong and Beresford 1998: 59–61). Nonetheless, Hanoi had clear goals on reunification. It aimed to extend the pre-1975 northern model of development to the whole country (Fforde and de Vylder 1996: 4). The way Vietnam was reunified after 1975 owed much to the process of postwar recovery and socialist construction after 1954.

The French handed over the city of Hanoi on 10 October 1954. They left it denuded, not simply of economic infrastructure but more importantly of a large part of its population. About one million people moved from north to south after the Geneva Agreement (Vietnam, Phu Tong uy Di cu Ti nan, c1958: 60). They were replaced in Hanoi by Viet Minh loyalists. Who were these people? Some came from the south, combatants and cadres, others from the USSR and China, returned after a tour of study. Most were from Vietnam's countryside. Many had spent years in the Viet Bac resistance headquarters. Some had fought against the French at the battle of Dien Bien Phu. Some were highlanders. Georges Boudarel recalled the celebrations: "If a surprised Vietnam is discovering itself in its infinite diversity, some ideologues, as hypocritical as they are short-sighted, say they are shocked to see women with naked breasts dancing with men in loincloths" (Boudarel 1997: 129). These exotic features of national unity—the unreserved portrayal of ethnic minorities as members of a new multicultural nation—did not last long: nakedness and loincloths were soon banished from such performances in conformity with cultural norms in the capital. Yet they signaled the beginning of a process whereby Vietnam's diversity, and above all the diversity of its lowland provinces, would be represented on Hanoi's streets and in Hanoi's homes. As Nga My noted:

> After 1954, migration for family reunion became common as many people stayed in Hanoi to join in the building and construction of the capital. As a result, it is no coincidence that up to two thirds of Hanoi's population today are people from other provinces. (Nga My 1997: 57)

In this city, officials of the Democratic Republic of Vietnam (DRV) formulated policies on the mobility of the population. Unlike in China, there was no major deurbanization, although U.S. bombs provoked evacuations after 1965. Urban centers were, in fact, developed as bases for the country's industrial policies, although there was no rapid growth in urban population. Hanoi was exceptional, expanding from 293,000 (1953) to 643,000 (1960) (Thrift and Forbes 1986: 88–91) with the arrival of soldiers and cadres of the revolution and their families, to replace the old elite vanished to the south. Overall low urbanization was the result of the 1955 institution of household registration (*ho khau*). Urban households registered their members with the police and reported births, deaths, and migrations (Thai Binh, So Cong an 1972: 18–21). This system, based on a Chinese model, aimed to restrict urban expansion, controlling how many people moved to the city and, more importantly, *who* moved (see Hardy 2001). The *ho khau* system was subsequently extended to the countryside, and local surveillance networks were established to ensure that every citizen lived and slept in their place of registered residence. It became an instrument of such tight regulation that, as one man complained, one of its principal effects was the prevention of extramarital affairs.[1]

As this system took effect, other changes affected rural-urban migration. With nationalization in the late 1950s, economic incentives for spontaneous mobility diminished. A coupon rationing system was developed, restricting supplies of basic commodities (food, fuel, cloth) to state employees (Hoang Thi Thu Ha 1999). Expansion of state employment provided opportunities for rural people to break away from their home village (*thoat ly*), which at this time became "a lifestyle fashion for peasants" (Luu Dinh Nhan 1991: 8). State jobs, and the migrations for family reunion they occasioned, became the main route to urban life. The DRV vision of urban development aimed at mobility along controlled channels. One observer noted: "migration to the city was almost impossible if one could not get a job in the state sector, either in production or administration" (Le Bach Duong 1998a: 28–29).

Collectivization from 1958 placed further limits on mobility. Membership in the cooperative determined access to economic and social benefits. Without household registration, membership could not be obtained. One village policeman told me that if people moved without transferring their registration, they *couldn't work on the paddies (which belonged to the cooperative), couldn't trade (it was illegal), couldn't work for wages (nobody hired wage laborers). They had to rely on other people for everything.*[2] Migration outside of state structures became both illegal and economically unattractive.[3]

In practice, this system did not abolish spontaneous migration. It just made it expensive. As in the cities, so in the countryside: policy became the major determinant of settlement (Le Bach Duong 1998b: 38). A few people still migrated without reference to the state, in moves described as "illegal," "secret," or "clandestine" (Nguyen Hong Minh 1993: 3; De Koninck 1999: 81). Others could transfer their household registration if they moved in state-approved directions (urban-to-rural, lowland-to-highland) or if they cultivated relations with village authorities. Numerically, however, the largest category comprised those on state migration programs. Between 1961 and 1966, more than one million people were recorded as going to national agricultural and forestry enterprises and new economic zone cooperatives in the highlands.[4] Not all of them stayed there, but this ambitious search for a "rational distribution of the productive force" remained a major feature of Vietnamese state policy for decades to come (Le Ngoc Luan 1995: 19; see also Evans 1992: 277).

Upon reunification, these state vehicles of migration had the same aims as after 1954. They opposed a vision of order to the chaotic patterns of mobility caused by the war, a time of rupture especially in the south when people moved in large numbers to safeguard their interests and security. Tuong Lai identified three objectives to postreunification migration policy:

> To reduce the long-standing *population pressure* in the Red River Delta, a place with excessively high population densities, and the coastal plains of central Vietnam.
> To restrain the rate of population growth in urban areas, especially in the two large cities: Hanoi and Ho Chi Minh City.
> To correct the population distribution within provinces and between regions, at the same time to allocate labor for *productive development* and establish regions of population to serve the interests of *security and defence*. (Tuong Lai 1998: 11. My emphasis)

Historically speaking, what exactly did these three objectives consist of?
Population pressure in the northern deltas had troubled colonial authorities and influenced DRV policy. One official described the thinking behind the migration program, which was announced at the Third Party Congress in 1960:

> Nowadays there is little paddy land in the delta region, and too much labor. Every year the population rises. According to documents of the Central Rural Committee, in the coming Five Year Plan, to improve the people's welfare and develop the economy, we must plan the migration of around 1.5 million people to regions of new economy.[5]

Welfare improvement in the plains was combined with economic development in the highlands. At the Congress, Le Duan explained that the policy "should help the highlands catch up with the plains, the highlands and border areas catch up with the heartlands, the ethnic minorities catch up with the Kinh [majority population]" (Le Duan 1960: 6). The northern mountains were slated to become culturally progressive areas as well as productive regions of intensive agriculture. In these early years, however, public emphasis was laid on the highlands' contribution to the lowland economy: the plains would supply population to the highlands, and resources produced in both regions would feed the state's industrialization policy. Over the five years from 1961, 550,000 hectares of new farmland were to be opened up, mainly by means of population redistribution (Pham Do Nhat Tan 1992: 43–44).[6]
This view of the highlands as a hinterland resource persisted on reunification. A district official in the lowland province of Thai Binh told me how he mobilized people for migration programs in the late 1970s, asking them to imagine *what the village will be like in the year 2000 if the birth rate continues like this.*[7] People were asked to move to the hills not only to improve their own situation but also "to contribute to the whole nation's enrichment."[8] After 1975 northern lowlanders continued to play a major part in the migration process. Pham Van Dong reported that "labourers from the North have already taken the first steps in the implementation of the pre-eminence of the socialist collective model in the South, contributing to the order and security of society there, and reinforcing strong people's government in their new homes" (Pham Van Dong 1978: 6).
In 1976 security and defence received greater attention in official statements. Le Duan was emphatic, at the Fourth Party Congress, that "the construction of the

country must go together with the protection of the country, these are the survival requirements of the nation" (Le Duan 1977: 58). The combination of economic and security imperatives was clear in population policy in the cities. According to one analysis, the deurbanization of the south that took place in the late 1970s responded to three concerns. These were "economic-practical" (withdrawal of U.S. support meant that cities could not support large populations, especially of war refugees), "economic-internal security" (the urban middle class constituted a threat to the state) and "moral" (cities symbolized capitalist iniquities) (Thrift and Forbes 1986: 129). Moving people out of the cities became a major priority, particularly as the 1975 exodus was not comparable in size with what occurred in the north in 1954—only 140,000 people left with the Americans before the fall of Saigon (Robinson 1998: 18). Authorities imposed socialism on an urban population far less malleable—and perceived as such—than that of Hanoi twenty years before. This model and the manner of its implementation was to provoke a further exodus—of the boat people.

Migration policy also served imperatives of security in the highlands. In 1954, the Viet Minh had swiftly dismantled autonomous highland territories created by the French (notably among the Thai in the northwest, and the Nung in the coastal province of Hai Ninh).[9] But after 1975, they were faced with a major ethnic insurgency in the Central Highlands, the FULRO.[10] While autonomous zones instituted after 1955 were abolished in 1976, in-migration by Kinh people from the plains was maintained. Establishing Kinh communities in what one settler called a *tense region* was an important part of the SRV's strategy for internal security.

It was also crucial for national defense. China's relationship with Cambodia gave violent Khmer Rouge incursions across Vietnam's borders a distinctly menacing meaning. After the 1979 invasion of Cambodia, the Central Highlands became a gateway and a rearguard base for Vietnamese forces there (Burchett 1980: 4; Salemink 1997: 494). The military importance of the migration programs would have been clear to readers of provincial newspapers. In 1978, *Dak Lak* ran a story on "a young people's regiment from Thai Binh" involved in "economic construction" in the border area: "Along with their production work, the regiment has organized and reinforced self-defence teams, increased the number of patrols and the level of security; . . . they fight when necessary, to protect the borders of the Fatherland" (Vu Quang 1978: 1). At this time 100,000 people moved to settle the border with China, and "join the ethnic compatriots in fighting the war."[11] In a reference to the "Chinese reactionary gang and their lackeys," a government report later praised this movement, noting that "the organisation and mobilisation of people to move and open up agricultural and forestry land over the last five years has a deep meaning, not only in economic terms, but also in terms of politics, society and defence.."[12]

Order and economic development: policy affecting people's place of residence served an ambitious and totalizing vision for the future of reunified Vietnam. But what form was this vision to take? Or, to ask the question in more pertinent detail, how were these patterns of settlement and migration organized? As for policy aims, so for its forms: northern models in place since the early 1960s were reproduced. State-run farms and forestry enterprises, as well as settler cooperatives, were the vehicles of migration in rural areas, with employment in government service and family reunion the main means of movement to the city. Systems of household registration and collective production were extended to all.

The key vehicle of agricultural migration was built on the ruins of French agriculture. Colonial plantations of coffee and rubber, abandoned to tenants in 1945, came under state control during the war. After 1954, they were formally established as "national agricultural enterprises" (*nong truong quoc doanh*) (Duong Hong Dat 1994: 83). The very pinnacle of socialist agricultural production, these were large-scale mechanized farms employing hundreds of people, in addition to auxiliaries such as the "assault youth" (*thanh nien xung phong*), young people recruited to help out with construction and land clearance. National forestry enterprises followed the same model in the management of forest land. As the following description of a forestry enterprise in Tuyen Quang indicates, these were all-encompassing institutions, not just forms of economic organization:

> Minh Dan is one of eight brigades belonging to the Tan Thanh forest enterprise. These units were not only a method of production management, but also a way to arrange housing and social conditions for employees. Thus, the brigade was a physical place, a center for working and social activities. It had rooms for offices, daycare and kindergarten for children, school and health services. The workers did not pay for the services, including housing. Around the central yard there were long row-houses where the forestry workers lived. (Liljestrom et al. 1998: 45)

Some national enterprises, moreover, were administered by the army, in a model of soldier-settlement that owed as much to traditional Vietnamese borderland policy as it did to the Soviet model. One of the earliest was set up at Dien Bien Phu with demobilized veterans of the 1954 campaign. In 1961, thirty military farms in the highlands employed 14,000 people from the plains (Nhan Dan June 18, 1961: 1). By the late 1980s, the model had been extended to the south and there were forty-three such enterprises throughout the country, all of them "developing the economy and ensuring security and defence at important points on the border."[13]

The following account gives a sense of the imagination that inspired these Soviet-style enterprises and the spirit in which they were meant to be built in the early days. Xuan Vu was a writer who fought for the Viet Minh in the south, before moving north in 1954. He was looking for a subject for his next book:

> At this point in 1954, there was no more war, so martial glory was out. Building socialism was in. The great themes of personal sacrifice and reconstructing the nation could be displayed in peace as well as in war. And maybe best on the kolkhoz, the collective farm.
>
> If Balzac was my guiding star, on this project Mikhail Sholokhov could be my patron saint. Sholokhov had written *the* great epic of rural Soviet life, *Virgin Soil Up-*

turned. Now socialist Vietnam was starting its own historic experiment in collectivisation. How would people respond to the new values, to brotherhood and the common good? The drama of making barren land productive and the simultaneous
drama of personal transformation among the farmers beckoned. Vietnam would
have its own Sholokhov—and who better than me?
    To pursue this vision I got myself sent to one of the new collective farms, around
Vinh, south of Hanoi. (Chanoff and Doan Van Toai 1996: 74. His emphasis).

This may have been the Song Con national agricultural enterprise, whose director had a more bureaucratic view of the venture:

After the August Revolution succeeded, our Government took over [the plantation's]
management. That was wartime, and it was impossible to develop normally, with just
a few former workers, still working on principles of autarkic subsistence. After the signature of the Geneva Agreement in 1954, in early 1955 the State promoted the development of the Agricultural Enterprise with workers freely arriving in greater numbers
every day. In mid 1956, machinery and equipment became available. People who rallied from the South, soldiers who changed their profession, joined the Agricultural Enterprise. From fifty people, the number of people in processing grew to 1,700 by mid
1956; the farm usually had 2,000 to 2,500 people in production as a whole.[14]

It is unlikely that farm workers shared all the enthusiasm of intellectuals and
cadres for this experiment, although hindsight should not let us underestimate
the energy and optimism with which the prospect of building an independent, socialist nation was greeted by many ordinary people. However, even these accounts
concur that the national enterprise did not live up to its promise. Looking back,
Xuan Vu recalled his frank disappointment: "I couldn't for the life of me see that
any noble human motives were transcending all this grimness." The director of
Song Con also regretted that mistakes during land reform caused morale on the
farm to fall in 1957 (and with it the number of workers—by 25 percent). He was
not discouraged, however, noting that by 1960 the workforce numbered 2,000
again and "individualist thinking among the workers was strongly criticized, so
nowadays socialist thinking has a stronger position among them."[15]
    Socialist thinking and a spirit of voluntarism were hallmarks of the other major
vehicle of organized agricultural migration: the settler cooperative. Known as "clearing the wilderness" (*khai hoang*) and "economic and cultural development of the
mountains" (*phat trien kinh te van hoa mien nui*), the resettlement program was
launched in 1960, establishing cooperatives in highland and coastal areas to reclaim
land from the forest and sea. The number of returnees from these settlements and
the way in which the model was redeployed after 1975—joining nationalized enterprises and migrant cooperatives into "new economic zones" (*vung kinh te moi*)—
have since given them a rather poor reputation (Le Khanh 1983: 19; Desbarats
1987). At the time, however, this was a vision of "new economy," an innovative contribution to national development. We cannot simply assume that propaganda
brought "revolutionary meaning"—shorthand for socialist construction and

defensive reinforcement—into people's decision making (Dang Van Sinh 1964: 2). But there is evidence that socialist/patriotic motivations were important. Even now, the phrase *going to make the economy* (*di lam kinh te*), with its resonance of nation building, is current in people's terminology for the program. Some families even by-passed lowland organizational structures, appealing directly to highland authorities for a chance to migrate (Liljestrom et al. 1998: 20). In most cases, however, the decision took the form of a dilemma: either believe the state vision and take a risk in the highlands, or stay home and risk poverty in the crowded delta. One old lady, a 1960s migrant, put it bluntly: *to go was miserable, to stay was miserable.*[16] Many went for the sake of their children.

Persuasion aimed to change people's perception of their world. Long-standing models of migration, built around village and family networks, and lowlanders' desire for farmland were invoked to convince them to uproot. Ancient proverbs such as *dat lanh chim dau* (where the land is lush, birds will alight) and *mot chon doi que* (one destination, two homes) were reworked as slogans to mobilize people to move. The phrase *que moi que cu* (new home, old home) appeared in the press, with its implication that migration did not mean abandonment of the ancestral village. This was a clear attempt to transfer home loyalties from village to nation. It became particularly pronounced after reunification. *Dat nuoc dep giau dau cung que huong* (beautiful land, rich country, everywhere is home) read a 1991 propaganda poster, with its bright images of cheerful folk boarding buses for the highlands and boats to the islands.[17]

Reunification saw the reproduction of this vision of socialist modernization in the south. Throughout the southern provinces, cooperatives and national agricultural/forestry enterprises were set up to build the new society. As Pham Van Dong urged, national enterprises were to "go first, being mirrors and schools for the cooperatives" (Pham Van Dong 1975: 42). Kinh resettlement in the highlands was implemented in tandem with a program of sedentarization (*dinh canh dinh cu*) among the ethnic minorities (Pham Van Dong 1978: 12). Initiated in the north in 1968, sedentarization aimed to stop highlanders' perceived destruction of the forest, to teach them up-to-date farming practices, and to "rationalise settlement patterns" in line with the state's desire to improve the governance and security of the highlands. By 1982, nearly 50,000 minority families (267,580 people) were living in sedentarized settlements (Khong Dien 1995: 171). Land was freed for other uses and ethnic harmony was supposed to result from incorporation in collective agriculture. Pham Van Dong quoted a 1968 party document offering a vision of this new life of patriotic solidarity: "the highland economy will become prosperous, meaning that there will be a denser population, the people will eat their fill, wear warm clothes, enjoy better health, educational opportunities and transport facilities; small towns will appear, making the highlands economically rich, politically firm and defensively strong" (Pham Van Dong 1978: 12).

The numbers involved in the realization of this vision exceeded even the 1960s heyday of socialist construction. Between 1976 and 1990, 6.6 million migrations were anticipated in three Five Year Plans, and statistics recorded 3.92 million people actually moving (Pham Do Nhat Tan 1992: 49). Pham Van Dong reported on the program's early results:

> Over a period of less than two years (from 1976 to September 1977), nearly one million people, nearly half of them laborers going to new economic zones, have already set up several hundred new communes and cleared more than 300,000 hectares of land. In particular, we have mobilised hundreds of thousands of people in the cities and towns of the south, especially Ho Chi Minh City, to move from urban areas back to their native village or to make a living in new economic zones. (Pham Van Dong 1978: 6)

The purpose of this was a new society, organized on ethical lines for the prosperity of all. A fine vision was one thing, however, and its successful implementation was another. The limits to the practicability of the socialist vision of development became clear after reunification. Early signs of strain came in the south.

LIMITS

Long before reunification, some DRV cadres had understood that socialist construction was not working as planned. Resources were underutilized and the goals of rapid urban industrialization and effective rural collectivization could not be achieved, even before the U.S. bombing. Explanations could, however, be found for the wide gap between vision and reality. The most persuasive after 1965 was the war, providing a motive for endurance, as well as aid from socialist countries. Shortfalls were never so severe as to challenge the possibility of the vision's fulfillment. After 1975 the psychological support of war was lost, and overseas aid fell dramatically (Fforde and de Vylder 1996: 4; Kerkvliet 1995c: 407–8). Socialism was implemented in changed material and psychological circumstances. Expectations were high and resources suddenly low.

Socialism was also implemented in the south, by people from the north. The army that entered Saigon in April 1975 was made up of soldiers from throughout the country, and Saigon was, during the first days, administered by cadres of southern origin. They were soon joined by "tens of thousands of cadres, workers, administrators and the majority of the people who had previously rallied from the South to the North, who came, along with their families, to live and work in the South" (Khong Dien 1995: 173). The contact of these people of the north with the southern population, who had for twenty years followed a different road to development, was to have effects unforeseen in Hanoi.

After 30 April 1975, people could move freely throughout Vietnam. One memoir related the "tremendous psychological impact" of free travel between north and south. Travel, of course, was not entirely unrestricted. Transportation and permission had to be obtained and interprovincial checkpoints negotiated. Nonetheless, "for people who during French colonial days had to have a passport to go from one region to another, and who were kept apart by the demilitarized zone during the Vietnam War, it was exhilarating to be able to circulate freely from one end of the country to another. Reunification made the population feel as one again. Families could be reunited, and ties that had been severed were re-established" (Elliott 1999: 414). Nor were the benefits limited to families. Informal commercial ties were established, in an explosion of consumption in the north fueled by a flow of goods from the south: "This spontaneous activity took place without any prior planning from individuals who were primarily cadres, soldiers, family members visiting their relatives, and to some extent, merchants" (Dang Phong 1998: 103).

A new socioeconomic reality emerged in persistent contrast to the socialist vision. The important contrast, moreover, lay not in the gap between vision and reality, which had always existed, but in the difference between market conditions before and after 1975. The coupon system continued to function but now worked alongside a thriving black market (Dang Phong 1998: 106). In the development of this two-tier economy lay the seeds of the Doi Moi reforms. Reunification was a veritable turning point, "because to the military and political victory of the North was superimposed the triumph—ideological and commercial—of the liberal economy of the South" (Papin 1999: 147). This was to constitute a major limit to the vision of socialist construction throughout Vietnam.

In the south, it may not have seemed this way at the time. Socialist construction, aimed at transforming urbanites from consumers into producers, entailed the deurbanization of migrant-swollen cities.[18] A "return home" (*hoi huong*) program got underway during the first few weeks after reunification. Employees of the former regime presented themselves for reeducation. People with political records volunteered for movements like the Vanguard Youth Corps, building roads and clearing land (Elliott 1999: 417). This was followed by socialist economic policies: a new currency, the taxation and reform of capitalism, nationalization of industry, and agricultural collectivization.

As in 1950s Hanoi, the capitalist economy of the south was dismantled quickly—over the months through to 1978 (Amer 1996: 79–82). Not all its consequences were immediately apparent, but the speed of the process and its marginalization of large sections of the population constituted a further limit to the vision of socialist development. This was particularly pronounced in the deurbanization policy. Many people for whom there was no space in the new urban society (700,000 from Saigon by 1977) found themselves on the road to a new economic zone (Condominas and Pottier 1982: 106). Few, however, found life tolerable in these far-flung settlements, many of which were on the Cambodian border and subject to Khmer Rouge incursions. One report noted that ineffective management and poor conditions in new economic zones had led to "a loss of the people's confidence."[19] Marginalization, moreover, did not end there. Rules about household residence, eligibility for employment, and access to coupons applied to all citizens after reunification. Many returnees from new economic zones had to wait before citizen rights were restored. One man related his departure from a zone in Rach Gia:

> Everyone who had been sent to my zone eventually returned, like me, to the city. . . . I walked back to Saigon from the camp, and when I arrived I had nothing to lose any more. I couldn't get a job, because my past history meant I was unemployable. I didn't have a ration card, because I was a nobody, without my citizen rights restored. If I went back to my village, my villagers and relatives would have to be responsible for me to the authorities—and if I escaped, they would have to answer for it. So I went to Saigon, and lived from one house to another, choosing empty places and houses where the communists were unlikely to come and search. I stayed with people who fed me and took care of me. I lived like that for more than two months. (Mr. Tran, in Hawthorne 1982: 176–77)

This man eventually found his way to a boat.[20] There and in camps throughout Southeast Asia, he would have met many new economic zone pioneers, along with others from both northern and southern Vietnam whose numbers reached 331,725 by April 1980 and a cumulative total of 839,228 in countries of first asylum by 1997 (Condominas and Pottier 1982: 90; Robinson 1998: 294).

Who were the boat people? The question provoked more polemic than analysis at the time: "For some, they were runaways, former collaborators with the Americans or individuals unable to get down to work; for others there were simply fugitives seeking to escape the ravages of the communists: clichés which moreover each contain an element of truth" (Condominas and Pottier 1982: 53). Whatever their motivation, however, figures show that the majority of boat people in the late 1970s were ethnic Chinese and most were from the south (90). In addition, a further 250,000 crossed the northern border into China (Alley 1980: 6).[21]

One of these was Lin Pao Hua, interviewed in Guangxi in 1979. He had joined the Vietnamese revolution in 1945 and during the subsequent war went to Hanoi:

> After the defeat of the French in 1954, he organized a trading company to deal in Chinese products, and also set up a worker's cooperative. He helped as well as he could to implement Premier Zhou Enlai's directive that all overseas Chinese should become loyal citizens of the country they lived in, and take its nationality, obey its laws. He even did his best to better relations between China and Viet Nam, but when certain oppressive measures were introduced, he felt it his duty to speak out against them, one in particular being the prohibition against teaching Chinese in overseas Chinese schools. For this he was sent to jail in 1972, and was there three years and nine months. Emerging he found that his assets had been seized, so borrowed money to bribe a small official to grant him a permit to sell congee in the streets, which he did for two years, until 1978. Then with the help of friends he and his wife came to China by train. (Alley 1980: 43–44)

This account is incomplete and, published in Beijing, conveys an official Chinese view of events. Yet it highlights two features of Vietnamese policy that contributed to the exodus of Chinese. The first was their involvement in newly prohibited economic activity—whether it be compradore capitalism or small-time trading. The second was the gradual breakdown in Vietnam's international relations, first articulated in antagonism with China, and by early 1979 in war on two fronts, with China and Cambodia. Assimilationist policies gave way to official encouragement of Chinese departures, as well as practices of covert cooperation and outright coercion.[22]

The crisis culminated in 1979, when 68,748 people arrived in Hong Kong alone. The pressure on the British colony impelled Prime Minister Thatcher to call for an international conference. Held in Geneva on 20–21 July 1979, delegates cannot have been ignorant of the irony of their assembly on the twenty-fifth anniversary of the signature of the Geneva Agreement, which led to Vietnam's first major refugee crisis. Most representatives, however, despite appeals from China to address the "root causes of the exodus," focused on the humanitarian aspects of the crisis. Resettlement commitments were made, and pressure placed on Vietnam to impose a moratorium on departures. At the same time, the first agreements for legal emigration from Vietnam were completed: on 30 May 1979, the U.N. High Commission on Refugees (UNHCR) and Vietnam signed a Memorandum of Understanding, laying the foundation for what later became the Orderly Departure Programme (Robinson 1998: 50–58).

The refugee phenomenon cannot be understood as a simple failure of diplomacy. Nor was it even the expression of two competing Vietnamese nationalisms in migration decisions by some on the defeated side. These were important in the late 1970s, but the refugee flow continued into the 1980s, increasingly involving people from the north. During only two years—1984 and 1985—did the number of Orderly Departures exceed that of boat arrivals (Hitchcox 1990: 75). Interviewed in countries of first asylum, boat people typically declared they were refugees from communism. But, what—apart from the need to establish a profile for resettlement—lay behind such statements in the circumstances of the 1980s?

The beginning of an answer to this question is provided by the Vietnamese Immigration Department, which presented the following analysis to a 1988 conference in Hanoi.

> Of the number of people who left, apart from those who wished to be reunited with their family, some acted out of class reaction and were basically enemies of the revolution, some owed money to the people, and a rather large number were deceived and aroused by the gang of imperialists and reactionaries; the majority left because they could not deal with or adapt to our new society, sympathise with the country's difficult conjuncture, or recognise their responsibilities to society and their fatherland at a time when it faced hardship in many areas, especially economics and society, etc. (Vietnam, Ministry of Interior 1988: 10a)

This analysis went on to note that the prolonged crisis was a legacy of war, the previous regime in the south, and U.S. aggression, before concluding that it was also due to:

our own country's shortcomings in the administration of society and especially of the economy, with its direct influence on the living standards of the people, difficulties which could not be overcome in a short period of time, requiring a long-term and complex process of change. (Vietnam, Ministry of Interior 1988: 10a)

These official observations offer a closer perspective on the boat people. By the 1980s, boarding a boat was no longer a response to specific fears or experiences of exclusion from Vietnam's new society. For many, it constituted an act of resistance to the government's vision for the future, a radical frustration with the "shortcomings" of a system unable to provide for its people's basic needs, a rejection of the "difficulties" the government expected people to endure for a cause in which they no longer believed. Over the decade from 1975, when people had left out of fear, the movement transformed itself into an expression of far broader socioeconomic grievances and desires. People started leaving not in fear but in the hope of finding new opportunities in a more favorable environment. By 1988, this dimension to the exodus was clearly understood in countries of first asylum and resettlement. Frustration with life under communism, expressed in this desperate act, was no longer deemed sufficient for people arriving on boats to qualify for the status of refugee. The 16 June 1988 cutoff date in Hong Kong, after which "economic migrants" were screened out from "genuine refugees," reflected this, as did the 1989 Comprehensive Plan of Action establishing the principle of repatriation for economic migrants (UNHCR 1998: 5).

What gave rise to the discontent that prompted so many people to drastic action? There exists, as yet, no social history of Vietnam in the 1980s, but social analysis is required, dealing with the impact of everyday situations on the decisions of families, or individuals within families, to leave their homes in rejection of Vietnam's socialist vision. An indicator of the difficulties of these years, in urban areas at least, may be gained from examination of pig-breeding practices there. One young woman, growing up in a fifth-floor apartment in the northern town of Hai Duong, recalled to me her daily chore of "bathing the pig." Unable to make an adequate living on salaries alone, the family raised a pig in their living room, feeding it with kitchen scraps. A second example of the same practice, common throughout the towns and cities of the north, offers insight into the social significance of the phenomenon. An official in Hanoi made space in his bathroom for two pigs, raised for sale to private traders. His house was situated near prestigious Phan Dinh Phung street, an area normally inhabited by senior officials and experts. Only better-off families had access to capital for a small pig. Less fortunate people raised chickens.[23] Agricultural production in the urban home became a sign of affluence.

In the countryside, recourse to contracts for activities within the cooperative system provided some income for farmers, additional to the 5 percent private land from which most of them obtained their primary income. However, inroads into the collective system in the mid-1980s did not necessarily bring immediate gains (Fforde and de Vylder 1996: 309). One settler in the Central Highlands explained the difficulties of collective farming in the context of a new environment: *no one knew how to farm this land; there were wet and dry seasons and no one knew how to react to them. But even if they did, it wouldn't have made any difference, because the work program was arranged by the cooperative. So the people would go out to the fields and spend eight hours there, doing a bit of work, but talking and having fun, so work wasn't hard as it is now.* He was clear about the consequences of this: *no one ate till they were full, everyone was hungry.*[24]

Employment scarcity, in a situation of rapid demographic growth, was mentioned often in official accounts of the country's problems. In a country where the state remained the main employer, only 10 percent of the one million annual entrants into the labor force found work in the state sector (Fforde and de Vylder 1996: 11). From 1980, in payment of Vietnam's national debt, a labor export scheme was instituted to socialist bloc countries.[25] More than 250,000 people secured contracts to work in Germany, Bulgaria, Czechoslovakia, and the Soviet Union (Vietnam, Vien Thong tin Khoa hoc Xa hoi 1995: 225). Jobs overseas went by priority to state workers who relinquished their tenured employment and to rural people with relatives who had died in the war.[26] The fall of the Berlin Wall in 1989 and the collapse of the Soviet Union caused the return of many of these laborers.[27] Some, however, opted to remain in the former socialist countries, most of them involved in commerce, enjoying a higher standard of living and remitting money and goods to their relatives at home (Dang Phong 1997: 10–11).

In many cases, however, even economic hardship fails to explain the decision to leave. Family situations, petty conflicts, frustrated hopes, boredom, and minor difficulties with the authorities were also of great importance. The following are extracted from UNHCR monitors' reports after interviews with repatriated boat people in 1989–1990.

[She] said the reason for her departure was to see Hong Kong taking the advice of an astrologer of a great opportunity.

[She] left for Hong Kong in August 1988 after a quarrel with her husband.

The family had been relatively well off in a comfortable house because of the head of the family's secure employment [as a welder] prior to the departure. . . .

His wife died a long time ago and his cousin stated that he left for Hong Kong because he had nothing particular to do and thought his notions on how to pilot a boat could be useful.

They all claimed that the reason for going to HKG [Hong Kong] was poor living conditions and with the hope to seek a better life somewhere else, and they also thought it should be easier for them in HKG due to the fact that they were ethnic Chinese.

We learned that he had deserted the army before his departure from HKG.

The wife said Mr Thanh had left Vietnam because they had family problems, with his second wife. (UNHCR 1998: 16–23)

Some people even became refugees by accident, like one Khanh who walked to Laos to visit relatives there. "In Vientiane, he got curious about what it might look like on the other side of the Mekong River. Over on the Thai side of the river he was arrested by local police and brought to Phanat Nikhom from where he asked to be repatriated" (UNHCR 1998: 27). Perhaps the most telling case was that of Tung, again extracted from the monitor's report, after a visit was made to his family:

"Tung is the only wayward child in the family; the rest are model citizens in government posts," Dad reported. Upon return in 1996, Tung was charged with having embezzled the equivalent of US$3,000 from the State Bank Branch where he worked until 1989. Mom had rejected the union of Tung and his girlfriend, and thus the money was to buy freedom for the lovers in Hong Kong. Mom and Dad and sibling cadres visit Tung when the prison allows, on the 1st and 15th of the lunar calendar (Buddhist Holidays). With irony, it is Mom who is distraught over Tung's singleton status. (UNHCR 1998: 7)

Like the others, Tung's account was recorded in Vietnam, where people were careful about what they said to foreign officials. Still, it offers real reasons for departure to compare with the ritualized complaints about communist rule made in refugee camps. Above all, it does not contradict them. A black sheep in the family, a young man frustrated in love, a crime committed: the only explanation we have here is that of opportunity. With U.S. $3,000 in hand, Tung left because he could. The key question, however, remains: why did he choose to go abroad?

There was, in the 1980s, a major failure of vision among the people. Describing socialist construction in the Soviet Union of the 1930s, Fitzpatrick has underlined the importance of utopian ideology. She shows how powerfully the idea of a socialist paradise on earth helped people accept supposedly short-term hardships (Fitzpatrick 1999: 66–71). Before 1975, the vision of peace represented a sort of paradise for Vietnamese. However, the war ended and, as early days of optimism faded into years of even greater hardship, many became profoundly disillusioned. Disillusionment often focused on the government and was described in official parlance in terms of a "loss of the people's confidence."

Visions of paradise, however, did not die. Indeed, emigration created new images of utopia, based on the relations established between migrants and nonmigrants. This phenomenon spread quickly from south to north and has been explained as follows:

The most widespread and common form of relation was that between families who stayed and members who left. Of course, the majority of those who stayed had no particular fondness for the communist system. As for those who left, the very fact of their departure demonstrates that they could not put up with the system existing at that time in Vietnam. So the relations between those who stayed and those who left were reinforced by their feelings of resentment towards the new system. This resentment in turn increased the tendency to respect foreign things, in particular the tendency to long for American civilization.

These relations, therefore, stimulated the development in the South after 1975 of an attitude of longing for foreign civilization, of reverence for the West. A notion of the West took shape and increasingly grew out of all proportion. The West took on the meaning of a promised land. For those people who wanted to leave, that was where they wanted to go. For those who could not leave, or for one reason or another did not wish to, the West was a promised land in terms of goods and lifestyle. It seemed almost like a paradise. (Dang Phong 1999: 12)

These relations between emigrants and those who stayed took the form of letters, goods, and money remittances. The remittances, moreover, were estimated by 1980 at 150 million dollars annually (equivalent to Vietnam's export earnings to nonsocialist countries) and may have been as high as 300–400 million (Condominas and Pottier 1982: 64; Dang Phong 1999: 26). Carefully posed color photographs offered rosy-hued portraits of the civilization across the sea. It should not be imagined, moreover, that this desire was focused exclusively on western countries. One former worker in the Soviet Union explained his decision to accept the offer of a job there by saying *you know in those days, we all thought that Russia was a country of greatness.* Russian greatness, moreover, was mediated in the same way. Returning workers brought with them goods, money, and stories with which they regaled their friends and neighbors.[28] These exerted a powerful influence over many imaginations: it was possible, in the early 1990s, to meet people for whom everything abroad must, by definition, be valuable. Vietnamese people have been described as "lacking a tradition of overseas migration" (Indra 1987: 1). During the 1970s and 1980s, they invented one.

Desperation and desire combined in decisions to leave. One young woman, who spent five years in Hong Kong, related her father's unemployment, her mother's lucrative (private) butcher's shop in Hanoi, the confiscation of their house, and then the day she and her dad went "on holiday" to the beach resort of Do Son. I wrote down what she said:

Her father had long [since 1980 she said] had the desire to leave. He'd read books [what books? she wasn't sure] and received letters. He definitely knew a lot about those countries.[29]

They left in August 1988, two months after screening was introduced in Hong Kong. As we have seen, screening was a response to increased boat arrivals in early 1988. Indeed, statistics showing a rapid upward curve in the late 1980s require some explanation.[30] One scholar in Hanoi saw this as the psychological effect of Gorbachev's reforms in the USSR, formally ratified in Vietnam at the Sixth Party Congress in December 1986. People were exhausted with the hardships of a system that had not worked for decades, and with the effort of believing in it. The admission of the vision's failure was a final straw: while intellectuals wrote politically risqué novels, ordinary people headed for the boats.[31]

Doi Moi, moreover, facilitated the practicalities of departure. In the words of a UNHCR official:

Before, if you lived in Hanoi and had a brother in Haiphong and wanted to visit him, you had to go to your boss and get permission. Based on his judgment you brought it to the political commissar of your work unit then to the local police and then maybe it was permitted for a certain period of time specified in the permit. When you reached Haiphong you had to go with your brother and announce your arrival to the local police and leave your ID card to be retrieved on your departure. Then you had to report back to the Hanoi police for your work unit. If you had carried two eggs in your pocket from Hanoi to Haiphong or back that would have been illegal trade. In 1987, road barriers to Haiphong were lifted. Suddenly, you didn't need to work for the state anymore. In fact, the state wanted to lay off 25 per cent of its workers. Cooperatives were going bankrupt. A lot of things happened very quickly. People were very insecure and unsure about what to do. The rumours about screening in Hong Kong were very unspecific. People could actually go to the coast and they could leave. Before, they had protected the coastline; they were shooting people. (Robinson 1998: 199)

Ironically, in both psychological and practical terms, the onset of reform brought the overseas utopia closer. It was only later, as relations with the rest of the world took on the grayer hues of reality, that new opportunities were perceived closer to home.

The boat people phenomenon was both the symptom and result of social, political, and economic changes taking place since 1975. As Tuong Lai put it:

This "exodus" has left a deep scar in the pain of the nation, among both those who left and those who remained, which history cannot efface, a scar of those years before and after 1975. Only in understanding those journeys away can we see the price which had to be paid for the struggle for independence and reunification of the country. (Tuong Lai 1998: 10–11)

Those journeys constituted another limit to the state's vision of socialist construction. Understanding them is to seize both the reality and a powerful image of resistance: people voted with their feet, or they saw others do so, or they received letters and remittances, and wondered whether to leave themselves. As Evans and Rowley point out, the boat people probably did more damage to Vietnam's image abroad than the invasion of Cambodia (Evans and Rowley 1990: 54). Compassion fatigue among countries of first asylum and resettlement, and the repatriation program implemented since 1989, undoubtedly played a part in reducing the flow. It was only with the end of socialist construction, however, and the real gains achieved under Doi Moi—experienced in people's everyday lives—that the boat people phenomenon was halted. By the late 1990s, some of those who returned to Vietnam expressed their relief at having done so.[32]

DOI MOI

The vision of socialist construction did not end suddenly. At the Sixth Party Congress, after a stinging indictment of the errors of the past, Truong Chinh emphasized the need for its "renovation" (Doi Moi) (Truong Chinh, quoted in Vo Nhan Tri 1990: 182). Despite shortfalls in many areas, some of the goals set out in 1976—in migration policy at least—had been achieved. Highland regions had been settled by Kinh people from the plains. The growth of large cities had been contained. Some policies—such as the diffusion of urbanization among smaller cities and towns— had enjoyed considerable success (Papin 1999: 53–57).[33] But the vision itself— ethical prosperity along socialist lines—did not materialize, and the limits mentioned above underlined the fact and undermined the vision.

Prior to Doi Moi, a system of employment, residence control, and restriction of non-state economic activity had the effect of channeling population movement. As we have seen, this system had never been watertight. After reunification it became progressively less so. How was it challenged in the 1980s? And how exactly did it change?

At the heart of the Doi Moi transition lay the process of land decollectivization and it was this, above all, that undermined the state's control over population mobility. Decollectivization proceeded from its seeds in the clandestine or "sneaky" contracts of the 1960s and 1970s, through the legalization of contract relations between cooperatives and families (Directive 100 1981), to the important Directive 10 of 1988. This law "destroyed the rural basis of the command economy" by granting extensive freedom of economic activity to cooperatives. Benedict J. Tria Kerkvliet observes that discontent in the mid-1980s manifested itself in "reports of people refusing to pay quotas, peasants quitting their fields in disgust, and villagers continuing 'sneaky contracts' that went beyond the new system." These forms of resistance and the opening up of new spaces for activity led to the wholesale carve-up of use rights to land, which were distributed to cooperative members at different times in different places (Fforde and de Vylder 1996: 157; Kerkvliet 1995c: 410–12).

As rural families' discontent with the failing cooperative system grew, so did migration. Use rights to land, distributed for a period of twenty years, could now be bought, sold, and mortgaged. The owners became free to dispose of the land's product—over and above their duty to pay taxes—as they wished. They could, above all, sell it in the free market (Kerkvliet 1995c: 412). In short, by the 1990s farmers were legally entitled to sell up and leave, temporarily or for good. Indeed, the structure of Vietnam's economy, offering low returns from the production of rice, promoted this option. As one analyst put it: "Strong fiscal pressure and weak profits came together to favorise rural migration and the informal economy. Three forms of behaviour emerged. Either peasants moved towards production which paid, and fed the urban markets by transporting goods on shoulder poles, or they left the countryside and went to join the cohorts of day-laborers working in the cities . . . , or they turned directly to the informal economy" (Papin 1999: 157).

Decollectivization depended for its success on the existence of other employment opportunities. The emergence of an informal sector was indeed a major agent of change. The effectiveness of the socialist model after 1975 became increasingly constrained by the existence of two economies: one organized by the state, with a fixed price system, and another operating according to laws of supply and demand (Le Bach Duong 1998a: 30). Built on the foundations of the consumption explosion of the first months after reunification, and fed by overseas Vietnamese remittances, autonomous trading was an important influence on the process of transition (Dang Phong 1999: 26).[34] The employment opportunities it created, termed "interstitial liberties," contributed to many livelihoods (Papin 1999: 134). Increased participation expanded the interstitial space for maneuver. And while interstitial liberties could be practiced at home—in villages and roadside markets—demographic pressure on scarce resources meant that opportunities were more often available elsewhere. Two destinations emerged: the Central Highlands and the cities (especially Ho Chi Minh City and Hanoi).

The regional reach of this mobility became clear to me in conversations with those men in green fatigues, the *xe om* drivers who stand at Hanoi's street junctions. Tien was waiting by the post office when I met him in 1998. I wrote down his experiences:

> He's from Xuan Truong district in Nam Dinh and came to Hanoi thirteen years ago. He has left his wife at home to tend the paddy fields while he goes off, and doesn't want to move his household residence to Hanoi, where land is too expensive. In the early 1980s, he went to "make the economy" (*lam kinh te*) in Dong Nai. He didn't want to go, but the economic situation forced him to go. He grew vegetables there.
>
> He returns home once a month from Hanoi (a three-and-a-half-hour ride) but from Dong Nai could only come back once a year. I asked if he went on a government program. He said, "I had relatives who told me about the place." . . .
>
> In the past he also went to saw timber in the Nghe An forests. I said he was a jack-of-all-trades. That, he said, is the destiny of the poor. Then he added that if he didn't look for waged work, his family wouldn't have enough to eat. Those who don't go are the really poor.[35]

In late 1990s Vietnam, where country roads are full of buses and motorbikes, it is hard to imagine the difficulty of travel in the past without state documentation and funding. Removal of restrictions on private business, legislated at the Sixth Party Congress in 1986, and the flourishing growth of transport companies have facilitated the act of migration (Li Tana 1996: 4). By the 1990s, it was possible to buy tickets in the Central Highlands for bus travel not only to nearby towns, and hubs like Hanoi and Ho Chi Minh City, but also directly to distant destinations in the north, such as Thai Binh, Hai Duong, and Cao Bang.

Tien did not tell me how he dealt with the problem of travel—whether he went by bus, train, or on foot, whether he carried the authorization papers necessary to buy tickets and negotiate administrative hurdles. But he was not the only free migrant to Dong Nai, even in the early 1980s. While some were leaving state settlements in the Central Highlands, others were heading there, relying on their own networks of information and resource (Dang Nguyen Anh 1998: 18, 20). These fortune seekers moved freely, outside the migration program. Once arrived they found it convenient to seek the advantages offered in terms of infrastructure, administration, and relationships by integration into existing settlements. Initially reluctant, local authorities were obliged to welcome them.

By the mid-1990s, spontaneous migration had integrated the Central Highlands to the economy of the whole country. Officials in Lak district (Dak Lak) informed me that in-migrants came from every province in the country with the exception of Ho Chi Minh City.[36] The development of a commodity market, particularly around the production of coffee for export, attracted migrants to new economic zone sites but also to clear areas of forest without any reference to local authorities (Tan 2000). By 1993, the Central Highlands became home to an almost certainly underestimated 419,000 such migrants (Tran An Phong 1996: 56). This transformation altered perceptions of highland settlement back on the plains. When I visited a village in the Red River delta province of Thai Binh in 1997, I met an older man who had seen the new economic zone pioneers boarding the buses twenty years before. Seeing them head off toward the hills, he breathed a sigh of relief: he was not among them. But in recent years, he said, he had heard that they were doing rather well. Initially sceptical—*I didn't believe a word of it*—curiosity got the better of him, and he made the long trip down to visit his family in Dak Lak. *Amazing!* he exclaimed. *The coffee; it's so profitable! They are incredible; they're all rich!* He was palpably jealous. His younger neighbors were preparing for their own departure.[37]

By the mid-1990s, this movement had replaced planned migration as the major redistributive vehicle of Vietnam's population. It remained true that spontaneous settlers in the Central Highlands contributed to the state's geopolitical project there: the securing of a long-disputed territory by means of agricultural expansion (De Koninck 1996: 231–32). The new dynamic nevertheless caused considerable administrative anxiety. Part of this was due to the large number of ethnic minorities from the north involved in the movement (300,000 according to Tran An Phong 1996: 56).[38] Migrants' ability to bypass state structures, and consequent loss of administrative control, occasioned further worry. The focus turned to negative impacts associated with migrants: social order (shorthand for "social evils" like gambling, drug addiction, and theft, as well as conflicts over land with indigenous inhabitants), difficulties of administration, the incidence of malaria, and the loss of forest and biodiversity (Nguyen Hong Minh 1993: 27; Jamieson et al. 1998: 15; De Koninck 1999: 81).

Deforestation has undoubtedly been a major cost of internal migration. A. Terry Rambo emphasizes the shift in demographic balance, particularly in the northern highlands where the number of Kinh people increased from 640,000 to almost 2.6 million over the thirty years to 1989, tripling the population density (Rambo 1997: 16–18). Nowadays, only 8–10 percent of the land is wooded in many parts of this region, where the forest was described as recently as 1973 as "green gold," "an inexhaustible resource" (Phan Huu Dat 1973: 336, cited in Rambo 1997: 20–21). Much of this resource was exhausted by pressure of population, as well as by inappropriate exploitation practices. Among the most damaging was a tendency to fulfill land clearance targets without planting the land, which was quickly degraded. In 1974 the Central Committee for Agriculture felt it necessary to remind cadres that to fight erosion, land clearance should aim at "increasing the land under cultivation, meaning that once cleared it should in fact be farmed."[39]

The shortcomings of the command economy were not the only agents of deforestation. In the Central Highlands, the arrival of spontaneous migrants and the displacement of ethnic minorities had a major impact on the forest cover, although there remained in the late 1990s large tracts of as yet uncleared woodland. Commercial logging, run by state-sponsored enterprises or by illegal entrepreneurs, was also a significant factor (De Koninck 1999: 48–49, 81, 85). Timber traders made use of lowland labor, and many *xe om* drivers shared Tien's lumbering experiences. I asked Dung, as he drove me through Hanoi's streets, whether people like him normally just come to the city: *No, they move around a lot,* he replied, as I noted down after the ride:

> He said Nghe An was the main destination, where *people saw wood.* We were traveling along the dyke road. He pointed out a small bulldozer, a yellow vehicle with large round wheels. *They go and cut down great trees, with trunks as big as that wheel there. Yes and they go up to the mountains in Tuyen Quang.* Asking then, I said, *but Laos is too far, I suppose?—No, people do go to Laos, to the place where Kho Mu people live.*[40]

This practice was far from new. Most of these men were from Nam Dinh, a province described in 1937 as follows: "The men of this region have the profession of lumberman or wood trader. They sojourn in the unhealthy regions of upper Tonkin."[41] In Lao Cai, a quarter-century later, an official reporting on spontaneous migrants there—some of whom were timber workers—noted that many already knew the place: "Most migrants have relatives or friends already living here, the husband will come up first and once he knows the area will go home to bring his wife and children up."[42] Dung himself gave me an insight into this regional tradition, when I asked how people know where to go. He said his father knew. *So, I asked, you and your father went off and did that work together? —That's right, people don't go on their own. They go in small groups, with friends. A bit like,* he added, *if I say to you, let's go and then the two of us go off and do that.*[43]

Dung and his colleagues were all men seeking to supplement the family income with work away from home. The timber trade was only one of their activities. Dung said people also did sandalwood collection, gold digging, fishing, and cross-border trading. One man even went off to Vung Tau to saw wood, before meeting up with a group of people there and jumping on a boat to Australia. Then from the late 1980s, as urban economies developed under Doi Moi, they found it advantageous to seek work in the city. In all these cases, their families remained home and the husband returned regularly, in particular to help bring in the harvest. The men departed, in effect, as sojourners, long-term temporary migrants living off their labor and remitting their income.[44]

There's not enough work, so off they go. They all go to Hanoi. But when harvest time comes, they return. This is especially since market relations developed. This was the opinion of a Peoples' Committee official in Quang Xuong district (Thanh Hoa) when asked about migration in the area. *The women do the fields, and go off trading in nearby markets. Their men don't go for the whole year. At harvest time, they return. The women can't do the carrying. It's heavy. So the men return. But for the rest of the year, they work in Hanoi, doing construction and carpentry, or general labor, doing whatever work they can find.*[45] Seasonal migration is an old phenomenon in northern Vietnam (Nguyen Thi Thanh Binh 1998: 29; Gourou 1936: 222–23). And Doi Moi created new forms for it, as I discovered when I made my way from Quang Xuong to the commune of Quang Loi.

One of the villagers there told me she has four *sao* of rice land, hardly enough to feed her family of eight. Binh had grown used to her husband's absence. First he went off as a soldier (1969–1976), before his appointment as a village official. Then, after resigning this post, he left for Hanoi, where in 1990 he met an old army friend working for the Hanoi Seed Company. This man found him casual work there, which became a formal contract in 1992. Binh said he now returns three times a year, bringing money that helps tide her over the five hungry months between harvests and pays for four of the children's school fees. When I asked how the family reached the decision for him to leave, she said he discussed it with her and she was *unanimous that he should go,* leaving him free to decide how long to be away, according to the state of his health.[46]

This man did well to find a contract offering him secure employment. Other successes include those men driving *xe om,* many of whom bought their bike after years pedaling a *xyclo.* Less stable work may be had by men who stand at labor markets (*cho nguoi* or *cho lao dong*), gatherings of day laborers on streets like Giang Vo, Nga Tu So, Dai Co Viet, and Cau Giay. One Quang Loi resident told me of his time at the labor market on Hanoi's Truong Chinh street. *Exhausting work,* he called it, and has since retired with poor health. He lives off a small rice field—enough for the family for three to four months a year—and borrows for the rest. But his neighbor, a trader constantly worrying over customers' unpaid debts, expressed envy for the men in Hanoi: *if they have work, they work; if they don't, they rest; they have no need to worry. It's hard work, but they're free.*[47]

Theirs is, of course, a highly conditional freedom. A recent study noted that one impetus behind the renewed movement of seasonal migration was a return, under Doi Moi, to the household organization of agriculture. Migration thus becomes part of a household economic strategy: "it is not the individual but the family household which decides who will migrate" (Nguyen Van Chinh 1997: 34). Intricate social networks ensure that contact is maintained with home: "the household economic structure, the gendered distribution of work within the family household and community relations within the village and lineage are the forces drawing and keeping people back in the countryside" (37). DiGregorio showed how this worked for people involved in Hanoi's waste recycling, where the combination of circular migration and agricultural production—held together by relations of village, kinship, and informal association—freed families from complete reliance on market relations (DiGregorio 1994: 128–29).

Similar strategies are used by young women seeking employment as maids (called *o xin* in popular parlance, after a Japanese TV show aired in 1996), or—after very different, individual decision-making processes—in karaoke and massage parlors, or brothels (these women are commonly known as *ca ve*, in a humorous corruption of the French word *cavalière*). Many of them remit money to their families, and some hope, after a few years in the city, to go home with enough money to set up as traders. A number, however, aim to escape their mothers' lives in the paddy fields by settling away from home.[48]

The decisions of this last group provide insight into social relations in the family and village. An interview in Hanoi, with a forty-year-old itinerant trader, offered the beginnings of a gendered perspective on migration practice. She is the family's main breadwinner, with her baskets of vegetables shoulder-carried around the city, and was twenty kilometers from home when I spoke to her. Avoiding comment on the practices of prostitutes in the city, she described in great detail some of the difficulties faced by women in the village. While men mainly went off for economic reasons, young women's experiences often took a different turn, reflecting the society they live in. As she put it: *the countryside, it's terrible* (*nha que, no kinh lam*). One woman couldn't stand her husband, so left. An unmarried girl got pregnant, the man wouldn't marry her, so she had to go. Two lovers failed to get their parents' blessing, so eloped. One woman became pregnant in her husband's absence, he got angry on his return, so both left in separate directions. Between embarrassed refrains—"*am I talking too much?*"—two phrases recurred in her account. One was *she left at night*; the other, *she escaped to the south*.[49]

There were, by contrast, few "escapes to the north." This constitutes a major north-south difference in migration pattern. Most migrants to Hanoi were born in the north.[50] But in Ho Chi Minh City only a quarter of migrants were from the Mekong delta; 15 percent were from the Red River delta, with a further 30 percent from other parts of the north and center (Ho Chi Minh City, Institute for Economic Research 1996: 60; Ho Chi Minh City, Institute for Economic Research 1997: 33). Ho Chi Minh City pulled people over far greater distances.

There may be historical reasons for this. Khong Dien suggests that north-south is Vietnam's "traditional" direction of migration (Khong Dien 1995: 173). But how do we understand tradition here? Regional differences in social organization play a role. Migrants in Hanoi live and work in clusters by district/village of origin, excluding outsiders, while in Ho Chi Minh City they are scattered, concerned to live near their place of work (Ho Chi Minh City, Institute for Economic Research 1997: 49). Networking is also important. Low levels of northward migration, both historical (e.g., 1954) and state-sponsored (post-1975), mean that few southerners can find a "base" in Hanoi. Data for Ho Chi Minh City show how crucial contacts are: 84 percent of respondents in one survey said they knew someone when they arrived (Ho Chi Minh City, Institute for Economic Research 1997: 41).

Full explanation, however, must take account of the economic opportunities available in Ho Chi Minh City. This is particularly the case for women, for whom jobs are plentiful in light industry, such as garment production, and services.

These are reflected in the statistics. While only 30 percent of migrants to Hanoi are female, more women than men are registered as temporary residents of Ho Chi Minh City (Li Tana 1996: 26–28; Ho Chi Minh City, Institute for Economic Research 1996: 58–59). Employers favor workers from the provinces, who are cheaper, work hard, and remain with the factory longer than city people (Bond 1999: 37). In short, there is simply more space—socially and economically—in Ho Chi Minh City than in urban centers in the north.

The phenomenon of "escape to the south" should make us pause before affirming people's undifferentiated attachment to their village. Many migrants were villagers who stepped out of the social norms on which community acceptance was based. But others became economically excluded, as I discovered in Quang Loi. According to village authorities, people who most commonly escaped to the south were those in debt. The grocer there was owed 170,000 dong by a couple who ran off in January 1999. Another family lost livestock to an epidemic, so they went too. *They leave for a short time, intending to return, but in the end they don't come back.* The grocer had no statistics of this sort of move, but emphasized that cases were *numerous.* People go to the south, to find relatives who moved in 1954 or after 1975. Or they might, quite simply, see the south as a new place where no one knows them. They could start again.

It is possible, in Vietnam today, to use a migration to start again. Attitudes of resistance against the constraints posed by both state and society could be turned into acts. In talking to the authorities at Quang Loi, however, I understood some of the difficulties of such ventures. We had arrived at the People's Committee at a time set aside for people to do their paperwork with officials. Many were there with requests for birth certificates. During our discussion afterward, one of the officials related the case of a woman, a divorcée who had gone to the south and started a new relationship there. When her child needed to go to school, she returned to the village to declare the birth. Officials told me they could only issue a certificate for a child born out of wedlock. She had no new marriage certificate, and as a result, her new relationship was not recognized by the law.[51]

This case is significant, as it highlights both the changes wrought by Doi Moi and the limits to those changes. A problem with an undeclared relationship may be regarded as normal. What had changed by the 1990s was the fact that she had no problem with her household registration. She probably saw this as irrelevant to her needs in her new home. Certainly household registration procedures no longer affected every aspect of people's lives as they used to, including where they bought their groceries and how much they paid. And this is reflected in the statistics. Of 202,100 in-migrants to Ho Chi Minh City in 1990–1994, only 26.6 percent had obtained a permanent residence permit (compared to 44 percent of the 178,000 arriving in 1986–1990 and 64 percent of 125,800 in-migrants in the early 1980s).[52]

Doi Moi brought about changes, but those changes had their limits. On the one hand, free movement has been enshrined in Vietnam's constitution since 1992:

"Citizens have the right to free circulation and residence throughout the country, as well as the right to leave the country and return from abroad, according to the regulations of the law" (Vietnam, Vien Thong tin Khoa hoc Xa hoi 1995: 209). But on the other hand, old administrative structures, created to restrict movement, still regulate the law. The result is a hybrid system operating in internal contradiction. A key interface is the issue of permits for temporary residence (*tam tru*). By 1994, the majority of migrants to Ho Chi Minh City recorded by the city's statistical office held such a permit. Of those who moved after 1989, 62 percent were accepted as "temporary long-term residents" by 1994 (based on an extendable three- or six-month stay) (Ho Chi Minh City, Institute for Economic Research 1996: 52–53). Interviews carried out in 1999 with the police in Hanoi show that the authorities are keen to get people signed up, according to a 1997 law facilitating the issue of both household residence and temporary resident permits to migrant applicants.[53]

Labor policy also demonstrates the hybrid—or transitional—nature of migration law. The Hanoi police emphasized that applicants for temporary residence did not need to show stable employment—a reasonable regulation given the temporary nature of most migrants' work. The Hanoi Labor Department, however, insisted they carry identification for the time of their stay in the city. Under a system established in 1995, the department issued them with a "labor card," indicating the bearer's name, age, place of origin, ID card number, temporary resident permit details, and the time period permitted to work in the city. When I met them in 1999, however, officials at the department complained that they could not issue the card, for which there was a fee of 10,000 dong. From 1996, they could not collect the fee, as it is contrary to national labor law, which states that *laborers have the right to seek work freely.*[54]

The rationale for these methods of control is easily comprehensible. Worries about the city's infrastructure were consistently raised by officials in Hanoi, particularly in the context of a crisis in the disposal of the city's rubbish (Nong Thon Ngay Nay, To Phong vien Chinh tri Xa hoi 1999: 3; Xuan Binh 1999: 4). Security officials also pointed to a deterioration in social order, particularly as migrants gather in specific areas based on their place of origin—*xe om* in the Hoan Kiem area are mainly from Xuan Truong district (Nam Dinh), while laborers on Truong Chinh street are usually from Thanh Hoa. This leads to situations of competition over work in different urban spaces, which one official euphemistically described as *bullying*, and of the influence of professional gangsters. The importance of regulations for ordinary police work was also emphasized: *all we want is to know who people are*, so as to *control people* and *enforce the law for the nation's citizens.*[55] A ward-level official in Hai Ba Trung district (Hanoi) summarized the effects of migration:

> From the time laborers from other provinces started coming to this area, the political and security situation, as well as social order and safety, has undergone complex problems. Their living conditions are unhygienic, disputes over work involving fights

and arguments have taken place, furniture is left on the pavements and streets. In addition, there has been gambling, thefts and swindling.[56]

These practical issues of urban management were not the whole story. Behind them lay a bureaucratic psychology formed by administrative structures created by the socialist vision. The reason for this, as one official noted, lay less with government departments who struggle with the everyday problems of running the city, many of whom were clearly working in the interstices of a legal system in transition. He complained instead of a lack of legislation on which everyday administrative decisions could be based. One Labor Department official accepted the importance of migration to Hanoi's development but expressed frustration at this lack of regulatory guidelines:

Nowadays, we do not yet have a policy for the administration of people registering to live in cities, but only the household registration management policy, which is the government's Decision 51-CP of 10 May 1996. But in reality in the market system, management of the process of free migration to the city cannot escape influences from many directions, and lies in the realm of general urban administrative policy, including: the administration of housing for in-migrants, the administration of housing construction in accordance with regulations, the prevention of squatting, the administration of temporary residence permits, the administration of recruitment of labor by businesses in every economic sector.[57]

This official went on to describe the temporary regulations issued by the department as well as requests to the government for further regulations, "while waiting for the Government to promulgate a Decision concerning the administration of free migrant labor." As one commentator noted in 1995, writing of migration to the highlands, "In fact, up to now, there is still no clear and consistent policy on this migration flow. . . . Should it be encouraged or prevented?" (Vietnam, Vien Thong tin Khoa hoc Xa hoi 1995: 222).

NEW VISION, NEW DECISIONS?

The Vietnamese government after 1954 sought, by exerting close control over population mobility, to promote migration to rural and highland areas, and to restrict urbanization. This policy, as we have seen, was extended to the whole country after 1975, but socioeconomic processes associated with reunification caused the government's control to falter. Free migration in the 1980s was at the same time a cause and effect of the loss of control. The government had to accept this and called the new situation Doi Moi, confirming preexisting trends toward freer internal and international migration.

The socialist vision was swept away by these changes, although some of its rhetoric remained. A further feature of socialism also remained: the administrative system. One symptom of this system's persistence into the late 1990s has been the low level of rural-urban migration, by Southeast Asian standards. By the end of the decade, statistically recorded migrants made up less than 10 percent of Hanoi's population—230,000 people out of a total of 2.6 million (March 1999). In Ho Chi Minh City, they were (under)estimated at 14 percent of the population—700,000 people (1997), out of 4.9 million (1996).[58] In comparison with the situation before 1975, the lack of a floating population and squatter settlements in Ho Chi Minh City is striking. By contrast, large areas of the Central Highlands are in the process of becoming expanses of squatter villages, cut straight from the forest.

These migration patterns reflect a legacy of pre–Doi Moi administrative practices, which have not yet completed a process of transition. The existence of reformed versions of policies suited to the original socialist vision is evidence of the relevance of Pham Van Dong's comment that "we are going along a road without a map." There remains no readily discernable destination or new vision, articulated in terms of new regulatory arrangements. The government is, in effect, using outdated, microlevel administrative tools in the running of a system now requiring macrolevel management.

As the transition remained incomplete, policy on migration, as well as on many other areas of activity, remained at the level of dilemma. In the early years of Doi Moi, the government's margin of maneuver as it sought its way forward was primarily defined inside of Vietnam (despite the U.S. offer of a "road map" to normalization). But in the late 1990s, in the context of the country's entry into the Association of Southeast Asian Nations (ASEAN) and negotiations with global organizations such as the World Trade Organization, the dilemma of governance has been made more acute. What started as Doi Moi, defined by the decisions, actions, and resistance of ordinary Vietnamese people, is taking on a global dimension. Unfocused dilemma is being recast as a choice. Vietnam could choose increased engagement with global capitalism and acceptance of restrictions on administrative reach, or that reach could be maintained, at an unknown social and economic cost.

NOTES

The research for this chapter was made possible thanks to support from the Australian National University and the National University of Singapore.

1. Interview, Hanoi, July 2001.

2. Interview, Thai Binh, January 1997. Quotations from informants are presented in italics, to convey the overlap implicit between their voices and the author's, which impinges by means of language, fieldnotes, and translation.

For administrative purposes, Vietnam is divided into provinces, districts, and communes. Here, the names of smaller administrative areas are specified with the mention *district* and *commune* respectively, while the names of provinces are left without the repeated mention of *province*.

3. For details of the link between *ho khau* and access to benefits, see Kleinen 1999: 117–18.

4. General Land Clearance Office (Tong cuc Khai hoang), "Bao cao tong ket cuoc van dong dong bao mien xuoi tham gia phat trien kinh te mien nui trong ke hoach 5 nam lan thu nhat va phuong huong nhiem vu nhung nam toi" [Summary report on mobilization of lowland compatriots to participate in highland economic development in the first 5-year plan and tasks for the coming years], Hanoi, July 1966.

5. National Archives of Vietnam Centre No. 3 (hereafter NAV3), Ministry of Labor (hereafter BLD), 961(vv), Minister of Labor to Central Committee for Overseas Vietnamese, 12 April 1960.

6. A separate figure for the land to be cultivated is given in a 1966 report: between 1961 and 1966, a reported 250,000 hectares of forest land were reclaimed for cultivation, plus 100,000 hectares of other land, "fulfilling the five year plan." Of the 250,000 hectares, however, only 20 percent were in production in 1966. General Land Clearance Office, "Bao cao tong ket."

7. Interview, Thai Binh, June 1996.

8. BLD, "Bao cao so ket cong tac dieu dong lao dong dan cu xay dung kinh te moi 1981–1988" [Report on the distribution of labor and population to build the new economy 1981–1988], undated (c1989).

9. These included the Territory of Hai Ninh (Territoire de Hai Ninh, autonomous in 1947) and the Thai Federation (Fédération Thai, established in 1948) which were included, with Central Highlands' provinces, among the Crown Domains (Domaines de la Couronne) in April 1950. Service Historique de l'Armée de Terre (Vincennes) 10H 1040, "Statut Provisiore du Pays Thai," 28 February 1948; "La question Nung," 1954; "Ordonnance No 6 du 15 Avril 1950" signed by Bao Dai.

10. The acronym stands for the French name: Front Uni pour la Libération [or Lutte] des Races Opprimées. For a fuller account of the movement after 1975, see Ngo Van Ly and Nguyen Van Dieu 1992: 205–9. This describes FULRO's links with "reactionaries disguised as religious elements" and "Polpot and Ieng Sary's gang," as well as periodization of the conflict (1975–1977 postliberation period, 1978–1979 link with Cambodia period, 1980–1992 guerrilla warfare period). For analysis in English, see Hickey 1982: ch. 3.

11. Central Committee for the Distribution of Labor and Population (Ban Chi Ddao Phan bo Lao dong Dan cu Trung uong), "Bao cao tong ket tinh hinh thuc hien ke hoach 5 nam 1976–1980 va phuong huong nhiem vu 5 nam 1981–1985 va nam 1983 ve cong tac phan bo dan cu, xay dung vung kinh te moi" [Summary report on the implementation of the 1976–1980 Five Year Plan, and directions for 1981–85 and 1983 concerning the distribution of population and the construction of new economic zones], undated (1982). The war also caused substantial population movements away from the border areas, mainly of ethnic minorities.

12. Ministry of Agriculture (Bo Nong nghiep), "Bao cao tinh hinh khai hoang va phan bo lao dong, dan cu di khai hoang xay dung vung kinh te moi 5 nam 1976–1980" [Report on land clearance and the redistribution of labor and population to clear land and build new economic zones, during the five years 1976–80], Hanoi, January 1982.

13. BLD, "Bao cao so ket cong tac dieu dong lao dong."

14. NAV3, Bureau for the Management of National Agricultural Enterprises (Cuc Quan ly Nong truong Quoc doanh, hereafter CQLNTQD) 140(vv), Bo Nong truong, Nong truong QD Song Con, Nghe An, "Bao cao tong hop tinh hinh Nong truong Song Con," 23 September 1960.

15. CQLNTQD 140(vv), "Bao cao tong hop tinh hinh."

16. Interview, Thai Nguyen, October 1996.

17. Migration eastward took two forms—to land reclaimed from the sea and to islands. A settler cooperative on reclaimed land, Nam Cuong in Tien Hai district (Thai Binh), was founded in 1960 and subsequently became a model for others, although district authorities note that the cost of land reclamation has become prohibitive. Migration to islands continues. In March 1999, authorities in Quang Xuong district (Thanh Hoa) recruited eighty fishing families to set up a new economic zone on Co To, an island off Haiphong that lost most of its population as boat people (UNHCR 1998: 22). Anecdotes circulating in Nha Trang suggested that some families had settled an island in the Spratley archipelago, as a showcase for Japanese tourists. The tourists, however, never showed up. Interviews, Thai Binh, July 1995; Thanh Hoa, September 1999; Nha Trang, November 1996.

18. The war and the import economy in pre-1975 South Vietnam led to high growth in the urban population. The number of people living in Saigon in 1975 had doubled since 1960, to 4.5 million. In regional centers, growth was even faster. Between 1960 and 1971, Can Tho grew by 214 percent, Cam Ranh by 237 percent, Nha Trang by 308 percent, Da Nang by 321 percent, and Qui Nhon by 509 percent. In the early 1970s, about 43 percent of the southern population (which totaled 18.7 million in 1971) lived in urban areas, many of them slums. As one observer put it, "Up to 1972, about 4.8 million people in the south had to leave their village and go to the city for work. That meant that about one third of the population of South Vietnam had to migrate" (Khong Dien 1995: 168, 204–5; Thrift and Forbes 1986: 125, 154).

19. BLD, "Bao cao so ket cong tac dieu dong lao dong."

20. At the time of the interview transcribed above, he lived in Australia.

21. Refugees were counted at arrival, leaving out those who did not survive the journey or tried to leave and failed. Amer reckons at 600,000 the number of boat departures to September 1979 (excluding departures in April 1975) and accepts the Chinese figure of 250,000 arrivals in China (1991: 107–8).

22. For detailed analysis of this issue, see Evans and Rowley 1990: 48–54; also Amer 1996: 79–88.

23. Interviews, Hanoi, September 1999. The difficulties of 1980s urban living in southern Vietnam receive sensitive portrayal in Viet Linh's film *Chung Cu* [Collective flat], Ho Chi Minh City, 1999.

24. Interview, Dak Lak, May 1996.

25. Relevant legislation included two decisions: Council of Ministers' Decision 46-CP of 11 February 1980, concerning workers' and cadres' overseas training, and Decision 362-CP of 29 November 1980, concerning labor export to socialist countries.

26. Interview, Hanoi, September 1999.

27. Note that by President of the Council of Ministers' Decision 73/CT of 13 March 1990, labor export was permitted to nonsocialist bloc countries. By 1999 figures from the Ministry of Labor's Department of Overseas Labor report that about 20,000 Vietnamese were working abroad, and opportunities were opening up in Taiwan, Japan, the Middle East (Libya and Iraq), Laos, Argentina, and "the islands" (Samoa and Palau), as well as in former socialist countries in Europe. Minh Quang 1999: 7.

28. Note that stories from socialist bloc countries not only stressed their material wealth, but also poked fun at socialism. Many political jokes (*tieu lam*) still circulating in Hanoi are of Soviet origin.

29. Interview, Singapore, June 1999.

30. Hong Kong arrivals rose from 2–3,000 (mid-1980s) to 18,417 (1988) and 34,622 (1989). Arrivals in all first-asylum countries rose from 19,527 (1986) to 28,056 (1987). Hitchcox 1990: 75, 98.

31. Interview, Hanoi, September 1999.

32. This was the feeling of a returnee from Hong Kong, interviewed in Singapore (she came there on business, this time by plane with a Vietnamese passport), June 1999.

33. Legislation concerning policy on the urban district town is summarized in Le Thanh Nghi 1979: 7.

34. More detail on the evolution of the free market can be found in Fforde and de Vylder 1996: 175–79.

35. Interview, Hanoi, May 1998.

36. Interview, Dak Lak, May 1996.

37. Interview, Thai Binh, January 1997.

38. In Dak Lak province alone, 166,612 spontaneous migrants were counted in 1975–1995. Officially figures show that one-third were Kinh. The rest were Tay, Nung, Yao, and other ethnic groups (Vietnam, Uy ban Dan toc Mien nui 1996: 40).

39. NAV3, Central Committee for Agriculture (Vietnam, Uy ban Nong nghiep Trung) 99 (vv), "Chuyen huong manh me nhiem vu mo rong dien tich, phat trien san xuat nong nghiep cuoi nam 1974 va nam 1975, xuc tien hoan chinh cac nong truong quoc doanh va xay dung cac vung kinh te moi" [Strong changes in the opening up of land and development of agricultural production at the end of 1974 and 1975, to step up the completion of national agricultural enterprises and building new economic zones], 1974.

40. Interview, Hanoi, September 1999. The lives of men sawing timber in the forest are vividly portrayed in Vuong Duc's film *Nhung nguoi tho xe* [The sawyers], Hanoi 1999, based on a short story of the same title by Nguyen Huy Thiep (1999: 254–89).

41. Centre des Archives d'Outre-Mer (Aix-en-Provence), Guernut Commission 92, Statement by Nguyen Van Ngac, auxiliary primary school teacher, Truc Ninh district, Nam Dinh.

42. One of the largest migrant groups there was from Nam Dinh (with Thai Binh and Ha Nam). NAV3, BLD 1030(vv), So Lao dong Lao Cai (Lao Cai Labor Office), "Bao cao tinh hinh nhan dan mien xuoi len thi xa Lao Cai trong nam 1960 va thu thang 1-1961 den 4-1961" [Report on lowland people moving up to Lao Cai town in 1960 and from January to April 1961], 5 May 1961.

43. Interview, Hanoi, September 1999.

44. For further details of sojourning practice in contemporary Vietnam, see Hardy 2000.

45. Interview, Thanh Hoa, September 1999.

46. She said he usually brings 2–3 million dong per year. Interview, Thanh Hoa, September 1999.

47. Interviews, Thanh Hoa, September 1999.

48. Interviews, Hanoi, September 1999.

49. Interview, Hanoi, September 1999.

50. Labor Department data show that five northern provinces (Nam Ha, Thanh Hoa, Ha Bac, Ha Tay, and Hai Hung) were home for 75 percent of Hanoi's migrants in 1999. Li Tana's data showed even smaller proportions of migrants from "other provinces," making up only 3 percent of her sample. Li Tana 1996: 19.

51. Interview, Thanh Hoa, September 1999. She refused this solution.

52. Data from the Ho Chi Minh City Statistical Office 1994, cited in Truong Si Anh et al. 1996: 14.

53. Interviews with police departments in Hanoi, September 1999. The text of the 1997 law (Government Decision 51-CP of 10 May 1997) may be found in Pham Thanh Binh 1997: 61–72.

54. Interview, Hanoi, September 1999.

55. Interview, Hanoi, September 1999.

56. Hanoi Labor Department document, dated 1997.

57. Hanoi Labor Department document, dated 1999.

58. Statistics from Hanoi Labor Department; Dang Nguyen Anh and Nguyen Binh Minh 1998: 32; Ho Chi Minh City, Institute for Economic Research 1998: 7. This data is poor, as one scholar noted: "Statistics of migration into urban areas—Hanoi for example— vary greatly from one source to the next, and no one can say exactly what the flow of people in and out of Hanoi might be in any given month, just as it is hard to know exactly how many unregistered people are living in Hanoi now" (Nguyen Thanh Liem 1998: 1). The Ho Chi Minh City figure is low, and local data show migrant populations of 16–37 percent in poorer urban wards (Bond 1999: 20–22). However, migration to Ho Chi Minh City, compared to the past, but also to other Southeast Asian cities, does not appear high.

5

Upland Areas, Ethnic Minorities, and Development

A. Terry Rambo and Neil L. Jamieson

Both Vietnamese and foreigners tend to think of Vietnam in terms only of its lowlands and the Kinh (ethnic Vietnamese) who live there, but this view fails to include a significant portion of the population and land area of Vietnam. Almost three-quarters of Vietnam is covered by hills and mountains, and about 20 percent (14 million persons) of its people live in the northern midlands and mountains and the Central Highlands, its largest upland regions. Many of these people belong to ethnic minority groups. Thus, problems of upland development are tightly intertwined with the situation of the ethnic minorities that are mostly found living there.

ETHNIC DIVERSITY IN VIETNAM

Vietnam is a multiethnic nation with fifty-four officially recognized ethnic groups. Table 5.1 lists the ethnic groups with populations exceeding 100,000 in order of size.

The Kinh form the vast majority of the national population, numbering almost 66 million in 1999. Ethnic Vietnamese (now commonly called *Kinh* or "people of the capital") account for slightly more than half of the total population of the uplands and are a large majority in several provinces such as Dak Lac and Lam Dong in the Central Highlands and Phu Tho and Thai Nguyen in the northern midlands and mountains. In 1999, Kinh constituted 4.3 million of the 9.6 million people living in the thirteen northern midland and mountain provinces and 2.7 million out of 4.1 million people in the Central Highlands (Vietnam, General Statistical Office 2001b).

Members of ethnic minorities constitute slightly less than 14 percent of the total population. The Tay (1.5 million), Thai (1.3 million), and Muong (1.1 million) are the three largest groups, all living in the Northern Mountain Region. Thirty-six

Table 5.1.   Population of Major Ethnic Groups of Vietnam in 1999

Official Name (alternate names)	Population
Kinh (Viet)	65,795,718
Tay (Tho)	1,477,514
Thai	1,328,725
Muong	1,137,515
Kho-me (Khmer, Cambodian)	1,055,174
Hoa (Chinese)	862,371
Nung	856,412
H'mong (Mong, Meo)	787,604
Dao	620,538
Gia Rai (Djarai)	317,557
E De (Rhade)	270,843
Ba Na (Bahnar)	174,456
San Chay	147,315
Cham	132,873
Co-ho	128,723
San Diu	126,237
Hre	113,111

Source: Vietnam, General Statistical Office 2001b: 21, table 1.6.

groups have populations below 100,000, of which the Si La, Pu Peo, Brau, Ro Mam, and O Du all have populations of less than 1,000, with the O Du numbering only 301 persons.

There is no entirely satisfactory way to classify the great diversity exhibited by these groups. They speak a variety of languages belonging to three major language families: the Austro-Asiatic, the Austronesian, and the Sino-Tibetan. Most groups (including the Kinh), speak languages belonging to the Austro-Asiatic family. Several groups speaking Austronesian (Malayo-Polynesian) languages—the E De, Gia Rai, Cham, Raglai, and Chu Ru (Chru)—are in the Central Highlands (Tay Nguyen) and adjacent foothills. Sino-Tibetan–speaking groups with relatively small populations are found along the border with China and sometimes straddling the border (Lo Lo, Cong, Phu La, etc.)

Almost all of the minority groups live in the hills and mountains. Only four ethnic groups traditionally lived in the lowlands: the Kinh; the Khmer; the ethnic Chinese (known as the Hoa); and the Cham. The remaining fifty groups are all residents of the uplands but otherwise share few common characteristics. Some groups, such as the Thai, Tay, and Nung, are primarily wet rice farmers whose villages have been in the same locations for generations, even centuries. Others, such as the E De and Gia Rai, are rotational swiddeners, whose settlements are relatively fixed. A few groups of H'mong and Dao conform to the Kinh stereotype of the ethnic minorities as nomadic shifting cultivators, but some H'mong in Lao Cai and Lang Son have constructed wet rice fields on elaborately terraced hillsides and have lived in the same spot for many generations. A few very small groups, such as the Ruc of Quang Binh, followed an essentially hunting and gathering mode of life until recently.

THE CHANGING WORLD OF UPLAND PEOPLES

Until the mid-twentieth century, the uplands were inhabited almost exclusively by ethnic minorities. Some groups have been living there for many centuries, if not millennia. Others have arrived more recently, with some entering Vietnam even in the twentieth century. They lived by practicing diverse forms of subsistence agriculture including long-fallow swidden (slash ʹand burn) agriculture, often combined with some wet rice cultivation where appropriate, supplemented by hunting and gathering. They engaged in extensive trade networks to obtain necessary goods from the lowlands (salt, metal, ceramics).

Each community had its own system of land tenure, its own institutions for natural resource management, and followed its own distinctive way of life. Decisions about resource management were largely in the hands of villagers themselves. Knowledge was essentially "local knowledge" and, as has been observed in other cultures, the local ("little") traditions were more important than any national ("great") tradition. Upland communities, although not completely isolated and always engaged in some trade, and often subject to political demands by lowland states, were in many respects autonomous (Rambo 1997).

Certainly, the larger world impinged on upland communities in the form of invading armies and eruptions of banditry, but in most areas these interventions were episodic and usually of short duration. The French made a more sustained effort to establish control over the uplands, but in most areas their presence was limited; they preferred indirect rule through native chieftains. Colonial taxes and demands for corvee labor (conscripted work providing little or no remuneration) placed a growing burden on upland people, but intrusion of external forces into day-to-day life remained limited. Only a few Kinh, mostly traders and government officials, lived in the uplands. All this has changed drastically in the past fifty years.

DEVELOPMENT TRENDS IN THE UPLANDS: AN OVERVIEW

We have elsewhere suggested (Jamieson, Le Trong Cuc, and Rambo 1998) that the Vietnamese uplands are in a state of deepening environmental and social crisis, and we argue that unless current trends are reversed, there is a real danger that in coming decades the uplands will suffer widespread environmental disaster and massive human tragedy. We now see the situation to be even more complex and unpredictable than we did in 1998, and we are less sure now than then that *crisis* is the right word to describe the situation in the uplands of Vietnam. The negative forces are still very real and very strong, but there are countervailing movements, stronger than we had expected, that make the long-term outcome more uncertain.

Signs of crisis are numerous and readily visible. Very rapid population growth has placed excessive pressure on an already degraded environment. Deforestation has seriously depleted the natural resource base. Biodiversity has plummeted. The length of swidden fallow periods has been greatly shortened, undermining the sustainability of existing agricultural systems. Soil erosion has reduced fertility on millions of hectares of land. Vast areas of formerly forested land are now classified as "barren hills" (or, euphemistically, "land not yet in use"). Restoration of full productivity to these areas will require a very long time, even if further degradation could be instantly stopped, which is unlikely to happen.

It is increasingly difficult for millions of households in the uplands to meet their basic subsistence needs. Many suffer from food shortages and nutritional deficiencies. According to virtually all development indicators (e.g., per capita income, life expectancy, educational levels, food security, etc.), people in the uplands are much worse off than people in the lowlands. Moreover, the gap between the uplands and lowlands is widening rather than narrowing.

Inequalities are also increasing within and between upland regions and among different sectors of the upland population. On the whole, ethnic minorities are much worse off than Kinh. Gender inequalities appear to be worsening as many families preferentially devote scarce cash to educating sons while daughters are kept at home to provide labor for household-operated farms.

Most serious of all, cultural and social dislocations of various kinds over many years may have impaired the capacity for adaptive change that is demanded by a rapidly changing context. Overstressed people and communities lack the psychological resources and social capital required to initiate positive changes. Apathy and self-destructive behavior (alcoholism, drug addiction) is one outcome; enlistment in nativistic movements, such as the millenarian cults currently flourishing among the H'mong of the northwestern mountains, another. The extensive and fairly rapid conversion to Protestantism of certain ethnic groups in the Central Highlands may be related to this phenomenon.

Most upland ethnic minority groups have undergone incredible change in their lives in recent decades, but the physiological, mental, social, and cultural consequences of this have received very little attention from researchers. Little research has been done that would enable us to go beyond speculation based upon anecdotal evidence in identifying and assessing the extent and specific nature of the damage such extensive change may have induced, nor in specifying the causes and probable consequences.

Most observers of the situation in Vietnam's uplands will agree with us that the current situation there is fairly grim, whether one is talking about poverty, or the environment, or erosion of cultural identity. There is probably much less unanimity regarding the direction of change now taking place. We have argued that things in general are getting worse, that the uplands may well be caught in a vicious downward spiral. Many other observers do not perceive any clear direction to the changes taking place, and some even believe that things are tending to get better.

ARE THE UPLANDS CAUGHT IN A DOWNWARD SPIRAL?

To reach any conclusion about the overall trend of development in the Vietnamese uplands, one must look at what is happening in a systematic manner rather than focus on specific changes within any single element or dimension of the situation. Most discussions of upland development in Vietnam (e.g., Rambo et al. 1995) tend to focus on describing specific sectoral problems such as deforestation or poverty or gender inequity. Such problems, of course, are important in their own right; but it is the complex and poorly understood interactions among these many different sectoral elements that collectively shape development trends in the uplands.

Several sectoral problems in the uplands (e.g., population pressure, resource depletion, poverty) interact in a manner such that a worsening in any of them has a negative impact upon the others. Conversely, of course, improvement in one factor is likely to have a positive impact on all the others. In other words, more attention needs to be directed toward what we see as a self-amplifying positive feedback system that drives upland development in a spiral that may be either "virtuous" (upward) or "vicious" (downward), depending on the balance between positive and negative trends among its many elements and the way these elements interact. The systematic nature of this situation is important and worrisome because such self-amplifying systems are notoriously unstable. They can easily run out of control as change occurs at faster and faster rates. It is this self-amplifying system, rather than any of its individual elements, that defines the nature and direction of the development spiral in Vietnam's uplands.

Before discussing the direction of change in the uplands, a general description of this system is in order. Five key elements in the current system function as driving forces of the development spiral: (1) population pressure, (2) environmental degradation, (3) poverty, (4) dependency on extralocal systems, and (5) social, cultural, and economic marginalization (figure 5.1).

Population Pressure

Absolute population densities in the uplands are much lower than in the lowlands, but the pressure exerted by population on land resources is actually much greater than is suggested by absolute densities. As table 5.2 shows, nutritional densities (persons per hectare of cropping surface) are actually quite high in four northern upland communities that were surveyed in 1999, although still not reaching the level of the Red River delta, which is one of the most densely populated rural areas in Southeast Asia.

Nutritional densities vary considerably among provinces within the same upland region and between different upland regions. Nutritional density is much

STRUCTURES OF POWER   STRUCTURES OF KNOWLEDGE

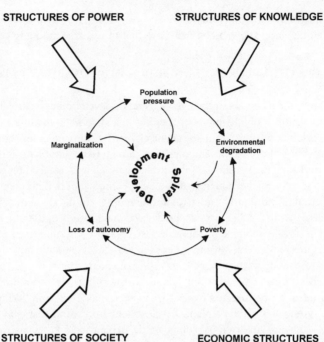

STRUCTURES OF SOCIETY   ECONOMIC STRUCTURES

Figure 5.1.   The Development Spiral in Vietnam's Uplands

lower in the Central Highlands than in the northern uplands. Within the northern uplands, it is lower in some provinces (i.e., Lai Chau, Son La) than in others (i.e., Ha Giang, Lao Cai). But—and this is a vitally important point that has not yet received adequate recognition—the relative situation of the uplands is actually much worse than is indicated by comparison of nutritional densities with the lowlands.

Nutritional density is simply a measure of the number of people who must try to obtain a living from each hectare of cropping surface. It does not take into account the productivity of that area—and this is where huge portions of the uplands are seriously further disadvantaged. Thus, in the Red River delta, good wet rice lands yield from six to nine tons per hectare per crop. One plot typically yields two rice crops per year, plus a third crop of maize or tubers. In the uplands, however, constraints of soil, water, climate, and (to some extent) lack of modern agricultural technology result in much lower productivity per unit of land. Only a tiny fraction of agricultural land in the uplands is suitable for wet rice cultivation, the only sustainable high-yielding system of cereal crop production in Vietnam. Wet rice yields in the mountains are only two or three tons per hectare per crop. Dryland fields, meaning most of the upland agricultural land area, produce at best about one ton of grain per hectare and that for only a single crop each year. Often, fields must be fallowed for from three to ten years to allow the natural vegetation to restore soil fertility before they can again be cropped for three or four years. Thus, overall, the carrying ca-

Table 5.2. Comparison of Population Densities and Nutritional Densities in Four Upland Communities and a Red River Delta Village (persons/ha)

Community	Absolute Population Density	Nutritional Density
Khe Nong (Nghe An Province)	0.08	3.8
Tat (Hoa Binh Province)	0.59	5.8
Thai Phin Tung (Ha Giang Province)	1.01	3.6
Ngoc Tan (Phu Tho Province)	4.36	6.4
Nguyen Xa (Thai Binh Province, Red River Delta)	14.97	9.5

Sources: Le Trong Cuc and Rambo 2001 (Khe Nong, Tat, Thai Phin Tung, and Ngoc Tan); Le Trong Cuc and Rambo 1993 (Nguyen Xa).

pacity of one hectare is much lower in the uplands than in the lowlands. Table 5.3 presents information on the total production (in unhusked rice equivalents) obtained from all agricultural and forest land used by each person in four upland communities in comparison to a village in the Red River delta.

Although the Dan Lai in Khe Nong use almost six ha per capita (more than 116 times the area available to each person in Nguyen Xa in the Red River delta), the total value of production obtained from this very large area is actually lower than that of the vastly smaller area in Nguyen Xa. This reflects the fact that most of the land used by the Dan Lai is covered with protected forest so that the amount of products that the people are allowed to extract from it is very limited. The Da Bac Tay people of Tat exploit a per capita area fourteen times larger than the Kinh in Nguyen Xa,

Table 5.3. Comparison of Total Production from Area of Land Used Per Capita in Four Upland Communities in the Northern Mountain Region with a Red River Delta Village

Community	Land used/per capita (m²)	Total annual production/per capita (kg unhusked rice)
Khe Nong (Nghe An)	57,259	546
Thai Phin Tung (Ha Giang)	2,536	448
Tat (Hoa Binh)	6,886	644
Ngoc Tan (Phu Tho)	1,162	1,269
Nguyen Xa (Thai Binh)	492	722

Sources: Le Trong Cuc and Rambo 2001 (Khe Nong, Tat, Thai Phin Tung, and Ngoc Tan); Le Trong Cuc and Rambo 1993 (Nguyen Xa).

but the latter obtain higher total production than the Tay. Most of the land in Tat is on steep mountain slopes that can be cultivated for only two or three years before being fallowed for several years, so that a household is actually only able to exploit a part of its total landholdings in any given year. Thus, when differences in land productive capability are taken into account, population pressure in the uplands is actually more severe than it is in the lowlands. In many areas the population has already surpassed the carrying capacity of the available agricultural land.

Not only is population pressure already very severe, but the population of the uplands is growing very rapidly. Between 1960 and 1984 the population of the northern uplands increased by more than 300 percent. Population growth in the Central Highlands (Tay Nguyen) has been even more dramatic. In 1900, the Central Highlands population was only about 240,000. By 1960, the population had climbed to slightly over 600,000; by 1976 it was 1,225,914; then between 1976 and 1985 the population doubled again, reaching 2,013,900, and then doubled again to 4,059,928 in 1999. It is still rising at a rapid rate.

These figures reflect both very high local growth rates and the effects of massive in-migration. Birth rates for upland ethnic minorities are well above the national average. And the extension of public health services into even the remotest mountain areas over the past forty years, an effort in which Vietnam can take legitimate pride, has dramatically lowered mortality rates. Consequently, growth rates exceeding 3 percent are not uncommon. Such natural increase has been greatly augmented by massive resettlement of Kinh into the uplands. Accurate statistics are hard to come by, but more than four million and perhaps as many as five million people have moved from the lowlands to upland areas since 1954.

In the northern uplands, roughly a million people were resettled from the lowlands (many of them from densely populated Thai Binh province in the Red River delta) into the midland and upland provinces, mainly during the early 1960s. This was known as the "clearing the wilderness" (*khai hoang*) program. The flow of lowlanders continued at a modest rate during the war and then increased again in 1976. The Kinh population was 639,000 in 1960 and grew to 3,215,832 by 1989, an increase of nearly 500 percent in just 29 years. (Khong Dien 1995: 95). It reached 4,329,204 by 1999.

In 1934 there were only about 33,000 Kinh in the Central Highlands. As late as 1943 the population of the Central Highlands was 95 percent indigenous. In the Saigon-based Republic of Vietnam the Special General Commission for Land Development established 225 "land development centers" in the uplands between 1957 and 1963. Some 274,945 people (many from Quang Nam and Quang Ngai) were moved into these centers. Resettlement of Kinh (mainly from Ha Tinh and Nghe An) accelerated after 1975. By 1979, the Kinh population in the region had grown to 836,831; by 1989, to 1,607,555. By 1989 the Kinh constituted over 70 percent of the population of Dac Lac and over 76 percent of the population of Lam Dong (Hickey 1982: 439; Khong Dien 1995: 96–97; Dang Nghiem Van 1989: 75–76).

While in recent years state-sponsored, planned migration programs have been greatly reduced, unplanned or spontaneous migration has increased greatly. Kinh from overcrowded Nghe An and Ha Tinh provinces continue to move south on their own to join relatives already resettled there by government programs. During the 1990s many tens of thousands of ethnic minorities have moved from the northern uplands to the Central Highlands. In particular, many Nung and Tay people have moved from Cao Bang province along the border with China (where the resource base is badly depleted) to the provinces of Dac Lac and Lam Dong where more land and forest remain to be exploited. The demonstrations over land rights by minorities in Dak Lac province in February 2001 may be explained in large part as a response to the ever-increasing competition for land between native people and migrants.

Despite strong government support for family planning in recent years and the acceptance of birth control by many upland women, the current high rate of population growth will almost certainly continue for some time. This is in large part a reflection of the fact that the upland population is an extraordinarily young one. Over 40 percent of the population in the uplands is under fourteen years old. It would appear that demographic momentum is built into the system for decades, regardless of how vigorously family planning is promoted. The population will almost certainly double again in little more than twenty years.

We see no way in which the subsistence needs of such an expanded population can be met. Even now, very few if any upland communities can grow sufficient grain to meet the minimal caloric needs of its inhabitants. Community surveys in four northern upland communities in 1999 (Le Trong Cuc and Rambo 2001) reveal that only a small percentage of households in supposedly subsistence-oriented communities are actually food self-sufficient. In Khe Nong (Nghe An province), the poorest and most subsistence-oriented community studied, not a single household produces enough carbohydrates (rice, corn, cassava) to meet its consumption needs for all twelve months of the year, while 90 percent of households only produce sufficient carbohydrates to meet consumption requirements for six months or less. To some degree, households in the uplands are able to supplement their own production with grain purchased from the market. On average, households surveyed spend from 25 to 40 percent of their cash incomes on purchasing grain. However, many poor households do not have sufficient cash to purchase all the extra grain they need. Consequently, many suffer from hunger, especially in the late spring when all of the past harvest has been consumed but the new crop is not yet ready for harvesting. Neo-Malthusianism is not fashionable these days, but we have no doubt that population growth is a major driving force for negative changes in Vietnam's uplands.

Environmental Degradation

Rapid population growth in the uplands of Vietnam is especially worrisome because it is occurring in the context of an already severely degraded environment. The quantity and quality of natural resources is much lower than it was just one generation ago and the ability of the environment to support people has correspondingly been rapidly reduced.

Fifty years ago dense forests covered most of the uplands. Forest cover has dropped everywhere, however, to less than 10 percent in the northwestern mountains. Most remaining forests are of poor quality with only a low volume of valuable timber. Species of high economic value have become rare. Simply obtaining wood to build houses and for cooking fuel is now a major problem for many upland households.

Some statistics suggest that the severe deforestation of recent decades has been halted. A recent survey by the National Institute of Forest Survey and Planning (FIPI) concluded that forest cover in Vietnam had increased from 28 percent five years earlier to 33.2 percent in the year 2000. In some areas, notably in the mid-land provinces such as Phu Tho and parts of Yen Bai, for example, allocation of lands to household management has resulted in dramatic regreening of formerly barren hills (Le Trong Cuc et al. 1996).

While some progress has been made, we suspect such areas are not the norm. Assessments of what is happening to Vietnam's forests depend heavily on how one defines *forest*. In many parts of the uplands, the rate of reforestation cannot keep up with the rate of cutting. Worse, what is being cut is diverse stands of high value, old growth primary forest. What is being planted is mostly monocultural tree plantations, low-value eucalyptus and pine, or stands of coffee, rubber, cashew, or fruit trees.

Land degradation is a widespread and still growing problem. Throughout the uplands, erosion and leaching of nutrients has reduced soil quality. Yields in swidden fields have declined to as low as 400 to 600 kilograms of rice per hectare (compared to the six or more tons now frequently achieved in the delta regions). As a result of population pressure and loss of forest land, the fallow period in swidden farming is steadily declining. In many places, fields are cultivated for three or four years, then left fallow for the same period, when a rest of ten to fifteen years is needed to fully restore productivity (Tran Duc Vien 1998).

Shortened fallow periods result in decreased soil fertility and increased weed competition. Farmers, primarily women, have to work longer and harder for ever-decreasing yields. In favored locations, farmers have begun to spontaneously diversify and intensify production, as exemplified by the composite swidden system of the Da Bac Tay minority people of Tat hamlet in Hoa Binh province (Rambo 1998; Fox et al. 2000). In most of the northern uplands, however, and in large parts of the Central Highlands, there are currently few economically viable and environmentally sustainable alternatives to swidden farming. So people must continue to practice swidden farming despite low and declining returns and accelerating environmental damage.

Biodiversity is also declining. Many species of plants and animals have disappeared or become very scarce. Both direct overexploitation and loss of habitat contribute to this trend. Hunting, gathering, and fishing have always provided important supplementary sources of food, medicine, and income for many upland people but can no longer meet their needs. The declining availability of wild tubers that were the main famine food in times of crop failure has a particularly severe impact on the poor.

A growing (and largely illegal) border trade with China poses a significant and continuing threat to the environment. The Chinese market for agricultural and forest products—especially plants and animals used for medicinal purposes or consumption as exotic food—seems to be insatiable. The prices of the tail of an anteater or certain snakes can equal a year's income for upland households; the price of a bear's gall bladder, several years' income. The flow of such resources across the border to China is perhaps the principal cause of the marked decline in populations of wild plants and animals in the northern mountains today. Effective government control of this trade is virtually impossible (Donovan 1998, 1999).

Numerous other forms of environmental degradation are taking place. Small-scale mining activities pollute local water sources with arsenic and mercury. Dam construction that provides energy and flood protection mainly to the lowlands submerges precious wet rice fields. The Hoa Binh reservoir forced many thousands of Muong and Tay families to abandon their rice fields in the now submerged valleys to eke out meager livelihoods by practicing swidden cultivation on the steep slopes above the reservoir. The proposed Ta Bu dam in Son La province will, if constructed, force more than 100,000 people, mainly Thai, to move to much less desirable areas. Grossly inefficient factories and processing industries create localized air and water pollution, although the problem is not yet widespread due to the slow rate of development of industrial activities in the uplands.

Poverty

Vietnam is one of the poorest countries in the world. The poverty situation in the mountains is much worse than that in the lowlands. The northern mountain area contains 18 percent of Vietnam's people but 28 percent of its poor (Vietnam and World Bank 1999: 17, table 1.5). In 1998, 59 percent of people in the northern uplands and 52 percent of people in the Central Highlands lived below the total poverty line (15, table 1.4). Even worse, while in 1996 18 percent of rural households in the whole country were below the food poverty line, 23 percent of households in the northern mountains and 29 percent of households in the Central Highlands were classified as "hungry" (Vietnam, General Statistical Office 1999a: 70, table 1.27).

Ethnic minorities are particularly vulnerable to poverty. Minorities constitute only 14 percent of the national population, but in 1998 they accounted for 29 percent of the poor (Vietnam and World Bank 1999: 15, figure 1.4). The depth of poverty among many minority groups is hard to believe unless one has witnessed it personally. A 1999 survey of four ethnic minority communities in the northern mountain region found that the percentage of households falling under the food poverty line is 100 percent in Khe Nong (Dan Lai), 93 percent in Thai Phin Tung (H'mong), 43 percent in Tat (Da Bac Tay), and 22 percent in Ngoc Tan (Cao Lan). The sole Kinh community in the sample, Lang Thao (Phu Tho province), had a poverty rate of 15 percent. In Khe Nong, the poorest community in the study, average per capita cash and in-kind income is estimated to be only 332,000 VND per year (barely 22 U.S. dollars) (Le Trong Cuc and Rambo 2001).

Because these are largely subsistence-oriented economies, cash income may not be the best measure of poverty. The incidence of hunger is probably a more reliable measure of levels of well-being. The genuine depths of poverty suffered by people in the uplands is revealed by the large number of households that report suffering from hunger at least some months each year. At Khe Nong (Nghe An province), which is an extreme but not unique case, only a single Dan Lai household has enough to eat in every month of the year! Fifty-five percent of the households report that they suffer from hunger for three or more months each year, with 35 percent going hungry for five or more months. The food situation is somewhat better for the H'mong in Thai Phin Tung (Ha Giang province) where 18 percent are hungry for three or more months during the year, Tat (Hoa Binh province), where 9 percent suffer hunger during three or more months, and Ngoc Tan (Phu Tho province) where only 5 percent suffer hunger for three or more months.

Looking at this evidence, and seeing the abject poverty in which many upland people live, one could readily conclude, as we did in 1998, that the poverty situation in Vietnam's uplands is one in which there is virtually no hope and that the region is in danger of falling into a vicious downward spiral. We could marshal an impressive array of facts and figures to support this position simply by quoting from the pages of *Nhan Dan*, the official newspaper of the Communist Party of Vietnam. This is not the way, however, that the people themselves perceive their situation. Most of the people living in these villages see their current situation as being better than it was five years ago and they expect the future to be even better than the present. That people's subjective perceptions accurately reflect positive changes in their living situations is supported by macrolevel analysis of poverty trends.

National sample surveys show that in recent years the incidence of poverty in Vietnam has fallen everywhere, including in the mountains. Nationally, the percentage of poor people declined from 58 percent in 1993 to 37 percent in 1998 (Vietnam and World Bank 1999: iii, figure 1). In the same period, the incidence of people living in poverty in the northern uplands declined from 79 percent to 59 percent and in the Central Highlands from 70 percent to 52 percent (15, figure 1.4). By late 2000, despite application of a new, higher poverty line, the poverty rate had declined to 36.1 percent in the Central Highlands and to 34.1 percent in the Northern uplands (*Vietnam Economic Times*, 3 November 2000).

This is an amazing performance by any standard, and it certainly is not what one would expect to find if the uplands were truly falling into a vicious downward spiral. If the situation is actually getting worse, how can so many households be climbing out of poverty so quickly?

For one thing, the methods being employed in national assessments may not accurately measure poverty in the uplands. The national poverty surveys, while carefully done, are based on measuring household expenditures, not household assets. Expenditure levels are highly responsive to short-term changes in income.

And income can quickly be increased by nonsustainable "mining" of natural resources (e.g., collection of nontimber forest products to sell to the Chinese market) and by increased flows of government transfer payments linked to specific development projects. Both of these factors are currently strongly affecting income levels in the highlands.

Given the very low level at which the poverty line is set in Vietnam, even under the revised criteria, it doesn't take a very large inflow of new income to shift a substantial share of households above that line, but the gains may be short-term with people falling back into poverty as soon as the stimulus runs out. This was the fate of many frontier "ghost towns" in the American west that enjoyed brief booms until their timber or mineral resources were exhausted.

One cannot argue that the perceptions of the people themselves are merely a statistical artifact. And we believe the people are correct in their perception that their living conditions have been and are improving. The situation of many people is in fact better now than it was in the past. One can argue that this reflects the sad reality that their situation in the past was so bad that even a small improvement is perceived as highly significant. In the late 1980s, before the cooperatives were dismantled, people in the uplands were desperately poor and almost always hungry. Today most are still poor, but not so many are hungry.

Freed of the burden of the cooperatives, local food production has increased and households retain a greater share of the food they produce. Policy changes now allow free movement of grain from the lowlands to the uplands, so local shortfalls in production can be made good by purchasing imported food. Better quality and cheaper consumer goods are also available in much greater abundance than before. Life really has gotten somewhat better for most people, but very few people have become well-off. Most live on the margins of poverty with only a single crop failure or other misfortune needed to throw them back below the poverty line. This vulnerability reflects the very limited assets base of most households. The 1999 survey of four ethnic minority communities in the northern mountain region found that the average total value of all household assets (land, house, and material possessions) was only 3.2 million VND in Khe Nong, 6.3 million VND in Thai Phin Tung, 11.6 million VND in Ngoc Tan, and 12.7 million VND in Tat (Le Trong Cuc and Rambo 2001). Thus, the net worth of an average household in the poorest community was barely 200 U.S. dollars and was less than 1,000 dollars in the best-off communities.

Loss of Autonomy and the Problems of Dependency

The uplands are rapidly becoming ever more deeply enmeshed in larger politico-administrative, economic, social, and cultural systems in which the locus of authority is extralocal.

In the politico-administrative sphere, every village, no matter how remote, has its People's Committee, its party cell, its Women's Association, and other mass organizations, all tightly linked into higher-level organizational structures that extend upward through the district to the province to Hanoi. This complex administrative apparatus serves to transmit a stream of instructions from the central government to the people. It transmits the ideas of the people back to Hanoi to a much lesser degree.

This extralocal administrative system plays an important role in guiding the livelihood activities of upland villagers. Control of exploitation of natural resources (e.g., allocation of land, permission to cut trees) although often implemented by local organs (people's committees, cooperatives), must now conform to policies and guidelines set by the central government. Cutting of forest or hunting and gathering of wild plants and animals that were formerly regulated by custom and traditional village institutions are now subject to national laws.

In the economic sphere, households and villages are increasingly involved in and dependent on the world beyond their experience. This integration into larger systems is occurring at an incredibly rapid rate, as illustrated by observations of a long-term CRES/EWC project being carried out in Ban Tat, a Da Bac Tay ethnic minority hamlet in Hoa Binh province.

When the study began in 1992, the villagers produced almost everything needed in their daily life and had extremely limited involvement in the larger market system. There was only one very poorly stocked shop selling salt, matches, and kerosene. Almost no manufactured consumer goods were to be seen. People relied on kerosene lamps for light within their houses and used bamboo torches when walking outside after dark. Transportation was rudimentary, with perhaps one vehicle per week passing through the hamlet on the dirt track linking it to the district capital. People had to walk half a day to reach the nearest market.

Today, barely a decade later, the hamlet has become much less isolated. Daily bus service links it to the outside world. Motorcycle taxis carry people to the market. Traders arrive in the village from China to purchase nontimber forest products. People are deeply involved in the market economy. There are now several well-stocked shops in the village. Households devote much of their effort to the production of goods for sale and have become much more dependent on manufactured consumer goods in daily life. Battery-powered flashlights have almost wholly displaced bamboo torches. Virtually all houses have electric lights powered by micro-hydropower generators imported from China. Most households have transistor radios and one-third of them have television sets.

In the cultural sphere, local knowledge is increasingly considered to be secondary to, and often inferior to, national culture as it is processed and distributed by the mass media. The rate at which traditional ethnic dress is being replaced by modern lowland styles is rapid and accelerating. Young people are increasingly abandoning traditional dress in favor of blue jeans and T-shirts, attempting to copy the styles seen on television. Changes in dress or the pursuit of commodities associated with the lowlands or with more "developed" countries do not, however, necessarily signify an abandonment or rejection of ethnic identity. For some people, they may express a desire to modernize and hence valorize that identity. They may simply be a means of contesting the imposed stereotype of their identity as "backward."

Although it may potentially have liberating aspects, this process of integration into a larger cultural system also decreases local control over information flow, weakens local symbols of identity, and converts upland people from producers into consumers of culture. Their lack of fluency in the national language and low level of literacy put many segments of the upland population at a gross disadvantage in dealing with these new flows of information.

Of course, growing integration into extralocal systems is not in itself necessarily undesirable. Many people in the uplands are eager participants in this process and believe themselves to be its beneficiaries. Population growth, although threatening to the environment, is itself partly caused by the reduction of previously high mortality rates brought about by the extension of national public health services into the uplands. People want more of such services, not less. The ability to meet the needs of an increased upland population is also dependent on the introduction of new productive technologies and the opening up of new opportunities to exchange resources with other regions. If deprived of grain from the lowlands, the nutritional status of upland people would be much worse than it already is, and the degradation of the environment would be accelerated. Building roads and improving transportation systems are important elements in reducing poverty in the uplands.

Integration into extralocal systems is negative, however, to the extent that the relationship is one of dependency rather than partnership. Unfortunately, experience in upland areas around the world demonstrates that when control over management of resources and decision making about the directions of development passes out of the hands of local people, dependency is the most common outcome. Such dependency on external forces will probably accelerate the process of marginalization that is already taking place.

Social, Cultural, and Economic Marginalization

Marginalization of upland populations has reached the point that it can become a significant component of a downward spiral. It interacts with and exacerbates problems of population growth, resource depletion, and poverty; and it is in turn amplified by their growth. This process has economic, social, and cultural dimensions.

Marginalization has steadily increased for the past fifty years, but recently the pace and scope of this process has been accelerating, as improvements in transportation and communication have increased interaction with the larger world. Resettlement programs in both the southern and northern halves of the divided country brought large numbers of Kinh into upland areas. The Central Highlands suffered horribly from war, with great numbers of people killed and many more dislocated (Hickey 1993). Then, when the war ended in 1975, the flow of Kinh into the region became a torrent. As late as 1943, the entire Central Highland population was about 95 percent indigenous. In Dac Lac province, the Kinh accounted for over half the population by 1976, for 61 percent by 1979, and 70 percent by 1999. The E-de, who dominated the province demographically fifty years ago, were at last count only 14 percent of the population.

Postwar development of Dac Lac also took a heavy toll on the traditional way of life in the late 1970s and into the 1980s. Some sixty-four state farms and forty-two state forest enterprises took over 86 percent of the land in the province, including much of the best agricultural land, but employed only about 20 percent of the population. The remaining 80 percent of the population (including most of the E-de) had to eke out a living on less than 14 percent of the land (Dang Nghiem Van 1989: 96). Many Kinh cadre saw the matrilineal social organization and longhouses occupied by extended families as key elements of "backwardness." Efforts were made to move E-de out of their traditional longhouses on stilts into smaller houses on the ground and to replace matrilineal extended family residences with nuclear families (76–111). Dac Lac is an extreme case although similar, but less dramatic changes have occurred almost everywhere in the uplands.

Many upland groups are not only poor, undernourished, and burdened by poor health; they are also poorly educated, especially the women, and many lack fluency in the national language. They lack adequate access to many different kinds of goods and services. They are underrepresented in the civil service and private enterprise. And they are victimized by negative stereotypes that portray them as backward, superstitious, and conservative. While local cultures have suffered serious dislocations, many upland people still lack the means to participate effectively in the new dominant national culture.

Literacy rates are fairly high for some ethnic groups (Kinh, Tay, Muong) but remain dismally low for most minority groups, particularly for the H'mong and the Dao—and literacy rates do not seem to be rising. Indeed, for some minority groups they seem to have been falling, especially for those in remote highland areas. The low literacy rates reflect the low levels of school attendance of many ethnic minority children. Table 5.4 shows data on school attendance by males and females in four ethnic minority communities surveyed in 1999.

The quality of education in the uplands is generally lower than it is in the lowlands. The physical state of schools in many poor and remote communities is

Table 5.4. Rates of School Attendance in Four Communities in the Northern Mountains

	Percentage of People Age Seven and Older Ever Attending School	
	Females	Males
Khe Nong (Dan Lai)	10	14
Thai Phin Tung (H'mong)	18	53
Tat (Tay Da Bac)	70	83
Ngoc Tan (Cao Lan)	100	95

Source: Le Trong Cuc and Rambo 2001.

shockingly bad. Teachers are often poorly trained, badly paid, and frequently absent from their classrooms while they carry on sideline activities to supplement their inadequate salaries. The situation of young Kinh women sent to teach in remote schools is particularly difficult. Not only must they live under difficult conditions but their chances of finding suitable husbands are very low. For reasons that remain unclear, teaching in minority languages was largely abandoned after 1975 and has only been revived in recent years. Not surprisingly, children from groups such as the H'Mong, where few people speak the national language fluently, experience great difficulty in learning.

The educational gap between the Kinh majority and ethnic minorities nationwide is revealed by 1998 figures on school enrollment rates by ethnicity. At the primary school level 93.3 percent of Kinh children and 82.2 percent of minority children are enrolled in school. At the lower secondary school level 66.2 percent of Kinh and 36.5 percent of minorities are attending school. At the upper secondary school (high school) level, it is 31.9 percent and 8.1 percent and by the postsecondary school level (beyond high school) it is 10.5 percent and 1.4 percent (Hainesworth 2000). This means that very few ethnic minority students get enough education to qualify for positions of leadership or professional positions.

The percentage of ethnic minority cadre in the government work force in the uplands is low, and it has not been rising. Few extension workers, school teachers, office managers or clerks, bank officials, policemen, health care providers, or others who provide public services (and serve as "gatekeepers") come from ethnic minority groups or can speak minority languages. The underrepresentation of minorities in government jobs is not a reflection of concealed ethnic prejudice. In fact, the government has tried hard to recruit more ethnic minority cadre. But, largely as a consequence of the lack of educational opportunities in the uplands, only a handful of minorities can meet even minimal academic standards for employment.

The essence of marginalization is that upland people learn—in schools, mass media, and daily social life—to judge themselves by lowland standards and to internalize their inferiority. As is the case in many other places (i.e., Li 1999: 298, 301–2), these people are too often defined and judged by what they are perceived by outsiders to lack, by the ways in which they differ from the dominant culture. The extent to which such negative stereotypes have been accepted by the minorities themselves is shown by the results of a 1999 survey of four minority communities and one Kinh community in the northern mountains (table 5.5).

Among both the Dan Lai and the H'mong, the majority of respondents accept the outside stereotypes that their groups are ignorant, superstitious, and backward. They also see themselves as being tradition-bound rather than rapidly accepting change. The Da Bac Tay are not as likely as the Dan Lai or H'mong to describe themselves as ignorant, superstitious, backward, or tradition-bound. Interestingly, however, they are more likely than members of any other group to perceive themselves as dishonest, cheap, and unkind. Although about one-fifth of Cao Lan respondents see their own ethnic group as ignorant and superstitious,

Table 5.5. Self-Perceptions of Characteristics of Own Ethnic Group, by Percentage of Respondents

Characteristic	Khe Nong (Dan Lai)	Thai Phin Tung (White H'Mong)	Tat (Da Bac Tay)	Ngoc Tan (Cao Lan)	Lang Thao (Kinh)
Ignorant	55	60	33	22	5
Superstitious	35	50	24	20	5
Lazy	5	0	2	3	0
Backward	65	78	29	7	0
Dishonest	5	0	22	2	2
Tradition-bound	55	100	29	4	8
Cheap	0	0	19	0	2
Unkind	0	0	10	0	0

Source: Le Trong Cuc and Rambo 2001.

only a very small percentage perceive their culture as being backward or tradition-bound. In general, the Kinh have a very positive self-image with only a small percentage attributing any negative characteristics to the Kinh culture.

The extent to which such negative stereotyping of minority cultures is widespread is poignantly evidenced by the remarks of Vu Dinh Hien, a young student from the uplands in Lai Chau province who won acclaim for successfully passing the entrance examinations for three universities: "When I went to Tuan Giao district high school to study, many friends disregarded me because I was from the highlands so must know nothing and be ignorant. I felt angry and sad but did not lose heart and resolved to study hard in order to make everyone understand more clearly about people from the highlands" (Doan Trung Tue 1997). Hien is evidently a strong-willed individual who struggled to escape the fate to which others had consigned him. But how many upland youths are defeated before they ever have a chance to excel? For how many children is the main lesson in school one of their own inferiority?

Anecdotal evidence suggests that the incidence of drug addiction, alcoholism, gambling, spouse abuse, and other disorders is rising in the highlands. Figure 5.2 displays information on the perceived frequency of occurrence of such problems in five communities, four of them inhabited by minorities and one by Kinh, in the northern mountains. The incidence of social problems is lowest among the Dan Lai and the H'mong, the groups that most strongly retain their traditional cultures and have the lowest level of involvement in the larger social system. Problems occur more frequently in the Da Bac Tay and Cao Lan hamlets, which are much more tightly integrated into the larger society, but problems are highest of all in the Kinh hamlet.

Of course, social problems of this sort, as well as suicide rates and the incidence of mental illness, are also commonly believed to be increasing in lowland villages and cities, where they are generally attributed to social and psychological dislocations caused by rapid change (*South China Morning Post,* 2 January 2001). Empirical studies are simply too limited to indicate if the situation is better or worse in the uplands than in the lowlands. There is, however, ample evidence from around

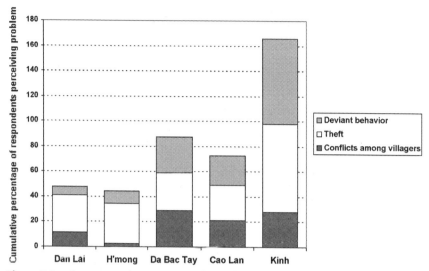

Figure 5.2.   Frequency of Occurrence of Social Problems in Five Upland Communities
Source: Le Trong Cuc and Rambo 2001.

the world to demonstrate that serious social impairment can result from the kinds of marginalization processes that are widespread in the uplands of Vietnam today.

THE STRUCTURAL DETERMINANTS OF THE DEVELOPMENT SITUATION IN THE UPLANDS

The interacting elements of the downward (or upward?) spiral—population pressure, environmental degradation, poverty, dependency, and marginalization—are indicative of deeper structural forces. The situation in the uplands is certainly not the intended outcome of government policy, nor is it the product of chance events or historical accidents. The strong similarity in basic patterns of (under)development that the Vietnamese uplands display with mountain areas in other Asian countries, and even with the United States, suggests that more systematic factors are at work. The interacting elements of what we have posited to be a downward spiral—population pressure, environmental degradation, poverty, dependency, and marginalization—are themselves in large part the product of deeper structural elements, what may be thought of as a higher system level. In Vietnam, it appears that the uplands development process is powerfully shaped by the workings of four underlying structural factors. These are the structures of power, of social organization, of the economy, and—especially—structures of knowledge.

The Structures of Power

What is happening in the uplands is strongly influenced by the structures of power that guide and implement development efforts. These structures include the party, the state and its multiple agencies (including the multitude of state-owned enterprises), local community structures (including cooperatives, mass organizations, etc.), and to some extent international development assistance agencies, nongovernmental organizations (NGOs), and foreign investors. It is within these institutions that key decisions are made about the course of upland development. The structures of power are little studied and poorly understood, but overall they display a number of special characteristics.

Centralized Decision Making

As might be expected in a relatively centralized state like Vietnam, development planning tends to be concentrated in national agencies in Hanoi. This means that critical decisions about the course of upland development are made in lowland urban areas, often by planners with little personal knowledge of the uplands. Implementation of policies is also largely in the hands of cadre assigned to the uplands from the lowlands or of local cadre who have assimilated the worldview and knowledge structures of the larger society. The practical effect is that development policies are rarely tailored to fit the special conditions of the uplands and that implementation is too often mechanical and inflexible under circumstances calling for adaptability and flexibility.

Underrepresentation of Upland Minority People in National Decision-making Organs and in the Civil Service

Although ethnic minorities played a large and important role in the struggle for national liberation from the French, with many (especially members of the Tay and Nung minorities) achieving high positions in the party and the state, their participation in such bodies has probably declined in recent years. Recently, however, strong efforts have been made to increase minority representation in the National Assembly. In the 1997 election, 78 minority representatives (17.3 percent of the total body) were selected (*Nhan Dan* 18 September 1997: 3). The former chairman of the National Assembly and now the general secretary of the Communist Party, Nong Duc Manh, is the most prominent minority representative, frequently making public appearances throughout the country.

Many provincial and district people's committees in the uplands are headed by members of minority groups, but relatively fewer individuals born in the uplands, either members of minority groups or upland Kinh, hold key positions in the ministries and state agencies that implement national development policies. This means that individuals with deep personal knowledge of the realities of upland life have relatively little voice in key decision-making processes about upland development. Upland people are also generally underrepresented in the ranks of cadre responsible for implementing and managing development projects and activities in the uplands. Their absence is particularly evident in the technical branches of the civil service, which is a reflection of their relative lack of access to advanced education. State farm and forest enterprises are also most often headed by Kinh of lowland origin.

Disproportionate Strength of Extralocal Institutions

Many of the most powerful and best-endowed development initiatives have been implanted into the uplands from the outside. They did not evolve from a local base and are thus free from many of the constraints on behavior that influence decision making about resource management in long-established communities. State-owned enterprises, especially the state farms and forest enterprises, are funded from the national budget and are managed and often staffed by Kinh brought for that purpose from the lowlands. Despite the national focus on assigning forested hillslope lands to individual households, six million of the first seven million hectares of forest lands allocated were allocated to state forest enterprises and collective organizations. Such extralocal institutions are likely to become privileged enclaves whose survival depends on continued external support rather than serving as efficient engines of local development.

Weakness of Local Structures of Power

The structures of governance in the uplands are much weaker and less able to implement programs than comparable agencies in the lowlands. The cadre of commune, district, and to some extent even provincial administrative organs are on the whole poorly educated and few have advanced technical education in their fields of specialization. Many of them are lowland Kinh assigned against their wishes to remote areas, people who have little motivation to do their jobs well. Not surprisingly, problems of corruption and bureaucratic inertia are widely evident.

Administrative capability tends to be weakest at the local level, that of communes and villages. In the northern uplands from the late 1950s through the 1980s, traditional local institutions for allocating and managing resources atrophied as their functions were assumed by the cooperatives and their informal leaders displaced by members of the formal bureaucracy. The subsequent decline of cooperatives and the reduction of the authority of their leaders has left many, but not all, upland communities with diminished ability to make or implement decisions about resource management above the household level. In the Central Highlands the war seriously disrupted most villages, and then resettlement and efforts to establish cooperatives further weakened indigenous institutions after 1975. Although allocation of hillslope and forest land to households is in many cases leading to improved management of individual plots, it is further diminishing community capacity to make and enforce measures for the common good.

The Structures of Society

In the uplands, the structures of society—both internal ones and those linking the uplands to larger systems (including national and international)—are important determinants of the development process. Some key structural features are briefly described below.

Cultural Diversity and Social Fragmentation

The great cultural and social diversity of the uplands is simultaneously a potentially valuable resource and a major constraint on development. On the one hand, these diverse cultures represent a rich storehouse of indigenous knowledge and are the source of a legitimate national pride in the multiethnic character of Vietnamese national society. On the other hand, the division of the upland population into many different local groups is an obstacle to the emergence of a shared consciousness of upland problems. Few social structures exist that integrate people from different groups, minority and Kinh alike, and that can articulate the interests they share in common as residents of the uplands.

Differentiation Between Elites and Common People

The cultural gap between leaders and common people is much greater in the uplands than in the lowlands. In the lowlands, cadre and villagers share a common language, have common cultural values, and have all had access to formal education of the same type. The leaders may have more advanced education and greater knowledge of modern technology but the difference is a quantitative one. In the uplands, however, the common people have both less and lower-quality formal education, are often illiterate, and lack fluency in the national language. In contrast, members of the leadership, particularly the senior leaders at district and provincial level, are increasingly the products of advanced education. For example, 78 percent of ethnic minority representatives to a recently elected National Assembly had university-level educations (*Nhan Dan* 18 September 1997: 3). This cultural gap impedes communication between the leadership and the people who are the object of development projects.

Uneasy Coexistence of Local and National Social Structures

The uplands are a complex matrix of local social structures overlaid, often very unevenly, with national institutions. Informal structures dependent on local customs and resources interact with a variety of formal state institutions dependent on external validation and resources. Negotiations between these structures are complex and fraught with misunderstanding and conflicting interests. Implementation of the national land law provides an illustrative example.

Although the land law sets out a standardized model of land allocation to households, actual implementation of the law is in the hands of local authorities. Consequently, great variation exists from community to community in how land is actually managed. The effect may be positive, when reflective of local knowledge and interests, but it is too often distorted by the power of extralocal institutions that manipulate the land allocation to maintain their special privileges.

Links to state or party spheres of influence, membership in cliques based on wealth or educational background, and other sources of special influence or consideration can distort programs to the detriment of the poor, the unconnected, or those out of favor. For example, the new model of commercial farms (*trang trai*) is increasingly resulting in inequity in access to land. There are now at least 120,000 "commercial farms" in Vietnam, most of them in the uplands. These entities receive tax benefits and privileged access to capital, technology, and especially to land. In provinces where there is only one hectare of arable land for eight to ten people, virtually all these new farms are well over one hectare, many are five to ten hectares, and some are ten to thirty hectares. In some places, new commercial farms can be found that are over a hundred hectares in size (*Saigon Times Weekly*, 26 February 2000).

The rationale for this program is that it will stimulate the use of more advanced technology, bring "unused land" into production, raise productivity, and create jobs for the poor; but its actual impact remains to be seen. If land is scarce, when some households or entities get additional land (for whatever reason), it must be at the expense of someone else. To some unknown but surely not insignificant extent, many poor households will lose access to land the government may have labeled "barren," or "land not yet in use" (*dat chua su dung*) but which is in fact being used heavily for subsistence purposes (as swidden land in fallow, as a source of fuel, fodder, medicinal plants, etc.). Who specifically is gaining access to resources and who specifically is losing access? And with what effects? Questions of equity are raised that intersect with issues of class and ethnicity in ways that do not yet seem to have received adequate attention from those responsible for upland development.

Scarcity of Social Capital

The efficacy of development efforts, particularly in rural communities, is closely linked to the amount of "social capital" available (Putnam 1993). A primary component of social capital is mutual trust and understanding among the individuals and households that make up a community. Social capital promotes cooperation, reduces transaction costs, and makes possible more optimal solutions to a vast array of problems in natural resource management, economic ventures, and the creation of various public benefits. In many upland communities, however, social capital is a very scarce commodity, although this is frequently concealed by the prevalent rhetorical invocations of solidarity when local people are questioned about social relations in their community by short-term visitors from the outside, as happens all too frequently in hastily done participatory rural appraisal (PRA) studies.

Because of the scarcity of social capital, efforts to decentralize resource management by returning control over assets into the hands of local communities may not be as effective, especially in the initial phases, as many expect. In recent years the concept of "community-based resource management" has gained considerable popularity among forestry departments, NGOs, and international development assistance agencies as solutions to problems of environmental degradation in Southeast Asia's uplands (Ford Foundation 1997).

In the uplands of Vietnam, as elsewhere in the developing world, proponents of community-based resource management have paid too little attention to the actual internal social organization of villages and the existing levels of social capital within villages (Agrawa and Gibson 1999). The range of capacities among villages to manage the resources entrusted to them is largely unknown. Such capacity cannot be assumed to be high and may in some cases need to be created almost from scratch. Empirical research has revealed that some upland communities are deficient in supplies of social capital (Rambo and Tran Duc Vien 2001). Rather than being naturally cooperative, these communities are characterized by high levels of interhousehold competition, pervasive distrust among members of unrelated households, and a near-total absence of community solidarity. Indeed, it can be argued that in such villages social capital is in shorter supply than financial capital. In such situations, the villagers, whatever their individual intentions and desires, lack the institutional capacity to manage resources for the common good.

Of course, many communities, such as some H'mong and Dao villages, retain strong traditional institutions and display high levels of solidarity. The Black Thai communities in Son La studied by Thomas Sikor and Dao Minh Truong display strong internal organization and an abundance of social capital (Sikor and Dao Minh Truong 2000).

Economic Structures

The economic system of the uplands is complex, poorly understood, and rapidly changing. In some ways it resembles a "dual economy" of the sort that European economists once thought typified colonial and excolonial countries, in which the market sector and the peasant subsistence sector were seen as totally isolated from each other. But the dual economy model ignores the most important fact about the economic system of the uplands: all of its components and sectors are in fact interrelated and interdependent and are increasingly tied into larger economic systems, national, regional, and international. Key characteristics of the upland economy include: dependency on external economic structures, unfavorable terms of trade, shortage of investment capital, and asymmetry of resource flows.

Dependency on External Economic Structures

Local economies are becoming increasingly dependent on larger economic structures. Even those people who are primarily subsistence farmers rely on goods and services produced outside of their communities and must in turn sell goods and services to external markets to obtain the cash needed to purchase the former. The food security of many upland communities, which are no longer able to produce sufficient grain to meet daily needs, now depends on trade. The transboundary trade with China of nontimber forest products (e.g., medicinal plants, wild animals) has become a major source of cash, as well as a major source of environmental degradation (Donovan 1998, 1999). Even entertainment is now derived from outside the boundaries of local communities as radios, cassette recorders, and televisions have become high-prestige consumer goods. This process is most advanced in areas served by well-developed transportation systems and with advanced participation in the market economy, such as along Route 13 running from Ho Chi Minh City through Buon Me Thuot to Pleiku and in the Lao Cai–Yen Bai–Vinh Phuc corridor along the valley of the Red River. It has had much less effect in more remote and inaccessible areas, such as the interior districts of Lai Chau, but clearly this trend is widening and deepening through the uplands.

Many upland provinces are heavily dependent on government transfer payments to maintain their administrative systems. Lai Chau province, for example, gets at least 80 percent of its budget from the central treasury. Routine administrative expenditures from central funds, special development assistance projects, salaries of government officials and military officers, pensions paid to veterans and retired cadre, and so on all add up to a massive cash influx to remote provinces. In a poor H'mong village in Ha Giang near the border with China, 16 percent of household cash income on average is derived from government transfer payments. It is difficult to imagine how those villagers would be able to survive if these flows were halted. Such situations represent increases in local dependency upon external agencies over which these people have no control.

In the northern mountain region, state-owned enterprises (SOEs) account for from 35 to 50 percent of GDP in most provinces; and 40 to 60 percent of that comes from SOEs managed by central authorities rather than local authorities. The role of external forces is probably even higher in the Central Highlands, where an extensive plantation economy has been developed largely under the leadership of vertically integrated general corporations (*tong cong ty*) belonging to the government. Commodity production dominates the economy in huge areas where production of coffee, rubber, cashew nuts, and cotton has been forcefully expanded.

Although much of this commodity production takes place on state farms and state forest enterprises, smallholders have been vigorously encouraged to plant these same commodities in hopes of achieving economies of scale in technology, processing, and marketing. While this approach has produced significant revenue and growth in exports in terms of national averages, it has also rendered many relatively poor households vulnerable to market fluctuations and crop failures, not to mention the organizations that they become heavily dependent on for inputs, processing, and marketing of their crop. The recent severe drop in coffee prices has demonstrated the vulnerabilities of smallholders dependent on an unstable world market. Indeed, Vietnam has become the second largest exporter of coffee in the world, and Vietnam's rapid increase in production has been a factor in the decline of coffee prices.

Unfavorable Terms of Trade

Goods and services imported into the uplands are expensive relative to the prices received for goods and services sold by upland communities. For example, a cloth that a Thai woman spends ten days weaving sells for the equivalent of one day's wages in Hanoi. The flashlight batteries that a worker in Hanoi or Shanghai produced in a few minutes cost her the equivalent of several days' income. It is in the nature of things that remote upland communities must sell cheap and buy dear. Terms of trade are unfavorable because:

• High transportation costs add a significant markup on goods passing in both directions. Only goods with a very high value to weight ration (like opium) can be profitably exported from the high mountains.
• Markets are highly imperfect, often de facto monopolies offering uplanders "take it or leave it" prices.
• Market information is inadequate and unreliable.
• Transaction costs are high, in part due to dispersed populations and the lack of highly concentrated areas of production. Goods tend to pass through the hands of several sets of middlemen before reaching the ultimate consumer.

Shortage of Investment Capital

Allocation of investment disfavors the uplands, where returns on capital are low compared to the lowlands, reflecting the scarcity of profitable investment opportunities and the high costs of management. Extending credit to small farmers who lack collateral is particularly expensive and difficult. Micro-credit projects are one of the most popular features of many upland rural development projects and NGO initiatives, but even the most successful projects reach only a tiny percentage of potential borrowers.

Given the continued availability of favorable investment opportunities in the lowlands, Vietnamese private capital is unlikely to enter the uplands on a large scale, although entrepreneurs have been quick to seize investment opportunities in sectors such as tourism and transboundary trade that offer a quick return. Private foreign capital has also been almost wholly focused on the lowlands.

Asymmetry of Resource Flows

Even when development projects are undertaken in the uplands, it is not always the case that the economic benefits are captured locally. It is a truism among specialists concerned with mountain area development everywhere in the world that profits from development flow downhill while costs flow uphill. For example, most benefits from the Hoa Binh hydropower project have gone to the lowlands (e.g., flood protection, cheap electricity). The costs, in the form of loss of productive farmland and displacement of local people from the area flooded by the reservoir, have been borne almost exclusively by the uplands. The proposed new dam at Ta Bu, built in part to protect and extend the life of the Hoa Binh dam, will destroy many more hectares of precious farmland and necessitate the relocation of tens of thousands of local people.

Even development that appears to benefit upland people through providing employment, such as the growth of tourism at Sapa, may carry high hidden costs in the form of environmental degradation, cultural disruption, and the spread of social problems (prostitution and AIDS), while most of the profits are captured by enterprises based in Hanoi (or abroad).

Structures of Knowledge

The system of concepts and beliefs that guides people's decision making is perhaps the most basic structural influence of all; it shapes all others in many ways. Anthropologists have devoted a great deal of effort to describing the structures of knowledge of indigenous peoples in the uplands of Southeast Asia. As a result we understand quite a lot about how groups like the H'mong or the Mnong Gar conceptualize the world and their place within it. Such studies are fascinating, and valuable. Our concern here, however, is with a different level, the national elite level, in particular the structure of knowledge of the policymakers who are responsible for formulating and implementing upland development policies.

National policymakers have little awareness of the extent to which their personal categories and assumptions are arbitrary cultural artifacts that often do not correspond very well to ground reality. Their view of the uplands is culturally constructed to an extent that is not surprising to one who has read the literature on such matters in other places but that would come as a great shock to most Vietnamese officials. It is important to call attention to the implicit, underlying, and unexamined assumptions upon which development policies are based in Vietnam, because Vietnam is very much a unitary state. Policies are formulated in the capital and are supposed to be uniformly applied everywhere in the nation. There is little provision for regional or local differences. With a "one-size-fits-all" approach to development planning, it is important to understand the structures of knowledge of the elite. Unfortunately, this is not yet a topic that attracts the attention of ethnographers.

In the case of Vietnam, these elite individuals are usually members of the Kinh ethnic majority. They are born and raised in the lowlands and live under urban conditions. They are almost always males, and they most often have university-level education in technical fields, not the social sciences or the humanities. They largely share a common, culturally specific worldview and base their actions on a common body of beliefs and assumptions. Their structures of knowledge are very different from those of the poor, illiterate, rural ethnic minorities who are the object of the upland development programs conceived by the elite.

In the elite worldview, development is assumed to take place in an orderly, predictable fashion that reflects the Marxist version of nineteenth-century evolutionary thought. This lineal scheme assumes that evolution has a purpose and inevitably leads to a good end. It is further assumed that social evolution is unilinear, leading through a set number of universal stages through which all human groups must pass. According to this worldview, some groups move more quickly up this evolutionary path than others. Movement up the evolutionary ladder is equated with "progress" (Jamieson 1991). Cultures of the upland ethnic minorities are perceived to be especially "backward," and it is the duty of more advanced groups (like the Kinh) to transform them in conformity with the natural order of evolution to a higher stage. The concept of cultural relativism is virtually unheard of and ethnocentrism is widely prevalent.

Elements of minority cultures perceived to be "backward" (like shifting cultivation or matrilineal kinship systems) or "superstitions" (like animistic religious beliefs) are to be eliminated as obstacles to progress. However, since the determination of which cultural traits are "backward" or "superstitious" is self-evidently possible only from the vantage point of people who are themselves more "advanced" and more "rational," efforts have been made to impose change upon upland minority groups from the top down, in accord with lowland standards and perceptions. Members of minority cultures have only passive roles in this process. They are objects, not subjects of development.

These general assumptions about the nature of historical progress underlie all development planning in Vietnam, but the specific form given to development programs in the mountains is based on a particular set of specific assumptions about the nature of the uplands. These can appropriately be labeled the "conventional wisdom." These beliefs, held unquestioningly and with little or no testing against empirical experience, are important because development policies are based on them. To the extent to which they are at variance with reality, they result in misguided development policies. Some of the key items of conventional wisdom are as follows:

- The uplands are inhabited mainly by ethnic minorities.
- The upland ethnic minorities are involved in closed subsistence economic systems and resist involvement in the market economy based on buying and selling of commodities for cash.
- Minority cultures are backward; their cultural practices are irrational and based on superstitions.
- Minority cultures are static and actively resist change.
- Most upland minority peoples are nomadic shifting cultivators.
- Environmental degradation of the uplands is due mainly to shifting cultivation by the minorities.
- The uplands are underpopulated and contain large areas of unused land that is available for future development.

Many of these beliefs are clearly false and none of them are unambiguously correct. Still, they powerfully shape the way in which development policies are formulated and implemented. Not surprisingly, given the inadequacies of the knowledge base, resultant policies often fail to achieve their goals and all too often produce unanticipated negative results.

Fortunately, the structures of knowledge are not set in cement. They are subject to change as new information, new ideas, and new paradigms for development become available. In Vietnam in the last few years there has been a remarkable amount of new thinking about the problems of the uplands. Empirical research has begun to call elements of the conventional wisdom, especially assumptions about the ethnic minorities, into question. Policy makers have shown themselves to be increasingly open to frank discussions of development problems. Some development projects are experimenting with new approaches to tapping local knowledge to reduce the top-down character of the development process. So the picture is not entirely a bleak one, but the pace of change seems painfully slow considering the urgency of the problems. The penetration of new ideas among policy makers is still extremely uneven, and most of the fundamental concepts underlying official upland development policy making have not yet been adequately challenged by persuasive empirical studies.

DIRECTIONS OF CHANGE

We have discussed five key elements that interact to shape development in the uplands. We have explained why we wrote several years ago that this system was facing a "crisis" and seemed in danger of being caught in a "vicious downward spiral." We have also identified some positive indicators that suggest that the direction of the spiral may be changing in a positive direction. The picture as we see it now is, like the uplands themselves, one of bright peaks and dark valleys. Overall it is bleak; but, as we have noted, it contains some very bright spots and is not as bleak today as we previously expected it to be.

It is highly significant that the majority of people in the uplands—including many of those with whom we have interacted to reach our conclusions—do not agree with our pessimistic view. They believe that their lives and communities have improved and will continue to improve. Many recent statistics support this view. The percentage of households living in poverty has been declining, not increasing. While we have numerous caveats and questions about this phenomenon, it is clear that genuine progress has indisputably been made. The loss of forest cover, after plummeting for decades, really has been halted in many places and reversed in some. Infrastructure is being rapidly improved. Roads and bridges are being built at a more rapid rate, improving access to markets and government services for many remote communities. Construction of markets and school classrooms and health stations has also been accelerating.

There is some basis for arguing that what we saw as a "vicious downward spiral" several years ago is in fact becoming a virtuous one, in which improvements in some areas are leading to improvements in other areas. We now see the situation in the uplands as more complicated, and more ambiguous, than we did previously. Were we wrong? Perhaps. But we think the question is still very much open. Certainly, the inexorable growth in population will continue to increase pressure upon very limited resources of land and water for agriculture. And while the percentage of people living with genuine hunger and in absolute poverty is declining, most upland households are still very poor and the gap in living standards between the uplands and the lowlands is increasing. In relative terms, the upland populations are still getting poorer, and marginalization shows no signs of decreasing.

An important reason for adopting a less pessimistic view is the improvements that have become visible in the development process itself. The Vietnamese government, aided by international development assistance agencies such as SIDA and the World Bank, and numerous international NGOs, has launched an astounding array of programs aimed at rapidly improving life in the uplands. It is impossible to compile an even partially comprehensive list of these state initiatives but the following are some illustrative examples of major policies and programs that currently exert influence on villagers in the uplands:

- Iodized salt campaign
- Family planning program
- Policy to subsidize prices for essential commodities in mountains (salt, kerosene, school notebooks, etc.)
- Reforestation programs such as the 327 program and the more recent 5-million-hectare program
- Policy to allocate forest lands and "barren hills" to households, commercial farms, and social units
- Creation of national parks and nature reserves
- Campaign to suppress planting of opium poppies
- Anti-illiteracy campaign
- Program to eradicate hunger and reduce poverty in 1,715 poorest communes
- Special rural credit programs from Bank of the Poor and Bank of Agriculture
- Prohibition of logging in natural forests
- Program for sedentarization and fixed cultivation of minorities engaged in shifting cultivation
- Creation of district and provincial boarding schools for ethnic minority students
- Program to develop "cultural villages"
- Projects to supply clean water to rural households
- Extension of national electric grid to rural areas in uplands
- Expansion of highways and roads in mountain areas
- Hydropower projects (Hoa Binh Reservoir)
- Rural development projects funded by international development assistance agencies (SIDA, World Bank, EU, GTZ) and international NGOs

This list is far from complete but it gives a sense of both the urgency with which the state views its mission to develop the uplands and the extent to which people's daily lives are being impacted by the development activities.

The government has initiated a massive Program for Hunger Eradication and Poverty Reduction. Over the past eight years, and especially over the past several years, this effort has grown in size and in sophistication. Much better targeting is in part responsible for lowering the poverty rate. The poorest and most remote communes have been identified and receive priority assistance from several agencies and from donors.

The Politburo Directive on Grassroots Democracy issued in February 1998 has been another source of improvement. Uneven but nevertheless very real progress has been made in decentralizing the development process and empowering local authorities to take greater account of local conditions in planning and implementation of development. Transparency has increased, and local authorities are more accountable to their citizens than ever before. Under the slogan of "The people know, the people discuss, the people implement, and the people monitor" (*Dan biet, dan ban, dan lam, dan kiem tra*), villagers now have more influence on the planning and implementation of development efforts that affect their lives. While many problems and weaknesses remain, real progress has been made.

In 1999 a Poverty Working Group (PWG) was established that brought together government agencies, donors, and NGOs in a concerted effort to eliminate poverty in Vietnam. On the whole, this has been an active and fruitful collaboration. Also, partly due to increased collaboration, the level of funding for upland development in general and poverty reduction in particular has been increasing. Donors pledged about 2.4 billion dollars for Vietnam in 2001, and an equal amount for 2002 (*Viet Nam News* 13 December 2001: 3). A large share of these aid funds are earmarked for upland development.

To the extent that a vicious cycle does exist, as we have posited, it is being combated more vigorously and more effectively than ever before. The rate of improvement in several aspects of the development process has exceeded our expectations.

We have also discussed the underlying structural forces that ultimately shape upland development, the structures of power, social organization, the economy, and knowledge. These structures, which are rarely visible and never transparent, are durable and highly resistant to change. Unless they are identified, described, analyzed, and in some cases reformed, it will be difficult to sustain an upward spiral. Here again, though, the picture has become more complicated.

We see some signs of improvement in the structures of power (a trend toward some decentralization, more democracy, more participation) and of the economy (some SOE reform, somewhat higher levels of investment). However, there is still considerable cause for concern because these economic and political structures remain so opaque and susceptible to manipulation by privileged elites. These processes are largely invisible and there is no tradition of critical sociology or investigative journalism to expose abuses. The press may occasionally expose inefficiencies or even corruption in certain upland development programs but there is as yet no systematic public scrutiny of these massive efforts. One knowledgeable Vietnamese official has privately remarked that the government might as well burn 70 percent of the funds being spent for all the good these expenditures are doing. There is a lingering tendency to undervalue the local, the indigenous, and the sustainable in favor of an uncritical faith in science and technology and in the virtues of "progressive" elements in upland society. Such biases can unwittingly have devastating impacts upon the most vulnerable members of upland society.

Ultimately, the most important element in the entire situation may be the structures of knowledge. We have been very critical of the structures of knowledge and decried the lack of empirical foundations for these assumptions. While these problems persist, and the situation is still troublesome, here again there has been noticeable improvement. Many officials have shown themselves to be willing to listen to criticism, to rethink some assumptions. The social and natural scientists who do research related to upland development have learned from experience (in Vietnam and in the region) and are becoming more sophisticated in their applied research. Also, a growing number of research groups are crossing disciplinary boundaries and seeking new and more appropriate models for dealing with the challenges of upland development in the twenty-first century.

Overall, many programs and agencies are improving. It remains to be seen if they can improve rapidly enough to counter the tendencies toward a downward spiral that we have elaborated above. They face immense challenges, and the depth and importance of the structural factors that shape development trends are not yet adequately recognized. The development process in the uplands, like the uplands themselves, is complex and poorly understood. None of us can predict the future with confidence. While progress in upland research and development is encouraging and highly commendable, there is still cause for deep concern that the spiral of change will turn out to be a vicious spiral rather than a virtuous one.

6

Clean, Green, and Beautiful: Environment and Development under the Renovation Economy

Michael DiGregorio, A. Terry Rambo, and Masayuki Yanagisawa

High above Hoan Kiem lake in central Hanoi, a billboard summarizes the Vietnamese Communist Party's goal for national development in one concise slogan. In large red letters it proclaims, "push forward industrialization and modernization." Long wars of national liberation and defense, internal social and economic struggles, international embargoes, and the collapse of socialist economic aid had hindered attempts to attain these goals over a nearly forty-year period. Now, sparked by market reforms intended to "unleash the full capacities of the people" and by a focus on global economic integration, they seemed tangible. Aware of its own agenda for social transformation and the dislocations involved in market-oriented development, however, the party could not leave these goals without a moral enjoiner. That enjoiner is recorded as a target on the second line on the billboard. "Industrialization and modernization" should not be considered goals in themselves, but rather, as the means of creating a "rich people, strong country, fair and civilized society." Across the street from this billboard, a much smaller sign, framed in green, comes almost as a warning. In the process of "industrialization and modernization," as we build a "rich people, strong country, fair and civilized society" we must be vigilant in our efforts to create "a clean and beautiful environment."

Although current public attention given to the linkages between environment and development is new, the problem is itself an old one in Vietnam. Efforts to promote rapid industrialization and modernization did not begin with renovation policies in 1986 and the massive environmental problems associated with development did not begin with the arrival of foreign direct investment in the mid-1990s. Unlike other countries in Southeast Asia, Vietnam entered this period of industrialization and modernization with a large catalog of unresolved environmental problems. It already had a large rural population and had depleted many of its natural resources, especially forests, so that it had no natural storehouse to draw on in the way that Indonesia had oil and Malaysia timber. Over the past ten years, however, as the pace of change has increased, environmental issues have taken on a new force. Deforestation and loss of biological diversity, land degradation, industrial pollution, overuse and pollution of water sources, and air pollution are already widespread and rapidly increasing. Such environmental problems pose an immediate threat to the health and welfare of Vietnam's seventy-six million people, cause undesirable costs associated with loss of productivity and health care, and create long-term barriers to economic growth. For these reasons, environmental protection has become an urgent concern as the nation seeks to become an essentially "modern and industrial country" by the year 2020.

Recognition of the need to protect the environment could not be more important. Vietnam has now entered a prolonged period of risk transition in which new risks to human health and the environment are being added to the common risks of the past. In an ideal world, improved public health measures and regulation of the environment would simultaneously reduce the impacts of new risks, such as industrial pollution and vehicle emissions, while lowering the prevalence of the old risks, such as waterborne diseases. In fact, this ideal world has never been attained. Vietnamese, like people in other countries undergoing rapid economic and social changes, are being confronted with a wider range and greater intensity of environmental threats to health and well-being than they have ever known. Furthermore, because of its history and current social situation, Vietnam as a nation is poorly equipped to cope with these risks and effectively manage the environment.

In this chapter we review the major environmental problems facing Vietnam and discuss their causes. We then assess Vietnam's difficult passage through the risk transition, examining the different threats that traditional and modern environmental risks pose to the health and well-being of Vietnamese people. Finally, we look at how Vietnam is responding to its environmental problems.

A DIVERSE COUNTRY WITH DIVERSE
ENVIRONMENTAL PROBLEMS

Vietnam is a large and environmentally diverse country strung out along a north-south axis, backed by mountains and fronted by seas. Its climatic zones, determined by latitude and elevation, are fed by monsoon rains. Its flora and fauna are influenced by similar factors, as well as by its position on the border of two great biological regions, Himalayan and Indo-Malayan. It has multiple cultural zones, mountain and lowland, urban and rural, with each suffering different environmental problems reflecting the ways in which Vietnam's fifty-four officially recognized ethnic groups carry out their lives.

Given this diversity, it should come as no surprise that each region, locality, and ecological zone faces a somewhat different mix of environmental problems. For the sake of simplicity, however, the country can be treated as if it were divided into three main human ecological zones. The deltas and coastal plains are characterized by a dense population of Vietnamese-speaking (Kinh) wet rice farmers. Hill and mountain areas are characterized by a much lower density of ethnic minority and Kinh majority people practicing shifting cultivation and plantation agriculture on the slopes and rice cultivation in river valleys. Urban areas are extremely densely populated by mostly Kinh inhabitants who depend primarily on industry and services, including public services, for their livelihoods (figure 6.1).

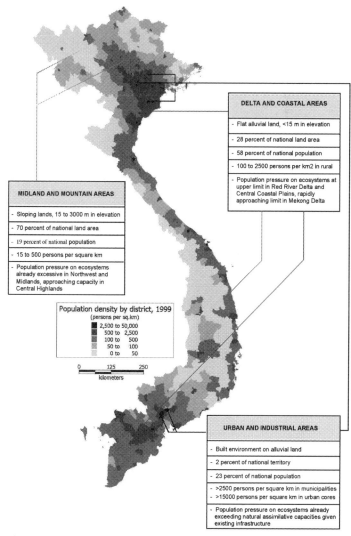

Figure 6.1. Human ecological zones

ENVIRONMENTAL PROBLEMS

Each of these human ecological zones are characterized by particular sets of chronic and emerging environmental problems. In highland areas, deforestation, loss of biodiversity, and land degradation are the most important problems. In lowland agricultural areas, land degradation is also an important issue, as is contamination of water sources. In urban and industrial areas, most impacts are related to contamination by residuals of industrial processes, disposal of domestic and industrial wastes, and changing consumption patterns. Of course, problems in each of these zones have impacts on the others. Ecology, as a science, is about relationships. Although we cannot begin to detail the entire catalog of relationships between human communities and the environment in Vietnam, some important problems can be noted and illustrated.

Deforestation

Deforestation is considered by many Vietnamese to be the most serious environmental problem facing the nation. Statistics that the percentage of area covered by forest has fallen from 45 percent in 1943 to less than 30 percent today are often cited (Vo Quy 1998). The data base is poor, however, and such figures should best be taken as approximations. There is no question, however, that much forest has been lost in the period since 1945, especially in the northern midlands and the Central Highlands. Perhaps more important, the quality of remaining forest has been badly degraded so that the diversity of species in standing stocks is much lower than in natural forests, and the quality of remaining timber is low.

There are numerous causes for deforestation and forest degradation. Shifting cultivation (slash-and-burn farming) by supposedly nomadic ethnic minorities is the most commonly cited cause in Vietnamese sources. Defoliation with chemical herbicides during the American war, illegal logging, unplanned clearance of land to plant cash crops such as rubber and coffee, and forest fires are also frequently mentioned causes of forest loss. Less commonly noted are the effects of planned settlement and exploitation.

Shifting cultivation is actually much less of a threat to Vietnam's forests than it is commonly believed to be. Only a few ethnic minorities still practice pioneering shifting cultivation, with most using a much more sustainable type of rotational slash-and-burn farming (see box 6.1). Conversion of forest land to permanent cash crop farms, often by Kinh migrants into the uplands, has been a much greater cause of forest loss. Vast areas of forest in the Central Highlands have been destroyed since 1975 to plant rubber, cashews, and coffee. At the same time, excessive logging, often done by state-owned forestry companies, has degraded huge tracts of forest. The companies were required to replant cut-over areas but often failed to do so. Even when reforestation has been undertaken, however, the transplanted seedlings are given little care and survival rates are low. Many areas have been "reforested" several times but remain largely barren hills while even successfully reforested sites resemble tree farms more than natural forests. More effective has been the policy of allocating hill lands to individual households to restore and protect. Given an economic stake, over the last decade Vietnamese farmers in the northern midlands have regreened large areas of formerly barren hills with a diversity of fruit, medicinal, root, and timber species (Le Trong Cuc et al. 1996).

Deforestation is perceived as a serious problem because of loss of valuable timber, loss of biodiversity, and especially because it is believed that it results in the occurrence of natural disasters such as floods and droughts. In fact, however, floods and droughts have been recurrent problems throughout Vietnam's known history. Records covering the ninety-five years from 1806 to 1900 for Hung Yen province in the Red River delta show that flooding due to breaks in the dikes occurred

---

Box 6.1. The impact of shifting cultivation on the environment

The prevalent view in Vietnam is that shifting cultivation practiced by nomadic ethnic minorities is the most important cause of deforestation. In fact, only a few minority groups, and not all representatives of these groups, engage in forest-destroying pioneering shifting cultivation in which primary forest is cleared, crops planted for up to ten years until the soil fertility is exhausted, and the area converted to permanent grassland. Some or all members of the pioneering group then move on in search of new forest to clear.

Most of the minorities practice a much more sustainable form of shifting cultivation known as rotational swiddening, a form of agriculture in which secondary forest serves as fallow between cropping periods. Fields are cleared in secondary forest and brush land, farmed for two or three years, and then allowed to revert to natural vegetation. After a rest period of several years, the field can again be cleared for planting. Although the diversity of species in forest fallows will be reduced, as long as population densities remain low (less than twenty persons per square kilometers), rotational swiddening can be a sustainable form of agriculture for generations. A study done of a Tay ethnic minority community practicing rotational swiddening on the hillslopes together with some permanent wet rice agriculture in the valleys in Hoa Binh province (Fox et al. 2000) found almost no loss in forest cover over a forty-year period, despite an increase in population density from less than ten persons to more than seventy persons per square kilometers during that period. Only in the past decade has forest degradation become evident in this community as a consequence of increased population density forcing more frequent clearance of plots before the forest has time to regenerate fully. Probably the most damaging form of slash-and-burn farming is practiced by Kinh migrants to the Central Highlands who log, cut, and burn ancient primary forest to clear land to plant permanent commercial crops, principally coffee. In recent years, many Tay, Nung, and H'mong ethnic minorities from the overcrowded uplands of northeastern Vietnam have also migrated to the Central Highlands, where they have destroyed large areas of forest in their quest for land to cultivate.

in twenty-four years (Miribel 1904, reproduced in Rambo 1973: 423–26). It is thus unlikely that even successful implementation of the national plan to reforest five million hectares will eliminate floods and droughts, although regreening of barren areas may have many other beneficial effects.

Only a few small areas of forest have survived in lowland areas of Vietnam. In the north, there are remnant and recovering mangrove forests in the marshlands around Ha Long bay, Hai Phong, and at the mouth of the Red River. In the south, remnant mangrove forest still exists in the mouth of the Saigon River near Ho Chi Minh City and in Ca Mau province in the Mekong River delta. In inland areas, pockets of cajeput (*Melaleuca* spp.) forest remain in the U Minh forest (Kien Giang province) and in the Plain of Reeds (Dong Thap and Long An provinces). Balancing rural development and protection of the environment in these remaining forest areas has been difficult, to say the least. The recent history of reclamation in the Plain of Reeds gives us an example of this difficult balancing act.

Dong Thap Muoi, commonly known outside Vietnam as the Plain of Reeds, is a large swamp east of the Tien Giang River. During the wet season (April to September), flood waters can rise three meters with high ground appearing as islands in the sea. During the dry season (October to March), evaporation draws acids in the underlying peat to the surface. This process, called acidification, produces the area's characteristic acid-sulfate soils. The presence of these soils, which have a pH of 2–3, and the extreme hydrologic regime are the main reasons why the Plain of Reeds was not converted to wet rice cultivation in the past. Rather, until recently, it had remained largely covered with cajeput forests and reeds (*Eleocharis* spp.). Where soils were less affected by acidification, local people combined the cultivation of floating rice with low-impact exploitation of the natural environment.

Beginning in the late 1970s, migrants from the densely populated Red River delta of northern Vietnam were encouraged to migrate to this area. The early migrants cut cajeput forest and constructed paddy fields typical of their northern homeland. The Vietnamese government supported these migrants through canal construction, technical assistance, and financial support. In this way, the Plain of Reeds has become the major source of new rice land in Vietnam which, in addition to increased productivity on existing rice lands, has contributed to the country's current rice surplus.

Strict focus on expanding rice land and increasing yields in the Plain of Reeds has had a number of negative social and environmental impacts. First, we note marginalization of the area's original inhabitants who had combined floating rice cultivation in the wet season with livestock grazing and forest exploitation in the dry. According to research conducted by Le Dien Duc at the Center for Natural Resources and Environmental Studies in Hanoi, given the degree of subsidies required to make rice cultivation profitable in the Plain of Reeds, former combinations of floating rice, livestock, and forest exploitation provided higher incomes per unit of land than current wet rice cultivation. Second, we note a loss of biodiversity as mixed cropping was replaced by rice monocropping. This is particularly important because the Plain of Reeds is an important nesting and feeding area for a number of rare and endangered migratory bird species, included the red-headed crane. Third, we note problems with flooding, acidification, and salinization brought about by reduction in the size of this important flood retention and groundwater infiltration basin. The gradual rise and fall of flood waters in the Mekong River delta is due, in part, to large retention basins in Vietnam and Cambodia. As these areas have been brought into cultivation, the severity of seasonal flooding has increased. The Vietnamese government has responded by constructing more and larger drainage canals. But by draining water out of these retention basins more quickly, the lower delta has lost an important source of freshwater flow through its underground aquifers, particularly in the dry season. As the flow of fresh water in underground acquifers is reduced, more salt water is able to intrude through the coast. Combined with acidification in areas like the Plain of Reeds, salinization threatens to reduce gains in the total rice output of the Mekong River delta.

Loss of Biological Diversity

Vietnam, because it is on the border between the Indo-Malayan and Himalayan biological realms, has an extremely high number of plant and animal species for a country of its size, including many endemic species found only there. For this reason it is considered a biodiversity "hot spot" and is the focus of much ecological research. The process of inventorying its natural wealth is still underway and new species are being discovered with surprising frequency, including six new mammal species recently found in the steep, jungle-covered mountains of the Truong Son range in central Vietnam. More new mammal species have been recorded in Vietnam in the past ten years than in the rest of the world since the turn of the century, and the number is still growing.

In the past decade, particularly since the opening of its border with China to trade, Vietnam's biological diversity has been seriously threatened. A number of factors are contributing to the rapid loss of species, habitat loss due to deforestation and overexploitation of wild plants and animals for commercial purposes being in the main. The Chinese market is rich and insatiable, border controls ineffective, and opportunities to make quick cash too attractive to resist. The collection of wild species for trade with China, and to a lesser extent with affluent Vietnamese, has become a major source of cash income to many rural people. Medicinal plants and animals believed to enhance male potency are particularly valued both for sale to China and for use in Vietnam.

Vietnam has taken major steps to try to protect its biodiversity. By 1999, the government of Vietnam had established eleven national parks and forty-seven natural area reserves and strengthened the Forest Protection Service. But since most parks are surrounded by poor, often hungry people, and Forest Protection Service staff have little authority over authorized exploitation of natural resources by economic branches of other government units, poaching continues, and the long-term survival prospects of most valuable wild species are bleak. Some success has been achieved with captive breeding of wild animals such as deer and bears, renewable exploitation of nontimber forest products such as bamboo and rattan, and cultivation of ornamental plants, medicinal plants, and fungi, particularly in buffer zones surrounding national parks. This form of low-impact exploitation may offer the best prospect for the preservation of species, albeit in a more domesticated environment.

Land Degradation

For a country like Vietnam with an economy largely based on agriculture, land degradation poses a serious problem. The threat is particularly strong in the hills and mountains that cover three-quarters of the surface area and are home to one-third of the national population. Land degradation is also occurring in the lowlands, however, where wet rice land is being lost to urban sprawl, construction of industrial parks, expansion of roadways, and disposal of wastes.

Land degradation is most serious in the uplands. Although able to support a rich growth of natural forest, upland soils are particularly susceptible to degradation. Shifting cultivation on steep slopes, for example, often results in unsustainable soil losses of sixty to two hundred tons of soil per hectare per year. Equally, lateritic soils in areas such as the midlands around the Red River delta take on a bricklike consistency when exposed by land clearance to the direct rays of the sun. Explosives must be used on these barren hills to blast out holes for tree seedlings. Regreening is very slow, however, and even eucalyptus trees, famous elsewhere in monsoon Asia for their fast growth on poor soils, remain stunted after many years. On some hills in Phu Tho province, eucalyptus planted in the late 1980s has not yet achieved harvestable size. Restoration of soils on such barren hills will take decades if not centuries.

Soil erosion has negative impacts both on the welfare of upland farmers and on the larger society. Yields of hill rice, which used to be over one ton/ha, have dropped to as low as 400–600 kg/ha. As a result, most upland areas can no longer produce enough grain to meet local needs and must rely on rice imported from the lowlands to make up for the deficit. The need to obtain cash in order to buy rice is a powerful incentive for upland people to overexploit wild forest products, thus contributing to biodiversity loss. The downstream consequences of land degradation in the mountains are also severe. Soil washed from swidden fields is carried by rivers into dams and irrigation systems. The reservoir of the Hoa Binh hydropower station, which had a design life of several hundred years, is now expected to be filled with sediments in only a few decades.

Solid Waste

Problems associated with the collection and treatment of solid wastes have emerged as an important public concern as the volume and types of wastes generated in urban and rural areas have changed over the past ten years. This change in waste generation patterns reflects a major cultural shift taking place in Vietnam, the shift from a low-consumption, thrift-conscious society whose products are largely derived from organic materials to a high-consumption, consumer society whose products are more frequently of industrial origin. To understand the importance of this change, it is necessary to take a step back. Up to the mid-1980s, waste treatments in urban and rural areas of Vietnam were similar in many ways. Most waste was organic and what could not be fed to livestock or used as fuel was often buried on house plots or left to rot at the end of lanes. Small fractions of waste that had value—wastepaper, scrap metal, duck and chicken feathers, glass bottles, bicycle tires, old plastic sandals—were retained for sale to itinerant junk buyers. In urban areas, sanitation companies, organized in the early part of this century, were responsible for the collection and disposal of the remaining fractions of solid waste and, in the north, nightsoil. The former was accomplished through regular street sweeping and transport to open dumps, generally former clay pits and fish ponds within the urban limits. Nightsoil was collected from latrines and septic tanks and used in aquaculture and agriculture. The major impacts of this system on the environment and human health were restricted to problems associated with acidic leachate at dumpsites, odors, pests (such as rats and flies), and parasites associated with the use of uncomposted nightsoil in vegetable gardens.

Since the early-1990s, this system of waste management has been pressed into new responsibilities as it deals with wastes generated by the growth of an unevenly affluent, consumption-oriented, industrializing society. A waste materials dealer in Minh Khai village, northern Vietnam's most important plastics recycling center, described this transition as one from a society where goods are used "once and forever" to one in which they are used "once and thrown away." For urban sanitation companies, this has meant increasing waste loads, increasing needs to segregate waste, and increasing needs to improve treatment.

The chart below illustrates the difficulty Hanoi's Urban Environment Company faces in collecting the city's wastes. Although the collection rate increased from roughly 45 percent to about 60 percent of the wastes generated within the city over the five years between 1991 and 1996, increases in the total generation rate have kept the gap between generation and collection fairly stable at about 400 tons per day.[1] Roughly half of this, nearly all materials with value, is collected by private recyclers within the city. Some of the uncollected waste is burned on site; some is fed to livestock, while the remainder is dumped into canals or ponds, negatively affecting drainage.

Ho Chi Minh City faces similar problems with solid waste management. In 1995 HCMC's 3.9 million people generated around 3,000 tons of waste per day. Of this, roughly two-thirds was disposed in the Dong Thanh landfill, about 35 kilometers north of the city center. When this site was first established in 1989, it was one of many small landfills in the municipality and received only between 100 and 200 tons of waste per day. The site received nearly 4,000 tons of waste

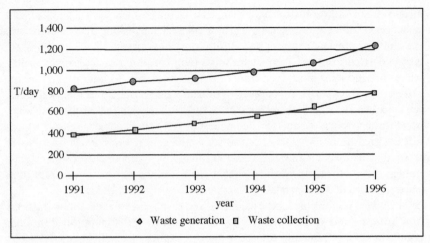

Figure 6.2.   Waste generation and collection in Hanoi, 1991-1996

(600–700 truckloads) per night in 1998. Inadequate preparation of the landfill site has resulted in groundwater contamination, problems with pests, foul odors, methane gas fires, and methane migration to wells in neighboring villages. Residents of these villages also have high prevalence rates for diseases associated with poor sanitation (Hong Van 1998 and Trinh Hai 1997).

The search for treatment facilities for growing mountains of waste has occupied much of the attention of Urban Environment Companies in both Hanoi and Ho Chi Minh City. From 1991 to 1999, Hanoi URENCO has moved its landfill facilities four times, successively overfilling and abandoning each in an arc around the city that has progressively moved treatment farther into the countryside. Tam Hiep (1991–1993), Me Tri (1993–1997), and Tay Mo (1997–1999) were each designed to buy time while a site was sought for the construction of a comprehensive municipal solid waste facility. Each of these landfills was abandoned under public pressure. The new facility, a seventy-three-hectare landfill located forty-eight kilometers north of Hanoi in Nam Son subdistrict, has been opened prematurely. As a result, serious environmental impacts have emerged in what was supposed to be Vietnam's premiere solid waste treatment facility.

Industrial Pollution

Industrial pollution in Vietnam is both a legacy of the past and a product of the present. As a legacy of its past, contemporary Vietnam has inherited old industrial complexes, built at a time when environmental concerns were minimal and subsidies for energy and materials promoted inefficiencies. In many such complexes, production technology dates back to the 1950s. Energy and material waste is high, products are inferior, and without the support of cheap subsidized credit and pro-

Box 6.2.   Environmental Equity

Complaints by neighbors of Hanoi's landfills are not uncommon, although they are not always reported. After a severe typhoon in August 1992, for example, URENCO was forced to pay about $3,000 in damages caused by leachate leakage into rice fields and fish ponds belonging to a cooperative adjacent to its landfill in Tam Hiep. In August 1997 residents of Me Tri village southwest of Hanoi blocked the road leading to a landfill nearby for three days, demanding closure of the site and compensation for losses. The village had suffered declining water quality and crop losses to rats ever since the landfill was established in 1993. The site was scheduled for closure in 1996. Most of Hanoi does not know these events ever occurred.

Thus it came as a huge surprise when garbage began to pile up in the early evening of September 13, 1999. Residents of Nam Son commune, with the support of local authorities, had blockaded the road leading to Hanoi's new landfill site. At the same time, residents of Tay Mo commune, a recently closed landfill site in Tu Liem district, refused to allow vehicles to enter. With no other alternative, URENCO staff began piling up wastes in vacant lots and along wide sidewalks while negotiations pressed on. At the heart of the conflict were two issues: impacts of the sites on the local environment and compensation for affected residents. Nam Son had been put into operation prematurely. At the time, URENCO officials considered this a temporary measure forced on them by closure of the Tay Mo site. They attempted to deal with mounting environmental problems with sandbags, plastic sheets, and limestone. Despite these measures, black acidic leachate trickled out of the site, into a neighboring stream, and from there into surrounding rice fields. Rice not harmed by leachate was scourged by rats that swept out of the landfill during the evening. As in most rural areas, nearby residents rely on rainwater, groundwater, and well water for cooking, drinking, and bathing. The landfill had begun to affect all three. Residents wanted compensation for losses imposed by the landfill and, strengthened by Vietnam's environmental laws, they knew they had the right to claim compensation from known polluters. According to sources in URENCO, the 164 households bordering the landfill have been granted 27 billion VND, about U.S. $193,000, in direct compensation and have been promised an additional 27 billion VND in improvements of the site. Residents of Nam Son have also been given scavenging rights to the landfill.

tective tariffs, many would have already collapsed. In industrial centers like Viet Tri, Thai Nguyen, Bien Hoa, Hanoi, and Hai Phong, these industries have become major sources of concern to regulators due to the expenses required to renovate them, the environmental and health consequences if renovation is not carried out, and the jobs at stake if closure is required.

New problems have been added to old with the introduction of Industrial Zones (IZs) and Export Processing Zones (EPZs). There are currently 63 IZs and 3 EPZs in Vietnam, the majority in and around Ho Chi Minh City. As of June 1999, less than a quarter of the land in IZs and EPZs was occupied. Under these conditions, IZ management boards are under pressure to attract new and to keep current industries by any means possible. In practice this means that IZ boards are rarely able to create industrial zones around related producers, which would facilitate waste management, and are frequently required to expedite permitting, including environmental impact assessments (EIAs). Environmental monitoring is complicated by IZ charters, which create virtual states within states. Although mandated to comply with environmental regulations, management boards often act as screens between Department of Science, Technology, and the Environment (DOSTE) monitors and individual firms within their sites.

The stalemate between environmental regulators and management boards has rarely been broken except in reaction to public complaints. This is the case of Vedan, a producer of monosodium glutamate located in the Long Thanh IZ in Dong Nai province, not far from Ho Chi Minh City. When fishermen on the Thi Vai River reported fish and shrimp kills downstream from the Vedan plant, regulators moved in to inspect. Monitoring revealed that Vedan had been releasing highly toxic organo-chloride into the river. Chemical process charts included in the plant's EIA did not include organo-chloride as a byproduct of production, although the chemical equations clearly indicated its likelihood (Dara O'Rourke, personal communication). The plant was closed and fined. Within a year, however, it was once more in the news for disposing waste at sea, this time under permit. The company justified disposal on the grounds that its wastes were largely composed of fertilizers and could have a beneficial effect on the marine environment. More recently, the company's disposal of a chemical fertilizer, Vedagro, along dikes in the Mekong delta raised concerns that it was once again disguising its waste (*Vietnam News*, 20 Jan. 1998: 11). In 1998, despite these concerns, Vedan received permission to expand its operations in Vietnam at another suburban site.

Large-scale industries are not the only sources of industrial pollution in Vietnam. Small-scale, unregulated industries in urban and rural areas have also attracted the attention of environmental monitoring agencies. These workshops are particularly difficult to regulate since their small size makes "best practice" solutions designed for larger firms impossible to introduce, and their location in dense urban areas and village lanes makes them hard to regulate. As in other cases of environmental monitoring, and in the absence of formal EIAs, DOSTEs must rely on public complaints to attract their attention to offending firms (Ha Hong 1998: 1).

Degradation of Water Sources

Water sources are being degraded in Vietnam through four main contaminants: agricultural chemicals, industrial waste, poorly managed dumpsites, and urbanization. While some impacts are clearly either urban or rural, many occur across environments due to flows of water above and below ground, siting of urban landfills in rural areas, and the increasing need for urban areas to draw water supplies from distant well fields and reservoirs.

Agricultural Chemicals

The misuse and overuse of agricultural chemicals, especially pesticides, is becoming an increasingly important factor in the degradation of water sources. Farmers spray at the wrong time, overspray, use banned chemicals, and they improperly store chemicals, dispose of packaging, or wash equipment (*Vietnam News*, 26 Dec. 1998: 21). Improper application often results in the extermination of predators (like spiders) along with pests. As a result, when infestations occur they quickly become plagues. This has been the cause of several serious outbreaks of brown leafhoppers, a major rice pest, over the past decade. In addition, improper application of chemicals tends to select for the hardiest and most pesticide-resistant pests. As a result, farmers have to use more and more pesticides just to keep pests in check.

Urban consumers, aware of this situation, follow news reports about pesticide dangers closely, resulting in the sudden collapse of markets in fruits and vegetables that might be affected. In the countryside, farm households often segregate a small plot on which they grow pesticide-free vegetables for their own consumption, although they are not as able to avoid chemical residues in well, pond, and rainwater. Some shops in Hanoi now sell "clean" vegetables under the slogan of "good for your health and for the health of farmers, too." While this movement is a positive sign, because clean vegetables and fruit are sold at a premium, mixing of pesticide treated and pesticide-free fruits and vegetables is common and consumer confidence is low.

Drainage and Sanitation

Like solid waste treatment methods, drainage and sanitation systems in use in Vietnam rely on biological assimilation to treat wastes. Modeled on rural practice, biological wastewater treatment systems, such as those used in Hanoi, drained wastewater from septic tanks into underground drains and canals linked to a network of urban and suburban ponds. Fish raised in the ponds grew quickly on algae in the nutrient rich water, and through their own biological activity, prevented eutrophication.

Extensive systems such as these approach collapse as the byproducts of industrialization and modernization—oil, grease, household chemicals, and industrial effluents—increase. Lower levels of most Hanoi lakes are now anaerobic and bottom-dwelling species are completely absent from some (Dang Thi Sy 1998). Rivers originating in the city—the To Lich, Set, and Kim Nguu—have become open sewers along their entire lengths. Each also passes through industrial areas in the city's southern suburbs where, in addition to their loads of organic waste, grease, and oil, they receive chemical, acid, and heavy metal waste as well. Only thirty years ago, the To Lich River was deep and, although not free of pollutants, it was swimmable and fishable. It is now composed *entirely* of wastewater. The Nhue River, to the west of Hanoi, is scheduled to fill a similar function in the future, regardless of the fact that this river flows out of western Hanoi into farming areas in two provinces to the south before draining into the Red River.

In Ho Chi Minh City, the situation is similar, although the wastewater treatment system was never as well organized as in Hanoi. Vu Kim Quyen, head of the city's Water Supply and Sanitation Management Board, estimates that the city generates between 800,000 and 1 million cubic meters of wastewater per day. More than 80 percent of this wastewater is from household sources (Quang Vu and Nguyen Pho 1997). Currently HCMC has about 1,000 km of underground drains built by the French, American, and Vietnamese governments. As in Hanoi, these drains flush sewage into canals and rivers. Unlike Hanoi, no treatment takes place beyond this point other than natural decomposition. As a result, rivers and canals flowing through the city have low levels of dissolved oxygen and high levels of ammonia (Dang Thi Sy 1998).

Urban Air

In the late-1980s, morning rush hours in Hanoi and HCMC were punctuated by the sounds of bicycle bells, the slow steady sounds of pedals, and the rhythmic

---

Box 6.3. Hanoi, Green and Beautiful

Lakes and trees provide Hanoi with its most endearing natural amenities and important natural infrastructure. Trees lower ambient air temperatures and filter particulate matter from the air. Lakes help to cool the city through the updrafts created by evaporating water. Lakes also provide storage for storm water and open space for boating and fishing in crowded urban areas.

In the early 1980s, Hanoi had forty lakes and ponds with a total area of about seven hundred hectares. These lakes and ponds were, and are, managed by three "surface water exploitation" companies, one within the central city, one in the suburbs, and one in West Lake. All of the city's ponds and lakes, with the exception of Hoan Khiem in the city center, have been used for wastewater treatment and aquaculture.

By 1997, only seventeen of Hanoi's lakes remained. West Lake, with an area of about 375 hectares, is the largest of these, comprising about 85 percent of the total surface water area. Between 1992 and 1994, West Lake lost twenty-three hectares to encroachment. By 1998, another seventeen hectares were lost. Approximately eight hundred households are now living on illegally "reclaimed" land on the shore of West Lake. In individual cases, the process of encroachment is simple: a small piece of shorefront property is obtained legally, then a bamboo barrier is constructed in the lake which is gradually filled with household and construction waste. In cases where larger pieces of land are encroached, personal and political connections are required. In order to protect the remaining area of West Lake, the Hanoi People's Committee has approved a U.S. $46 million project to build a nine-meter-wide, seventeen-kilometer-long promenade around the lake. About three hundred meters have already been constructed—and immediately encroached upon by nearby fish restaurants. The remainder has been held up by negotiations with shoreline residents, many of whom have no legal claim to the land. (*Vietnam News,* 23 Aug. 1998: 2)

scraping of street sweepers' brooms. The view along major city streets was long and clear, with only an occasional smoke-belching truck raising ire among others on the road or sidewalk. Air pollution, where it existed, was largely restricted to areas around aging factories, predominantly those using coal furnaces or producing construction materials.

The situation began to change in the early 1990s as the number of motorcycles on city streets began to overtake the number of bicycles. Motorized transport is the single most important source of air pollution in Vietnam's urban areas. Monitoring of CO_x NO_x and SO_x, common vehicle emissions, in Hanoi and HCMC between 1992 and 1997 all show general increases in these indicators. These general increases have come *despite* site-specific reductions due to a gradual closure of old urban factories and conversion of industrial power plants from coal to gas. Meanwhile, pedicabs, a nonpolluting means of transportation in Hanoi and HCMC, have been banned on many streets as conflict for road space with more affluent motorcycle owners has increased.[2]

The noise caused by motor vehicles has become another source of concern. Currently, all major intersections in Hanoi and HCMC surpass noise level standards. Noise levels at main traffic intersections in HCMC range from 83–84 dBA during the daytime, 13–14 dBA above the limit. Transportation authorities in HCMC expect an increase of 0.4–1 dBA per year over the next few years as the number of vehicles continues to increase and present vehicles age. HCMC has more than 1 million motorized vehicles including 113,000 cars and 1.2 million motorbikes (*Vietnam News,* 8 July 1998: 4). The current daytime average noise level for major intersections in Hanoi is 83 dBA. Some attempts have been made to reduce noise, such as restrictions on the size of air horns, but they have had little effect. Meanwhile an ambitious public transportation plan for Hanoi envisions 1,457 buses on the road by 2001, with a ridership that includes 60–70 percent of the population by 2010 (*Vietnam News,* 8 July 1998: 4). Given the accommodations already made to Vietnam's motor vehicle industry, motor vehicle taxes or restrictive maintenance standards, two means of reducing private vehicle use, are not likely to be put in place. At the same time, the expansion of road networks to serve the bus system will likely provide incentives for continued growth in private vehicle use, while buses themselves are likely to become major pollution sources. As one indication of the future, Hanoi's traffic police, whose occupation forces them to be in the middle of this mixture of dust, noise, and chemicals, suffer ear, nose, and throat disorders at rates far greater than the general population.

CAUSES OF ENVIRONMENTAL DEGRADATION

Vietnam's current environmental problems are the outcome of interactions among many different factors including the natural setting, historic legacies, cultural values, and institutional structures. These factors provide a backdrop for more recent environmental change brought about by expansion of the market economy, population pressure, urbanization and industrialization, inappropriate or poorly implemented development policies, and lack of adequate knowledge and understanding of the environment.

The Natural Setting

Vietnam's natural environment is characterized by great diversity, a high level of natural hazards, a relative poverty of natural resources, and a fragility in the face of overexploitation. It is one of the more difficult settings for human settlement in Southeast Asia. Although classified as a tropical country, Vietnam extends across sixteen degrees of latitude and displays great variations in elevation, ranging from sea level to more than three thousand meters above sea level, with nearly three-quarters of the surface area classed as hills and mountains, so that it has a much greater climatic diversity than is typical for other Southeast Asian countries. Its location astride the typhoon belt and on the southern edge of the East Asian continental climate zone, with most of the northern and central provinces subject to cold winter winds from Siberia, contributes to an extremely high level of environmental risk. The rivers of the north and center have steep gradients and flow from small watersheds causing their flood regimes to be violent and unpredictable. Settlement of the Red River delta is consequently dependent on construction and maintenance of a vast system of protective dikes. In contrast, the Mekong River has a much more gradual and predictable flooding cycle.

In general, groundwater sources are abundant, although dry season water shortages are problems in parts of the northern mountains and the western Mekong delta. Although natural forests in the mountains are luxuriant and endowed with a great wealth of species, the underlying soils are generally thin, of low fertility, and unsuitable for continuous cultivation of annual crops. Small areas of rich basalt soils in the Central Highlands are well suited for growing rubber, coffee, and other tree crops, however. The Red River and Mekong delta soils are well suited for wet rice cultivation and their fertility is renewed by periodic flooding, which brings in fresh deposits of silt eroded from the uplands. Upland soils are deficient in iodine, so that goiter was a widespread disease until the government began a program to distribute iodized salt in the early 1990s. The plains are mercifully free of malaria, but this mosquito-borne disease is endemic in the mountains and, despite major efforts to eliminate it undertaken over the past thirty years, remains a major threat to public health.

Historical Legacies

Virtually no place in Vietnam has escaped human intervention over the past four millennia. Since 1945, warfare, large-scale migrations, urbanization and industrialization, and efforts to achieve rapid increases in agricultural production have all adversely affected the natural environment. War has been especially important, both because of its direct negative effects on the environment (destruction of forests by chemical herbicides, dispersal of mines and unexploded ordinance) and, perhaps more important, because of the extent to which it has absorbed so much of the nation's energies and talents for much of the twentieth century.

Cultural Values

Many Vietnamese see their traditional culture as one that valued people living in harmony with nature (Le Trong Cuc 1999). Human beings are seen as sharing the same living space with natural objects (trees, water, mountains) and supernatural beings associated with nature. In this worldview, humans were part of a natural order and their behavior was expected to maintain balance with other elements of that world. One must ask, however, how did the majority of Vietnamese conceive of nature? They certainly did not regard nature in the Western sense as a wilderness outside human history. Rather, truly wild nature was generally perceived as dangerous and hostile to humans. Forests were feared as places filled with ferocious animals and evil spirits.[3] Such places should be avoided or, whenever possible, cleared and transformed into cultivated landscapes. The nature that was valued was a domesticated nature, a landscape filled with paddy fields, bamboo groves, canals, ponds, and villages, an ordered and largely humanized nature. Thus, traditional Vietnamese were *not* conservationists in the Western sense. Indeed given the density of settlement in the Red River delta there was virtually no space for wild nature, regardless of the values of the people. Even today, to the extent that popular support exists for protecting forests it is derived from pragmatic considerations such as a belief that forests prevent floods and are natural storehouses of products for human benefit.

Institutional Structures

The Kinh, the majority population of Vietnam, have lived for many centuries as citizens of a society ordered by the hierarchical institutions of a bureaucratic state. In such a system, decision making was highly centralized and uniform policies were expected to be implemented everywhere within the national boundaries. Deviations from policy that took into account local diversity were not officially tolerated, although the state rarely had adequate resources to directly implement its policies at the local level. Thus, in practice, national policies have always been modified, often in very significant ways, at the local level. Despite this, a fiction of national uniformity was maintained through official discourse.

This institutional legacy has strongly affected the way Vietnamese bureaucratic institutions have been organized in modern times. As in the past, the governmental system maintains an official discourse of uniformity with regard to implementation of decrees, directives, guidance, and laws while tolerating local-level experimentation and negotiation. Such deviations from official policy, however, can have both positive and negative effects. In some cases, positive deviations, such as the gradual return to the household economy, have subsequently been incorporated into state policy. In other cases, deviation and compromise has only covered over local-level corruption with a mask of conformity. Thus, despite a national ban, illegal logging has continued almost unchecked in many localities, and only the most flagrant of such violations have been prosecuted as examples for others who may be involved in similar activities. For example, 35 officials in Binh Thuan province were recently sentenced to a total of 225 years in prison after their illegal logging operations were exposed (*Vietnam News*, 4 Oct. 1999: 3). It is not clear whether such prosecutions will have long-term impacts, however, given the demand for wood and the ability of some to continue forest exploitation in various other guises.

Expansion of the Market Economy and Changes in Consumption Patterns

Although the adoption of market mechanisms has been widely applauded for freeing the productive capacity of the people, it has been accompanied by a pre-occupation with making short-term profits regardless of long-term costs, human or environmental. It has also set off a consumption revolution. During the cooperative period, northern Vietnamese dreamed of owning thermos bottles and bicycles. Now they strive for motorcycles and three-storey houses. The consumption explosion that began in the mid-1980s has placed extreme pressure on forests for construction materials and furniture; stone and sand for cement; clay for tile, porcelain, and ceramics; coal for furnaces; gas for cooking, and petroleum for motor vehicles. At the same time, the affluence of a minority is fueling trade in rare and endangered plant and animal species, cultural artifacts, and land. Individuals with the means to do so now consume more per capita than at any time in Vietnamese history. Meeting these new needs places heavy demands on natural resources and generates larger quantities and types of pollutants.

Export has added to these problems. By exporting, Vietnamese producers are able to capture the effective demand of markets in richer countries. The export of medicinal plants and animals to China is one example that we have already noted. To this must be added export-driven agricultural sectors such as coffee and rubber; expanding manufacturing sectors such as pulp and paper; and exports of materials such as cement and natural resources such as ocean fish. While capturing effective demand in wealthier countries may be necessary in the medium term as a means of building industrial capacity and national wealth, the environmental costs of this strategy cannot be overlooked.

Population Pressure

The issue of effective demand is important when one considers the role of population pressure in environmental issues. Vietnam is one of Asia's poorest and most densely populated countries. Rural densities in the Red River delta now exceed 1,000 persons per square kilometer. About 45 percent of Vietnam's rural population falls below its official poverty line (Vietnam and World Bank 1999). The northern uplands, with 18 percent of the national population and 28 percent of the poor, is the poorest region in Vietnam.

Most rural Vietnamese rely heavily on the local environment for their livelihoods. For this reason, high population densities place intense pressures on natural resources. Thus, although often referred to as a country richly endowed with natural resources, when these are allocated on a per capita basis, Vietnam faces serious shortages, especially of arable land but also of timber and other forest products, minerals, and energy. When the effective demand of Vietnam's newly affluent and export-oriented industries are included in this equation, the source of growing resource conflicts becomes more clear. Land required to fuel an export coffee industry cannot simultaneously remain part of a rotational swidden system. Bottom land in the upper reaches of major rivers cannot be simultaneously used for rice cultivation and hydroelectric generation. Mangrove forests cannot be simultaneously reserved for low-impact exploitation and converted into export-oriented shrimp farms. While these various enclosures take place, policy remains preoccupied with food security, particularly rice production. Even this preoccupation is underlain with an export orientation. The expansion of rice-growing land in the Mekong River delta presently generates a large surplus that has made Vietnam the world's second leading rice exporter, after Thailand. Within twenty years, however, this surplus will be needed internally to meet the needs of a growing population.

Urbanization

Between 1975 and 1990 the percentage of Vietnam's people living in urban areas barely changed, fluctuating between 19 and 20 percent (Brockerhoff 1998). There are many reasons for this low rate of urbanization. Some of the most notable are low levels of industrialization, particularly in the north; an anti-urban bias; an economic structure that discouraged spontaneous migration; forced resettlement programs; and the flight of refugees (Forbes and Thrift 1987). As the economy began to open, however, opportunities for work outside the state sector have made it increasingly possible for people to move in search of work. This trend was strengthened by Vietnam's 1992 constitution, which guarantees a citizen's right to search for employment anywhere in the country.

By 1999, the percentage of Vietnam's people living in urban areas had grown to 23.5 percent (*Vietnam News*, 14 January 2000). In Ho Chi Minh City, the annual rate of population growth between 1976 and 1996 is divided nearly evenly between natural growth (1.5 percent) and artificial growth (1.7 percent) (Le Van Thanh 1998). By 1996, migrants accounted for about 80,000 new residents per year in HCMC and about 22,000 in Ha Noi (Doan Mau Diep et al. 1998).

As the urban population has grown, so has the urban land area. In 1960, for example, urban Hanoi had a land area of 58 square kilometers. By 1998, this had grown to 91 square kilometers. According to development plans, the city's urban land area is expected to increase to 121 square kilometers by the year 2010 (Le Anh Ba 1998). Ho Chi Minh City center, the former Saigon, had a land area of only 1 square kilometer at the beginning of the twentieth century. By 1995, HCMC's urban land area had grown to 210 square kilometers with an expectation that this will reach 350 square kilometers by 2010.

Migration and natural population growth alone cannot account for this expansion, however. Urban residents who have the financial capacity are buying suburban land and building homes as fast as they can in view of limited space and high land valuations in central city areas. For example, in 1995 the per capita floor area of housing in Hanoi was only five square meters (Le Anh Ba 1998). Moreover, roughly one-third of the city's population has less than three square meters of living space. The search for land for new housing has been driving valuations far higher than the speculative bubble that occurred as representative offices were established in Ha Noi and Ho Chi Minh City. Thus, although this rental boom has faded, it is still not uncommon to find unrenovated homes on hundred-square-meter plots in the central city for sale in the range of $150,000 to $200,000. In nearby suburbs, housing values are three to five times lower.

The rush to buy land and build houses is occurring well ahead of the construction of environmental and transportation infrastructure. Houses appear in former agricultural areas almost overnight with infrastructure consisting of little more than a dirt path large enough to transport building materials by hand cart, telephone and electrical lines strung along bamboo poles, a deep (and untested) well for drinking water, and an underground septic tank for sanitation.[4] There are many reasons for this, not the least of which is a sense of urgency. Registration and permitting is difficult and many people do not expect it to become easier. This leads perspective home builders to simply "make an agreement" with ward-level authorities, build quickly, and hope that when land administration is "rationalized," their rights will be legalized. As a result, only about 10 percent of private housing in Hanoi has a legally defendable title to land and permit to construct (Le Anh Ba 1998).

The immediate impact of this pattern of construction on the environment is negative. Reliance on individual wells in deltaic regions generally results in soil subsidence. Homes without proper footings become structurally unsound. Meanwhile, use of septic tanks adds to pollution levels in groundwater which, as it is drawn down, gradually affects drinking water sources. At the same time, poor drainage leads to flooding and since many new housing areas are outside the jurisdiction of publically owned solid waste management companies, the hazards of periodic flooding are compounded by leachate and runoff from uncontrolled dumps and landfills.[5] If the experience of other countries in the East and Southeast Asia can serve as an example, the various agencies in charge of specific aspects of urban development will not be able to catch up with the pace of development for many years to come and, as a result, one should expect that incremental rather than planned development will be the major means by which urban areas in Vietnam expand.

Ambitious Development Policies

After 1954 in the north and after 1975 in the whole country, development policy emphasized rapid creation of heavy industry and the undertaking of massive infrastructure projects. Natural resources, especially forests, were unsustainably exploited as a source of capital or resources for industrialization. This rush to industrialize led to concern with production targets (the quantity of output) at the expense of quality or the externalized costs of resource degradation. At the same time, subsidies encouraged inefficient use of materials and energy as well as overinvestment in fixed capital. This has left behind a legacy of large polluting industrial complexes that cannot compete in the market economy but must be supported for the jobs they represent.

While industry was promoted, agriculture was starved for investment. Under these conditions, achievement of local level food self-sufficiency became a major policy objective, one that ignored issues of comparative advantage and environmental degradation. As each individual cooperative and collective struggled to meet its own needs and that of the district in which it was located, the amount and types of food available for sale declined to unprecedented levels. At the same time, land marginally suitable to rice cultivation was pressed into this service at the expense of more suitable uses. The conversion of cajeput swamp forest in the Plain of Reeds, mentioned above, is just one of many examples of this focus on rice self-sufficiency.

Other huge and unsustainable projects have followed since the 1986 reforms. The most recent of these include the expansion and collapse of the sugar industry, the cyclical expansion and collapse of coffee and rubber plantations in the central highlands, the expansion and collapse of silk production in Lam Dong province, and the yet to be realized expansion of pulp and paper production in Gia Lai province.

Lack of Knowledge and Experience

Although last on our list, lack of knowledge is the reason that government officials most often mention as the primary cause of environmental degradation in Vietnam. Thus, deforestation is blamed on ethnic minorities whose continued practice of shifting cultivation is attributed to their supposed cultural backwardness and their lack of knowledge of better methods of cultivation. Field research has shown that minority farmers are well aware of the problems associated with shifting cultivation but persist in using this means of cultivation because no alternative methods for producing grain are successful in the mountains. In other cases, such as the

‑al pesticides by lowland farmers, lack of knowledge of the dangers is newly introduced technology is indeed part of the explanation. ‑rs avoid using pesticides on crops grown for home consumption of knowledge is not the sole explanation. Equally, small-scale ‑ot unaware of the environmental and health impacts of their production methods, but disciplined by competition, they lack the means to address these issues individually. Besides, compliance with Vietnam's environmental standards are generally beyond the means of most small producers considering the technology they employ and the scale of their production.

CAUGHT IN THE RISK TRANSITION

Where do environmental and health issues stand in this period of industrialization and modernization? We wish to frame the answer to this question through an elaboration and expansion of a concept first developed by K. R. Smith (1997): the risk transition. People in all societies face numerous environmental risks, but there is a significant difference in the kinds of risk that afflict agricultural societies and industrial ones. As industry and commerce begin to play a larger economic role in societies that formerly relied more heavily on agriculture, forestry, and fisheries, material culture changes and with it the types and mix of risks faced by its population. Old and well-known risks (e.g., infection with intestinal parasites spread by night soil used as fertilizer) will still afflict many, while a variety of new risks (e.g., contamination of food and water with industrial chemicals) will appear. The newly affluent, as a vanguard of development, can often insulate themselves from these risks. The poor are less able to do so. In the ideal scenario, overall risks would begin to decline as lifestyles change, poverty is reduced, and modern risks are more effectively controlled. In practice, however, this transition is never easy and, where poverty and discrimination remain or are growing, old risks can exist alongside new risks for generations. Thus near epidemic rates of "traditional" risks, such as tuberculosis, occur among the poor even in urban areas of the "modern" world.

In Vietnam, the risk transition has entered its most dangerous phase, the time when old risks remain serious but new risks are rapidly appearing. Public health and environmental management institutions, already overstretched trying to cope with traditional risks, are ill-equipped to take on the additional burden of emerging modern risks.

This is not to say that Vietnamese are not acquainted with risks and have no institutions to cope with them. Traditional rural society in northern and central Vietnam was characterized by a very high level of risk to individual survival including threats associated with the natural environment, a predatory state, bandits, and war. In response to these risks it had evolved strong social institutions to help individuals cope with the all too frequent disasters that befell them. The "closed corporate" peasant villages of the Red River delta, in which individual households were tightly integrated into largely autonomous self-managing communities, can be seen as an adaptation to an unpredictable environment characterized by frequent natural disasters (floods, droughts, crop failures), banditry and social unrest, and intense competition for land and other scarce resources. In trast, the much more benign environment of the Mekong River delta fa evolution of an "open peasantry" in which local settlements lacked a well-developed capability for self-mobilization to meet threats (Rambo 1973).

In contemporary Vietnam, many of these traditional natural hazards still threaten the survival of villagers. *Nhan Dan*, the party newspaper, may be the only national newspaper in Southeast Asia that features a daily front-page column reporting on current natural disasters and preparations to better cope with impending ones. The year 1999 was a particularly bad one, with the central provinces first devastated by the most serious drought in a century followed by massive flooding in many localities. Plagues of grasshoppers and locusts and outbreaks of rats damaged the harvest in many Mekong delta provinces. Whirlwinds and hailstorms wreaked havoc in several parts of the northern mountains. Less frequently noted, but still all too prevalent in the countryside, are the less spectacular daily environmental risks to which villagers are exposed: infection with intestinal parasites, malaria, Japanese B encephalitis and, in the smoke-filled houses of ethnic minorities in the mountains, eye infections and respiratory illnesses.

At the same time, modernization and industrialization have resulted in the modification of many traditional risks in ways that make them more dangerous. Flooding in the Mekong River delta, for example, has always occurred but local society had evolved ways of coping that minimized the damage it inflicted. Houses were often constructed so as to be easily dismantled and transported to safe areas in years of deep floods. Modern-style masonry structures cannot be moved. Floodwaters also quickly drained away through the vast network of streams and canals that crisscrossed flood-prone areas. In recent years, expansion of the road network (which creates barriers to drainage) and conversion of flood retention basins to agricultural uses have made the impacts of floods more serious and longer lasting.

The resurgence of malaria and the rapid spread of dengue fever in recent years offer other examples of modification of old risks into more dangerous threats. In the case of malaria, troops returning from Cambodia introduced chloroquine-resistant varieties that have now become a serious health problem in many areas of the Vietnamese highlands. The spread of dengue-hemorrhagic fever, on the other hand, has been facilitated by careless disposal of a modern product, plastic bags, which provide ideal breeding habitats for the *Aedes* mosquito that carries this disease.

In addition to these old and modified traditional risks, modern risks are being introduced at a frightening pace. We have noted many of these new risks above in this chapter. They include increases in the amount and types of air, noise, and water pollution; chemical residues in food; exposure to agricultural chemicals; traffic and workplace hazards; and new environmental risks associated with large-scale monocropping.

RESPONSES

Unfortunately, new threats to human health and the environment cannot be reversed by turning back to a simpler time. The process of modernization that is the source of these new risks is both the problem and the cure. In this regard, we expect responses to environmental and health problems to reflect, paradoxically, the simultaneous development of new structures of governance and new opportunities for individual and collective expression. We cannot predict how these social conventions will develop in Vietnam, although we can attempt to point to some possibilities. For simplicity, we have grouped these into three categories: regulatory responses, public awareness, and for-profit environmental services.

Regulatory Responses

Since the mid-1980s, the government of Vietnam has been active in environmental protection through the creation of natural area reserves, sponsorship of research projects, and capacity building in its regulatory and monitoring system. Many of these efforts were inaugurated in preparation of change. Among these, the most notable are efforts to regulate and monitor environmental impacts. Many others look back, carrying with them a clear sense of the need to preserve Vietnam's natural and cultural heritage. Among these, we include efforts to create and manage national parks and reserves, as well as the major programs on re-greening of upland areas.

Environmental issues were first raised to national consciousness through the Draft Conservation Strategy, a document prepared in 1985 by the Center for Natural Resources and Environmental Studies with assistance from the International Union for the Conservation of Nature (IUCN). The preparation of this document, and the research activities that preceded it, provided a means for a diverse group of academics to focus their thoughts around the issues that were pressing at the time: the rapid and unsustainable exploitation of natural resources that followed reunification. Many personal relationships grew out of this activity, and although the draft document was not accepted by the government, its agenda for research and action was carried over into the two major national environmental programs of the 1990s.

In 1990, a conference was organized in Hanoi with support from the United Nations Development Program, the International Union for the Conservation of Nature, and the Swedish International Development Agency around the theme of sustainable development. Shortly thereafter, Vietnamese participants of the conference submitted a framework for action[6] to the Council of Ministers (now the Office of Government). This framework, which included seven programs of action,[7] was accepted by the government in 1992. A corresponding program of research, the National Research Program on Environmental Protection, was inaugurated at around the same time (1991). This four-year program was divided into seventeen research projects grouped around four themes: regulation and monitoring, environmental abatement technology, environmental management, and social impacts. Much of the baseline data that appeared in research articles and conference papers through the mid-1990s was generated through these two programs.

The government of Vietnam has been attempting to establish a comprehensive structure for environmental management. The basic legal framework for environmental regulation in Vietnam is the Law on Environmental Protection (LEP), put into effect on January 10, 1994. The Ministry of Science, Technology and Environment, created in 1993, plays the major role of enforcing provisions of the LEP. Among other things, the LEP requires environmental impact assessments (EIAs) of new industrial plants and land use plans, authorizes the government to levy environmental taxes or charges, requires MOSTE to issue ambient and source standards for various types of pollution, and authorizes inspections pursuant to these requirements. MOSTE carries out its regulatory responsibilities through the National Environmental Agency (NEA), established in 1995, which works through provincial and district offices of MOSTE to monitor compliance with environmental standards.

The LEP appeared first as an enabling legislation that laid out rights, responsibilities, and relationships rather than legal stipulations. The LEP thus goes to great lengths to identify structural relationships between ministries, political-administrative units, economic units, and individuals through which the law will be carried out. It is important to note here that these relationships take precedence over actual legal stipulations in the LEP. For this reason, it may be best to regard the LEP as many Vietnamese do: as a sign that the Communist Party and the government of Vietnam, represented by the National Assembly and the various ministries, had reached a consensus on the *importance* of environmental issues and the *need* to regulate environmental impacts.

Having reached a consensus through the National Assembly, the real task of creating guidelines for implementation shifted to the prime minister's office, the Office of the Government, and the ministries. These offices have since issued a constant stream of decrees, decisions, circulars, and guidelines. Among these we include two of the most important with regard to environmental monitoring and regulation: the Environmental Standards issued by MOSTE in 1995 and, more recently, guidance on legal proceedings concerning the violation of stipulations related to the environment (1996). These two documents are the core regulations governing the environment. To them are added specific regulations for industries and sectors issued by relevant ministries including the Ministry of Health, the Ministry of Industry, the Ministry of Construction, and the Ministry of Agriculture and Rural Development.

In its efforts to develop regulatory capacity, the government of Vietnam has been bound both by the past (ministries are responsible for enforcement for enterprises under their jurisdiction) and by its anticipation of the future (many of the regulations have been borrowed from developed countries). This places MOSTE in a bind. Although charged with monitoring and enforcement of environmental regulations, regulators may be hampered in these efforts by a variety of conditional factors. These conditions include economic stability (particularly with respect to small producers and state-owned enterprises), ambiguity in the regulations, and conflicts between MOSTE and specific guidelines issued by ministries relating to their own productive activities. Conditionality of this sort breeds red tape, ineffective enforcement, and corruption. At the same time, conditionality provides an opening for local consensus-building and regulatory adjustments. This is, apparently, one of the intentions of the law as Article 30 states:

> Organizations, individuals engaged in production, business and other activities that cause environmental degradation, environmental pollution, environmental incidents must implement remedial measures as specified by the local People's Committees and by the State management agency for environmental protection, and shall be liable for damages according to regulations by the law.

For foreign companies who enter this ambiguous situation it may all seem unfair, especially if their notion of fairness is based on an equal application of legal structures outside human relationships. For many Vietnamese, however, such a structural approach to regulation seems inhumane since it cannot accommodate difference. In the West, there have been increasing trends to negotiate settlements over environmental disputes within the *framework* of the law. In Vietnam, the trend may be in the same direction but with a different outcome: negotiating settlements as a means of gradually *implementing* the law. This distinction is particularly important because many of the regulations issued by ministries and offices, including some of MOSTE's environmental standards, look forward to conditions of "industrialization and modernization" that do not reflect the current conditions.[8] Without some means of negotiating staged compliance and the modification of standards, there would be no end to the issuance of fines, and no limit to the workload of regulators.

Public Awareness

Public awareness of environmental issues, regulations, and their rights to prosecute offenders has been an important feature in pressuring government agencies to both enforce laws and address grievances. Environmental stories appear almost daily in the popular press and are frequently featured on television news programs. The press has been encouraged to promote environmental awareness both directly through provision of environmental training courses for journalists and indirectly through the constitution (Article 74[9]), the Law on Environmental Protection (Article 43[10]), and circulars such as 36 CT/TW (1998) on "enhancing environmental protection in the period of industrialization and modernization."

Although many of the stories presented in the press contain inaccuracies, sensationalisms, and stereotypes, they nevertheless have helped to raise public awareness of environmental issues. This is not to say that citizens never complained about environmental issues in the past (see DiGregorio et al. 1995). Rather, these complaints have received greater standing in public consciousness and an institutional structure for negotiation. In accordance with the LEP, citizens are requested to make complaints through local People's Committees. If complaints cannot be resolved locally, outside authorities may be brought in to negotiate a settlement. If grievances cannot be settled through this procedure, citizens have organized, and the state has accepted, public protest as a means of pressuring for a resolution.[11]

The significance of the LEP can easily be underestimated by foreigners who are unaware of its role as an enabling document and outline of rights, relationships, and responsibilities. It can equally be mistaken for a copy of similar legislation in other countries, complete with requirements for Environmental Impact Assessments, environmental standards, fines, charges, and other economic instruments. But as Dara O'Rourke (2001) has pointed out, public complaints and media exposure have served an important, though post-impact, role in negotiating compliance with environmental regulations. What is lacking in this process, and what makes it inefficient, is difficult access to information (such as provincial "State of the Environment" reports) and rights to public review (such as the review of EIAs). Finally, it is not clear how settlements will be enforced without the participation of the legal system. As yet, there is no framework for citizens to present a class action suit against environmental offenders. Although this will likely serve only as a last resort in stalled processes of negotiation, such class action suits are likely to become necessary in the future. Referring back to the case of Nam Son landfill in Hanoi, although a settlement was negotiated between residents and the Hanoi People's Committee, this settlement must rely on goodwill rather than legal standing to insure implementation. Since the dispute began with noncompliance issues and escalated into a public protest, there is no guarantee without participation of the legal system that noncompliance issues will not emerge again.

For-profit Environmental Services

Over the past fifteen years, foreign donors have assisted Vietnam in building regulatory capacity and raising public awareness of environmental issues. Much less effort has been expended on developing economically motivated private environmental services, the third pillar in the environment governance structure. That is not to say that environmental service providers have not emerged, especially in urban areas. With regard to direct services, they include companies and individuals that install and maintain sanitation systems, set up and maintain water supply systems, provide advice and equipment for environmental impact abatement, plant trees, and collect and recycle wastes. Indirect services include a variety of both Vietnamese and foreign technical and law consultancies, the former often linked to government or university research institutes. Environmental service providers have appeared in response to economic incentives, including the need for information and advice in order to comply with regulations, such as environmental impact assessments. They are likely to increase in number and variety as environmental regulations are increasingly enforced.

The private environmental services sector is currently underdeveloped in Vietnam largely because many of the functions that could be carried out in the private sector are carried out by the public sector. We do not wish to suggest a wholesale conversion of these activities from public to private as a means of improving environmental management. For example, experience has shown that public sector management of domestic solid waste is necessary to provide cross-subsidies between more-affluent and less-affluent residents of urban areas (Lee 1997). This does not mean, however, that there is no space for a mixture of public and private services. In Hanoi, for example, the public sector manages the majority of domestic, clinical, and industrial waste while private recyclers, including those who collect food wastes to feed pigs, manage the remainder.

In summary, there are clear indications that the environmental regulatory apparatus, which grew out of public concern expressed through the National Assembly, will be augmented by a more environmentally conscious public that has been empowered by the constitution, law, and recent experience to file complaints and demand compensation for environmental impacts. Lagging behind, a for-profit environmental services sector is also developing. This sector, motivated by economic incentives, is currently strongest in direct services and indirect research and advisory services conducted through private and university-based research institutions. Other areas of the environmental services sector, such as environmental law and advocacy firms, will develop as the implementation of environmental regulations improves.

We opened this chapter with reference to a pair of slogans. We wish to end with a further reference to these slogans. The first, which encourages the nation's citizens to "push forward" development, is displayed on a huge sign hung prominently in what to many is the heart of Vietnam's cultural identity, the site where, almost a thousand years ago, the nation and its capital were proclaimed. The slogan on the second sign, smaller and on the side of the road, is less prominent, but what matters is the fact that it is there at all. In the various development booms that swept across East and Southeast Asia following World War II, environmental concerns were rarely, if ever, regarded as anything more than a needless obstacle to development. Environmental awareness arose only as the real costs of pursuing this obsession with national gain—measured by savings and investment rates, incremental capital-output ratios and gross national product—began to be recognized. For the newly affluent, their newfound wealth lost a bit of its gleam when measured against decline in the noneconomic quality of life brought about by degradation of the environment. For the poor, environmental degradation resulted in a loss of critical natural resources on which they depended for their livelihoods and declines in health and comfort caused by ever-increasing pollution. As these two very different types of environmental awareness converged, they became the basis of social movements that have sought environmental justice for some and the improvement of environmental quality for all (Lee and So 1999).

We have heard many times through press releases that the leadership of the Vietnamese Communist Party and the Vietnamese government are learning from the experiences of neighboring countries and we believe that the appearance of environmental protection on the national development agenda is one indication of this.

NOTES

Much of the research on which this chapter is based was conducted by the authors while they were associated with the Center for Natural Resources and Environmental Studies (CRES) of Vietnam National University, Hanoi. We would like to express our deep gratitude to Dr. Le Trong Cuc, CRES director, and his staff for all of the assistance that we have received over the years.

This chapter was drafted at a writing workshop held at the Center for Southeast Asian Studies, Kyoto University. Michael DiGregorio's participation in this workshop was funded from a grant to the East-West Center from the John D. and Catherine T. MacArthur Foundation.

1. In 1997, three new districts (Thanh Xuan Bac, Ho Tay, and Cau Giay) were added to Hanoi's urban area. The figures presented here only concern the historic urban core of Ba Dinh, Hoan Kiem, Dong Da, and Hai Ba Trung districts.

2. Since 1992, non-Hanoi residents have had their pedicab licenses revoked. At the same time, many streets have been closed to pedicab traffic. Although subject to fines, harassment, and confiscations, many rural pedicab drivers continue to work on forged residency papers.

3. The "sacred forests" that survived until recently in many areas of the Red River delta were often associated with gravesites.

4. In at least one way, however, this is preferable to planned unit developments: farmers can earn profit on the speculative value of their land. Land valuation is one of many sticking points in the conversion of agricultural land. State construction companies working alone or in joint ventures with foreign companies attempt to pay for land at its agricultural value (measured in rice yields) rather than its speculative value (measured in comparison to other housing projects).

5. It is not uncommon for owners of fish ponds in urbanizing areas to *ask* neighbors to fill their ponds with household and construction waste as a means of converting them to housing land.

6. National Program on the Environment and Sustainable Development: Framework for Action.

7. Urban development and population control, management of watershed forests, management of coastal regions and river mouths, protection of wetlands, maintenance of biodiversity, creation of reserves and parks, pollution control, and waste treatment.

8. For example, Article 29 of the LEP, which "strictly prohibits" burning of forests, automatically relegates swidden cultivation of all forms to the category of environmental offense.

9. The citizen has the right to lodge complaints and denunciations with the competent state authorities against the illegal doings of state organs, economic bodies, social organizations, units of the people's armed forces, or of any individual.

10. Organizations, individuals have the right to complain, denounce to the state management agency for environmental protection or other competent state agencies about activities in breach of environmental protection legislation.

11. In the case of protests at Hanoi's landfill, the actions of local residents were supported by local authorities who could then play an intermediary role in resolving the conflict.

7

Gender Relations: Ideologies, Kinship Practices, and Political Economy

Hy V. Luong

In the era of economic reforms and globalization in the 1990s, gender relations in Vietnam were at the intersection of major crosscurrents. In the village of Hoai Thi in the northern province of Bac Ninh, for example, patrilocal residence was practiced de rigueur. Throughout northern and north central Vietnam, patrilineages were strongly revitalized. Kinship relations became more male-oriented in many aspects. Yet, at least in the village of Hoai Thi, daughters enjoyed a good share of family inheritance, probably more than at any point in its contemporary history. Similarly, beyond the kinship domain, in the 1990s, on the one hand, female bodies were commodified with the resurgence of prostitution throughout the country. They were also victimized in any police crackdown, as it was generally the prostitutes and not their male customers who had to undergo reeducation. Customers might be asked to pay only small administrative fines. They had to stand trials only if they engaged in sexual relations with underage prostitutes. On the other hand, in the 1990s, the post-1975 decline in women's political representation was reversed: women played a more important role in political leadership toward the end of this decade than in the preceding fifteen years. The full understanding of these and other contradictory currents requires a historically grounded analysis of gender relations within the larger political, economic, and ideological frameworks.

In this chapter, I focus on how gender relations among ethnic Vietnamese were shaped by the interplay of ideologies and political economy in the 1990s. I draw heavily upon the findings on ethnic Vietnamese in the northern part of the country, since little systematic research has been conducted among other ethnic groups in Vietnam and since there have been relatively fewer field research projects in southern and central Vietnam.

VIETNAMESE KINSHIP AND GENDER ROLES:
HISTORICAL PERSPECTIVES

Vietnamese women historically played a fundamental role in the Vietnamese economy and in generating household incomes through commerce, handicraft production, and agriculture. As early as 1688, a Chinese traveler to Hanoi remarked: "Trade was the domain of women. Even the wives of high-ranking mandarins were not concerned about losing face [through their trading activities]" (Thanh The Vy 1961: 91; see also Dampier 1906: 608).

Barrow, who visited the trading port of Faifo in central Vietnam at the end of the eighteenth century, similarly observed:

> In Cochinchina it would appear . . . to be the fate of the weaker sex to be doomed to those occupations which require, if not the greatest exertions of bodily strength, at least the most persevering industry. We observed them day after day, and from morning till night, standing in the midst of pools of water, up to the knees, occupied in the transplanting of rice. In fact, all the labours of tillage, and the various employments connected with agriculture, seem to fall to the share of the female peasantry; while those in Turon, to the management of domestic concerns, add the superintendance of all the details of commerce. They even assist in constructing and keeping in repair their mud-built cottages; they conduct the manufacture of coarse earthenware vessels; they manage the boats on rivers and in harbours; they bear the articles of produce to market; they draw the cotton wool from the pod, free it from the seeds, spin it into thread, weave it into cloth, dye it of its proper colour, and make it up into dresses for themselves and their families. (Barrow 1975: 303–4; see also Crawfurd 1970b: 270)

The findings on nineteenth- and early-twentieth-century Vietnam support Barrow's observation on Vietnamese women's active roles not only in commerce but also in agriculture (including land ownership) and manufacturing. In agriculture, in the early nineteenth century, female landowners made up 22 percent and 17.5 percent of the landowners respectively in the northern provinces of Ha Dong and Thai Binh (Phan Huy Le et al. 1995: 26; Phan Huy Le et al. 1997: 465), and 6–34 percent of those in a sample of six hamlets in the six southern provinces in the nineteenth century (Nguyen Dinh Dau 1994: 159–60). In manufacturing, for example, at the turn of the twentieth century, women owned two of the three largest ceramics kilns in the famous northern pottery center of Bat Trang (Luong 1998).

Despite women's major roles in the economy and their wealth accumulation through mercantile and other activities, both Vietnamese public life and the Vietnamese kinship and household system were strongly male-centered.

In the public arena, until the introduction of French colonial education, education and bureaucratic positions were strictly a male domain. Despite the legendary prominence of some women as troop commanders or literary figures in Vietnamese history, before the twentieth century, women had access neither to formal Confucian education nor to positions in the national mandarinate or in local village administrations.[1] They had no official roles in village communal houses, which served as the seats of local power and local tutelary deity worship. Their worship fora were restricted mainly to local Buddhist pagodas and various shrines.

Women's lack of public authority had its parallel in a male-centered kinship system familiar to students of East Asian kinship. It was a hierarchical model in which descent was traced mainly through men; postmarital residence was predominantly patrilocal (a newlywed couple residing with the husband's parents after marriage); inheritance was heavily in favor of sons who were responsible for ancestors' worship and patriline continuity; and authority, both domestic and public, rested with men (see Luong 1992: 71ff.). In the internal logic of this model, the marriage of a man to many wives in a polygynous relation was to ensure the birth of sons and the male-centered continuity of the patriline. When a first wife was late or incapable of bearing sons, she might take the initiative in arranging for her husband to take another wife, and she held special maternal responsibilities toward the latter's sons (75). Although the Vietnamese family and kinship system was also underlain by an alternative bilateral model that stressed children's additional linkages to their mothers, this model did not operate strongly in the northern and central parts of Vietnam and among the Confucian-educated elite (76–77). The male-oriented kinship model was reinforced by the Confucian ideology that emphasized women's threefold subordination to their fathers, husbands, and sons. Women's visible roles in the economy were intended not to replace their domestic duties but to increase the financial resources of the households for which they were responsible (see Luong 1989). In the ceramic-manufacturing center of Bat Trang, for example, it was in many cases women's entrepreneurship that sustained their households' livelihoods and enabled men to concentrate on studying in pursuit of bureaucratic careers (see Luong 1998). While a woman's important role in household management was acknowledged with her appellation as *noi tuong* (domestic general), this acknowledgment and her significant financial contributions did not necessarily lead to any increase in her authority.

The French colonial period witnessed the opening of education and low public-service positions (such as schoolteachers and nurses) to women. The ratio of female to male students in primary education increased from virtually no female students in 1880, to 1 to 12.5 in 1930 (Indochine 1931: 19–20). However, neither the male domination in the public domain, nor the dominant male-centered model of kinship and household relations, was fundamentally transformed in the French colonial era (see Marr 1981: chap. 5).

THE POST-INDEPENDENCE ERA

After independence from France in 1954, in both the U.S.-allied south and the socialist north, Western ideologies of both non-Marxist and Marxist varieties underlay the significantly improved access of women to educational opportunities (including in higher education), their inroads into the political arena, as well as the legal prohibition of polygyny. However, it was in the north that the state launched a more frontal attack on the material and ideological foundations of the male-oriented kinship and family system by collectivizing most land, undermining patrilineages, specifying the equal inheritance rights of both sons and daughters in the 1959 family and marriage law, and encouraging the replacement of sacred ancestral worship with commemoration of parents and grandparents among Communist Party members and beyond (Nguyen Duc Truyen 1997: 51, and Pham van Bich 1999). However, the male-oriented kinship model remained powerful in shaping gender relations, even in the socialist north. Postmarital residence remained overwhelmingly patrilocal, and household division of labor, heavily male-centered. The male-oriented kinship model continued providing an influential conceptual framework that undermined to some extent the state's attempts to restructure gender relations in the public and domestic arenas.

By 1989, in Vietnam, the gender gap had virtually been eliminated in primary education, and significantly reduced at higher levels. As seen in table 7.1, there was no longer much difference in the school attendance rates of boys and girls below the age of 10. In the next age group, 81.7 percent of boys and 73.2 percent of girls attended schools at the time of the 1989 census, revealing a gap of 8.5 percent. Among teenagers from the age of 15 to 19, 27.9 percent of boys and 19.3 percent of girls still attended schools at that time, showing a similar gap of 8.6 percent. This gap continued in postsecondary education as 61 percent of the postsecondary degree holders in 1989 were male, and only 39 percent were female (Vietnam, National Census Steering Committee 1991, II: 359).[2] However, from a historical perspective, the gender gap in education in the post-independence era had been considerably narrowed from that in the French colonial period.

Table 7.1.   Gender and Education in Vietnam in 1989 and 1999

	Male			Female		
Age Group	(1)	(2)	(3)	(1)	(2)	(3)
1989 Census						
5–9	60.5	.8	36.2	59.8	.9	39.2
10–14	81.7	13.4	7.4	73.2	18.4	8.3
15–19	27.9	64.8	7.2	19.3	73.1	7.6
1999 Census						
5–9	75.5	.8	23.6	75	.9	24
10–14	87.4	9.5	3.1	83.3	13.1	3.6
15–19	49.3	46.6	4.1	38.6	56.7	4.7

Sources: Vietnam, National Census Steering Committee 1991, III: 12–13; Vietnam, National Census Steering Committee 2000: 145.
Note: (1) currently attending school; (2) having stopped attending school; (3) never attending school.

The narrowing gap in education went hand in hand with the wider participation of women in public life, both through a wider variety of occupations and through a more visible participation in the political arena.

The percentage of women in the state bureaucracy of unified Vietnam reached 51.4 percent in 1989, although they were still overwhelmingly concentrated in certain domains like education, health care, and accounting or finances, which accounted for 70.1 percent of the bureaucratic workforce (see table 7.2).[3] At a higher level, by 1989, while women still occupied a little more than one-sixth of the managerial positions in the Communist Party and government (table 7.3), and while there had never been any woman in the all-powerful Political Bureau (Politburo) of the Vietnamese Communist Party and only one woman full minister in Hanoi, this figure already represented a significant achievement over the pre-independence period. The percentage of woman deputies in the pre–Doi Moi and largely symbolic National Assembly steadily increased from 2.5 percent in the first election in 1946 to 32.3 percent in 1976 (table 7.3). Women's greater access to public power was partly facilitated by the historical context of the American war, during which millions of men were mobilized into armed services. In the north, the state exhorted women to shoulder three main responsibilities (*ba dam dang*): for production and work, for the family, and for national defense (Le thi Nham Tuyet 1975: 291–319).

After the end of the American war in 1975, women's participation in the public domain suffered a precipitous decline. The percentage of female deputies in the largely symbolic National Assembly dropped steadily from 32.3 percent in 1975–1976 to 17.7 percent in 1987–1992. Those in People's Councils dropped from 28.6 percent in 1985–1989 to 11 percent in 1989–1994 at the provincial level, from 19.4 percent to 13 percent at the district level, and from 19.7 percent to 16.5 percent at the commune and ward level for the same period (Tran thi Van Anh and Le Ngoc Hung 1996: 202).[4] Toward the end of this period, the percentages of women in managerial positions in the government and in enterprises were also low

Table 7.2.   Women in the Vietnamese Bureaucracy in 1989, by Percentage

	Female	*Male*
Managerial positions in government and in the Communist Party	16.9	83.1
Managerial positions in enterprises	12.9	87.1
Law and inspection	22.8	77.2
Financial and planning	48	52
Technology	26.8	73.2
Culture and arts	34.7	65.3
Education and research	65.6	34.4
Health care	72.5	27.5
Other	46	54
Total	**48.6**	**51.4**

Source: Vietnam, National Census Steering Committee 1991, III: 11, 15.

Table 7.3. Women in the Vietnamese National Assembly, by Percentage

Period	1946–60	1960–64	1964–71	1971–75	1975–76	1976–81	1981–87	1987–92	1992–97	1997–02	2002–
Percentage of Women	2.5	11.6	18	29.7	32.3	26.8	21.8	17.7	18.5	26.2	27.3

Source: Tran thi Van Anh and Le Ngoc Hung 1996: 2000; and Vietnam-General Statistical Office 2000a: 102.

at 16.9 percent and 12.9 percent, respectively (table 7.2). The percentages of women in top leadership positions were even lower: in 1991, women made up only 1.4 percent and 2 percent, respectively, of the chairs of the district and provincial people's committees (heads of district and provincial governments); 2.2 percent and 2.4 percent of district and provincial party secretaries (heads of Communist Party organizations at the district and provincial levels), 8.2 percent of the membership of the Central Committee of the Communist Party, and 0 percent in the supreme Politburo of the party (Vietnam-General Statistical Office 2000a: 100, 101, 109–13).

On one level, the decline in the percentage of woman deputies in the National Assembly and probably in other domains reflects the return of male war veterans, many highly decorated and inducted into the Communist Party during the American war. They displaced many women who had filled managerial and leadership positions during the war years.

On a deeper level, the aforementioned decline reflects the socialist state's partial ideological concession to the male-centered model in the kinship and family domains and the fairly popular support for this model in people's daily lives. For example, a major policy address on women by the late first secretary of the Communist Party, Le Duan, elaborated at length on the significance of the family and the unique domestic role of women in the child-rearing process (Le Duan 1974: 57–69, see also Werner 1981b: 187–88).[5] At the local level, in the commune of Hai Van in the northern province of Ha Nam Ninh, the father in a family shared an average of 20 percent of the domestic chores with his wife and children, even when heavy chores such as well-water transportation were included (Houtart and Lemercinier 1981: 175–76; cf. Ngo thi Chinh 1977: 69–70). When male soldiers and cadres returned to this commune from the war in 1975–1976, the number of women in the active local workforce decreased by 251 (14.8 percent) in a two-year period, at least partly because many women found heavy the double burden of both domestic work and paid labor participation. The ratio of females to males in the local agricultural and industrial workforce dropped dramatically from 1.45 in 1974 (1,695 women and 1,167 men) to .92 in 1978 (1,355 women and 1,473 men; Houtart and Lemercinier 1981: 37).

In the northern ceramic production center of Bat Trang, the highest-ranked female manager since 1954, the president of a ceramics cooperative from 1985 to 1988, elaborated on some of the difficulties of being a female manager in her narrative to me:

> The job of the president of Hop Thanh cooperative . . . was a demanding job, requiring frequent travel and extensive contact throughout the district and in Hanoi city. Although other people could represent me, or normally accompanied me whenever it was necessary to travel to other provinces, I still had to show up on the more important occasions. Upon returning home, I had to take a rest.
> . . . the time was also irregular. At times, I was still at work at 10 at night. At 2 o'clock in the morning, if a cooperative member came back with raw materials, I had to mobilize members to work to move them to the right areas in the cooperative. On occasions,

I was so sick that I could not eat much, but I still had to go. Nobody demanded it, but without me, without orders from above, cooperative members would be reluctant to proceed with tasks.

[How did you handle domestic chores during your terms as the cooperative president?] I was not good at all in domestic work. A cooperative president had no time left for domestic chores. I relied on my husband. [Did your husband take care of domestic chores?] My children did. My daughter was already 16 in 1985. She did well in her school and attended a school close to our home. She could therefore help with the work at home. But at times, the entire family lost sleep because at mid-night, I was called by a cooperative guard.

In this case of the female president of the Hop Thanh cooperative in Bat Trang, even her supportive husband contributed little to domestic chores. She could assume the position partly thanks to the help of a teenager daughter at home, and partly through the informal contact that, despite her gender, she had developed over the years in order to obtain credit and other forms of assistance. Female managers with younger children or older sons would have encountered the problem of domestic chore arrangements both for regular daily work outside the home and for extensive travel. This was not a problem faced by their male counterparts.

The persistence of the male-oriented model for kinship and family relations extended well beyond the domestic division of labor. In a survey of three hundred agricultural cooperative presidents (mostly male) in northern Vietnam, 71 percent of the respondents who had only daughters were determined to continue the procreative process until a son was born (Do Long 1985: 33). Many men still justified having multiple wives on the basis of the need for sons to continue the patriline. In a village in Tam Dao district of Vinh Phu province, forty-four cases of polygyny were identified in the 1977–1982 period, including a case of a man with four wives and three cases of men with three wives each (Duong thi Thanh Mai 1985: 67). In another village in Ha Bac province, the three daughters of a family having no son reportedly had to yield their ancestral home to their father's patrilineal nephew although he already owned a house in the neighborhood because the latter could worship the father after the father's death (Trinh thi Quang 1984: 48). A large number of women in all three regions of Vietnam also shared this male-centered need for sons to continue patrilines. In a regional comparative study in a northern, central, and southern commune in 1990, 41 percent of female respondents without sons in the northern commune of Van Nhan would like to stop having children, while 80 percent of those with one son and 90 percent of those with two sons would like to stop reproductive processes. In the central Vietnamese commune of Dien Hong, the corresponding figures were respectively 39 percent, 56 percent, and 86 percent, while in the southern commune of Than Cuu Nghia, they were 31 percent, 62 percent, and 95 percent (Nguyen thi Van Anh 1993: 39).

Postmarital residence remained overwhelmingly patrilocal. In a systematic and longitudinal analysis of demographic patterns in 1,300 households in thirteen communes and towns in Nam Dinh, Ninh Binh, and Ha Nam (lower Red River delta), Hirschman and Nguyen Huu Minh have found that 79–80 percent of men and women married in the 1956–1985 period lived with husbands' parents upon marriage. (The majority of remaining couples [about 15 percent in the aggregate] established separate households [Nguyen Huu Minh 1998: 223.]) A couple normally lived with the husband's parents for a period, then moved off to form their own household, leaving one of the husband's brothers and his wife staying with the parents on a long-term basis.[6] This accounts for the fact that about 75 percent of the households in the Red River delta in 1989 were nuclear, while patrilocal postmarital residence was still the norm.[7] In the Mekong delta village of Khanh Hau where I have conducted field research over the years, of the 738 full or disintegrated couples in a random sample of 340 households, 67 percent lived with the husband's parents upon marriage, 9 percent lived with the wife's parents, while 22 percent established their own residences (cf. Luong and Diep Dinh Hoa 2000: 52, 58).

In general, the majority of newlywed Vietnamese couples still lived with the husbands' parents at least for a number of years before establishing their own households. This pattern of postmarital residence added considerable psychosocial pressures on women. They had to take care not only of their nuclear families, but also their husbands' parents and even the latter's nonadult siblings. They had to adapt to daily patterns and food preferences in their husbands' families (further elaborated below). Parents-in-law, and mothers-in-law in particular, seldom allowed their sons to alleviate the daughters-in-law's domestic burdens, since domestic chores were considered the primary responsibilities of women. I would suggest that the continuing strength of patrilocal residence contributed to the persistence of domestic labor division and to the emphasis on women's economic contributions simply as a part of their *domestic* duties, which in turn exerted a major adverse impact on women's abilities to participate on an equal footing with men in the political arena (cf. Werner 2002).

KINSHIP AND GENDER RELATIONS IN THE ERA OF ECONOMIC REFORMS AND GLOBALIZATION

Sociocultural and political economic crosscurrents on gender relations intensified in Vietnam in the 1990s when the country became more integrated into the regional and global economies. The male-oriented kinship system continued its resurgence at the same time that women generally gained more economic opportunities, as well as a greater visibility in the political arena under the Vietnamese state's affirmative action program.

In May 1994, the Central Committee of the Vietnamese Communist Party issued decree 37, an affirmative action plan to increase the number of women in governmental and economic management positions. As a result, the percentage of female deputies in the Vietnamese National Assembly increased sharply from 18.5 percent in the 1992 election to 26.2 percent in 1997 and 27.3 percent in 2002 (table 7.3). The percentages of women in local People's Councils also increased from 11 percent in 1989 to 20.4 percent in 1994 at the provincial level, and from 13 percent to 18.1 percent at the district level in the same period. In the more powerful executive branch of the Vietnamese government, by the end of the 1990s, women had headed one ministry (Labor) and filled the deputy minister ranks in some influential ministries like Finance.[8] The percentages of female chairs of People's Committees (heads of local administrations) increased from 2 percent in 1991 to 3.3 percent in 1996 at the provincial level, and from 1.4 percent to 4.5 percent at the district level in the same period. Within the powerful Communist Party, a woman was elected for the first time to the Politburo in 1996. The percentage of female Central Committee members also increased from 8.2 percent in 1991 to 10.6 percent in 1996. The percentages of female Communist Party secretaries increased from 2.4 percent in 1991 to 8.3 percent in 1996 at the provincial level, and correspondingly from 2.2 percent to 3.7 percent at the district level (see table 7.4).

Beyond the political domain, in the 1990s, women also participated more actively in the market-oriented economy, as white-collar workers, entrepreneurs, industrial workers, domestic workers, and sexual commodities. The Vietnam Living

Table 7.4. Women in Leadership Positions in the Vietnamese Communist Party and Local Governments, by Percentage

	1991–1996	1996–2001	2001–
Communist Party—National Level			
Politburo	0	5.3	0
Central Committee	8.2	10.6	8
Communist Party and Local Government—Provincial, District, and Commune Levels			
Provincial			
Party secretary	2.4	8.3	—
Chief of administration	2.0	3.3	—
Executive Administrative Committee	9.8	11.4	—
People's Council	11	20.4	—
District			
Party secretary	2.2	3.7	—
Chief of administration	1.4	4.5	—
Executive Administrative Committee	10.6	11.3	—
People's Council	13	18.1	—
Commune/Ward			
Party secretary	n/a	3.1	—
Chief of administration	n/a	2.5	—
Executive Administrative Committee	10	10.7	—
People's Council	16.5	14.1	—

Source: Vietnam-General Statistical Office 1998: 7; Vietnam-General Statistical Office 2000a: 100, 101, 109–13; Tran thi Van Anh and Le Ngoc Hung 1996: 202.

Standard Survey data reveal that women's earnings increased from 71 percent of men's earnings in 1992–1993 to 82 percent in 1997–1998 (Vietnam-General Statistical Office 2000b: 188). The growth of private mercantile activities, light industrial jobs in garment and footwear firms, and prostitution, all of which were dominated by women, might have helped to narrow the earnings gap between men and women, although further empirical research needs to be conducted on this issue. This narrowing income gap was facilitated by the fact that the gender gap in education did not increase with economic reforms. In 1999, among younger children below the age of ten, there was virtually no gap (table 7.1). Among children in the 10–14 years of age group, the gap was also narrowed from 8.5 percent in 1989 to 4.1 percent in 1999, while among teenagers from the ages of 15 to 19, the gap widened from 8.6 percent to 10.7 percent in the same period.

However, the greater visibility of women in the political arena and the narrowing wage gap between men and women did not result in a fundamental restructuring of gender relations within and beyond the domestic domain. In the labor market, paid maternity leave for women was reduced in the early 1990s from six to four months (Wong 1994: 14) and remained at this level throughout the 1990s. Women still had to retire at the age of fifty-five, in comparison to the retirement age of sixty for men. The debate in the Vietnamese National Assembly in 2000 that the law should give women the option of retiring at the age of fifty-five but the right to work until the age of sixty was inconclusive.

More pernicious within the context of a market economy and the growing class differentiation was the commodification of women's bodies through the significant growth of the sex industry and mistress arrangements. Government sources reported 40,000 female prostitutes in Vietnam in 2001, but this figure did not include the considerably larger number of hostesses in dancing clubs, karaoke and beer bars, and coffee shops, whose earnings came primarily from their sexual services (cf. Kolko 1997: 108).[9] The growing domestic prostitution in Vietnam since the onset of economic reforms results from the long-standing double standard of sexual mores in the Vietnamese sociocultural system, the growing wealth and inequality under economic reforms, as well as a gender bias in governmental clamp-downs on prostitution. Long-standing Vietnamese sexual mores considered men's pre- and extra-marital sex, while not ideal, less unacceptable than women's engagement in similar practices. While premarital sex among seriously dating young couples might be on the rise in urban contexts, virginity was expected considerably more of the woman at the time of marriage than of her husband (Gammeltoft 2002: 120ff.). This double moral standard also extended to extramarital sex. Second, emerging with the growing class differentiation, young women's greater concern with their own virginity, and the commodification process in society at large, were men with financial resources who were less constrained by social mores than their female counterparts. Even if they got caught in police crackdowns on prostitution, it was generally the female prostitutes and not their male customers who had to undergo reeducation. Besides small administrative fines, the strongest measure undertaken by the police on male customers of prostitution who were white-collar workers was to report their behavior to their work units, and not to their families, out of concern about the impact of the report on family harmony.

In the context of growing wealth differentiation, a number of poor young women were also trafficked to Cambodia and some other parts of East Asia as sex workers. Many poor women sold their bodies on a long-term basis to Taiwanese men in the hope of escaping poverty, which in many cases was brought about by illnesses in their families and the resulting indebtedness in the context of marketized health care in the era of economic reforms (see box 7.1).

Even if the market economy in Vietnam had not accentuated the commodification of women's bodies, in Vietnamese society under economic reforms, the wider economic and political opportunities for women were countered by the strong resurgence of a male-oriented kinship system as a result of the confluence of state policies on the one hand and household strategies and the gender socialization process on the other.

In the 1990s, the Vietnamese state redefined and contracted its role not only in the economic arena with the shift from a centrally planned to a market-oriented economy. It also restructured its role in the provision of social, medical, and educational services (see Luong's chapter on wealth and poverty), as well as relaxed its control of noneconomic and nonsecurity domains. In the relation between the household and the socialist state, the household became stronger in the 1990s than in the preceding three decades and a half, serving as the locus of economic, social, and cultural reproduction and transformation. This shift took place as the household shouldered greater shares of medical and educational costs, while protected less from consequences of the shocks of life-cycle-related mishaps (such as serious illness) and more vulnerable to market-induced economic shocks (e.g., dramatic changes in the prices of agricultural commodities, see my introduction to this volume).

Throughout the country, in the 1990s, life-cycle ceremonies (weddings and funerals) became considerably more elaborate, due to the need of households to maintain their informal networks of reciprocity, which could be mobilized in times of need (see Luong 1994 and Malarney, this volume). In the northern Vietnamese commune of Son Duong, where I did research over the years, if in 1991, the bride's and groom's banquets had had about 120 and 180 guests respectively, by 1998, the average size of a wedding banquet had reportedly increased to at least 240 guests. If the groom or one of the parents worked at a nearby state factory, the number of guests might reach 600 because coworkers from the state factory had to be invited. A death anniversary meal in Son Duong also increased in size from 20–30 guests in 1991 to 60–150 guests by 1998. The intensification of rituals and households' social networks was not restricted to Son Duong or northern Vietnam. It took place throughout the country (see also Luong 1994; Malarney, this volume; Kleinen 1999: chap. 8; Luong Hong Quang 1997: 169). The mutual assistance on the occasions of life-cycle ceremonies both reflected the strength of relations and reinforced them in

Box 7.1.   Trafficking in Young Women

PITIFUL SCENES OF A SPOUSE MARKET

It is too much to call it a "market." But it is really a market: it has sellers and buyers. It meets daily with hundreds of young women, mostly from the lower Mekong delta, sitting or standing around, waiting anxiously for wife-buying Taiwanese. This chaotic and pitiful scene takes place in a large neighborhood, in the Binh Thoi housing complex, in ward 8, district 11, in Ho Chi Minh City. Captain Vo Ngoc Thanh, the chief of police in ward 8 of district 11, speaks with a sense of disquiet: "People call it a love market, but it is more appropriately called a spouse market. The union is not based on love!"

Hundreds of Young Women Daily in the Market

They all are very young, seemingly between 18 and 20 in age, neatly dressed, carefully made up, but unable to disguise totally their rural roots. They all seem anxiously waiting. Their eyes brighten up to follow any male passer-by. . . .

. . . street corners are full of motorcycle-taxi drivers, . . . carrying cellular phones and ready to go. . . . Telephones ring constantly. From time to time, a few of them put the cellular phones in their pants pockets and roaringly head off with two or three of the young women. . . .

. . . In the afternoon of February 23, I incidentally stopped by the coffee shop of Ms. Six on 3A street which was also a gathering point for young women waiting to be examined. I felt quiet when the men taking them to examination places called them "goods." . . .

. . . At a refreshment stand at the corner of 1st and 6th streets, I sat down at a table where 2 young women had been sitting because other tables were full of "standing goods" (women). I was still trying to figure out a way to strike a conversation when a lottery ticket vendor invited me to buy lottery tickets. I shook my head and pointed to the two women at my table. The lottery ticket women disdainfully said: " I know these young women well. They look nice but have no money in their pockets. In my neighborhood, there are also young and nice-looking women, but they would rather sell lottery tickets than grabbing money in some other ways. . . ." I saw the two women lowering their heads. Concerned about their possible embarrassment, I quickly bought a few lottery tickets and gave one to each of them as a gift. I said half-jokingly: "God bless you and let you win the lottery, so that you do not have to live in far-away land. . . ." We quickly got acquainted. Loan, from Can Tho, had been there for 3 months; My, also from Can Tho, had arrived only 1 week earlier. . . . Loan spoke with tears in her eyes: "Little My is new here and not familiar with things. I am too fed up. I have been waiting daily, for months and in vain, for a man to choose me. My matron has said that if by the end of the month, nobody has chosen me, I will have to work as a beer bar girl or a prostitute to get money to pay [family] debts. . . ."

Many women in the spouse market do not hesitate to acknowledge that they need to marry Taiwanese men due to the need for money to provide assistance to their families. But like any woman, they also long for the happy endings of meeting husbands of their dreams. But reality is cruel. In the hasty transactions in the spouse market, financial arrangements are occasionally less than honest. How could we talk about love and obligations [in such market transactions]?

Purchase of a Wife to Work as a Call Girl!

". . . I swallowed the solution of marrying a Taiwanese husband simply because my mother wanted me to. I love my mother, my poor family, and my siblings. . . ."

. . . On December 11, 2000, through a matchmaker named Hien in the spouse market, Mrs. V.N.D. . . . decided to marry off her daughter H.M. to a middle-aged Taiwanese man named L.M.D., the owner of a bottled water company in Dong Nai [province].

"The old man asked me to go through a medical examination to make sure that I was still a virgin. Otherwise, he would not have agreed to marry me. I felt ashamed, but I did it anyway. The result met his demand. L.M.D paid the matching-making people, I do not know how much, who in turn gave my mother 7 million dong [less than U.S. $500]. . . ."

L.M.D. left with the young woman for a few days. Mrs. V.N.D. got worried and began searching for her daughter. The Taiwanese "groom" sent her [Mrs. L.M.D.] $100 through a third party to prepare for a wedding reception. He said that in conformity to Taiwanese customs, he and H.M. could not attend the reception!

"For a few days, L.M.D. took me to a hotel on Hoa Hao street, demanding sex. I refused because there was no wedding yet. He angrily called another woman to the room to have sex in front of me. Angry and embarrassed, I demanded to go home. . . . I refused to go along. . . . He forcefully raped me."

The daughter's narrative led Mrs. D. to file a grievance against the illegal group. . . .

"He [L.M.D.] told me that I was brave, and that he had deflowered over one hundred Vietnamese young women, few of whom dared to file a grievance against him because he could deal with anything with money. He said that the only woman filing a grievance saw her house destroyed by his gang from Taiwan. He advised me to work as a call girl, because he would be willing to introduce me to many Taiwanese male visitors to Vietnam. I only cry for my fate."

In response to Mrs. V.N.D.'s grievance, Captain Phan van Thanh, deputy chief of police in ward 8 of district 11, ordered ward police to look for L.M.D. in the hotels in the ward, but he had fled. . . .

Some women have found happiness, but this is rare. Mrs. Do thi Lan of Pham Ngu Lao ward in district 1 and Mrs. Bui thi Thu Ba in Cau Kho ward of district 1, revealed their secret: "We need to have education, to know a foreign language and the husband's customs, but most importantly, relations must be based, not on monetary gains, but on sentiments." This criterion is seldom met

among the women in the spouse market and among the Taiwanese men searching for wives.
Quy Phong, *Nguoi Lao Dong,* Feb. 26, 2001 and Feb. 28, 2001

BITTER FATE OF A SELECTED BRIDE

It was only 7:00 a.m. when 21 young Vietnamese women waited in the main lobby of hotel PL on Le van Sy street. They all looked tense and worried. In a short while, like commodities, they had to be lined up for customers to choose. I was lucky to be present at this selection event thanks to my friend T., a specialist in exit paperwork for Vietnamese women marrying Taiwanese men. T. was present at every selection meeting, so that if any woman was chosen, he would take her file from the matchmaker to different agencies for marriage registration, medical examination, and consular interview booking. T. would be paid U.S. $1,500 for all the paperwork, and had to cover all the fees and expenses out of this amount. I came to the hotel as his assistant. Within 10 minutes, three men, 2 Taiwanese and 1 Vietnamese, came down from the second floor. The Vietnamese man, I was told, was P., a major "matchmaker" in the city with 10–40 women from the countryside living in his house and waiting to be chosen. Whenever a prospective Taiwanese groom arrived, he was ready with his "goods." The older Taiwanese man, around 60, was the Taiwanese matchmaker. The third man was a prospective groom, about 40 years old.

"Why are there so many matchmakers?" I asked. T. explained:

"The Taiwanese matchmaking man is responsible for identifying those who need Vietnamese wives. A prospective groom pays him U.S. $8,000 to $10,000. The Taiwanese matchmaker will cover all expenses, including airfare from Taiwan and lodging and meals for 5 days here. The Taiwanese matchmaker will give his Vietnamese counterpart $4,500 to cover the expenses in connection with the selection process, wedding expenses, brideprice, and the paperwork for the bride's departure from Vietnam. . . ."

The Taiwanese "groom" looked carefully at each woman, up and down a few times, and then he shook his head in disappointment. . . . He returned to his room, leaving the space for other Taiwanese men. None of the 21 women was chosen by the 3 Taiwanese men. They quietly left with the motorcycle-taxi drivers. Each driver drove 2 women. . . . The matchmaker P. was impatient, calling nonstop with his cellular phone. Within a few minutes, 30 other women were driven to the hotel. This time, a Taiwanese "groom" selected 5 women for further interviews. The matchmaker P. acted as an interpreter. The former asked the same set of questions: "Are you still a virgin?" "Once arriving in Taiwan, you cannot demand to return to Vietnam." "Why do you want to marry a Taiwanese man?" Some women trembled during the interview and became forgetful of what had just been asked. . . . After the preliminary interviews, he chose 2 for the final round. This time, he looked carefully at the physical appearance, the walk, and finally selected one. For anybody selected from this group of young women provided by other matchmakers, P. had to pay $100 to the matchmaker providing the selected girl.

Instant Marriage

The selected woman could not return to her matchmaker's place. She had to go to the "groom"'s hotel room for the marriage to be consummated right away. The matchmaker P. immediately informed the bride's family that they had to attend a wedding the following day or within two days because the groom would stay in Vietnam only for 5 days altogether. The matchmakers controlled the timing in such a way as to reduce their own costs. The wedding dinner would have only 2–3 tables [20–30 people in attendance]. The fewer people in attendance, the more profit the matchmakers made. The Vietnamese matchmaker gave the bride's family 5 to 8 million dong. Few received as much as 10 million dong. Any jewelry to the bride would be a special gift from the groom. However, the matchmaker would keep the jewelry and gave them to the bride only when she was about to leave for Taiwan, in order to reduce the chance that she would disappear after receiving the money and the jewelry. From the wedding time onwards, the bride would have to live at the matchmaker's place. The lodging and meal costs would be covered by the groom, at about $100 a month, instead of on the basis of the exchange for a woman's domestic services as before. This amount would also cover the fees for her Chinese language lessons. . . .

[In response to my question about the reasons for Taiwanese men to marry Vietnamese women] T. thought for a while and then said slowly:

"First, we need to acknowledge that many Taiwanese marry Vietnamese women out of their real needs. The majority are peasants and taxi drivers . . . from Tainan and Kaohsiung areas, the more rural parts of Taiwan. Their lives are not easy as farmers. Some are not able to find spouses yet even at the age of over 40. Some have to borrow $9,000 or $10,000 to go to Vietnam to marry a wife. Many wives are disillusioned after arriving in Taiwan."

Kim Tuyen, *Saigon Giai Phong,* June 21, 2001.

Note: The Vietnamese press also occasionally reports the sale of women to rural China as brides due to the gender imbalance there which results from female infanticide.

the context of the state's partial disengagement from the public sphere. In the northern part of Vietnam, many people also actively established formal organizations to strengthen their own social networks and to fill the public space vacuum left by the state. Many of the male-centered organizations, such as patrilineages and the male-exclusive same-age associations, had been reinvented throughout northern Vietnam by the end of the 1990s (see Luong 2000; Kleinen 1999; Luong Hong Quang and Pham Nam Thanh 2000: 156–61; Phan Dai Doan 2001: 185–91). In its selective emphasis on tradition as an integral part of Vietnamese identity in an age of globalization, the Vietnamese state also became more tolerant of the proliferation or nonpolitical reinvention of traditional organizational forms.

In parallel, in the 1986–1995 period, in the thirteen northern communities studied by C. Hirschman and his colleagues, the percentages of men and women living patrilocally after marriages increased respectively to 85 percent and 83 percent from 79 and 80 percent in 1956–1985 (Nguyen Huu Minh 1998: 176–235).

Similarly, of the couples getting married from 1996 to 2001 in my sample of 340 households in the southern village of Khanh Hau, over 80 percent lived with the husband's parents, in comparison to 67 percent in the general sample. Nguyen Huu Minh's regression analysis of the data from northern Vietnam suggests that the younger the husband and wife were at the time of marriage, and the more they engaged in agricultural work, the more likely they would live patrilocally (Nguyen Huu Minh and Hirschman 2000: 47).[10] Patrilineages and patrilocal postmarital residence continued to be strengthened.

It is not surprising in the aforementioned context that the domestic division of labor to the disadvantage of women persisted in the 1990s. As revealed in a study conducted by the Center for Women's and Family Studies in Hanoi in the early 1990s, this division of labor pattern was fairly uniform across the Vietnamese lowlands. More specifically, in the communes of Thai Hoa in the northern province of Thai Nguyen, Hoa Phu in the central province of Quang Nam, and Khanh Hau in the southern province of Long An, in at least 63 percent of the surveyed households, women handled exclusively childcare and cooking, as well as other meal-related tasks (table 7.5). While parent-teacher meetings were attended by both men and women to almost the same degree, men participated more frequently in the more important public meetings in the hamlet and commune. The Vietnam Living Standard Survey data indicate that in 1992–1993, women spent an average of 15.52 hours a week on unpaid housework, while men spent only 10.91 hours. In 1997–1998, the gap remained, although the number of hours had been reduced to 12.75 hours for women and 8.31 hours for men, possibly due to the availability of household equipment and domestic helpers among the urban middle class, and to the lunch delivery services to office workers (Vietnam-General Statistical Office 2000b: 197, 199; see also Ha thi Phuong Tien and Ha Quang Ngoc 2001). In general, it was much easier for men than for women to maintain extensive public commitments.

The male-centered domestic labor division and patrilocal residence continued exerting a strong psychosocial pressure on young women as daughters-in-law. The anthropologist Tine Gammeltoft discussed a revealing incident about the local definition of gender relations in the northern commune of Vai Son, near Hanoi, when the mother-in-law in her host family one day slightly slapped her daughter-in-law, a local schoolteacher, with a stick in public. The mother-in-law told the foreign anthropologist:

> You see, this is what I told you. People don't know how to behave anymore, they don't know what is up and what is down [i.e., who is superior and who is inferior], they have no morality. How can I live with a spoilt daughter-in-law like this? She even tells me I cook too salty food. Would *you* ever dare tell *your* mother-in-law her food was too salty? (Gammeltoft 1999: 160)

Gammeltoft learned from the neighbors that the tension between the mother-in-law and daughter-in-law in her host family was not mainly over foods, but really over the upbringing of the eldest grandson who was more unruly than most

Table 7.5.   Division of Domestic Labor

	Commune								
	Thai Hoa (North)			Hoa Phu (Center)			Khanh Hau (South)		
Task	H	W	H+W	H	W	H+W	H	W	H+W
a. Cooking and other meal-related tasks	2.4	84.9	5.6	3	90	2	3.2	82.6	2.1
b. Child care	5	63.4	28.7	5	63.3	31.1	6.5	71.1	19.4
c. Purchase of consumer durables	60.4	12.6	24.3	29	33.3	33.3			
d. Sale of products	28.7	55.7	8.7	8.2	70.1	18	12.3	49.1	33.3
e. Parent-Teacher Association meetings	45.7	54.3		50	44.6		38.2	38.9	
f. Hamlet/commune meetings	59	28.8	56.8	26.3	40.3	36.4			

Source: Nguyen Linh Khieu 2001: 29, 36.
Key: H: husband; W: wife

boys of his age. Although the mother-in-law was known as hot-tempered and difficult, all the neighbors condemned the daughter-in-law. A neighbor explained: "No matter what her mother-in-law tells her, being a daughter-in-law she should still speak nicely and behave properly" (161).

In the commune of Vai Son, within the domestic domain, as Gammeltoft explained:

Women's everyday stresses and worries seem to be related to two central facets of their lives: first, the experience of *overwork*, i.e. very hard work every day and responsibility for both working the fields and for all domestic work including the management of the household economy, and second, the experience of *submission*, i.e., having to "please" (*chieu*) one's husband and his family. (162)

Chieu the husband means pleasing him both socially and sexually. In a patrilocal joint family context, pleasing the husband's family also means being attentive especially to parents-in-law's needs and wishes and being respectful of them.

The psychosocial pressures on young women due to patrilocal residence was not restricted to rural northern Vietnam. In her study of the relation between daughters-in-law and mothers-in-law in urban Ho Chi Minh City, Ngo thi Ngan Binh also suggests: "This situation [being a daughter-in-law in her husband's family] creates a challenge to the daughter-in-law's performance of roles, which demands tactful skills, endurance, energy, and time. If a working woman in a nuclear family has to perform double duty, balancing between career and family responsibilities, then her counterpart in the extended family has to face triple duty, balancing among work, home and *lam dau* [being a daughter-in-law] obligations."

(Ngo thi Ngan Binh 2001: 149) Those obligations were challenging for an urban daughter since the mother-in-law seldom adopted a liberal view on four feminine virtues (work, appearance, discourse, and character). She often emphasized a woman's domestic duties and the primacy of her son's consanguinal ties over his marital and affinal relations. In this context, while a mother-in-law in the urban south might not require a new daughter-in-law to make a strict adaptation to her family's lifestyle, the latter might still not be highly prepared for domestic chore demands since the young woman's own mother might have been relaxed regarding the young woman's domestic performance in order to facilitate the girl's pursuit of education and career.

The studies to date suggest that Vietnamese girls were socialized from an early age in preparation for their gender roles in both the domestic domain and beyond. In both a description and prescription of behavior, local people in Vai Son commune saw girls as mild, gentle, and enduring hardships, while boys were perceived to have hot and uncontrollable tempers. In a study on gender socialization in the commune of Thinh Tri in the same Ha Tay province, H. Rydstrom similarly reported that local definitions of girls and boys portrayed the former as gentle, responsive, obedient, easy to discipline, emphasizing sentiments (*tinh cam*), adjusting to situations, occupying little space, demanding little attention, and preferring quiet occupations. In contrast, they portrayed boys as mischievous, active, disobedient, difficult to discipline, emphasizing obligations, orchestrating situations, occupying much space, demanding much attention, and engaging in energetic games (Rydstrom 1998). While these definitions were stereotypical, they shaped expectations and the sanctioning of children's behavior: a disobedient boy who ignored a request for housework might be forgiven more easily than a disobedient girl, leading to a shift of housework to girls (121–22).

Beyond childhood and in the larger national arena, the rapidly growing self-help literature whose readers were mainly the members of the middle class advised women how to preserve happy family lives: by keeping feminine appearances and by providing their husbands with appropriate pleasures (Nguyen Vo Thu Huong 2002: 147–50). This literature plays a role in reinforcing the dominant definition of femininity inculcated in childhood. As the mass media became accessible even in remote parts of Vietnam in the past decade, and as advertising, mainly by multinational corporations, became an increasingly important part of the Vietnamese mass media, research would be useful on the extent to which the mass media contributed to the reproduction of gender stereotypes.

The definition of women's roles as domestic-centered, even when women worked outside the home, created enormous psychosocial pressures on women. In an illuminating study of the pressures on women in Dong Vang village (in the northern province of Ha Tay), which in 1999 had about two hundred women (aged from the early twenties to the late sixties) working as traders in Hanoi, Truong Huyen Chi reported their mental anguish about leaving their children behind in the village, despite the fact that this village was close to Hanoi:

as mothers and wives, they [woman-traders] struggle with restless feelings of insecurity and loss of chance to fulfill their nurturing and caring responsibilities towards their family members.... women are [also] aware of their *major* roles, not simply supporting, but generating cash income for the entire family. (Truong Huyen Chi 2001: 141)

On the one hand, a woman's undertaking of the hardship of trading in towns is good because it is driven by her sacrifice for her husband and children. On the other hand, her increasing absence from home should be criticized because it means she does not behave properly (*biet dieu*) toward her husband and children. (145)

While many urban middle-class women could rely on female domestic workers to alleviate their domestic burdens, this did not reduce their guilt about not personally providing better care for their children.

Obviously, Vietnamese women were not simply passive agents in the context of conflicting structural pressures on gender relations in the 1990s. According to Gammeltoft, to deal with psychological distress, a woman in the northern village of Vai Son might first of all confide in other women who, however, often counseled endurance (Gammeltoft 1999: 230). Or they could choose footdragging, performing work in a sullen manner. However, her children might suffer from her refusal to perform domestic work effectively. Third, she might refrain from eating, drawing other people's attention to her anguish. Fourth were the somatic expressions of illness that might make her husband more caring and her mother-in-law more compassionate (202–37). Ngo thi Ngan Binh also reports on a major strategy among daughters-in-law to gain more power through the control of their nuclear families' budgets and through an emphasis on their marital ties to their husbands (Ngo thi Ngan Binh 2001). In daily life, Vietnamese women might combine those responses with different degrees of effectiveness. I would suggest that women's heavy leaning toward Buddhism with its concepts of karma and infinite cycle of miseries was also a reaction to the problems that they faced in the Vietnamese sociocultural and economic systems.

CONCLUSION

In conclusion, marketization and globalization increased income-generating opportunities for many women. However, for many, this means an increase in their paid working hours on top of their unpaid domestic work. The contraction of the state's role in the public domain and the selective reinvention of tradition outside the government-controlled sphere also led to the resurgence of the male-oriented kinship model to the disadvantage of women.

On a theoretical level, as pointed out by Goodkind (1995), Vietnamese data on gender relations in the era of economic reforms and globalization do not support the hypothesis, rooted in modernization theory, that gender equality will increase with modernization. Neither do they support a Marxist theoretical framework that sees gender inequality as rooted in the feudal and capitalist modes of pro-

duction: gender inequality in Vietnam persisted even at the height of socialist reforms. The Vietnamese data on both the economic reform period and in the preceding centuries also challenge a non-Marxist economic-reductionist framework
that equates economic power with an increase in status: Vietnamese women's significant roles in the economy do not necessarily lead to a restructuring of gender
relations to their advantage. While research needs to be conducted in greater
depth on the regional, class, and ethnic dimensions of gender relations, as well as
on how women took advantage of and reacted to the changing opportunities and
constraints, the currently available Vietnamese findings suggest that the socioculturally and historically embedded definition of gender relations may be as
powerful as the political economic framework in reproducing and potentially
transforming gender relations in Vietnam (cf. Werner 2002).

APPENDIX: FEMALE-HEADED HOUSEHOLDS IN VIETNAM AND
THEIR SOCIOCULTURAL CONTEXT

Despite women's generally lower wages, study after study in Vietnam has shown
that female-headed households have higher average per capita income and/or expenditure than male-headed ones. The Vietnam Living Standard Survey data in
1992–1993 indicate that the average per capita *expenditure* in female-headed
households was 25 percent higher than in male-headed ones (1,448,000 dong versus 1,162,700 dong) (Vietnam-General Statistical Office 1994: 188). Average per
capita *income* among the former was 18 percent higher than among the latter
(1,255,300 dong versus 1,061,400 dong) (224). The data in 1997–1998 similarly
indicate that the average per capita expenditure in female-headed households remained 25 percent higher than in male-headed ones (3,496,000 dong versus
2,804,000 dong (Vietnam-General Statistical Office 2000b: 268, see also Vietnam
and World Bank 1999: 169–72). The average per capita income among the former
was 36 percent higher than among the latter in 1997–1998 (4,295,000 dong versus 3,151,000 dong) (Vietnam and World Bank 1999: 309).

Vietnamese findings are incongruent with those from numerous Western societies that have found female-headed households economically worse off than
their male-headed counterparts. I would suggest that this incongruence results
from the differences in sociocultural context. As Western households tend to be
nuclear, a female-headed household tends to be composed of a woman and her
dependent children. In the Vietnamese sociocultural and institutional contexts,
this is not necessarily the case. In a sample of 999 households in Ho Chi Minh City
in 1998, 43.5 percent of the so-called female-headed ones had the heads' husbands
in residence. In the Vietnam Living Standard Survey, 34 percent of the female-
headed households also had the husbands of the heads in residence (Vietnam and
World Bank 1999: 169). In-depth interviews in Ho Chi Minh City reveal that the
majority of those households officially declared women to be heads for household

registration purposes: the female heads were long-term residents of Ho Chi Minh City, while their husbands from other provinces needed to be registered for permanent residence on the basis of marriages to legally resident spouses.

In the Vietnam Living Standard Survey, even when the "female" headed households with husbands in residence are reclassified as male-headed, the per capita expenditures in the remaining female-headed households (i.e., no husbands in residence) were still on the average 11 percent higher than those in the male-headed ones (Vietnam and World Bank 1999: 169). In order to explain this apparent anomaly, we also need to take into account the higher frequency of extended and joint family arrangements in Vietnam, the developmental cycle of Vietnamese households, and women's generally greater longevity. For a sixty-year-old woman with a deceased husband, the per capita income and expenditure of her household may be significantly boosted by the incomes of her adult and working children and children-in-law still residing with her (cf. Nguyen thi Hoa 2001 and Scott 2001: 180–89).

NOTES

1. The prominent figures include Ladies Trung in an anti-Chinese campaign in the first century, Lady Trieu in a similar anti-Chinese uprising in the third century, Madame Bui Thi Xuan, a troop commander in the eighteenth century, and literary figures such as Ho Xuan Huong and Ba Huyen Thanh Quan in the eighteenth and nineteenth century (see Le thi Nham Tuyet 1975).

2. Data are not available for a *regional* breakdown on male and female access to education.

3. Unfortunately, figures are not available on the changes in the percentages of women in the bureaucratic system from 1954 to 1989.

4. Local people's councils officially exercise a supervisory role over local administrations. They meet once every few months to review local budgets and other major local issues.

5. The emphasis on women's duties to take care of their families inadvertently and indirectly led to their stigmatization in many cases in the collective era. In the village of Dong Vang in the northern province of Ha Tay, many women continued female villagers' tradition of rice trade in order to feed their children and other family members better during the collective era. They were stigmatized by the male-dominated commune government for pursuing private business, in the same way that mercantile activities had been stigmatized in the Confucian ideology in the pre-independence period (Truong Huyen Chi 2001). The stigma on private commerce was reduced with the economic reforms of the late 1980s.

6. However, the percentage of couples who reported living patrilocally for more than 3 years dropped from 68 percent for couples married in 1956–1960, to 60–61 percent for those married in the 1961–1975 period, and 46 percent for those tying the knot in the 1976–1985 period (Nguyen Huu Minh 1998: 176–235, and Nguyen Huu Minh and Hirschman 2000: 41–54; see also Mai Huy Bich 2000). A major change in the kinship and family domain involved the married couple's greater input into their spousal selection. Nguyen Huu Minh's analysis of data in 13 Ha Nam Ninh communes and towns indicates

that the percentage of nonarranged marriages increased from 32 percent for males and 37 percent for females in the 1956–1960 period, to 72 percent and 74 percent respectively in the 1960–1975 period, to 82 percent and 79 percent for the following decade, and to 86 percent and 85 percent in 1986–1995 (Nguyen Huu Minh 1998: 118). The dominant forms of nonarranged marriages involved the couple's decision with their parents' approval, and parents' decision with children's approval (see also Pham van Bich 1999).

7. The percentages of extended and joint households in the Red River delta and in the northern central panhandle were the lowest in Vietnam in 1989 (standing respectively at 17.7 percent and 21 percent). This percentage reached 25.6 percent in the northern highlands, 27.4 percent in the Central Highlands, 28.5–29.4 percent in the central coast, the southeast (around Ho Chi Minh City), and the Mekong delta (Belanger 1997: 98). The relatively low percentages of extended and joint households in the Red River delta and the northern central panhandle may reflect the division of a number of households in the aftermath of the 1988 land division when in a number of communities, each household could buy a certain amount of residential land at relatively low prices (see also Mai van Hai and Nguyen Phan Lam 2001).

8. In 1976, Mme. Nguyen thi Binh, who had been a minister of foreign affairs in the Provisional Revolutionary Government of South Vietnam and highly visible at the Paris Peace negotiation, became the first female minister in socialist Vietnam. She was later moved from the Ministry of Education to the ceremonial role of vice president. Over the years, a number of other women were appointed to minister-equivalent positions (president of the National Committee to Protect Mothers and Children, president of the Women's Union), but not to full cabinet positions. The current minister of labor is the second female full cabinet member in socialist Vietnam since 1954.

9. In May 2001, the Vietnamese government launched a nationwide crackdown on prostitution, drug use, and crimes, leading to the considerable slowdown in the business of dancing clubs, karaoke and beer bars, and "[hostess] caressing" coffee shops (*ca phe om*). It remains an open question whether the campaign would have a lasting impact, or would be shortlived like many other campaigns.

10. However, the percentage of men and women who lived with husbands' families for more than 3 years declined slightly to 42–43 percent in the 1986–1995 period. Nguyen Huu Minh and Hirshman attribute the reduction in the length of patrilocal residence over time to later marriage ages, the declining mortality rate, and the consequent increase in the number of siblings (2000: 51) in the context of a more crowded household and the need for only one couple to stay and to take care of elderly parents (Nguyen Huu Minh 1998: 209, 214–15). If the couple married earlier, if the husband's parents were older than 54, if the husband was the eldest son, and if the husband had fewer siblings, all these factors would increase the likelihood that patrilocal residence would last for more than 3 years. However, the more educated the couple was, the more likely they would stay longer with the husband's parents. Nguyen Huu Minh suggests that this might relate to the more educated's stronger expression of filial piety in conformity with social norms and governmental encouragement.

8

Return to the Past? The Dynamics of Contemporary Religious and Ritual Transformation

Shaun Kingsley Malarney

One of the most significant dimensions of social change in Vietnam over the past fifteen years has been a nationwide resurgence of religion and ritual. Beginning in the 1950s in the north and after 1975 in the south, the Vietnamese government had attempted to place religion and ritual under official control in order to advance its sociopolitical agenda to build a socialist society. These policies and the related restrictions they imposed greatly limited the types and forms of religious and ritual practices that people could perform. Since the mid-1980s, the government has relaxed its control over cultural affairs. In this less restrictive environment a blossoming of religion and ritual has occurred. This chapter's purpose is to examine the history and nature of this process in order to demonstrate two main points about the resurgence: first, that it does not represent the emergence of an innovative set of needs or desires on the part of those involved in their conduct and organization; and second, that the nature and direction of the resurgence do not represent the unhindered expression of popular interests. As I show, many of the contemporary changes are directly related to points of tension and resistance that existed during the reform years, and the way they have recently evolved has been the outcome of a process of negotiation between the state and the people, both of which continue to influence the form and direction of change.

The discussion that follows attempts to be comprehensive, but it should be considered provisional for a number of reasons. The Vietnamese government has only allowed serious, long-term research on these topics since the early 1990s, and then researchers in Vietnam have in many cases encountered difficulties gaining access to certain people, places, and materials. For example, research on some topics, such as the politics of contemporary Buddhism or the Hoa Hao, remains forbidden. Given the complexities of permits and other logistical factors, field research has also tended to cluster around the major urban centers of Hanoi and Ho Chi Minh City, particularly the former as it is the seat of the national government.

Finally, Vietnam was divided into North and South Vietnam from 1954 to 1975, creating disjunctures in the time and nature of the implementation of related policies. Nevertheless, with these caveats in mind, I attempt to provide as complete a discussion as possible.

RELIGION AND RITUAL UNDER SOCIALISM

North Vietnam's first constitution of 1946 enshrined "freedom of religion" (*tu do tin nguong*) as a central tenet of the new state. Although this indicated a potentially liberal attitude toward religion, the reality of the state's attitude proved much more restrictive. Official opposition to religion stemmed from a number of different sources. At the broadest level, the government recognized the potential for religious organizations to become a focus of political opposition. Vietnamese history is replete with cases in which religious groups, either in the form of institutionally complex groups such as Buddhists or Catholics, or the smaller millenarian groups such as the Cao Dai or Hoa Hao, posed a serious threat to state power. The group that generated the most concern for the government in its early years was the Catholic Church. During the Franco-Vietnamese War (1946–1954), Vietnamese Catholics and the church leadership had supported the French and were staunch opponents of the Vietnamese Communists. After the Communists succeeded in gaining control of North Vietnam in 1954, the government began to deal with the Catholic community by asserting control over church properties and institutional life. Fear and hysteria associated with the Communist ascension to power led to the flight of hundreds of thousands of northern Vietnamese Catholics to South Vietnam in 1954–1955 (see Gheddo 1970). Their departure greatly weakened the institutional strength of the church in the north. The government was also suspicious of organized Buddhist groups, although their relative lack of political organization in the north at that point in time made them a less serious threat. As the North Vietnamese state began to take shape in the post-1954 period, the government brought all organized religious groups under their control with the establishment in 1955 of the Buddhist Association of Vietnam and the Liaison Committee of Patriotic and Peace Loving Catholics. The formation of these organizations, whose membership included government officials and Communist Party members, ensured that organized religion did not become a focus of dissent and opposition.

Official opposition to religion also derived from the government's atheism policy. Like other revolutionary socialist governments, the Vietnamese government and Communist Party rejected all claims that any divine or supernatural entities existed or exercised an influence on human life. The state's adoption of this policy was undoubtedly informed by the progressive and anticlerical sentiments that had influenced revolutionaries in France and the Soviet Union, but officials in Vietnam were particularly concerned about eliminating what they considered to be the retrograde social consequences of these ideas. According to officials, many of the ideas that asserted the existence of supernatural forces or beings were part of the so-called feudal and backward cultural inheritance that previous regimes had bequeathed to Vietnam. As Ho Chi Minh stated, this assemblage of ideas was part of a "keep the people stupid policy" that made the Vietnamese easy to rule because it cultivated an attitude of resignation and passivity in the population. More pointedly, these ideas legitimized the social hierarchy of the prerevolutionary period, and with their emphasis on supernatural causality in human life, prevented the Vietnamese from understanding the true causes of suffering and inequality. The government wanted the people to develop the critical skills necessary to analyze their life situations and recognize that their destiny lay in their own hands, not those of the gods or spirits. A cultural primer written by officials in 1968 in the northern province of Ninh Binh cogently summarized this attitude when it noted, "When the masses still believe in the heavens, spirits, and fate, they will be powerless before natural changes and the difficulties that the old society has left behind. People will not be able to completely be their own masters, the masters of society, nor the masters of the world around them" (Ninh Binh, Cultural Service 1968: 6).

The revolutionary state labeled the complex of retrograde ideas included in this category as "superstitions" (*me tin di doan*). The primary defining feature of a superstition was the assertion that a supernatural entity existed and could influence human life. Thus, superstitions included such popularly held ideas as fate, temporal auspiciousness/inauspiciousness, and supernatural punishment for moral transgressions. It also included such popularly conducted practices as geomancy, astrology, divination, and spirit mediumship. In practice, the boundaries of the concept were often blurry. The state vigorously argued that fate, geomancy, gods, and spirits did not exist, yet it remained ambivalent about such entities as the souls of ancestors. Reverence for the dead, particularly officially approved heroes, was an important component in the government's efforts to legitimize its rule, thus the state never asserted that ancestral souls did not exist.[1] It was also frequently unclear in practice how to draw the line between a "superstition" (*me tin*) and a "legitimate religious belief" (*tin nguong*). The state might have valorized such heroes as the Trung Sisters who, in 40–43 A.D., led the Vietnamese in battle against an invading Chinese army, but it simultaneously sought to eliminate the idea that the sisters' spirits could be called upon to assist the living. What was clear about the label, however, was that the state reserved the right to decide upon its definition.

From 1954 onward, the government implemented a range of aggressive policies to control religious life and combat superstitions across North Vietnam. It is important to note that the establishment of the revolutionary socialist state represented an unprecedented level of intrusion of the state into local life.[2] The government set up a standardized administrative structure for all localities throughout the country and this structure was in turn dominated by the Communist Party. This gave the state an enhanced ability to monitor and control local social life. At the same time, it either disbanded or put tight controls on any nonstate social organizations, such as prayer groups, ritual associations, or religious societies. To give one example, there were three types of organizations that had played a significant role in social life in prerevolutionary Thinh Liet commune, a community near Hanoi. These were an advisory committee that assisted in the organization of activities at local Buddhist temples; a Mandarinal Association for elite men that regularly conducted rites devoted to Confucius; and village-based Elderly Men's Associations, composed of men fifty-five and older, that conducted rites throughout the year and assisted in members' funerals. These groups were all disbanded, as were many others in other communities that had provided contexts for the practice of religion or ritual. In their stead, the state established mass cultural organizations, such as the Youth Association, Women's Union, and Elderly Association. The guiding purpose of these new organizations was the advancement of official agendas.

A second armature for the assertion of control over religion and ritual was the appropriation of the material infrastructure that had supported such practices. This occurred first in the 1953–1956 Land Reform campaign and later in the establishment of agricultural cooperatives from the late 1950s. During this period, cadres generally refrained from confiscating or damaging churches or Buddhist temples, but other sites that were previously important foci of ritual practice, such as village communal houses (*dinh*), lineage halls (*nha tho ho*), and spirit shrines (*dien, den,* and *mieu*), were appropriated and in some cases damaged. The two former types of sites were appropriated because of their associations with the former elite and the politically influential local lineages, respectively. The latter types of sites, which were generally among the most severely damaged, were targets because they were the primary sites for the conduct of superstitious practices. Even if such sites were not damaged, local cadres prohibited the organization of rituals on their premises. They also confiscated and redistributed any lands associated with the sites that had been used to provide either agricultural products or land rentals to provision ritual practices. The implementation of these policies varied throughout North Vietnam. Some shrines experienced complete destruction, while others were left untouched. Some communal houses were turned into warehouses for agricultural cooperatives, while others were simply closed up. Regardless of the precise nature of the change, by the early 1960s revolutionary cadres had succeeded in bringing both the organizational and material infrastructure of religion and ritual under their control.[3]

After seizing control of the sacred sites, the government forbade the conduct of the rites, such as spirit medium ceremonies at shrines or communal house ceremonies formerly performed at the sites. Local officials also placed the sites under surveillance in order to ensure that residents did not return to the clandestine practice of prohibited rites. They did the same with the variety of specialists who conducted the rites. Villages across North Vietnam had featured a range of ritual practitioners, including spirit priests (*thay cung*), diviners (*thay boi*), and spirit mediums (*Ong Dong, Ba Dong*), who specialized in the conduct of particular rituals. From the 1950s onward, many of these individuals were arrested, placed under surveillance, and in some cases given special indoctrination sessions in order to persuade them to abandon their professions. Local cadres also disseminated official propaganda designed to discredit the practitioners as unscrupulous charlatans who did not believe any of the ideas they espoused and who engaged in their rites simply for material gain. Officials were particularly critical of the specialists associated with spirit mediumship and healing rites. These ideological assertions and portrayals were an important part of the official campaign to eliminate unsanctioned practices. While the government was ready to implement aggressive policies to bring forth the elimination of these ideas and practices, their primary goal was, through education and propaganda, to convince people to voluntarily abandon them. These efforts at persuasion were targeted at all sections of the population, but state officials particularly targeted the elderly and women, although especially elderly women, because they regarded them as the most enthusiastic and committed followers of unsanctioned practices.

Running parallel to the government's campaigns to clean up religion and ritual was another aggressive campaign to reform the set of life-cycle rituals performed by families. In the prerevolutionary period, Vietnamese across the nation had engaged in an elaborate set of rites for such occasions as weddings, funerals, and death anniversaries.[4] Although each of these individual rites had its own specific characteristics, they shared the common features of ritual engagement with family ancestors, the conduct of a feast, and the participation of friends, kin, and others. In the case of weddings and funerals, the rites also usually extended over a period of two to three days. The revolutionary government objected to numerous elements within these rites.[5] The feasts, which could include the slaughter of several animals and the consumption of large quantities of rice or other staples, were considered wasteful. The events' timing and duration, which often occurred during the daylight hours, interfered with maximizing production. Some elements, such as checking for the astrological auspiciousness of the bride and groom's union for a wedding to go forward, or the burning of votive paper objects for use by the deceased's soul, were considered superstitious. Other elements, such as the practice of daughters lying on the ground to impede the casket's progress to the grave site, were regarded as feudal.

Government reforms of the rites sought to eliminate these elements and their perceived negative consequences. Although the nature of actual reforms varied between locales across North Vietnam, some similarities were present. The new rites were to be shortened, taking place on one day only, and in the case of a preplanned event like a wedding, taking place ideally at night so as not to interfere with production. They were to consume a minimum of resources, thus feast size and the number of food items were to be reduced. They were to be purged of all feudal elements, and they were to become egalitarian. This latter goal was realized in a variety of ways, such as the simplification of wedding and funeral attire, the socially inclusive issuance of wedding invitations, and the provision of pallbearers and a standardized casket by the local agricultural cooperative. Perhaps most importantly, the rites were to be disengaged from the supernatural. At one level this involved the prohibition of certain rites previously associated with funerals, such as soul-calling ceremonies and the burning of votive paper objects, but it also entailed the removal of the symbolically critical propitiation of family ancestors by the bride and groom in the wedding ceremony. With regard to funerals and death anniversaries, the government argued on this difficult point that the rites were no longer dedicated to assisting the deceased's soul or providing it with support. Instead, the rites were to be strictly commemorative.

In order to achieve its ambitious goals of reforming life-cycle rites, government officials assumed responsibility for their conduct, particularly by inserting themselves into the rites. Given their relatively smaller size, this did not occur with death anniversary ceremonies, but in both weddings and funerals local officials assumed critical roles. Regarding the former, officials from the local Youth Association, a Communist Party mass organization that was dominated by members in their twenties, assumed responsibility for the organization and conduct of wedding ceremonies. This role reached its most spectacular form in the years 1954 to 1957 when couples in numerous communities across the north were married in "collective wedding" (*cuoi tap the*) ceremonies, an innovative rite that involved the marriage of several couples in one ceremony. The secretary of the Youth Association presided over this rite and delivered the symbolically critical wedding speech. In many communities officials also forced the removal of the rites from the participants' homes, where they had previously been conducted, and held them in public buildings or even communal houses (see Malarney 1998). Regarding funerals, the local branch of the Elderly Association (*Hoi Phu Lao*) assumed a pivotal role in organizing the rites and its representative took over the role of delivering the funeral oration in most funerals. The insertion of local officials into these rites, and particularly their assumption of control over the speeches, played a critical role in the realization of the government's agenda to transform the rites into vehicles for official propaganda. In all of the speeches, cadres were urged to celebrate or commemorate the participants based upon their revolutionary virtues (see Malarney 1996b and 2002).

The implementation of the new revolutionary policies toward religion and ritual dramatically changed the cultural landscape in North Vietnam. A wide array of formerly common practices, such as spirit medium ceremonies, soul-calling rites, and communal house ceremonies, disappeared from public life. Many that were not officially banned, such as rites or services held at Buddhist temples or Christian churches, experienced a steep decline in participation as many people felt uncomfortable attending services. Local officials often made note of those in attendance, and this information could create difficulties for people, notably in the form of accusations that they supported backward practices or lacked revolutionary spirit. Of those rites that did remain, such as life-cycle ceremonies, their character was often profoundly modified, although people continued to organize them. Officials did recognize, however, that it would be impossible if not counterproductive to completely eliminate organized ritual practice. Thus they established an array of secular holidays, such as those on the National Day (September 2), War Invalids and Martyrs' Day (July 27), and others. They also established a set of quasireligious cultic activities dedicated to the worship of revolutionary heroes (see Treglode 2001). Although this practice built upon the pre-revolutionary pattern of hero worship, these sites, and the officially approved holidays, never generated the same enthusiasm and interest as those they replaced.

DIMENSIONS OF RESISTANCE: 1954–1986

The reforms discussed above proceeded apace throughout the 1960s and into the 1970s. It is clear from the written evidence, notably in the form of official regulations published by the Communist Party, the Ministry of Culture, and a variety of provincial and district cultural and party organs, that while localities tended to conduct their reforms within the general boundaries established by the national government, there nevertheless existed a significant degree of variation in the specific details advocated by particular areas. Thanh Hoa province, for example, represented one of the most vigorous cases of revolutionary reform, while areas in and around Hanoi often took a less strident line. When the government first began implementing the reforms in the mid-1950s, it benefited from the general enthusiasm among many people that characterized the first years of the revolution. Once this began to fade, it then benefited from the establishment of the agricultural cooperatives in the late 1950s as these helped the state monitor and regulate resource consumption. Still, despite this new level of control, the party always had to contend with the fact that many people across the country resisted the new policies. Far from representing a stunning revolutionary triumph, the reform campaigns soon settled into a decades-long war of attrition between the state and the interests and desires of local communities.

The initial aspects of resistance to government reforms centered on their most extreme elements, such as the removal of weddings from the participants' homes or the elimination of rites to propitiate family ancestors. As far as is known, the experience of Thinh Liet commune near Hanoi is fairly representative, as only a handful of "collective" weddings were held there and by the end of the 1950s the conduct of the rites had returned to people's homes. Families had also insisted on maintaining the propitiation of family ancestors in their rites in order to demonstrate their continued devotion to the ancestors. This is not to say, however, that no official reforms succeeded. To the contrary, wedding ceremonies did become shorter and simpler in terms of the participants' dress and the overall ritual structure. In many communities, weddings also became more socially inclusive. Prerevolutionary invitation practices had reinforced social cleavages, yet the reform practice of inviting widely within communities often made them more inclusive than before. Regarding funerals and death anniversary ceremonies, the notion that the rites were to become strictly commemorative and not dedicated to assisting the deceased's soul was not accepted. The best evidence for this was the continued performance of such rites as the "soul-calling" rites as well as the clandestine production and utilization of votive paper objects (*hang ma*). These objects had played a prominent role in funerary rites. They were made of paper or paper wrapped around bamboo frames and represented a variety of common objects, such as money, gold, jewelry, or even bicycles or houses. Following their rites, people burned these objects with the idea that, through the medium of the smoke, they were transferred to the dead for their use in the "other world" (*the gioi khac*). The Communist Party regarded *hang ma* as the physical manifestation of superstitions and outlawed their production and consumption. The objects largely disappeared from public life, but their secret production in people's homes and an active trade conducted under the cover of darkness attested to their abiding importance.

With both weddings and funerals, the most enduring foci of resistance were the restrictions on resource consumption in feasting. The government championed the moral necessity of frugalness. This was vital, they argued, in order to build socialism and, after the American war began in the early 1960s, in order to help the North Vietnamese military fight on to victory. Despite intense public pressure, as well as the restrictions placed on people through their membership in agricultural cooperatives, many families still channeled significant quantities of rice, meat, and money into their feasts. On all of these points, it was clear that while many people were willing to implement reforms that made rites simpler or more egalitarian, they were unwilling to allow the state and its officials to dictate how they and their families should conduct important family rituals.

One of the most interesting areas of resistance during this period was the continued existence of informal Buddhist associations. Many northern Vietnamese communities in the prerevolutionary period had featured lay Buddhist groups composed of particularly devout Buddhists, often women who had advanced beyond their childbearing years. Often called by the name of *hoi chu ba*, these groups usually met at temples to chant and conduct rites, although in many communities they also assembled at people's homes to chant during funeral rites. From the mid-1950s onward the existence of these groups was threatened because of official pressures that discouraged the conduct of rites at temples and also because of the government's attempts to limit the formation of non-state-sanctioned social organizations. With these restrictions in place, many of these groups ended their public activities yet maintained an active private organization that did not congregate at temples but did clandestinely meet in people's homes to chant and participate in funeral rites. The politics of these groups were interesting because they often included the female relatives of local officials. The latter were frequently reluctant to publicly criticize or interfere with the women's activities, particularly if their female relations were their elders. Officials often had little choice but to let the groups continue their activities, especially the chanting at funerals. On the one hand, a good number of officials did not want to cross their female kin, but perhaps more importantly, many recognized the critical importance of funeral rites for families, and they held that it was better to allow people to conduct their rites as they felt most comfortable, provided of course that it remained in the privacy of their homes. The important consequence of this attitude, as Hy Van

Luong has noted, was that the Buddhist groups constituted the only unofficial social organization to persist from the 1950s onward (Luong 1993b: 271).

A critical reading of government documents from the 1950s and 1960s also demonstrates that antisuperstition policy enjoyed only limited success. As early as the Third Party Congress in 1960, officials complained that the government still needed to work with the people to help them "overcome superstitions" (Vietnam [Government of] 1962: 11). Just over a decade later, in a 15 January 1971 directive published on the regulation of local festivals (*hoi he*), the Ministry of Culture made a remarkable public admission of the problems it continued to encounter. The directive noted that after the ending of American bombing raids against North Vietnam in 1968, "tens of thousands of people from all provinces, cities, and places have been going to participate in festivals. The most crowded locations have been the city of Hanoi, Haiphong, and all of the provinces of the delta and midlands of northern Viet Nam" (Nam Ha, Cultural Service 1971: 6). What troubled the officials were the negative consequences that the festivals produced, particularly the blossoming of superstitious practices. The ministry recognized that some people participated for what it regarded as legitimate reasons, but a great many individuals went to engage in superstitions. The ministry issued the directive, in fact, in order to mobilize local officials and prepare them to prevent an even larger growth of the festivals and their superstitious practices in the early 1971 festival season. In the following years, officials continued to publish reports and regulations that reiterated the need to successfully "sweep clean" (*quet sach*) such remaining vestiges of superstitious practices as astrology, divination, and the production and consumption of votive paper objects.

The large-scale festivals just mentioned all took place with official permission and involved rites at major sacred sites, such as the Phu Giay Shrine in Ha Nam province. While such festivals indicated one measure of continued public utilization of sacred sites, one important question that has yet to be satisfactorily resolved is to what extent residents in villages made use of the smaller sites in their locales. Given official surveillance and state control over public buildings, it was difficult for Vietnamese to organize rites in many local shrines, temples, or communal houses.[6] This did not appear to mean, however, that the people completely abandoned all ritual activities in such sacred spaces. Small numbers of people did conduct rites at shrines and temples, for example. Village communal houses also appear in some communities to have entered into a liminal zone in which residents did not organize large-scale rituals, but they also did not completely renounce their sacred character. In many communities officials closed up their village communal houses or converted them to mundane uses, but there often remained a tacit consensus not to destroy the altars or all of the sacred ritual paraphernalia. To give one example, in the village of Giap Nhi of Thinh Liet commune, local officials had seized control of the communal house during the Land Reform in the commune in late 1954–early 1955, and had even taken the step of organizing a series of "collective weddings" in it soon after. A few years later they began using part of the interior as a warehouse and then in the 1980s constructed a meeting room at the front for official functions. Nevertheless, despite their appropriation of the communal house, officials still allowed the inner sanctum and a number of ritual objects to remain untouched. Unconfirmed accounts even assert that in some villages people surreptitiously continued to propitiate their local guardian spirits. The reluctance of officials in Thinh Liet and other communities undoubtedly derived from their concern not to seriously offend local constituents who did not support official policies.

After the North Vietnamese seized control of South Vietnam in the spring of 1975 the government began to implement many of the same cultural reforms previously carried out in the north. Unsanctioned practitioners were placed under surveillance, restrictions were imposed on unapproved rituals, and attempts were made to appropriate sacred sites. Reforms of weddings and funerals were also introduced, as were new heroes, such as the southern Communist Ton Duc Thang, chosen to replace the heroes and cultic figures linked to the old regime (see Giebel 2001). The government was particularly severe in its treatment of religious groups that had opposed the Communists. The Cao Dai and Hoa Hao experienced the seizure of many of the sacred and secular sites under their control, and like the southern Buddhists, also saw the arrest and detention of some of their leaders. However, unlike the rapid pace with which they had conducted the reforms in the north, the government proceeded more slowly and cautiously in the south. Details are difficult to come by, but it appears that from the beginning, many southerners openly resisted the government's proposed reforms (see Luong 1994). One area that appears to have been a major focus of opposition were official attempts to take control of local communal houses. In the north many of these had been transformed into functional spaces by agricultural cooperatives, but southerners, who were also resisting the establishment of cooperatives, in many cases retained a measure of control over the sites and prevented the government from completely seizing them. Luong reports that in such communities as Khanh Hau, officials attempted to seize control and limit the conduct of rites in the communal house, but residents resisted this and some rites were still performed (see Luong 1994: 95–97). Kirsten Endres notes that in the southern commune of Binh My there were few restrictions placed on communal house rites, although official permission was required to perform them, while in Long Dinh commune official opposition to organized rites was stronger (see Endres 1999: 210). As in the north, the government did attempt to implement reforms in the south, but it did so in a much gentler fashion and many southerners retained an active religious and ritual life.

RESURGENCE BEGINS: RECREATING FAMILY RITES

By the early 1980s the Vietnamese government had been actively engaged in attempting to reform religion and ritual practices for almost three decades, yet the results were mixed. Following the introduction of the Renovation policy (*doi moi*) in 1986, the government began to ease the pressure on cultural reforms. True, it did periodically continue to release directives and regulations that exhorted the citizenry to implement the reforms, but coercion by local officials largely disappeared and a level of freedom to organize rites and conduct religious activities appeared that was previously absent. In this more favorable political climate a resurgence of ritual practice began that continues to this day. The resurgence has taken place in two primary stages. First, families returned to the organization of large-scale weddings, funerals, and death anniversary ceremonies. This stage began in the late 1980s and picked up momentum from the early 1990s onward. Second, a wide range of "superstitious" and magical practices reemerged as local groups began to resacralize their previously closed-down sacred sites and organize rites there that had been neglected since the 1950s. This stage began in the early 1990s and intensified from the mid-1990s. It was unsurprising that life-cycle rituals made the earliest resurgence because, from a political perspective, they were less threatening to the government. Once that process had solidified the people began to assert themselves more forcefully regarding the conduct of other rites and practices, and the state accommodated itself to their demands while often simultaneously exerting pressures to channel the practices in particular directions. As discussed in the following sections, each of these stages involved their own particular dynamics, but their overall development represented a process of gradual negotiation between the state and the people. What stands out most clearly about the process is that while a resurgence has occurred, it is composed of a set of rites that are in many cases quite different from their prerevolutionary antecedents.[7]

When the resurgence of life-cycle rituals began in the late 1980s, it quickly became clear that women, particularly elderly women, were a driving force behind it.[8] From the 1950s onward, women had constituted one of the main foci of resistance to official policies. When the atmosphere began to improve, they began to assert themselves more forcefully in order to bring about changes. Female religious groups, such as the Buddhist Associations, became more prominent in local life. Their activities at temples became larger in scale and also more public. They also assumed a more public role in such activities as chanting at funerals. In both of these cases, the women tested the boundaries of what was acceptable and slowly forced the expansion of what local officials were prepared to accept. In many cases, women lobbied local officials, many of whom were their relatives, behind the scenes to get them to accept such changes, but in other cases they simply went ahead and did what they wanted. In one case from the village of Giap Tu in Thinh Liet commune, local women spearheaded the movement to renovate the village communal house, and local men grudgingly followed along. Women were able to play such a vital role for two reasons. First, as evident in the discussions above, many women had not renounced their religious practices during the reform years, thus when new possibilities emerged, they were able to bring out publicly that which they had privately retained for years. Second, given the male dominance of local politics and Communist Party membership, many women did not have the same political liabilities as men. A male party member who openly advocated the return of unsanctioned ritual practices could face party censure or the loss of opportunities for political advancement. Women were usually not as involved in the political structure, thus there were fewer effective sanctions that could be applied against them. Given this independence, women were more successful in advancing their vision of correct ritual and religious practice.

Many of the changes in resurgent life-cycle ceremonies affect their form or appearance. For example, many brides and grooms have adopted Western-style dress, some families will ignore concerns about astrological auspiciousness and conduct rituals on convenient days, and in many places the long series of gifts and meetings that took place prior to a wedding have been reduced.[9] Among the most interesting and important changes related to life-cycle rituals have been those associated with feasting. When the government loosened its control over production and consumption in the late 1980s, the long-standing resistance to official sumptuary restrictions began to transform into gradual increases in feast sizes for weddings, funerals, and death anniversary ceremonies. Research from the countryside has indicated that this process began as early as the late 1980s (see Luong 1993b; Malarney 2002). It has also occurred simultaneously in the cities. This transformation, however, has been characterized by two contradictory trends. On the one hand, many of the new feasts manifest a more egalitarian character than those prior to the revolution. This is particularly true of funerals and death anniversary ceremonies. Prerevolutionary society had featured social cleavages between elites and commoners, and in some instances these differences had been maintained by mutual exclusion at feasts. Revolutionary social reforms broke down many of these barriers (although they did introduce some new ones, such as between supporters and opponents of revolutionary policies), and in some communities a socially more expansive set of guests began attending feasts.[10] In these communities this change was regarded as the logical outcome of the egalitarian "sentimental" (*tinh cam*) relationships that people maintained and strengthened by attending each other's feasts. According to this argument, an egalitarian trend had always been present in feasting, particularly in the reciprocation of gifts that accompanied feasts, thus when revolutionary policies eliminated the social practices that had kept it suppressed, it correspondingly blossomed. These assertions, however, fail to recognize that the growth in feast size has also been characterized by increased conspicuous consumption and assertions of social status, particularly in weddings. Families employ various methods to assert their status through feasts. The simplest method is the choice of food items consumed at the feast. Up until the early 1980s, most feasts featured a standardized set of dishes, usually based upon pork, rice, vegetables, and rice spirits. By the early 1990s, these items began to change as more families began substituting prestige items into their feasts, such as chicken instead of pork, beer and wine instead of rice spirits, and imported cigarettes as opposed to Vietnamese brands. If one is to have a feast considered impressive by others, it is vital to provide such prestige items. Another important method for asserting status, which is possible only with weddings where guests are invited and not in funerals where guests come of their own initiative, is to invite large numbers of guests to the feast. Some people who invite overly large numbers of guests are accused of "buying sentiment" (*mua tinh cam*). Their status assertions are not lost on others. Families are financially able to invite large numbers because guests who plan on attending the feasts are obliged to provide the host family with a standardized gift, called a *mung* gift. It usually takes the form of a cash sum although other items, such as food, are accepted in the countryside. In recent years the size of this gift has increased. For example, in Hanoi in the early 1990s a guest at a feast was usually expected to contribute 10,000 to 20,000 dong, yet the contemporary gift is normally a minimum of 50,000 dong, although more can be expected. Many Vietnamese complain that they now receive so many invitations and have to pay out so much that weddings have become a burden for them. The combination of these changes has meant that, in many communities, the cost and size of feasts have risen dramatically, much to the government's consternation.

Another important area of innovation has been the set of changes associated with the position of women in weddings and marriages. The Vietnamese revolution had regarded a number of practices as feudal, such as arranged marriage, underaged marriage, the payment of brideprice, and the allowance for men to marry multiple wives, because they generated inegalitarian relations between men and women or children and parents. In contemporary Vietnam, several of these practices have been reduced significantly. Arranged marriage has largely disappeared, the average age of marriage has increased, and polygamy has for the most part ceased, although illegal cases do periodically come to light. Marriage is now for the most part monogamous and voluntary, although parents usually do have some input. One of the more interesting manifestations of unintentional change has occurred in the rites performed for the bride and groom in the wedding ceremony. Prior to the revolution, the bride's and groom's sides had negotiated the payment of brideprice, paid from the groom's to the bride's family, in order to finalize the marriage. The items included in the brideprice, such as meat, tea, liquor, and tobacco, had been used by the bride's family to invite guests and hold a small feast at her home prior to the wedding. The bride's feast was always much smaller than the groom's, largely because the groom's family invited a larger number of guests and also collected the *mung* gift from each guest that attended, which helped them defray the feast's costs. In many contemporary communities, particularly in the north, the disparity in the sizes of the bride's and groom's feasts has decreased as many brides and their families have become more assertive about celebrating a daughter's wedding in a manner comparable to that of a son. In some places this has taken the form of a large party for the bride and her friends on the evening before the wedding (see Luong 1993b), while in other places brides' families have begun to collect *mung* gifts for their feasts (see Malarney 1998 and 2002). Luong quotes an elderly man in one northern community who commented that regardless of their dissatisfaction with the increased demands for a daughter's wedding, most parents have little choice in the matter and "will have to pay quietly" (Luong

1993b: 279). It is true that the groom's feast does remain larger than that of the bride, but their increased parity points to a significant change in wedding practices.[11]

A final area of family-focused ritual growth in the post-1986 period has been rites dedicated to war dead. During the wars against France, the United States, China, and Cambodia, Vietnam lost hundreds of thousands of soldiers, many of whose bodies were lost or buried at the front and never brought home. Since the late 1940s, the North Vietnamese government has gone to great lengths to honor those who fell in battle. In addition to devising special social policies to assist their families, they also constructed commemorative monuments and special cemeteries for war dead, established the National War Veterans and Invalids Day, and during the American war developed a commemorative ceremony that local officials held in the dead soldier's home (see Malarney 2001: 52–58). While these efforts have been appreciated by the population, war death, particularly in cases where the deceased's body was lost or never brought home, created the possibility that the deceased's soul could never be put to rest and would be doomed to eternally wander the earth as a malevolent ghost.[12] For family members, this was the worst possible outcome. In response to this problem, residents of some northern Vietnamese communities during the war years created their own set of family commemorative rites to put the souls of their loved ones to rest (see Malarney 2001 and 2002). Since the wars ended in the 1980s, many families have begun organizing trips to locations throughout the nation to find their loved ones' bodies so they can put them to proper rest. Those fortunate enough to find the remains (and many do not) bring them home for final funeral rites. In most cases people conduct the rites in their homes, while in a small number of cases they install the soul in a Buddhist temple. Many families have also begun organizing two commemorative ceremonies and small feasts for their dead each year, one on the deceased's death anniversary and another on War Veterans and Invalids Day. In recent years, these have also grown in size and expense. (As Luong and others have noted, death anniversary ceremonies have generally increased in size [see Luong 1993b: 279; and Malarney 2002: 138–44.]) On this point, however, it should be well noted that official support for the commemoration of war dead is confined to those who died fighting on the Communist side. Soldiers who fought against the Communists can only be commemorated privately and in some cases cemeteries dedicated to such soldiers have been emptied out and converted to other uses. They have effectively disappeared from both the official government heroic war narrative and its associated ritual corpus.

RESURGENCE CONTINUES: RECONSTRUCTING
PUBLIC SPACES AND RITUALS

As the process of reemergence for family life-cycle rituals took hold in the mid-1990s, residents turned their attention to the resacralization of previously sacred sites and the construction of new ones. One of the simplest and least controversial early indications of this process was the refurbishment of family graves and the construction of modest sites for family tombs in many communities. The resacralization of larger sites was politically more sensitive because it involved the open renunciation of official control over space and the participation of nonstate social organizations. The roots of this transformation date back into the 1980s and earlier. As discussed above, many communities had covertly maintained sacred spaces within their communal houses, most Buddhist temples had remained open although only limited numbers of people attended rites there, lineage halls (*nha tho ho*) had been closed up but small rites continued inside, and many families had also maintained family shrines (*dien*) where they secretly conducted rites. As official controls relaxed, people began the process of refurbishing them and reclaiming these spaces for public rites. In some ways, the reappropriation of these sites was facilitated by the dissolution of the agricultural cooperatives, which no longer needed them for warehouses or other uses, but in many cases the most important factor was the begrudging acceptance by local officials of the reappropriation and refurbishment of the sites. Officials in some communities, such as Thinh Liet commune, even facilitated the process by donating money for the renovation of the sacred sites, but in most cases the funds for repairs have been provided by private individuals, oftentimes many people with very little money who contribute only a modest amount. The names of donors are often visible on lists hanging on walls inside shrines, temples, and communal houses across Vietnam. One of the most important groups involved in this process, particularly in southern and central Vietnam, has been overseas Vietnamese. Donations for the construction or refurbishment of sacred sites is considered a virtuous activity and many overseas Vietnamese have donated large amounts of money to build and renovate sacred sites in their native communities. The money that they have donated has resulted in some of the most spectacular sacred architecture in contemporary Vietnam, as any visitor to the fishing communities near Hue can attest. In recent years the process has moved beyond simply refurbishing older sites to the construction of new ones. This trend is most visible in the proliferation of new family shrines (*dien*) and altars in family compounds. In some cases, former officials and Communist Party members have even constructed new shrines.

Once the refurbishment of sacred sites was underway, the next pressure that officials faced was for the return of large-scale rites conducted at the sites. Generally speaking, the government has allowed these rites to go forward, although it seeks to keep them under control by demanding permission to organize the rites and by placing restrictions on some of the activities that can take place at them. Thus, for example, residents across the country travel to festivals at shrines and temples, but officials attempt to ensure that these festivals maintain their religious character and do not become arenas for antigovernment dissent or feature such officially undesirable activities as gambling, public drunkenness, charlatanry, fortune-telling, or superstitions. Still, in many cases, these efforts fail and such activities are readily evident. In a number of cases, such as the spring pilgrimage to the Perfume Pagoda

(*Chua Huong*) outside Hanoi or the festival celebrating the Trung Sisters, the government has changed its attitude and now embraces the celebrations as manifestations of venerable Vietnamese tradition. This attitude change has been extremely important because it has provided the government with a legitimate justification for encouraging rites it previously discouraged. Nowhere perhaps is this change more evident than with the festival conducted at Phu Giay shrine in northern Vietnam. In 1976, the Ha Nam Ninh provincial cultural service published a short text entitled "Here! The Reality of the Phu Giay Festival" (*Day! Thuc chat hoi Phu Giay*), which argued that the festival was little more than a convocation for superstitions, yet a 1997 volume on festivals published by the Culture and Information Publishing house listed the Phu Giay Festival as a "religious festival" (*le hoi ton giao*) (Ha Nam Ninh, Cultural Service 1976; Le Trung Vu and Nguyen Hong Duong 1997). Many other such reversals of official attitudes have also occurred.

One of the most important areas of negotiation between the state and village communities regarding public rites has been the organization of communal house rites to worship village guardian spirits. Officials in the 1950s had been keen to prevent the organization of these rites because the former elite had dominated their organization and conduct (see Malarney 1993). The state prevented their reemergence until the late 1980s, but when pressure to return to organized rites reemerged, officials in communities throughout Vietnam opted to manage instead of suppress the rites' return. How this played out in different communities has varied. In some communities, such as in the village of Giap Nhi in Thinh Liet commune, local women had spearheaded the movement to conduct communal house rites again, and the first ceremonies in the early 1990s were both led and dominated by women. Local men, however, found this situation intolerable. Thus, after two years of domination by women, the men produced a long-lost ritual charter that described the proper conduct of the ritual and began conducting it themselves. Local officials did not initially participate in the rite, but they did forbid the organization of a post-rite feast, and a number of retired officials played critical roles. By the late 1990s officials had inserted themselves into the ceremony and the president of the commune's People's Committee assumed the role of chief ritual officiant (see Malarney 2002: 189–207). In the northern village of Lang To, John Kleinen observed a different dynamic in which members of former elite families had a significant role in the return to and subsequent conduct of communal house rites. As in Thinh Liet, local officials had initially been reluctant to get involved, but ultimately did so (see Kleinen 1999: 162–65). A different pattern was observed by Endres in the southern communes Long Dinh and Binh My. Here again men played a vital role in pushing the resurgence forward, but in some villages an innovative egalitarian ritual organization was created, while in others they reverted to such inegalitarian prerevolutionary practices as one patrilineage exercising control over the rites. Interestingly, large feasts were a critical part of all communal house rites (Endres 1999: 211–14).[13] Each of these cases illustrates how the return to communal house rites has spurred the creation of new social organizations with which local officialdom must contend, and in each case the rites that resulted were markedly different than their prerevolutionary antecedents. Nevertheless, the overarching strategy employed by the state has been to accept communal house rites and endorse them as important components of Vietnam's cultural heritage. In doing so it can simultaneously meet local aspirations to conduct rites that celebrate local history and develop local pride, while also giving the state the opportunity to ensure that they do not deviate too much from the official line.

The government's approach to resurgent rites has enabled them to keep some measure of control over them, but the government must still periodically deal with the emergence of public rites that deviate from official dictates. In the north, one of the more spectacular examples of this has been the emergence of cultic activities associated with Ho Chi Minh. A common theme that runs throughout Vietnamese religious history is the worship of historical heroes, particularly those who have played a significant role in protecting Vietnam from foreign invaders (see Taylor 1983: 336). Prominent cults have developed around such heroes as the Trung Sisters, Trieu Thi Trinh, who led a rebellion against the Chinese in 248 A.D., and the famous general Tran Hung Dao, who devised the strategy to turn back the Mongol invasion in 1285. The logic behind hero worship holds that the hero's achievements were the result of supernatural assistance channelled through them or supernatural powers they possessed. After their death, these associated powers persist, and the living can enlist the hero's soul for assistance. For example, the spirit of Tran Hung Dao is regarded as one of the most powerful spirits in the Vietnamese pantheon who can be called upon to assist the living to secure good fortune or eliminate bad fortune. While he was alive, some northerners held that Ho Chi Minh belonged to this category of hero. Some describe him as a "living god" (*than song*) sent by the heavens to rescue Vietnam from foreign domination. Some also say that one can detect a third pupil in his right eye in official portraits, a marker of his divinity. After his death, the government sought to promote the reverence of Ho as a symbol of the socialist regime but discouraged the formation of cultic activities devoted to him. Since the 1990s, a number of innovative ritual practices have emerged. In some cases, Ho has been merged into preexisting rites, such as in the references that are made to him in rites devoted to the mythical hero Lac Long Quan in the Binh Da festival (see Phan Khanh 1992: 243–58). In other cases, cultic rites have been created. The largest was in Vinh Phu province where a group proclaimed that Ho was the eighteenth king in the mythical Hung dynasty that is regarded as Vietnam's first. Officials moved quickly to disband the cult (see Mydans 1996). At a more mundane level, many people worship Ho in their homes, and some villages in north Vietnam have also attempted to install Ho as their guardian spirit (see Malarney 2002: 189–207). Here again, officials have moved in to prevent the installation of Ho as guardian spirit.

The government manifests similar concerns about the worship of heroes in southern Vietnam, but in this case they have sought to prevent the emergence of cults associated with heroes not approved by the government. The Vietnamese

Communists came to power after the dissolution of the Nguyen dynasty in the 1940s and had historically opposed the monarchy. The people of southern and central Vietnam, however, had cults devoted to a number of heroes associated with the Nguyen dynasty, such as the worship of Marshall Nguyen Huynh Duc in Khanh Hau (see Hickey 1964). After 1975 the Communist government attempted to halt the worship of such heroes and replace them with those approved by the government. This move has not been particularly successful (see Luong 1994), but the government still wants to ensure that large-scale cults and festivals associated with those heroes do not emerge and become a focus of political opposition. With all of the resurgent public rituals, the government's continuing aim is to make sure that they remain arenas for the celebration of ideas that the government supports and do not become places where destabilizing forces could emerge.[14]

MAGIC, ECONOMY, AND SOCIETY

Since the introduction of market reforms in 1986, Vietnam has experienced tremendous economic growth. The country never succeeded in assuming a place among the "Asian Tigers" as many journalists and business people predicted in the early 1990s, yet it has nevertheless witnessed growth rates in excess of five percent for the past decade. The benefits of this growth are immediately visible in new construction and the proliferation of consumer goods one now sees on the streets, but while this growth has occurred, its benefits have not been evenly distributed throughout the country. As Luong notes in this volume, the poverty rate has dropped from 58 percent of the population living in poverty in 1992–1993 to 37 percent in 1998, but as the figures indicate, many people remain very poor. This has been particularly true in the countryside where economic opportunities outside of agriculture have remained limited. Alongside this poverty has been another complicating factor, the increase of uncertainty and indeterminacy in people's lives. It is indisputable that Vietnam, in the years before economic reform, was one of the world's poorest countries. All of the measures of poverty, such as gross national product, agricultural yields, or per capita income, demonstrated the dimensions of Vietnam's poverty. However, despite these figures, a social safety net still existed. Needy members of agricultural cooperatives, for example, received public assistance to help them through their difficult times, and although their quality and availability were modest, medical care and education were also available to all citizens. One elderly man described this situation to me in the early 1990s with the comment, "We were poor then, but we were all poor." The implementation of economic reforms has eliminated this safety net. Many people are now more vulnerable than before as they must provide for themselves and often have little to fall back upon.

As social and financial insecurity has increased, many people have correspondingly attempted to marshal the supernatural in order to provide security and success in their endeavors, particularly in the economic realm. Many Vietnamese hold the idea that one's individual and family financial success are linked to supernatural entities. The entities most directly responsible for this are the family ancestors. As one adage puts it, "one makes a living because of the graves" (*lam an duoc do mo do ma*), a metaphorical reference to the idea that well-cared-for ancestors will reciprocate by bringing good fortune to the living. While the correct engagement with the ancestors includes the general promise of success, many Vietnamese now directly engage the supernatural realm in order to achieve specific goals. Much of this activity can be described as magical, if we accept Max Weber's definition of magical activity as involving the "coercion of the gods" (Weber 1978: 422). One of the simplest forms of this is visible in the large number of students who flock to shrines and temples in Hanoi and Ho Chi Minh City around the time of the annual university entrance examinations. Many comment that they are not entirely sure if it will help, but, on the other hand, it probably cannot hurt. Young people also visit shrines and temples for more mundane reasons, such as to seek supernatural assistance in maintaining good health or even finding a good marriage partner. Some people also visit specific sites in order to achieve benefits for which that site is famous. For example, some northern couples having difficulties conceiving a child visit the Perfume Pagoda for assistance in becoming pregnant. One also sees large numbers of people making magical offerings at shrines and temples in the first few days after the Lunar New Year (*Tet Nguyen Dan*). From the 1950s to the 1980s people tended to concentrate on rites conducted within the home or in their villages, but now large numbers of people make trips to specific shrines in order to ask for health and good fortune in the coming year. The composition of the groups at these sites is mixed, although women and the young tend to be visible more often conducting such magical rites.[15]

The group in Vietnamese society that has perhaps become the most active in the conduct of magical rites are female market traders and other business people. Although the composition of the former group varies, from those who have successful stalls in established markets to those who simply sell a handful of items from a basket on the roadside, a common trend among them is to try to harness the supernatural in order to ensure success. Many women in these trades will begin their work day with a series of brief rites dedicated to a local spirit. For those who have an established place of sales, there is almost always an "Altar for the Spirits of Wealth and Fortune" (*ban tho than loc than tai*) dedicated to the guardian spirit of the land and a male spirit that brings wealth and good fortune to traders. These altars are normally located in small cabinets placed on the floor and are often visible from the outside. Beyond the daily rites conducted at these altars, many traders will also conduct special rites to the spirits in shrines and temples on the symbolically important first and fifteenth of every lunar month as well as around the Lunar New Year. People who are critical of these practices, usually men, like to comment that female peddlers and small traders are the most superstitious members of Vietnamese society. Some like to needle the traders by vociferously bargaining for goods in the early morning markets. Many traders assert that the quality of the interaction with the day's first customer will set the tone for the entire day, placing a premium on the avoidance of rancour and argument with the customer. The calculating hold that one can therefore get the lowest possible price at that time, thus it is best to bargain hard. After such an encounter, the trader might conduct a brief rite in which they burn an object made of paper or straw in order to eliminate any lingering malign influence brought by the customer. Beyond these traders, many other Vietnamese also propitiate the supernatural in order to achieve financial stability and economic success.

Several sites in Vietnam, such as Ba Chua Xu temple in Chau Doc and a number of Chinese temples in the south, have become renowned locales wherein the living attempt to harness the supernatural for economic success (see Do 1997: 77–78). Perhaps the most famous is the shrine of the Goddess of the Treasury (*Den Ba Chua Kho*) located in Co Le village of Bac Ninh province northeast of Hanoi (see Khanh Duyen 1994; Mydans 1996). The legend of the Goddess of the Treasury asserts that she was born into a poor family in Bac Ninh but later married a Ly king. A skilled teacher and administrator, she was greatly revered by local people during her lifetime because of her many achievements on their behalf. Not only did she bring prosperity to the local population by persuading the king to allow them to occupy fallow lands, she also turned a population of prisoners of war into prosperous farmers and managed the supplies of the local military during an incursion into the area by Sung Chinese troops. This link between her spirit and prosperity remained after her death as local residents began regularly worshipping her spirit on the tenth of the first lunar month. Although activity at the shrine almost ceased from the mid-1950s to the late 1980s, in the last decade it has seen a dramatic rise in ritual activity, much of it of a highly transactional character. People from across the north, particularly Hanoi residents engaged in commerce, visit the shrine in the first months of the lunar year to present offerings and "borrow" money from the goddess. This money does not take material form, but the amount is precisely stipulated. In borrowing the money, the borrower not only takes on the debt but also requests the goddess's support and assistance in their endeavors for the year. At the lunar year's end they must then repay the debt by returning to the shrine and presenting a tray of offerings to the goddess. They repay the debt by presenting the amount borrowed plus interest in the form of votive paper gold or money. After presenting the offerings and propitiating the spirit, supplicants burn the votive paper objects in an area behind the shrine. The government still considers these objects superstitious, yet the rear area is completely blanketed in ash and smoke. The shrine is busiest during the first and twelfth lunar months, a point evident in the packed roads between the shrine and Hanoi during those months.

An article in the 26 January 2000 issue of the newspaper *Phap Luat* indicates that not only is activity at the shrine expanding, so is the range of people now visiting there. During my first visit to the shrine in 1994, there were perhaps thirty stalls in its environs that sold a variety of different offerings to visitors, most of which could be purchased quite cheaply. The number of stalls now exceeds one hundred and an average set of complete offerings now costs some 200,000 dong. The clientele has also expanded from private entrepreneurs to representatives of state-owned organizations and businesses. The director of one enterprise from the city of Hai Phong was alleged to have purchased offerings worth a total of 60 million Vietnamese dong. This purchase was so enormous that it apparently required twenty people to carry it into the shrine (Lam Du 2000: 12). While some Vietnamese regard these extraordinary displays of ritual extravagance as a vital and worthwhile reengagement with the supernatural realm, they also have their critics. Those with an allegiance to the party or its cultural campaigns regard them as a waste of resources in activities that will have no empirical effect. Many with this attitude derisively refer to these practices as "buying and selling spirits" (*buon than ban thanh*). For them, the resources would be put to better use if invested in productive activities. For those who conduct rites for the Goddess of the Treasury or other spirits, their actions ideally give them an extra measure of security in their lives.

SPIRIT MEDIUMSHIP REAPPEARS IN THE PUBLIC DOMAIN

Attempts to harness the supernatural for financial gain and security are part of a broader reengagement with the supernatural visible in contemporary Vietnamese society. In a visit to any city or village across the country, one can easily learn who the most skilled diviners, spirit priests, or astrologers are, and in everyday conversations one regularly hears of people's visits to such specialists and their outcomes. One can also see a visible increase in the practice of geomancy, the consultation of horoscopes to determine when to conduct specific activities, such as weddings or beginning a trip, and the construction of sacred sites, such as altars or shrines, to meet people's spiritual needs. Slowly emerging back into public view alongside this general trend has been spirit mediumship. As discussed above, spirit mediumship never completely disappeared from Vietnamese society. Instead it became a secretive activity generally conducted in the privacy of people's homes, although it does appear that some cases were more public. In the early 1990s spirit mediums were still extremely reluctant to publicly perform their rites. By the mid-1990s they were becoming more open in their activities. Despite this presence, the government still officially regards spirit mediumship as a superstitious practice and regularly condemns it. However, officials today rarely crack down on mediums, thus mediumship has begun to flourish again.[16]

The reemergence of spirit mediumship manifests a number of important trends in Vietnamese social life. The most obvious characteristic of its resurgence is its gender dimension. As before, spirit mediumship involves a set of rites and ideas most commonly advanced by women. The set of ideas associated with mediumship is called the "Four Palace Religion" (*Dao Tu Phu*) or the "Mother Religion" (*Dao Mau*). It consists of a wide pantheon of spirits, such as former mandarins, ancient military heroes, and more mundane individuals, both male and female, that are worshipped at shrines (*den, dien, mieu,* or *phu*) and not at more traditional male spaces, such as communal houses. Both men and women possess a basic knowledge of the outlines of this religious system, such as its main spirits and practices, but it is more often women who engage these spirits. The vast majority of mediums are also women. Barley Norton has commented that most mediums experience some form of family crisis, such as the death of a newborn baby or the inability to care for children, that leads to their decision to be initiated as a medium (see Norton n.d.). Many also experience a call by the spirits to become a medium. Initiation then takes place in a rite conducted by a senior medium. In an interesting aside, Norton also notes that while there are more female mediums, male mediums generally enjoy greater social status, wealth, and influence. The most famous medium in northern Vietnam is male. He has presided over the renovation of a number of important shrines in both Hanoi and the countryside. In spirit medium groups (*hoi dong bong*), male mediums often exercise a leadership role, a point brought home to me when the women of one group outside of Hanoi excitedly invited me to witness their rites, but then quickly rescinded the invitation when a male medium in the group opposed the offer. Male mediums also tend to look after important public shrines. Women generally do not look after larger shrines, and rarely look after more than one. Those that they look after are generally smaller and less opulent, with the most common practice being for them to look after small, family-based shrines (*dien*) attached to their homes. Although male mediums may enjoy some influence in mediumship circles, their overall social influence is generally limited by the fact that most men regard mediumship as a female activity and many of the male mediums are considered "effeminate" (*dong co*). Many never marry, and some are homosexual, both of which place them outside of the standard expectations for masculinity and male social status. Norton also reports that entrance into spirit medium groups can create conflicts between women and their husbands who disapprove of their activities (see Norton n.d.).

Like the cases of people seeking supernatural assistance in their financial affairs, many people turn to mediums in order to solve problems they have encountered. Despite the decades of propagation of the state's secular ideology, many Vietnamese still retain an assortment of ideas which assert that a wide variety of supernatural forces or entities, such as fate, chance, or the activities of spirits, are the cause of human suffering and misfortune. Spirit mediums play a vital role in both the determination of the cause of misfortune and its redress. To give a characteristic example, an elderly woman living in a commune outside of Hanoi had, over a period of several years, encountered a long string of misfortunes, notably financial hardships and repeated illness among her children. Unable to determine the cause of her problems, the woman consulted a spirit medium who then organized a rite to diagnose the problem. The medium discovered that the woman's misfortune originated from a distant family ancestor who was punishing the family for neglecting him in family ancestral rites. The medium outlined a series of measures the family needed to perform to eliminate their misfortune. This they did, and their misfortune came to an end.

Spirit mediumship also plays an important role in explaining and diagnosing madness. Vietnamese folk theories of madness and mental illness often attribute them to the activities of spirits. Both benevolent and malevolent spirits can invade a person's body and cause behavior considered mad, such as outbursts of inappropriate speech or descent into a fully catatonic state. On these occasions, spirits are often suspected, and mediums are called in to mollify the offending spirit and force it from the victim's body. Recent research by Narquis Barak has demonstrated that residents of some rural areas in the north have maintained such ideas about the causes of mental illness, in spite of the institutional development of psychiatry throughout the country. Many people prefer to consult a medium rather than see a psychiatrist (Barak, personal communication). In all of these cases, it should also be noted that women are the most likely to turn to mediums to solve such problems. The reasons for this vary on an individual basis, but women in the Vietnamese family bear the primary responsibility for its well-being. This plays out in such different manners as making sure family members are fed, children educated, and the sick tended to, but it also entails a deeper responsibility to ensure that family life remains happy and harmonious. When problems occur, it is often the women who assume the most active role in solving them. Interestingly, it appears that most of the women active in spirit medium circles are still in their childbearing and parenting years, the time when such responsibilities are heaviest.[17] As they age, many women turn away from the more immediate solutions that spirit medium rites offer and become more interested in Buddhism, which offers more compelling answers to such important questions as what will happen after death.

On a final note, it is important to acknowledge the role of Vietnamese intellectuals in transforming the sociopolitical classification of spirit mediumship and its related system of ideas. One of the most politically charged semantic distinctions that exists in the Vietnamese language is that between "legitimate religious beliefs" (*tin nguong*) and "superstitions" (*me tin di doan*). With the advent of the revolution, the state assumed for itself the role of defining *tin nguong* and *me tin di doan*. The former category included such important phenomena and practices as ancestor worship or the veneration of national heroes, while the latter included the many ideas and practices discussed above, notably spirit mediumship. Since the early 1990s, a number of scholars, although particularly those associated with Ngo Duc Thinh and the Institute of Folklore, have begun to challenge this classification. Building upon an important component of Vietnamese Communist historiography which asserts that Vietnamese society was originally matriarchal but became patriarchal after Vietnam's conversion to Confucianism, Thinh has argued that the "Mother Religion" associated with spirit mediumship is a vestige of this matriarchal period. Thus, instead of exclusively representing a set of superstitious practices, "Mother Religion" in fact constitutes a set of indigenous ideas and practices that should be further examined and respected (see Ngo Duc Thinh 1996). It is true that this reclassification has yet to become a part of official ideology, indeed some government publications still refer to mediumship as a "social

evil" (*te nan xa hoi*), but it does slightly move the boundaries so that spirit mediumship and its associated ideas can become an object of legitimate academic inquiry, something that was impossible only fifteen years ago.

ORGANIZED RELIGION AND THE THREAT TO STATE POWER

The relaxation of restrictions on religious and ritual practices has represented a
scaling back of state influence in cultural affairs. However, while the government
has shown a more open attitude toward the above activities, it has continued to
vigorously maintain control over the institutional life of organized religions.[18] This
is accomplished through the activities of such organizations as the Office of Religious Affairs, the Communist Party–controlled Fatherland Front, and the state-
sponsored religious organizations, such as the Buddhist Association of Vietnam
and the Catholic Patriotic Association. Controls over these groups are maintained
in a number of different manners beyond requiring official permission to conduct
large-scale festivals. They include government censorship and controls over the
printing of religious literature, quotas on the number of religious specialists that
can be ordained each year, the vetting of candidates for ordination in order to ensure that they do not have unacceptable political backgrounds, controls over the
placement and transfer of religious personnel, restrictions on the number of seminaries or training schools and the number of students in them, requirements for
permission to hold religious retreats or previously unscheduled convocations, the
registration of all religious groups, the disbanding of unsanctioned religious organizations, limitations on charitable activities, and permission requirements to
build or repair religious buildings or facilities. Beyond these controls, the government also frequently issues statements that the members of the different religious
groups should be patriotic and not engage in activities that threaten national unity.
Exhortations against the latter in fact are backed by stiff penalties, including
imprisonment, for those who engage in actions that the government regards as
harmful to national unity. All of these activities and restrictions indicate that the
government still perceives organized religion as a potential threat to state power.
Government relations with the different religious groups over the last decade have
been both variable and contradictory, but a recent series of high-profile clashes has
shown that future instability related to religious issues is possible.[19]

The religious group that has been the greatest source of concern for the government is the country's Buddhists, particularly in southern and central Vietnam. During the period of the American war, several Buddhist organizations, notably the An
Quang sect based in Hue, took a highly critical stance toward the Saigon government.[20] Following unification in 1975, negotiations began to integrate the southern
United Buddhist Church of Vietnam (UBCV), which included the An Quang sect
and the formerly pro-southern government Vien Hoa Dao sect, into the official
Buddhist Association of Vietnam. While some southern Buddhists accepted inte-

gration, many associated with the An Quang sect opposed such a move and in 1981 these members of the UBCV chose not to join with the Buddhist Association of Vietnam. Since then, oppositional UBCV members have remained critical of the Hanoi government. Their leader, the Venerable Thich Huyen Quang from Hue, has been confined to an isolated temple in Quang Ngai province for almost twenty years. The situation with the UBCV boiled over in the spring of 1993 when a government crackdown on the headquarters of the movement at Linh Mu pagoda in Hue led to a series of large-scale public demonstrations in the city. A number of prominent monks were subsequently arrested and detained for long periods. Relations remained tense in the following years and further monks were arrested. Relations appeared to begin improving in the late 1990s, particularly as evident in the release in 1998 of three prominent UBCV monks, Thich Quang Do, Thich Tue Sy, and Thich Tri Sieu, under a general amnesty. However, other prominent UBCV monks, such as Thich Huyen Quang, Thich Quang Do, and Thich Nhat Ban, remain in detention.[21] While the government appeared to be improving relations with the Buddhists, it also further exacerbated them in early 1998 when the Office of Religious Affairs passed an ordinance that prohibited the small number of Theravada Buddhist monks and nuns from begging for alms. Although the vast majority of Vietnam's Buddhists, including the UBCV, follow the Mahayana tradition of Buddhism and therefore do not beg for alms, a small number of Buddhists in southern Vietnam follow the Theravada tradition that predominates in Cambodia, Laos, Thailand, and Burma. Many Buddhists saw the alms restrictions as an unnecessary insult to Buddhism. A 1999 United States State Department report on religious freedom in Vietnam comments that 1998 and 1999 saw no new arrests or detentions of monks, but tensions and suspicions remained unresolved. The government is fully aware of organized Buddhism's role in destabilizing the Ngo Dinh Diem regime in the early 1960s. With this in mind, it still prohibits prominent monks from that era who now live abroad, such as Thich Nhat Hanh, from returning.

The second group that is a cause for concern is the Catholics. There are presently some six to seven million Catholics in Vietnam (approximately 8 percent of the population), most of whom are concentrated in the northern provinces of Nam Dinh and Ninh Binh on the South China Sea coast, and in Ho Chi Minh City and its surrounding provinces. Unlike the majority of the country's Buddhists, who have a more diffuse identity of themselves as Buddhists, Vietnamese Catholics frequently have a strong self-identity as Catholic and thus constitute a more cohesive and unified social group. As with the Buddhists, government relations with the Catholics have been improving, although there have been points of tension. One of the issues that had bedeviled relations for years was the appointment of bishops. During the 1990s a number of new bishops needed to be appointed, but the Vietnamese government rejected the authority of the Vatican to do so. In 1998 the government allowed the ordination of a new archbishop of Ho Chi Minh City, a post that had been vacant for five years, and several other new bishop appointments followed. The government also relaxed the requirement that all clergy be members of the Catholic Patriotic Association, although apparently few clergy had actually joined previously. With this relaxation of relations, a number of delegations from the Vatican and other countries began to visit Vietnam and Vietnam's bishops went abroad to attend church meetings. The government also eased restrictions on religious education and charitable activities. Perhaps the greatest indication of the new openness toward Catholicism came in the enormous turnout for the annual Marian celebration at La Vang in northern Vietnam. It has been estimated that in both 1998 and 1999 tens of thousands of Vietnamese Catholics had traveled to that community to celebrate the Virgin Mary. United States' State Department figures put the numbers at 100,000, although this is difficult to confirm. All the same, it represents a significant change in government attitudes.

While positive changes were taking place, problems still remained. Church officials felt that there were still not enough clergy to tend to the nation's Catholics and that the six officially approved seminaries did not have the ability to meet their needs. Priests and church officials, who were generally free to travel around the country, also encountered difficulties when trying to work in Vietnam's northwestern provinces (these restrictions also applied to Protestant missionaries). And although some previously imprisoned priests have been released, several others remain in detention. The most persistent area of conflict has been Dong Nai province, just north of Ho Chi Minh City. Many of this province's Catholics settled here from North Vietnam after 1954 and the area has since been one of the most devout in the south. The mid-1990s saw the formation of a number of unsanctioned religious organizations, such as the Sacred Heart Group, the Holy Mother Group, the Holy Communion Youth, and others. In April 1997 the Provincial People's Committee issued Directive 1216 that ordered the disbanding of all of these groups and attempted to place the church under closer official scrutiny. These moves outraged many Catholics. The situation turned violent at the beginning of the following November when state officials attempted to sell land that belonged to a church in Tra Co. Protesters turned out in the thousands. They apparently burned down the homes of several officials, fought pitched battles with riot police, and blocked a section of National Highway One, the country's main north-south thoroughfare. Protests continued throughout the month, although the situation seemed to have eased by month's end. (These protests were particularly disturbing for the government because they occurred only a few months after the uprising in the northern province of Thai Binh, raising fears of a widespread protest movement throughout the country.) There have not been any other large-scale conflicts with Catholics since, although tensions in Dong Nai remain high and the government still looks on Catholics with suspicion. This has been made amply clear in the recent convocations between high-ranking government officials and church leaders in which the government has reiterated its position that Catholics need to be more patriotic and not engage in activities that threaten national stability.

The Vietnamese government has also remained suspicious of the country's Protestants. Unlike the Catholics, who primarily come from lowland, ethnically Vietnamese communities, most Protestants are members of highland minority groups, such as the Hmong in the north, and the Ede and Jirai in the Central Highlands. Denominationally, approximately half of the country's estimated 600,000 Protestants belong to small, charismatic "house" churches that operate independently and are not registered with the government. Half of these are Pentecostal churches. The remainder of the country's Protestants include "Good News" (*Tin Lanh*) churches that originate from early-twentieth-century missionary activities, and other groups. Some fifteen "Good News" churches constitute the only Protestant groups registered with the government. They have enjoyed better treatment from the government. Officials have acted much more severely against the house churches, especially among minority groups in the northwestern provinces. In these areas, officials have prevented the conduct of religious rituals and a number of Protestants have been arrested for their religious activities. It is likely in these cases that the government fears that Christianity, particularly the secretive house churches, will become a focus of resistance for minority groups that have had difficult relations with the central government.

The two final groups that remain a source of concern for the government are the Cao Dai and Hoa Hao in the south.[22] Each of these groups has somewhere between one and three million followers spread throughout the country. The largest concentrations of Cao Dai followers are found in Tay Ninh province near the Cambodian border, while most Hoa Hao followers live in An Giang province south of Ho Chi Minh City. Compared to the Buddhists and Catholics, these two groups have undergone much more severe repression that largely continues to this day. One of the primary reasons for the Cao Dai's repression was the opposition of almost all Cao Dai sects to the Communists. After 1975, the Hanoi government cultivated relations with the Do Thanh sect that had supported the Communists, but in the late 1970s the Fatherland Front took over the organization through the establishment of a "Management Committee of the Holy See." This committee, which is stocked with party officials and Cao Dai supporters, makes all of the important decisions regarding religious life and practice, notably the ordination and promotion of religious officials. In 1996 and 1997 the government brought the Cao Dai under even stricter government control. This occurred first in 1996 when, from June to September, the Communist Party organization of Tay Ninh province resolved to disband the Tay Ninh Cao Dai Church and replace it with an official Cao Dai Church that would exclude dissident church figures. Later in 1997 they abandoned the original charter for the religion, called the *Phap Chanh Truyen*, and replaced it with an officially approved document. The Cao Dai are allowed to congregate and conduct rites at their main facility in Tay Ninh (the temple there has in fact become a popular tourist destination), but their religious life is still severely restricted by the government. The establishment of the Management Committee has also produced an active resistance among some members, many of whom object to the committee's existence and the enduring vacancies for a number of high-ranking church positions. These dissidents now constitute a de facto oppositional church structure that opposes the official committee. Two Cao Dai leaders, Le Kim Bien and Pham Cong Hien, remain in detention in Kien Giang province.

Hoa Hao conflicts with the government have perhaps been the most severe. Given their armed resistance to the Communists from the 1950s onward, the Hoa Hao effectively ceased to exist as a religious organization after 1975. According to Vietnamese authorities, Hoa Hao remains as one of Vietnam's six religions, but as the government closed down all church buildings, both secular and sacred, and forbade the publication of sacred scriptures and the conduct of religious festivals, the religion ceased to publicly exist. Worshippers could, however, conduct rites in their homes. In 1998 the government softened its attitude for the first time and allowed the public conduct of a Hoa Hao festival in An Giang. Former Hoa Hao officials and practitioners are still under regular surveillance and several leaders, including Le Minh Triet, remain in administrative detention. At the end of 1999 frustrations among Hoa Hao members increased significantly due to the continued suppression of their faith and their inability to conduct public religious activities. In October two Hoa Hao leaders, the seventy-five-year-old Nguyen Thi Thu and sixty-eight-year-old Ha Hai, declared on separate occasions that they intended to take their lives by self-immolation in order to protest the government's restrictions on religion. They have yet to do so, but the government placed them under immediate surveillance to ensure that they could not. In December open confrontations broke out. One centered around an incident when a Hoa Hao follower attempted to publicly hang religious sayings and pictures of Hoa Hao founder Huynh Phu So. A policemen allegedly pulled them down and stomped on them, leading to a scuffle with local police. A second incident occurred when the police tried to prevent several hundred pilgrims from visiting Huynh Phu So's birthplace. The police arrested several individuals involved in this confrontation, but after the police station was besieged by angry family members the next morning, they released all of those arrested. It seems clear that given the extent of the Hoa Hao's suppression, such conflicts will continue to break out.

At present, the government continues to walk a fine line between allowing the members of different religious groups to practice their faiths while simultaneously ensuring that they do not become foci of dissent. At a national level, a general loosening of control has been evident as Buddhists, Catholics, and other groups renovate their sacred structures and organize larger and more public rituals. Some regions, such as in Hanoi and Ho Chi Minh City, have also allowed even greater freedom of religious practice than that allowed in some rural areas. However, the government remains firmly in control of these groups' institutional structures and officials do not hesitate to arrest religious figures they regard as political threats.

CONCLUSION

In the early months of 2000, the Vietnamese press featured five short but revealing articles. An article in a provincial newspaper from Vinh Phuc described the recent growth among poor residents of a sect established in 1971, Long Hoa Di Lac, that champions prayer and chanting to cure illness. The group had come under official criticism because of an incident in which a young boy who broke a bone died after adherents insisted on treating him with holy water and prayer (Minh Anh 2000: 4). An article in the Hanoi newspaper *An Ninh Thu Do* described a recent boom in which wealthy city residents have begun purchasing expensive coffins, sometimes for as much as $1,000, despite the government's efforts to encourage thrift in ritual practices (Hoang Van Quang 2000: 6). *Sai Gon Giai Phong* had an article that described a series of events in Cu Chi outside Ho Chi Minh City, where there has been an explosion of worship at a termite hill that some people regard as the incarnation of Avalokitesvara, the Bodhisattva of mercy. Some 200–300 people, mostly petty traders, worship there daily, although local authorities want to destroy the mound to prevent the growth of superstitions (*Sai Gon Giai Phong* 2 March 2000). The *Vietnam Economic Times* told the story of Ms. Phan Thi Bich Hang who, after being bitten by a rabid dog, gained the ability to speak with the dead. Working with others with supernatural powers, she has employed her skill extensively to help families discover the remains of dead soldiers killed in battle, reportedly with a success rate of over 70 percent (*Vietnam Economic Times* 11 April 2000). Finally, the communist periodical *Tap Chi Cong San* complained that many contemporary party members, even high-ranking members with many medals, engage in superstitious practices at temples and shrines. Apart from searching for success in business or high salaries, the article noted that some even conduct rites to avoid becoming victims of the party's contemporary restructuring efforts (Mai Thanh Hai 2000: 58–59).

The events described in the articles illustrate that despite the government's efforts to reconstitute religion and ritual, they remain vital and dynamic parts of contemporary Vietnamese life. People remain profoundly engaged with religion and ritual, and it is an important focus of social action and a destination for resource expenditures. The articles show that many of the ideas and values mobilized in these practices often conflict with official ideology. People assert the existence of the supernatural, conduct magical rites, attempt to heal through prayer, and devote significant quantities of their resources to these practices. They also demonstrate the many continuities with prerevolutionary practices. People engage Buddhist deities, seek to properly care for their dead, perform rites for good fortune or to cure illness, use expensive caskets to assert their status, and conduct rites at shrines and temples. Many of the reforms associated with these practices were foci of resistance during the reform period, and in a more relaxed environment, they have returned strongly. However, as the cases of the search for war dead and the sacred termite mound show, there is yet innovation in which preexisting themes or practices are adapted to accommodate contemporary circumstances. This latter point, which accords with the discussions in this chapter, is important to make. There has been a significant resurgence of older practices, but these have frequently been modified or transformed, and thus they do not constitute an unhindered return to the prerevolutionary status quo.

Perhaps the most significant point the newspaper articles revealed was that, in spite of the many contemporary changes, the state keeps a watchful eye on these matters and does not hesitate to voice its displeasure or even intervene to stop the practices. This latter point was shown in the 1998 passage of Directive 28 that imposes stiff penalties on people, although particularly officials, who make excessive expenditures in their family ritual practices. To implement this, in January 2000 officials in a large number of communes in Hai Duong province imposed a ban on brides wearing wedding dresses in their weddings because they contradicted policies encouraging thrift. Violaters were to be fined 300,000 dong and their grooms forced to perform community labor (*Phap Luat Thanh Pho Ho Chi Minh* 19 January 2000). It has also been evident in the closing down of cults devoted to Ho Chi Minh and the 1999 sacking of a high-ranking official in southern Vietnam for violating the sumptuary regulations. However, that latter's case also showed that those in charge of enforcing the regulations sometimes break them and are often reluctant to vigorously enforce them at the local level.

The issuance of these regulations and the periodic interventions by officials to control these practices, both of which have obvious antecedents in earlier decades, demonstrate that the resurgence process has not occurred in a context in which people have been free to do whatever they desired. Instead, they have had to contend with the state and its policies. Luong has aptly described this process as a "dialogic restructuration" of ritual practice (Luong 1994). Use of the word *dialogue* is particularly appropriate because the changes that have occurred and continue to occur have emerged out of this dialectic between these two main poles of social action. The contemporary status quo is indeed not the pure expression of the ideals of the state or its citizens. It is a combination of both. The material presented in this chapter demonstrates that Luong's insight on the dialogic quality of contemporary changes also extends further back into Vietnamese religious and ritual history. Thus, as we consider the changes of the past half-century, it is useful to speak of the "dialogic structuration" of religion and ritual, for both state and nonstate actors have had an important influence on the nature and direction of religious and ritual change. Benedict J. Tria Kerkvliet, in this volume, raises the question of the most accurate way to characterize relations between state and society in Vietnam since the commencement of the revolution. The history of religious and ritual transformation, which has not developed according to the mandates laid down by the state and its organs, demonstrates the deficiencies of the "dominating state" argument. It also demonstrates that in this realm the state has in some cases been successful in pursuing a "mobilizational corporatist" agenda, such as in the success of the Ministry of Culture and the Fatherland Front in setting publicly accepted parameters around certain activities.

However, the state has also needed to follow the lead of such nonstate organizations as the local Buddhist Associations that have played a vital role in directing change at the local level. As is clear in the case of ritual and religious transformation, no single explanation is fully compelling. Nevertheless, it is vital to recognize that the recent history of religion and ritual in Vietnam can only be understood by carefully examining the roles of and interplay between both state and nonstate actors.

NOTES

The author is grateful to Narquis Barak, Thien Do, Kirsten Endres, and Barley Norton for sharing their research, both published and unpublished, and to Hy Van Luong for his comments on an earlier draft.

1. The creation of new official heroes has been discussed by Giebel (2001) and Treglode (2001).
2. While the level of intrusion by the state into social life was unprecedented, Vietnamese governments had for centuries attempted to control cultural and ritual practices. See Tran Trong Kim (1954: 248–53), Whitmore (n.d.), Woodside (1971: 189).
3. Discussions of attempts to control sacred space can be found in Endres (2001), Luong (1994), and Malarney (2002: 41–51).
4. The work of Toan Anh (1968 and 1969) provides a useful, if at times somewhat overgeneralized, introduction to many prerevolutionary cultural practices throughout Vietnam. Phan Ke Binh (1990) provides a good introduction to many practices that existed in the early twentieth century. The classic discussion of the prerevolutionary communal house is Nguyen Van Khoan (1930). Leopold Cadiere (1992) is an excellent overview of prerevolutionary popular religious practices. Cleary (1991); Minh Chi, Ha Van Tan, and Nguyen Tai Thu (1993); Nguyen, Cuong Tu (1997); and Nguyen Lang (1977) provide useful historical information on Vietnamese Buddhism. Tran Anh Dung (1992) provides an introduction to Vietnamese Catholicism.
5. The dimensions of the reform campaign are discussed in Goodkind (1996), Luong (1993b and 1994), and Malarney (1993, 1996b, 1998, and 2002).
6. Discussions of the treatment of communal houses in different communities in the reform and contemporary periods can be found in Endres (1999 and 2001); Kleinen (1999); Luong (1992, 1993b, and 1994); and Malarney (1996a and 2002).
7. The following discussion focuses primarily on weddings. Changes associated with funerals in northern Vietnam can be found in Malarney (1996b). For the Saigon region see Ton Nu Quynh Tran (1999: 165–91). For other southern communities see Luong Hong Quang (1997: 170–79).
8. The role of women in the resurgence of ritual has been particularly pronounced in the north. Further research is needed to comparatively understand their role in southern and central Vietnam.
9. Simplifications of wedding ceremonies has also been reported in the Saigon region (see Ton Nu Quynh Tran 1999: 153–65).
10. One important question that has yet to be adequately answered is the extent to which wedding invitation practices have changed. In large communities that had a strong

256   *Shaun Kingsley Malarney*

mandarinal presence and sharp differences between rich and poor, such as Thinh Liet commune near Hanoi, wedding invitation practices did become more inclusive. Thinh Liet, which had a population of over 5,000 people and over a dozen different patrilineages in the colonial period, was a different case than small communities of less than a thousand people and few patrilineages. Thus, these changes have likely developed differently in different communities. Ton Nu Quynh Tran reports that in some contemporary communities in the Saigon region invitations have become more exclusive, while in others they have not (1999: 162).

11. The descriptions of both brideprice and feast items are drawn from northern examples. For a comparative case in the Saigon region see Ton Nu Quynh Tran (1999: 151–65); for other southern communities see Luong Hong Quang (1997: 155–70). Further research is needed to understand their constitution and variation in central Vietnam.

12. For a discussion of ideas associated with the soul and death, see Phan Chanh Cong (1993).

13. For a discussion of communal house practices in the Saigon region, see Ton Nu Quynh Tran (1999: 191–207). For other southern communities see Luong Hong Quang (1997: 85–89; 192–200).

14. Other aspects of religious and ritual change in southern Vietnam, such as activities at shrines, temples, and Cao Dai and Hoa Hao practices, are discussed in Luong Hong Quang (1997) and Ton Nu Quynh Tran (1999).

15. For a comprehensive discussion of contemporary religious practices in southern Vietnam, see Do (1995).

16. With the exception of Didier and Norton's research, little systematic work has been published on spirit mediumship in contemporary Vietnam. The two most comprehensive studies of Vietnamese spirit mediumship outside Vietnam are Fjelstad (1995) and Simon and Simon-Barouh (1973). Also valuable is Durand (1989).

17. More detailed comparative study needs to be done regarding the composition of spirit medium groups in Vietnam.

18. At present, the Vietnamese government acknowledges the existence of six "religions" in the country: Buddhism, Catholicism, Protestantism, Islam, Cao Dai, and Hoa Hao.

19. The most comprehensive discussions of the situation and politics of organized religion in contemporary Vietnam can be found in the United Nations Commission on Human Rights' December 1998 report on Vietnam, *Civil and Political Rights, Including the Question of Religious Intolerance*, and the September 1999 United States Department of State's *Annual Report on International Religious Freedom for 1999: Vietnam*. The former report is particularly useful for its extensive listing of the various directives and regulations enacted by the government to control religious life. Both documents have limitations, but they provide worthwhile introductions to the relevant issues.

20. Fitzgerald (1972) and Thich Nhat Hanh (1967) provide useful introductions to the politics of Buddhism in the 1950s and 1960s in South Vietnam.

21. Human Rights Watch/Asia (1995) discusses the dimensions of the UBCV problem.

22. Introductions to the Cao Dai and Hoa Hao can be found in Hickey (1964), Tai (1983), Oliver (1976), and Werner (1981a).

9

A Passion for Modernity: Intellectuals and the Media

David G. Marr

The idea of "society" (*xa hoi*) is closely linked with both intellectuals and the media in Vietnam. The word itself was borrowed by early-twentieth-century Vietnamese intellectuals from Japan, where "society" (*shakai*) had recently been coined to capture some of the connotations of the European concept—especially the notion of a large community existing separately from the ruler or the state. Vietnamese intellectuals quickly assumed responsibility for explaining "society" to the common people, and they often justified their own status by reference to this higher collectivity. The newly arrived printing press disseminated "society" and many other neologisms ("the people," "struggle," "progress," "democracy") far more widely than would have been possible with traditional ink brush or word of mouth. Other media followed, notably the cinema, radio, and eventually television. Each medium created new producers and consumers who helped to expand and redefine the meaning of "society." The state took a direct interest in the media, often cutting across intellectual aspirations. Intellectuals pursued their dream of using the media to transform reality, sometimes in close association with the state, sometimes in opposition.

"Put three intellectuals together and you've got a newspaper," was a joke I heard often among Vietnamese in Saigon during the 1960s. These words evoke nicely the passionate love affair between intellectuals and the printing press that began at the turn of the twentieth century, while also commenting wryly on the tendency of small groups of intellectuals to conduct polemics or indulge their own cultural pretensions. Being part of a publishing initiative—whether as editor, writer, printer, distributor, or avid reader—gave repeated generations a sense of community and empowerment, even if circulation figures were low or certain subjects excluded due to state censorship. The excitement of launching a new newspaper, literary journal, novel, poetry collection, or history book helped to frame the intellectual experience, with emotions being heightened by knowledge of the many obstacles encountered and overcome. Some of this exhilaration carried over to the launching of new movies, radio programs, or television series, although most intellectuals continued to reserve first ranking for the print media.

During the past decade, a new generation of media practitioners has arisen, eager to master advanced technology, able to access a far wider range of sources, not tied to a state-determined career path, and less troubled than their elders about treating information as a market commodity. The growing commercialization of Vietnam's entirely state-owned media bothers Communist Party leaders, who routinely talk ominously of tighter controls. Older intellectuals also complain about the fudging of news and entertainment, the drop to the lowest common denominator when searching for readers or viewers, and other such tendencies long familiar to inhabitants of capitalist countries. However, no one in Vietnam wants to return to the media system of earlier decades.

To appreciate what has changed in recent years, and what remains tied to the past, it is necessary to begin the story much earlier. This chapter explores the intellectual-media symbiosis in Vietnam, relates both elements to the state, and positions everyone within eighty years of challenge, experimentation, war, revolution, dictatorship, and socioeconomic transformation. Media content ("the message") is seldom discussed here—a deliberate omission designed to tease out factors not necessarily dependent on ideology, politics, or other topical preoccupations. Intellectuals who put ideas over everything, or see themselves as the conscience of society, may take exception to this approach.

PRECOLONIAL LITERATI

An intellectual can be defined as someone who articulates the hopes, fears, and symbolic values of his/her community. Vietnam has long been well endowed with such persons, commenting on nature, the universe, human experience, customs, and rules of behavior. Transmission has been formal and informal, written and oral, centrally sanctioned and locally inspired. The arrival of Chinese writing more than two thousand years ago gave a few individuals the opportunity to access prior recorded knowledge, inscribe their own thoughts, and hopefully transfer this accumulated wisdom to subsequent generations. Most writing was by brush, and even the eventual arrival of woodblock printing only served to multiply dissemination by fifty or sixty copies before new blocks had to be carved.

Prior to the twentieth century, the vast majority of Vietnam's intellectuals were dispersed in the countryside, making their way as teachers, priests, scribes, healers, and fortune-tellers. Most could read and write classical Chinese, although books and manuscripts were far from abundant. Despite respect, even reverence for the written word among the population at large, the literacy rate remained low. Intellectuals thus spent most of their time communicating verbally with fellow villagers, whether it involved consulting about taxes or dispensing medicine, selecting an auspicious date for a marriage or supervising a funeral.

Intellectuals might be scattered, but the precolonial Vietnamese state paid close attention to them. Most importantly, the state organized examinations to recruit

officials and to foster ideological orthodoxy. Those persons who passed a preliminary screening at district or provincial level could enroll for the regional compe-
titions. The limited number of men (women being excluded) who survived the
regional exams were eligible for the metropolitan and palace exams. Top-scoring
individuals had their names inscribed on dynastic stele and received choice
mandarin positions. Candidates marked a bit lower were offered jobs as district
officials, with hopes of eventual promotion to court if they managed to avoid
trouble. The thousands of literati who failed the exams at one level or another
could try again later, meanwhile retreating to their home villages.

A few families (perhaps one or two per district on average) became well known
for their capacity to produce successful examination graduates. Other families
would try to marry their daughters into these prestigious scholar families. Young
men arrived from distant villages begging to be accepted for instruction. Out of
these relationships local political alliances were forged, which might then extend
into the court, even the royal clan, when members of such alliances were appointed
to high position. Retiring mandarins normally returned home and endeavored to
reproduce their achievements among the younger generation. Few scholar families
managed to establish substantial library collections or private academies, however.

This left the royal court as the only focal point of intensive intellectual activity,
to include preparing historical chronicles, compiling gazetteers, offering policy
advice, annotating literary texts, and circulating poetry creations. Many a court-
based scholar received praise and benefactions from the emperor one year, only to
be disgraced and ejected the next. A palace school was established as early as the
eleventh century to train members of the royal clan and allied families. From
the late fifteenth century, sons of mandarins and a few youths recommended by
district education officials were permitted to study as well.

The founder of the Nguyen dynasty, Emperor Gia Long (r. 1802–1820), and especially his son, Ming Mang (r. 1820–1841), personally supervised the acquisition
of books from private Vietnamese owners, from Chinese merchants in Cho Lon,
and by members of routine tributary missions to the Middle Kingdom. Imitating
Chinese court practice, Ming Mang established the Historical Institute (Quoc Su
Quan) to codify what was held, to recopy and annotate selected texts, and to assist him in promulgating authentic knowledge (Woodside 1971: 114–15, 119,
123–25). This whole process of gaining control over the written record was an important attribute of kingship in Vietnam.

FRENCH COLONIAL ERA

The Printing Press Revolution

As French forces smashed their way into Vietnam from the 1860s on, intellectuals
at all levels tried to make sense of what was happening and respond accordingly.
Court scholars debated policy options, provincial officials dispatched urgent me-
morials, local literati petitioned the emperor in anguished tones. When all this

proved fruitless, intellectuals often acted according to their own lights, whether by attempting to organize armed resistance to the French or by accommodating themselves to foreign domination. By the 1890s overt opposition had been quelled. For the next forty years, most Vietnamese intellectuals accepted colonialism in the de facto sense, meaning that they eschewed violent attacks, learned the basic requirements of the new order, and sought opportunities to advance themselves without necessarily endorsing the legitimacy of French rule.

Attempts to fathom the roots of western power had begun among a handful of Vietnamese intellectuals from the mid-nineteenth century, but not until the first years of the twentieth century did this become a consuming passion. Classically trained scholars looked first to the Chinese "New Learning" books filtering into the colony, often recopying them by hand from one location to the next. Several hundred scholars and students managed to travel illegally to Japan and China, thenceforth contributing their own written observations, commentary, and recommendations. Meanwhile, a few intellectuals in Saigon possessed sufficient mastery of French to be able to translate and interpret works arriving directly from the métropole. First in Saigon, then increasingly in Hanoi as well, intellectuals chose to employ *quoc ngu*, the Roman alphabet linked to spoken Vietnamese, rather than continue to rely on the classical Chinese writing system. This shift became irreversible after the French discontinued the civil examinations in Chinese in 1915–1919.

Access to the modern printing press dramatically transformed Vietnamese intellectual behavior. The first movable type printing press arrived with the French occupation forces in the early 1860s, to produce edicts, a gazette, and official stationery. In subsequent decades a limited number of books and pamphlets appeared as well. Not until the turn of the century, however, did Vietnamese intellectuals establish a foothold in the colonial publishing business, as editors, writers, and proofreaders. With the rapid growth of the cities of Saigon and Hanoi, and the emergence of a dozen or more provincial towns as well, clerks, shopkeepers, and secondary school students looked for reading materials. Rural intellectuals visited these cities and towns increasingly, and some found ways to settle. The colonial telegraph system made newspapers current, and the postal system enabled the submission of manuscripts and distribution of publications with a speed and economy inconceivable before. By the early 1920s, fascinated by the potential power of the press, Vietnamese intellectuals formed small editorial groups, sought funding, and applied for authorization to publish a wide variety of publications. The printing press also depersonalized communication, with intellectuals moving from face-to-face contact to writing for a largely anonymous audience. While print depersonalization troubled some older intellectuals, younger modernists argued that it helped to break the static grip of the family and the village, in favor of dynamic "society" or "the people."

Testing the parameters of colonial print censorship became an art form among Vietnamese editors and publishers. When officials closed down a particular newspaper, the same team often managed to open up under a different masthead within months. French language publications encountered far less restrictions than *quoc ngu*, although they were not immune to police retribution. Text censored from a newspaper might be allowed to appear in pamphlet form. Materials banned in Annam or Tonkin could often be distributed in Cochinchina. Rules also varied from year to year.

The number of people able to read a Vietnamese (*quoc ngu*) newspaper or book may have doubled between 1925 and 1945, reaching ten percent of the total population (Marr 1981: 34). While still low by western standards of the day, such a literacy rate probably exceeded all other colonial societies in Asia with the exception of Singapore and the Philippines. During those two decades, at least thirty million bound publications were printed in Vietnam, or about sixteen to eighteen books per literate individual.[1] Some Vietnamese newspapers achieved circulation rates of 10,000 copies or more, but most had to be content with printing 2,000–3,000 copies. French language newspapers seldom exceeded 1,500 copies (Marr 1981: 46–51, 338). The number of periodical titles climbed remarkably, from 96 titles in 1922 to 153 in 1929; the government authorized 230 new periodicals to appear in 1936 alone, before numbers dropped sharply during World War II. Between 30 and 40 papers disappeared each year (Nguyen Thanh 1984: 31, 76; Woodside 1976: 78–82).

Vietnam's long scholastic tradition had imbued paper, pen, and ink with quasimagical significance. Now, thanks to modern publishing techniques and communications, it was possible for office clerks, primary schoolteachers, or hospital orderlies not only to read for their own edification or pleasure but also to submit their creations to editors and see them printed for thousands of other people to read. Most newspapers contained a letters-to-the-editor section. Taking up a French convention, the "Forum," Vietnamese periodicals identified certain topics worthy of public discussion, invited readers to submit short essays, published a selection, and then summed up opinion in a concluding editorial. Some papers offered readers an opportunity to participate in public opinion surveys, another innovation (Nguyen Van Ky 1995: 107–8). Such an exchange of opinion over such distances would have been impossible only a decade earlier. Nonetheless, post office staff were known to open personal mail on occasion, and certain periodicals were likely to become "lost" enroute to readers.

Authors scattered in the countryside submitted essays, short stories, and poems to faraway editors, and sometimes were taken on as regular contributors. When this didn't succeed, an author could still approach a printing house with a manuscript, agree on a total cost, pay thirty percent in advance, obtain censorship clearance, and then handle most of the publicity and distribution as well. Small groups of intellectuals pooled resources to do the same. Novelists often convinced a newspaper to serialize their work; if reader response was positive, republication was arranged quickly in book form (Marr 1981: 50, 154).

Cartoons appeared in Vietnamese periodicals from the late 1920s, and soon cartoonists were using this new medium to considerable critical and satirical effect. Good cartoons sometimes went on the front page, undoubtedly helping to sell papers. Cartoonists developed visual stereotypes to represent the French official, the

Vietnamese mandarin, the village headman, the westernized young woman, the exploited peasant, and many more. One cartoon character in particular, Ly Toet,
came to symbolize the anachronistic village elder, dressed in traditional black tunic, long hair tied in a bun, and toting his black umbrella as status marker. Ly Toet
was laughable in his encounters with modernity, yet cartoonists generally portrayed him as curious about the new, not stupid, and not hiding at home. Relations
between the sexes were another favorite topic for 1930s cartoonists, the humor often revealing a sense of insecurity among Vietnamese men about changes in the attitudes and behavior of women. During the Popular Front period (1936–1938),
cartoons took on a much sharper political edge, often condemning colonial inequality, exploitation, and physical repression (Nguyen Van Ky 1995: 193–228).

Editors and Readers

Editors became the most talked-about intellectuals of the 1920s and 1930s. They
rose or fell on their capacity to manage a volatile contingent of creative writers, literary critics, journalists, translators, and cartoonists, meanwhile usually producing
articles themselves, and maintaining good relations (they hoped) with financial
backers and the publisher who answered legally to the colonial authorities. The
earliest Vietnamese editorial luminary was Nguyen Van Vinh (1882–1936), who
began his press career under the tutelage of François Henri Schneider, owner of the
largest private printing and publishing business in Indochina. As editor of *Dong
Duong Tap Chi* (Indochina Journal), appearing between 1913 and 1918, Nguyen
Van Vinh mocked the knee-jerk tendency of most of his intellectual contemporaries to rely on Chinese or Japanese interpretations of western knowledge, instead
of going directly to French sources. He himself was a prolific translator from
French, deliberately using a freewheeling oral style compared to the Chinese-based
translations of his friendly competitor, Pham Quynh (1892–1945), whose paramount objective was to raise *quoc ngu* literature above its plebeian origins and foster a sense of majesty, ceremony, and refinement (Marr 1981: 150, 161; Woodside
1976: 75; Nguyen Van Ky 1995: 143, 173, 181).

The most extraordinary editor of the 1920s was Nguyen An Ninh (1900–1943),
a brash young law graduate who had observed journalism at its font, Paris, and
who proceeded to capture the imagination of French-reading intellectuals with a
series of saucy, incisive periodicals that came and went according to the reactions
of distracted colonial officials in Saigon. With *La Cloche Fêlée*, Nguyen An Ninh
not only wrote and edited most of the content but scandalized older intellectuals
by sometimes hawking his own papers on the street as well. Aspiring journalists
from Tonkin and Annam soon rushed to Saigon to emulate his efforts. Enduring
arrest and incarceration on a number of occasions, Nguyen An Ninh eventually
perished on the prison island of Poulo Condore (Con Son) (Tai 1992: 120–45).

Hoang Tich Chu (1897–1933), another student returned from France, moved in a
different editorial direction, aiming to attract readers with news scoops written in

matter-of-fact prose rather than flashy polemics or literary creations. He employed the international news services skillfully and captured reader attention with photographs and cartoons. Linguistically, the movement begun by Hoang Tich Chu to communicate in spartan sentences, with the least possible ambiguity, exerted a lasting impact on both written and spoken Vietnamese (Marr 1981: 164–65).

The preeminent editor of the 1930s was Nguyen Tuong Tam (1906–1963), better known by his pen name of Nhat Linh. Two years after returning from France in 1930, Nhat Linh took control of a Hanoi weekly called *Phong Hoa* (Customs), quickly transforming it into the most important cultural and social publication of the era. As Neil Jamieson has put it, Nhat Linh "worked day and night writing editorials, short stories, and novels; drawing illustrations; making staff assignments; soliciting manuscripts; calculating precarious financial projections" (Jamieson 1993: 114). Amid the text, Nhat Linh sprinkled lively cartoons and drawings in the manner of *Canard Enchaîné* (Paris), as well as the first Vietnamese crossword puzzles. What is now considered Vietnam's traditional national costume for women, the *ao dai*, was actually developed from week to week on the pages of *Phong Hoa*. Many novels that still captivate Vietnamese readers today were first serialized in *Phong Hoa*, then published in the *Tu Luc Van Doan* (Self-strengthening Literary Group) book series, also edited by Nhat Linh. In 1934, the same editorial team initiated *Ngay Nay* (This Day), modeled on *Paris Match*, featuring timely news articles, investigative reporting, and quality photographs (Nguyen Van Ky 1995: 99, 101–2, 105; Jamieson 1993: 113–14, 156–58).

The Vietnamese word for "intellectual" (*tri thuc*) appears to have been coined in Japan during the late nineteenth century to evoke the English meaning, thence being imported to Vietnam a few decades later. By the 1930s, to be a Vietnamese intellectual was more than the dictionary definition of "a person possessing knowledge, usually with fairly high education"; it also meant a commitment to modernity and progress, in contrast to those still wedded to "old" ideas, especially the classically trained literati, priests, and monks. Intellectuals formed small groups, debated each other on every topic imaginable, and tried to publish. More than anything, they thought, talked, read, and wrote about change. French officials often derided Vietnamese intellectuals of this era as half-baked, deraciné, neither fish nor fowl. Ordinary Vietnamese sometimes mocked them for putting on airs, lacing their sentences with French words, and claiming unique access to the truth. Looking back from the present, however, and painfully aware of what happened in between, it seems to me that intellectuals of the 1930s deserve admiration for their curiosity, optimism, and relative tolerance of alternative viewpoints. In a way not equalled since, some 1930s intellectuals had the ability both to involve themselves deeply in a group and to leap out of their own shadows occasionally to assess reality critically.

Also by the 1930s, the nature of reading had changed dramatically. If previously a few literate men had concentrated their attention on a very limited number of texts in characters possessing near sacred status, now perhaps 1.5 million people, including some women, could read a wide variety of books and serials printed in a decidedly secular roman alphabet. One might read extensively or intensively, for amusement or edification. Chinese characters did survive for ritual purposes, especially among Buddhist monks and spirit priests, even as it became necessary to print prayer books in *quoc ngu* for lay readers. Reading retained some of its aura of knowledge, power, and refinement (McHale 1995: 49, 156, 158–60, 180, 212, 242). It became common for middle-class families to accumulate a bookcase full of novels, short story collections, poetry, literary criticism, and history texts. Well-off intellectuals built substantial personal libraries. The expanding print media exercised tremendous influence on spoken as well as written Vietnamese. Thousands of new words entered the common oral vocabulary this way, pronoun usages changed, fresh sentence constructions could be heard. At the same time, printing had a standardizing impact on language, helping to cause some words and constructions to vanish (Nguyen Van Ky 1995: 131–42; Marr 1981: 167–75).

Other Media

Although the print media dominated intellectual activity during the 1920s and 1930s, other media aroused considerable interest as well. Western dramas attracted the attention of translators, with the first theatrical performance being a 1920 Vietnamese adaptation by Nguyen Van Vinh of Molière's "Le malade imaginaire." Soon original dramas were being written, but it was not easy to find persons willing to mount the stage to play the specified roles, given the risqué reputation of performers in the traditional theater (*tuong*). Aspiring dramatists recruited friends, spouses, and students as actors. The stage was well suited to exploring issues of individuality, the family, love, marriage, and morality—at a time when nothing was regarded as permanent or sacrosanct. The audience for such theater experimentation remained small, however (Nguyen Van Ky 1995: 171–81; Woodside 1976: 86–87; Marr 1981: 166–67).

The first moving pictures arrived in Indochina during the 1910s, mostly for viewing by French residents. Within a decade, however, Vietnamese city folk were frequenting the cinema as well. If in 1926 there were twenty-nine movie theaters throughout the colony, by 1939 this had increased to ninety-six establishments, including such out-of-the-way towns as Cao Bang, Tuyen Quang, and Lang Son. During the late 1930s, an average of 250 feature films were imported and screened each year. Charlie Chaplin films, Tarzan offerings, and *The Three Musketeers, Les misérables, The Hunchback of Notre Dame, Sinbad the Sailor,* and *All Quiet on the Western Front* attracted almost anyone who could afford the price of admission. Charlie Chaplin himself visited Indochina in 1936, causing a sensation. Vietnamese writers frequented movie theaters often, talked among themselves about actors, plots, and imagery, and contributed film reviews to periodicals. Each feature film was preceded by a news film laden with material favorable to France and the French colonial mission. In 1939, it became necessary for officials in Tonkin to discontinue these news screenings because Vietnamese members of the audience were jeering some passages (Nguyen Van Ky 1995: 184–91).

Radio arrived in Indochina in the early 1920s, initially as a supplement to cable and telegraph communications. Soon Vietnamese who worked in commercial companies, plantation offices, and some government bureaus were familiar with "wireless" (*vo tuyen dien*) circulation of shipping information and weather forecasts. Government transmitters in Saigon and Hanoi also began to broadcast news and music, aimed mostly at the 40,000 French residents in the colony. However, prosperous Vietnamese families purchased radio receivers too, around which curious neighbors sometimes grouped in the evening. As war clouds gathered in the late 1930s, the authorities ordered all radio equipment to be registered. During World War II, Vietnamese working in the Post-Telegraph-Telephone Service with access to shortwave radio receivers became valued sources of international information for their compatriots.

In the 1930s, western music became quite popular among Vietnamese urbanites, largely as the result of listening to the soundtracks of new movies, the radio, and Gramophone records. Listeners were particularly attracted to the songs of Tino Rossi, Maurice Chevalier, Josephine Baker, and Mistinguett. Although Vietnamese could only be consumers of film and radio media, they found novel ways to produce music. In the popular new dance halls, for example, Vietnamese musicians played alongside Europeans. Much earlier, the Catholic Church had introduced Vietnamese parishioners to four-part singing; some Catholic villages also boasted small bands for wedding and funeral ceremonies. The colonial army possessed several marching bands composed mostly of Vietnamese enlisted men. Musical notation was taught in secondary schools, and sheet music was sold in bookshops. Periodicals printed the scores of popular songs. Youths who could afford a guitar, mandolin, or harmonica were key members of singing groups formed at schools, offices, and within organizations like the Boy Scouts or Catholic Youth. It was common to create Vietnamese lyrics to go with French tunes, and by the late 1930s Vietnamese songs were being composed and published in European styles. By the early 1940s, a few young intellectuals were composing marching rhythms with patriotic lyrics, which spread from one town to the next and were soon being employed by Viet Minh adherents to drill thousands of villagers as well (Ebbesen 1997: 12–27).

WAR AND REVOLUTION

With the French declaration of martial law in September 1939, Vietnamese intellectuals found their activities circumscribed sharply. The number of Vietnamese language journals and reviews fell to 118 in 1941, and 92 in 1942 (Trinh Van Thao 1990: 316). Wartime shortages of paper and ink reduced printing to a trickle by 1944. During this time, despite the political and physical restrictions, some intellectuals managed to publish thoughtful essays, short stories, and poetry. Others retreated to quiet aestheticism. Still others engaged in illegal activities, which often brought them imprisonment or flight to the countryside. In late 1944, as information circulated about Allied victories in Europe and the Pacific, intellectuals gathered in small groups to ponder the implications for Vietnam. However, most were caught unprepared by the 9 March 1945 Japanese *coup de force* which abruptly removed the French administration and triggered a new era in the history of Vietnam.

During the early 1940s the Indochinese Communist Party suffered heavy losses, retreating to a tenuous clandestine existence and communicating largely by word of mouth or handwritten messages. The rudimentary gelatin and ink technique of duplication, employed by illegal groups since at least the turn of the century, could be used to print several dozen leaflets before having to re-etch the gelatin. Wax paper, purchased on the black market, could also be inscribed and then used like a stencil to print crude two-page newspapers. Locally fabricated rice paper substituted for newsprint. Because such conditions ruled out widespread distribution, individual copies were given to reliable Viet Minh followers, who were then expected to read the contents to a number of small groups in succession, each time encouraging discussion of content and memorization of simple slogans. This type of controlled instruction fitted well with Leninist principles, although it would be some years before both cadres and audience members understood what was expected of them (McHale 1995: 320, 343–44, 353–60; Woodside 1976: 179–80). As Viet Minh adherents took advantage of new political opportunities during the summer of 1945, the basic revolutionary message was conveyed mostly by anecdotes, songs, slogans, and the red flag with yellow star, not by printed materials (Marr 1995: 323–77, 386–401).

Once local groups moved to take power in the cities and towns in late August 1945, gaining custody over printing equipment became a high priority. Newsprint remained very scarce, but crude substitutes multiplied. Viet Minh intellectuals who had been producing primitive leaflets in the countryside were delighted to take control of well-oiled printing presses in Hanoi, Haiphong, Saigon, and a number of provincial towns. When newly arrived British forces ejected Viet Minh adherents from Saigon, the latter managed to carry away printing equipment and resume publication within weeks. The fledgling Democratic Republic of Vietnam (DRV) government in Hanoi issued censorship edicts and endeavored to supervise publishing in general, but this did not prevent a number of editors from bypassing state controls. In December 1946, the outbreak of full-scale hostilities between the DRV and France caused tens of thousands of people to flee the northern cities and towns.

Amid this exodus, printing presses were hastily dismantled, carried to various locations in the countryside, then reassembled. Within months, writers, editors, printers, and mechanics had gravitated toward the presses and begun to publish again. Paper was fabricated locally, while ink and spare parts could be found on the urban black market and smuggled back past French military posts. Probably the largest quantity of anti-French Resistance periodicals, booklets, leaflets, and official stationery originated in Interzone IV, especially the provinces of Thanh Hoa and

Nghe An. Hundreds of intellectuals had fled in that direction in early 1947, and the French seldom attacked the area in force for the remainder of the war. A substantial number of publications also emanated from the Viet Bac region, rugged home of the DRV central government during 1947–1954. In Quang Ngai, base area for Interzone V, another cluster of intellectuals published materials for the central coast provinces. Further south, in the Mekong delta, the French compelled DRV adherents to move printing operations on numerous occasions, yet readers hardly noticed the disruptions, with serials continuing to be distributed on schedule.[2] Meanwhile, some patriotic intellectuals remaining in French-controlled Saigon managed repeatedly to outmaneuver the censors, publishing essays, fiction, and poetry that amounted to a public indictment of the French authorities and their Vietnamese associates.

In the various resistance zones, intellectuals tried to avoid writing anything that might offer aid and comfort to the enemy. They kept quiet about abuses of power within DRV ranks, for example arbitrary property confiscations, detentions without trial, character assassinations, and purges. Intellectuals themselves were part of the deeper revolutionary tumult, wherein accusations of "reactionary," "feudal," or "counter-revolutionary" thinking or behavior surfaced often, and few formal procedures existed to evaluate such charges. Most accused persons were simply warned to correct their ways, but in other cases they faced ostracism, loss of rations, protracted interrogation, torture, indefinite incarceration, or even execution. Because most intellectuals could be seen to have benefited from the colonial system, they often felt vulnerable to popular criticism. On the other hand, they possessed the skills to read central DRV publications carefully, memorize entire passages from the speeches of Ho Chi Minh, and use this rhetoric when interacting with less educated compatriots. Throwing themselves into the mass movement, being part of the heroic national struggle, intellectuals could both satisfy their need to belong and protect themselves from censure. In this atmosphere, self-censorship came naturally.

The Communist Party Asserts Control

From 1948, the Communist Party endeavored to extend its control over all groups participating in the anti-French Resistance, to include intellectuals. At the Second National Conference on Culture, convened in July 1948, Party Secretary Truong Chinh delivered a long report on "Marxism and Vietnamese Culture" that established boundaries on intellectual activity that the party has continued to demand to the present day. The ultimate arbiters of truth and beauty were the masses, as represented by the party. A special role was delineated for literary and art critics who understood the needs of the revolution, the preferences of the masses, and the principles of socialist realism. According to Truong Chinh, a good critic was like a whip to make the horse rear up and perform effectively. He warned that no intellectual participating in the Resistance struggle could claim to be above politics, beyond the judgment of the masses, creating according to his own values. Indeed, to take such a position played into the hands of the enemy (Ninh 2002:

39–47). Parts of Truong Chinh's speech were reprinted in local periodicals, yet until criticism was mounted against specific authors or publications, most intellectuals remained uncertain about the implications for them personally.

In September 1949, the Association of Art and Literature convened a conference in the Viet Bac hills to provide an opportunity for members to engage in systematic self-criticism. The poet To Huu delivered the keynote address and stage-managed the subsequent outpouring of mea culpas, each speaker denouncing his own previous creative output and promising to reform. Follow-up sessions focused on the more recent work of selected authors present at the conference, with colleagues often accusing them of failing sincerely to revolutionize their thinking and become one with the people (Ninh 2002: 88–98). By this time, some intellectuals had already become disenchanted by their experiences within local Viet Minh organizations and begun to move back to French-held cities.

Even before establishment of the People's Republic of China in October 1949, a movement swept through both military and civilian units of the Viet Minh to learn from the Chinese revolutionary experience and emulate their success. Intellectuals competent in written Chinese busily translated manuals, literary compendia, and the works of Mao Zedong into Vietnamese. Party intellectuals were dispatched to China to learn the techniques of "rectification" (*chinh huan*), whereby each member of a group confessed his or her sins, accepted criticism, criticized others, worked toward collective absolution, and received unit clearance, it was hoped, from rectification cadres managing the proceedings.

During 1951–1953, Chinese-inspired rectification campaigns swept through Viet Minh units. The print media saw an upsurge in material dealing with class struggle, elimination of feudal thinking, and advancing the revolutionary role of poor peasants. Intellectuals also had to introduce these ideas to the literacy classes, which continued to be an important part of Viet Minh mass mobilization.

Besides the printing press, DRV leaders appreciated the power of radio to reach millions of citizens whenever equipment could be secured and technicians enrolled. On 31 August 1945, the Japanese Army released the main Hanoi radio station to the DRV provisional government, which quickly used the facility to transmit public pronouncements and official instructions to scores of localities possessing vintage receivers. In southern Vietnam, DRV adherents managed to spirit several old transmitters out of Saigon ahead of the attacking British and French forces. When hostilities broke out in Hanoi in December 1946, radio equipment for the DRV's *Voice of Vietnam* program was carried into the hills and was relocated a total of fourteen times over the next seven-and-one-half years (Viet Nam Thong Tan Xa 1995: 46). During this period, a network of transmitters and receivers was built up across Vietnam, Laos, and Cambodia, in the first instance to communicate confidential orders and reports, and secondly to disseminate government proclamations, news, short stories, and poetry. Intellectuals generated the bulk of this material, most of which had to be sent in Morse code, not voice transmissions. Local editorial teams depended on these radio receptions when producing a good portion of their broadsides, posters, and periodicals.

Early DRV cinema efforts were even more technologically constrained than radio, yet not without significance. In 1947, employing film stock, chemicals, and developing equipment purchased in Saigon, Viet Minh film teams followed guerrilla units and produced a series of short movies about the war (Woodside 1976: 78). In 1952 , a fully equipped Chinese cinematographic team joined Viet Minh writers, interpreters, porters, and guards to infiltrate past French posts to spend several months in the Red River delta, filming armed guerrillas, public meetings, production efforts, and local scenery. The eventual film was titled *Viet Nam Khang Chien* (Vietnam Resistance), with sound track added in Beijing. While aimed mainly at an international audience, the movie also was shown in Viet Minh zones, with some viewers delighted to be able to recognize themselves on screen. Nguyen Tuan, a well-known writer and participant in the original Sino-Vietnamese production group, noted how those evening moving picture presentations managed to reach directly into the hearts of audience members (Nguyen Dang Manh 1999: 745–57).[3] Chinese feature films also reached Viet Minh audiences, most notably *The White-haired Girl*, a lavish operetta-ballet.

Peacetime Renaissance and Repression

Following the May 1954 Viet Minh victory at Dien Bien Phu and the subsequent Indochina-wide cease-fire brokered at Geneva, millions of Vietnamese, including intellectuals, found themselves on the move, whether from north to south, from south to north, migrating to France, returning as victors from the hills and forests, or simply coming home after years of war and social upheaval. Most intellectuals felt that the cessation of hostilities offered an unparalleled opportunity to express themselves as citizens of an independent country. Writers and artists who had come to public prominence in the 1930s were especially anxious to make up for lost time. However, first in the north, then in the south, the central political authorities circumscribed intellectual activity in the name of ongoing revolution and defense against enemies foreign or domestic.

Within days of returning triumphantly to Hanoi in October 1954, the DRV resumed *Voice of Vietnam* broadcasts from the capital, utilizing two 7.5 kilowatt transmitters and several smaller machines to produce voice programs live in Vietnamese, French, English, Cantonese, Mandarin, Lao, and Khmer. A year later, big Soviet tape recorders arrived for the main station, and in 1958 Hungary donated smaller portable recorders, which enabled radio reporters for the first time to tape people in auditoriums, factories, cooperatives, laboratories, and schools. About the same time, a new 150-kilowatt Soviet transmitter boosted medium-wave broadcasts. Writers could now experiment with radio dramas, while a variety of musical groups performed regularly on the radio. *The Voice of Vietnam* became a large state apparatus employing several thousand reporters, writers, translators, editors, producers, and technicians. Very few families in the DRV possessed radio receivers. Instead, the state relied primarily on loudspeakers installed every few city blocks, or in front of village communal houses, to be able to relay Hanoi radio news, exhortations, and patriotic music each morning and evening. Somewhat later, the state subsidized the installation of small speakers in family homes, connected to local repeater stations. Persons with direct access to a radio receiver caught listening to the BBC, *Voice of America* (VOA), or other "imperialist" stations could be imprisoned. Still concerned about citizens listening to dangerous ideas, the DRV tried to jam some frequencies electronically.

Printing operations that had been dispersed for eight years in the north were soon concentrated back in Hanoi and Haiphong, with the party also moving to exercise closer supervision than before. Nonetheless, the DRV officially discontinued pre-publication censorship, private printshops continued to take business, and a host of small intellectual clusters prepared manuscripts for publication. Not only older intellectuals, but a new generation that had come to maturity during the Resistance, wanted to launch a Vietnamese cultural renaissance. Some of the more outspoken writers and editors were serving as members in the People's Army. No one contested party leadership of the government, and almost everyone was prepared to defer debate on sensitive political or foreign policy issues in favor of wide-open discussion of literature, the arts, education, science, and technology. What these intellectuals failed to appreciate, however, was the firm intention of most party leaders to exercise control over every facet of citizen behavior, in faithful conformity to the teachings of Lenin, Stalin, and Mao Zedong. More particularly, the party intended to break the influence of "petty bourgeois intellectuals" and to replace them with newly trained workers and poor peasants who had demonstrated unswerving allegiance to proletarian dictatorship.

Throughout 1955, a sort of shadow boxing prevailed, with party leaders warning intellectuals to practice restraint in the face of continuing enemy threats, and some intellectuals testing publication parameters with mildly controversial short stories, poems, or literary essays. In traditional fashion, a few intellectuals also petitioned party leaders with ambitious cultural reform proposals (Ninh 2002: 126–36). Amid these cautious maneuverings, however, a wild card surfaced in the form of increasingly frenetic, bitter campaigns of land reform. Intellectuals instructed to take part in local land reform efforts emerged shocked by the injustices they had witnessed. Others received word that their own families had been punished as landlords or rich peasants. Simultaneously, the party was conducting a purge of its own membership, especially targeting personnel who had operated underground in French-held areas. Stories multiplied and circulated orally of experienced, loyal province- and district-level cadres being humiliated, tortured, or executed. Party leaders like Truong Chinh and To Huu, who prided themselves on their intellectual credentials, now found it difficult to communicate with some writers, editors, and artists who had worked with them throughout the Resistance (Boudarel 1991: 172–93, 212–18).

In early February 1956, a small group of younger intellectuals convinced a private publishing house in Hanoi to release *Giai Pham Mua Xuân* (Spring Belles Lettres), a forty-eight-page Lunar New Year collection of essays, short stories, poetry, and musical scores obliquely critical of the status quo. The police confiscated most copies of the publication, and the Literature and Arts Association was convened to denounce the entire initiative. At that moment in faraway Moscow, however, the first secretary of the Communist Party, Nikita Khruschev, delivered his stunning speech denouncing the repressive legacy of Stalin and outlining a policy to relax ideological and organizational controls over society. Word of the speech soon spread among Vietnamese intellectuals, although the Hanoi media remained silent. In mid-April, the party Central Committee announced its resolve to conduct regular criticism and self-criticism sessions in order to correct the lack of intraparty democracy. The pressing issue at hand was not Stalin, Khruschev, or democracy, but how to deal with growing discontent over land reform implementation and the party purge. Three months later, the party suspended the current land reform wave and began a laborious process of "rectifying errors." Meanwhile, China had launched its Hundred Flowers campaign, encouraging intellectuals to criticize official policies. When no Hanoi newspaper published the details, students translated excerpts from China's *People's Daily* and displayed them as wall posters (Heng 1999: 81–88; Boudarel 1991: 134–41, 193–201).

On 7 August 1956, *Nhan Dan* chided the press for insufficient attention to criticism/self-criticism. Taking their cue with a vengeance, members of the Literature and Arts Association took the opportunity of a large, nineteen-day meeting of the organization to criticize the leadership for imposing narrow-minded, formulaic rules on creative activity in general. The same day the meeting closed, *Nhan Dan* carried Ho Chi Minh's open letter to the nation's peasants admitting errors in implementing land reform and promising rectification. Within days, a number of different editorial groups were putting together provocative material and finding publishers and printers willing to release it. Most notable was the revived *Giai Pham* and a new periodical called *Nhan Van* (Humanism), both of which brought together intellectuals who had come to prominence during the colonial period with younger Viet Minh era intellectuals. While ranging across a variety of literary, educational, legal, economic, and scientific topics, these journals conveyed a common message: national progress and personal creativity together were in danger of being stifled by functionaries wielding ideological clubs. The argument had now become openly political, whatever the intentions of intellectuals a year earlier (Heng 1999: 89–92; Ninh 2002: 136–53).

The last months of 1956 saw considerable confusion within the party over how to respond to major political setbacks, to include the land reform debacle, growing intellectual dissent, and Khruschev's disinterest in Hanoi's aspirations for national unification. In September, Truong Chinh was removed as party general secretary, a position he had held for fifteen years, yet he managed to hold on to his Politburo seat and continued to wield considerable influence, notably on questions of ideology and culture. In October, General Vo Nguyen Giap, hero of Dien Bien Phu, admitted on behalf of the party that "grave errors," including routine torture and unjust executions, had been committed in the land reform and party purification campaigns. On the other hand, To Huu, who remained in charge of the party's

Ideology Commission, persisted in admonishing groups of intellectuals face-to-face, while *Nhan Dan* ran commentaries and letters to the editor criticizing the instigators of *Nhan Van* and *Giai Pham*. *Nhan Van* editors felt confident enough to reveal the content of some "internal" (*noi bo*) encounters and to expose efforts by the local authorities to restrict supplies of paper and pressure printers and distributors to withdraw labor (Heng 1999: 93–101). For older participants like Phan Khoi or Dao Duy Anh, these confrontations in print must have recalled the heady days two decades prior, when intellectuals had dared to take on the French colonial establishment. Whether Truong Chinh saw the historical irony of himself moving from 1930s challenger of autocracy to late 1950s defender is unknown.

Events in faraway Hungary may have helped Truong Chinh and To Huu to stiffen the spines of party colleagues against political ferment at home. When liberal reforms in Budapest reached the point of jeopardizing local Communist Party rule, the Soviet Union intervened militarily in early November 1956. A month later, To Huu convinced the party committee of Hanoi city to prevent publication of the sixth issue of *Nhan Van* and to ban circulation of the five previous issues. *Giai Pham* and several other journals also ceased to appear. Nonetheless, public skirmishes between intellectuals and the party persisted through 1957, suggesting ongoing differences within the Politburo. Censorship was tightened in January 1958, and for the rest of the year DRV intellectuals were ordered to participate in criticism/self-criticism sessions. Newspapers published vitriolic personal denunciations by some writers of their peers, while other writers abjectly confessed to grievous errors and begged forgiveness. Scores of intellectuals were consigned to reeducation camps or manual labor in agricultural cooperatives, factories, or mines. Two years later, five persons who had participated in the publication of *Nhan Van* were put on trial and sentenced to three to fifteen years in prison (Heng 1999: 102–11; Ninh 2002: 153–63).

High Socialism

By 1960, all remaining private print shops and publishing houses in the DRV had been nationalized, and all production of books and serials placed under the control of specific party, state, or Fatherland Front organizations. Following Soviet precedent, the party Ideology Commission regularly instructed editors on the current political "position" (*lap truong*), critiqued output meticulously, and approved all editorial appointments. Editors had to be party members who had demonstrated unswerving loyalty, with publishing experience or intellectual reputation being of far less consequence. Each publishing unit also possessed a party committee that watched the editor, approved internal appointments, and checked texts prior to printing. From another direction, the Ministry of Culture issued identification cards, promulgated formal media regulations, and distributed supplies and equipment (Heng 1999: 55–72). With slight variations, this control system applied as well to radio stations, film productions, live dramatic and musical performances, and artistic exhibitions. Some media executives were intellectuals and indeed were not above using their positions to ensure that their own output received prominent attention. However, a large proportion of media executives possessed no more than primary or lower secondary school training, having mostly climbed party ranks due to correct class background, wartime survival, attachment to a powerful patron, and avoidance of controversy. Among the 630 highest-ranking cadres in the entire central apparatus of the DRV as of 1959, only 23 percent could claim university attendance, while 60.5 percent had seven years or less of formal education (Ninh 2002: 252).

Intellectuals had no choice but to obtain employment with a party, state, or Fatherland Front organization, as most sources of private income had dried up and state rations were distributed through those channels. Some intellectuals were treated quite well by the standards of the 1960s and 1970s, being assigned an apartment, given access to foreign commodities and preferential health care, selected to travel to fraternal countries, and able to place their children in the best schools. In return they had to repeat and embellish the party line, both in their intellectual output and whenever paraded by the authorities. Intellectuals who remained in the People's Army often received specialized overseas training in the sciences, engineering, and medicine that brought them new respect. However, the majority of intellectuals had to earn their salaries as "cultural workers" of one kind or another. Under Ministry of Culture auspices, for example, intellectuals established local "houses of culture" (*nha van hoa*), supervised amateur performing arts troupes, identified heritage sites, administered libraries and museums, escorted foreign cultural delegations, and helped to develop a national film studio (Ninh 2002: 164–203). Under the Ministry of Education, intellectuals helped to set up complementary education courses in state work units and agricultural cooperatives, and they taught at new vocational schools. At the tertiary level, a surprising number of intellectuals of bourgeois or petit bourgeois origin were permitted to teach the new educated elite, and the students themselves were drawn from a wider class spectrum than party doctrine indicated (Ninh 2002: 204–36).

During the 1960s and 1970s in the DRV, both intellectuals and the media became extremely compartmentalized. With the party having arrogated to itself the role of defining and articulating community values, hopes, and fears, most intellectuals sought solace in their own work units and specialized associations. Psychologically, their response resembled that of traditional villagers drawing together behind bamboo hedges. Some groups buried themselves in research and managed to produce impressive results, for example those working in archaeology, precolonial history, ethnology, folklore, linguistics, agro-biology, geology, and mathematics. In order to publish the results of such investigations it was still necessary to include a preface and conclusion that upheld the relevant party pronouncements, yet otherwise the book or article often avoided politics. This was not feasible with most social science research, which encountered ideological constraints at every turn.

For a poor country at war, the DRV generated an extraordinary amount of printed matter. Publishing was the responsibility of at least thirty different units, mostly located in Hanoi. The party produced *Nhan Dan* daily, *Hoc Tap* (Study-Practice) monthly, and a stream of collected speeches and official documents via Su That (Truth) Publishing House. The military produced *Quan Doi Nhan Dan* (People's Army) daily, while its publishing house proved more eclectic than that of the party, releasing not only speeches and training manuals, but also military histories, memoirs, and fiction and poetry written by members of the armed forces. Other publishers directed their periodicals or books toward scientists, social scientists, teachers, cultural workers, women, youth, or children. Although paper was very scarce overall, the party allocated huge quantities to publishing works by Ho Chi Minh, to ninety different ministerial journals and bulletins, and to official circulars, instructions, or forms to be filled out in multiple copies. The Soviet Union took charge of producing a 55-volume Vietnamese translation of *The Complete Works of Lenin*, with print runs of 60,000 hardbound copies per volume—the entire job consuming 3,500 tons of paper. By contrast, members of research institutes in Hanoi often had to wait two or three years for a government committee to release paper to print books on a title-by-title basis. Occasionally reader demand did influence publishing decisions, the most notable example being a four-volume collection of Vietnamese legends reprinted to a total of 533,942 copies between 1958 and 1975 (Marr 1988: 32–35).

Between 1955 and 1985, the Soviet Union helped to train more than 70,000 Vietnamese specialists. Possibly another 30,000 went to various Eastern European countries, and an equivalent number studied in China up to 1978. While perhaps half of these overseas trainees were administrative cadres or technical workers coming for limited periods, the remainder studied at a wide range of foreign academic institutions and saw themselves as career professionals. On return to the DRV, they effectively shaped the first and second postcolonial generations of intellectuals (Marr 1988: 16–18). Often they hoped to maintain contact with their overseas peers and to publish in foreign academic journals, but the party actively discouraged such long-term collegial relationships.

During the period 1964–1972, DRV intellectuals were swept up once again by war. With American troops in South Vietnam, and U.S. aircraft bombing the north, the party used the media to mount intense anti-imperialist campaigns. Most DRV intellectuals, outraged at U.S. aggression, were eager to make a contribution to the anti-American Resistance. Thousands of cultural cadres went south with People's Army units, while intellectuals in the north produced material designed to sustain morale on the home front. It was not a time for creative innovation, and many writers, artists, composers, and filmmakers of that era later looked back on their wartime output with embarrassment. They paid their dues as citizens, although the party consulted very few of them on major policy issues of the era. The security and control apparatus intruded as never before, so that intellectuals had to be careful about what they said informally, as well as what they produced for the cause. Ironically, it was not comments about the United States or the Saigon regime that landed some intellectuals in deep trouble, but rather remarks construed as support for Moscow's "revisionist" position in its dispute with Beijing. According to Russell Heng's calculation, at least twenty-nine media practitioners were implicated during the mid-1960s in what security officials came to label as "Revisionist, Anti-Party behavior," even though investigators found it impossible to establish criminal activity from their output (Heng 1999: 127).

REPUBLIC OF VIETNAM

Intellectuals in the Republic of Vietnam between 1956 and 1975 had very different media experiences from their brethren in the DRV. Initially the situation in Saigon was similar to Hanoi, with thousands of intellectuals and students arriving from the north and proceeding to establish dozens of journals and newspapers, which jostled on the newsstands with periodicals produced by established southern intellectuals. When the DRV closed down *Nhan Van* and *Giai Pham* at the end of 1956, RVN officials gleefully contrasted evil communist repression with their own high regard for press freedom. Simultaneously, however, they were moving against southern intellectuals deemed pro-communist, jailing some and dispatching a few across the seventeenth parallel to the north. By 1960, many intellectuals had become sufficiently concerned about President Ngo Dinh Diem's monopolization of power to voice their criticisms publicly. Diem retaliated by closing newspapers and jailing some critics. With each year the regime became more repressive and the press less lively, although it was still possible to publish experimental fiction and poetry in small circulation journals.

Following the overthrow and killing of Diem in November 1963, newstands filled once again with scores of periodicals representing a variety of noncommunist groups and opinions. Cartoonists flourished for the first time in three decades. Even radio stations voiced different positions. After General Nguyen Van Thieu outmaneuvered his military rivals in 1967 and became RVN president, the closure of newspapers and imprisonment of opponents resumed. Unlike in the DRV, however, many groups still were able to use mimeograph machines to circulate provocative information. Also, there remained many topics about which the RVN leadership showed little interest when it came to media exposure. Nor did intellectuals in the south have to affirm the political line to retain access to food and housing. As the war persisted, more intellectuals were drafted into the RVN armed forces, while others joined the communist-led National Liberation Front instead. Even so, the 1930s tradition of intellectuals clustering around a newspaper to attract a loyal readership remained alive if not always well in Saigon.[4]

Television came to South Vietnam in the mid-1960s, with the rapidly growing urban middle class purchasing Japanese black-and-white TV sets to watch mostly Hollywood movies and weekly features like *Dragnet, Batman, I Love Lucy,* and *The Ed Sullivan Show.* The issue of American cultural imperialism exercised many intellectuals who had no liking for the communists. By the early 1970s, rampant inflation made it difficult for intellectuals to set aside time to study or write, much less locate a viable book publisher. Thousands of intellectuals fled South Vietnam in April 1975, fearing harsh treatment by the victorious communists. On the other hand, some southern media personnel who did not leave eventually played catalytic roles in the 1990s reemergence of commercial newspapers

POST-1975 CHANGE

In the north, the end of the war brought a collective sigh of relief and tremendous desire for normalcy, after decades of upheaval, trauma, and sacrifice. Intellectuals pulled out motheaten manuscripts, tuned up their battered guitars, and talked eagerly of peacetime projects. Those able to visit postwar Saigon stocked up on western phonograph records, long-banned Tu Luc Van Doan novels from the 1930s, and scarce consumer commodities. Very soon, however, the party was demanding more sacrifices in the name of postwar reconstruction and socialist development. By 1978, new armed confrontations loomed with Cambodia, then China. The domestic security and control apparatus swung into high gear again. This time, despite the foreign threats and security campaigns that persisted into the 1980s, people found many ways to husband emotional space for themselves. Intellectuals chafed at media controls, conversed with far less restraint, and sought out foreign information aggressively.

Nowhere was this change more pronounced than with music. Already in Hanoi in the late 1960s, Latin American rhythms and dancing enjoyed by some students had raised the ire of older party cadres, yet the music could not be banned for fear of undermining Vietnam's intimate relationship with Cuba. In early 1975, Tran Minh Tuoc, editor of *Thong Nhat* (Unification) magazine, described to me his concern at hearing his grown-up son playing Latin American music and showing no interest whatsoever in traditional Vietnamese music. Tuoc had reacted by instructing his son for weeks about not only traditional culture, but also colonial exploitation, survival in jail, and the meaning of the August 1945 Revolution.[5] On the other hand, Hoang Tung, editor of *Nhan Dan* daily, told me he disagreed with the head of the Musicians' Association that Vietnam had to return to traditional musical forms; the younger generation would ignore such instructions in favor of modern music, and even dancing.[6] The subsequent liberation of records and tape cassettes from South Vietnam, and the regular return of students from Eastern Europe laden with western music tapes, provoked the authorities to launch public campaigns against listening to "blue music" (sad, pessimistic) and "yellow music" (romantic, sexy), to little avail.

Vietnamese composers and performers remained in a difficult position, however. Until the late 1980s they were prevented from reprinting, broadcasting, or performing romantic songs from the 1930s or from pre-1975 Saigon. Instead they were pushed by the Musicians' Association to continue producing and performing politically correct "red music," which radio stations obediently broadcast but which live audiences and private listeners increasingly ignored. The Vietnamese musical establishment vehemently supported party attempts to stem the flood of foreign audio cassettes and videos, easily duplicated around the country, yet rampant inflation and depreciation of state salaries forced musicians to look for opportunities on the open market, especially in the growing number of dance halls, hotels, and upmarket restaurants. From the mid-1990s the rapid expansion of Vietnam Television also offered new opportunities for composers to score soundtracks for shows and TV advertisements. Meanwhile, the party continued to attack "depraved" music, and the police launched periodic raids on shops and karaoke bars, but for the right price just about any kind of music was still readily available (Ebbeson 1997: 88–136, 144–60; Marr 1996: 3–9, 40–52).

Hoang Tung may have been prepared in early 1975 to let new consumer tastes influence music, but that proclivity did not carry over to his running of *Nhan Dan* daily, or to party management of the print media in general. Tens of thousands of RVN-era books and serials were destroyed in the south after April. Tight controls on content remained. There was no attempt to experiment with more attractive formats for newspapers or book covers. Big automated printing presses with color capacity languished in Saigon. Among intellectuals, however, attitudes and behavior were changing. Unapproved typescripts circulated more widely than anyone would have dared previously. Persons with access to shortwave receivers listened increasingly to foreign stations and shared the news with friends. Dire economic circumstances in 1979–1980 sparked intense questioning at the work unit level. As salaries fell further behind basic living requirements, intellectuals went beyond their work units to look for income. In the south, urban families began to receive material support from overseas relatives, which soon became visits filled with animated sharing of information.

In 1980, Nguyen Khac Vien published a thoughtful article in *Nhan Dan* calling for fewer controls on the circulation of information (*Nhan Dan*, 16-3-80). When summarizing his argument, Dr. Vien included a diagram that predictably placed the (party) leadership at the center of information activity, yet then proceeded to draw a direct link between the "scientific community" and the mass media. He urged increased grassroots discussion in the media of current policies and performance, including opinions contrary to official statements. He especially asked that surveys conducted by social scientists that produced unpleasant results not be restricted to a tiny official audience. Nonetheless, Dr. Vien still felt it necessary to draw a double line on his diagram that separated all intra-elite communication from the profusion of complex, contradictory data arriving from both within Vietnamese society and from the world outside. He also offered no solution for the extreme compartmentalization that had developed over the previous three decades between ministries, research institutes, media outlets, and other organizations, often making practical sharing of data or work assignments almost impossible. When senior officials did address the compartmentalization problem they almost always called for more centralization rather than reducing the barriers. Thus, a member of the State Science and Technology Commission urged unified administration of all foreign contacts and a halt to all inappropriate, localized, or frivolous interactions. Another official proposed that a single committee control whatever foreign currency the state was able to muster for

purchase of books and journals overseas (Marr 1988: 40–44). Such centralizing attitudes continued into the Doi Moi period, although leaders reluctantly relaxed controls when the alternative was economic disaster. Many lower-level barriers simply
faded away.

During the early 1980s, an occasional publication would attract attention for
the way it called the status quo into question. Usually it was a work of fiction, an
evasive tactic dating back centuries. Thus, one novel told the story of a state fishing enterprise adjacent to Ho Chi Minh City that was losing a large portion of its
catch to the black market. The author captured the tensions between northern
and southern cadres, between generations, between ideologues and pragmatists—
without neat solutions or an upbeat ending (Nguyen Manh Tuan 1982). Such
modest questioning of the system tested the rules of censorship and helped to
prepare the ground for the more ambitious criticisms to come.

In 1985, when a dramatic government attempt to grapple with prices, wages, and
the money supply ended in economic chaos, To Huu accepted responsibility and was
removed from the Politburo. In early 1986, word circulated that Le Duan, party general secretary for twenty-six years, had terminal cancer. In March, Mikhail Gorbachev announced his momentous program of political and economic reforms to
the Twenty-seventh Soviet Party Congress in Moscow, which Hanoi proceeded
to endorse cautiously. Vietnamese intellectuals now appreciated that the lead-up to
the next Vietnam Communist Party Congress, expected later that year, might prove
the most significant political event in decades. Some intellectuals who were party
members took part in unprecedented debates at work unit and city-level meetings to
elect delegates to the congress. Amid these meetings, in July, Le Duan died and
Truong Chinh replaced him as acting general secretary. For the first time in the fifty-
six-year history of the party, elements of the media became involved in promoting
one candidate as top leader versus another, although never being so indiscreet as to
name who they supported or opposed. Journalists suddenly became more influential
than ever before, especially by digging up embarrassing evidence on the clients of
particular Politburo members. It is likely that the candidacy of Le Duc Tho was com-
promised in this way. Much journalistic evidence was used to fuel the rumor mill and
never made its way into print. Journalists and editors alike took increasing risks. The
most striking example was the campaign mounted from September by a dozen different media units against Ha Trong Hoa, party secretary of Thanh Hoa province,
and a protégé of Le Duc Tho. Just prior to the opening of the Sixth Party Congress
in December, Le Duc Tho apparently proposed that three elderly leaders—himself,
Truong Chinh, and Pham Van Dong—step down simultaneously. The Congress then
elected Nguyen Van Linh as compromise general secretary (Heng 1999: 143–76).

THE LIMITS OF DOI MOI

As part of the new policy of Doi Moi launched by the Sixth Party Congress, newspapers and radio stations immediately began publicizing slogans such as "Struggle

against negativism" and "Tell it straight, tell it true, tell it openly." Nguyen Van Linh developed a tactical alliance with media practitioners, using the latter to improve his position amid Politburo colleagues who owed their careers to Le Duc Tho or the late Le Duan. He also began quietly to release *Nhan Van Giai Pham* participants from purgatory. The pace of investigative reporting increased, and soon spread from the central media to provincial and city newspapers and journals. At meetings of the Vietnam Journalists' Association, members compared notes and passed resolutions urging further relaxation of official controls. At the party's Ideology Commission, however, no one appears to have wavered in their conviction that the party must continue to direct change each step of the way. Meanwhile, journalists were joined by creative writers, literary critics, essayists, artists, and musicians, publicly encouraged by Tran Do, head of the party's Culture and Arts Commission.

The focal point for cultural discourse and new creative expression became *Van Nghe* (Literature and the Arts), a long-standing weekly journal of the Vietnam Writers' Association. For example, *Van Nghe* published several of Nguyen Huy Thiep's iconoclastic short stories for the first time, then printed criticisms that came in from readers. Thiep was significant because he went beyond the political controversies of the day to question the deeper agenda of progress and modernity that had prevailed among Vietnamese intellectuals since the 1920s, and he possessed an original prose style (Nguyen Huy Thiep 1992). Other writers of the late 1980s upheld personal as distinct from collective perspectives, renewed calls of the late 1950s and 1930s to liberate culture from political shackles, and suggested that "building socialism" failed to encompass many moral, aesthetic, and psychological yearnings of contemporary citizens.

The practical difficulties of carving out space for intellectuals to project themselves via a more open mass media were best exemplified by the rise and fall of Nguyen Ngoc as editor of *Van Nghe* from July 1987 to December 1988. While Nguyen Ngoc's reputation as a writer was minimal, he thrived on controversy and was particularly admired for having incurred the wrath of To Huu on several past occasions. As editor of *Van Nghe*, he personally cleared all copy and worked hard, together with Tran Do, to prevent higher echelons from interfering in decisions. Undoubtedly some of his own staff members reported to the Ideology Commission and the security services. As Russell Heng explains succinctly, Nguyen Ngoc "was not against literature being political, only against literature being politically controlled" (Heng 1999: 190). Nguyen Ngoc wanted *Van Nghe* to spearhead an expanding discourse on vital political and cultural issues, and to be able to examine systemic weaknesses, not merely expose "negative phenomena" on a case-by-case basis. Not least of all, he planned to review punitive state actions taken against writers in the past, beginning with the *Nhan Van Giai Pham* affair. Such public statements put Nguyen Ngoc on a collision course with key members of the Politburo. They also probably caused anguish among those intellectuals who hoped to be able to distance their creative lives from the hurly-burly of politics. Following Nguyen Ngoc's dismissal as editor, he still managed for several months to pursue an argument on the pages of *Van Nghe* with his immediate superior, Nguyen Dinh Thi, head of the Writer's Association (Heng 1999: 177–91, 193–204, 210–15).

Meanwhile, far from Hanoi, in the quiet hill town of Dalat, a small group of progressive-minded writers received permission from the provincial authorities to establish a journal titled *Langbian* (an ethnic minority designation for the region). Articles criticizing long-dominant cultural policies and exposing day-to-day censorship struggles with local ideology cadres soon brought *Langbian* to the attention of intellectuals nationwide. The editors also published poems by *Nhan Van Giai Pham* participants that had been banned for decades, and involved one of the purged poets, Huu Loan, in efforts to link up with like-minded groups elsewhere in central Vietnam. When permission was refused to continue publishing *Langbian*, the editorial team decided to travel from town to town collecting signatures on a protest petition that also publicized the threat to Nguyen Ngoc's editorship of *Van Nghe*. On arrival in Hue they met with editors of *Song Huong* (Fragrant River), second only to *Van Nghe* in literary experimentation during this period. Such forthright networking outside party channels was unprecedented, causing officials in both Hanoi and Dalat to order the *Langbian* team home for disciplinary action. The team pushed on to the capital nonetheless, arriving just as the head of the Ideology Commission was denouncing them for "factionalism" and preparing to remove Nguyen Ngoc from *Van Nghe* (Heng 1999: 191–93, 204–210, 214). Tran Do lost his position at about the same time.

In Saigon, the party had reversed its policy of isolating pre-1975 "bourgeois" intellectuals, instead encouraging those who remained in the country to participate in a range of new cultural projects. Most commonly, a topic was announced for deliberation, formerly ostracized writers and teachers were invited to workshops together with party academics (often migrants from the north), papers were presented, and a publication organized. Edited volumes on southern history, society, literature, and folklore proved particularly rewarding. On the other hand, a project on the history of Catholicism in Vietnam came to grief. The initial workshop was successful, the manuscript survived scrutiny in Hanoi by both the party and the state Commission on Religion, Catholic parishioners donated funds to print 20,000 copies, and Dong Nai Publishing House began typesetting—only to have the authorities change their minds abruptly in late 1989 and confiscate the text. The principal author, Nguyen Van Trung, was subjected to long police interrogations, ordered to turn in other copies of the manuscript, and refused permission to travel to Europe for further studies.[7]

Also in Saigon, prominent members of the anti-French and anti-American struggles had been lobbying since 1983 for permission to establish a mass organization under the Vietnam Fatherland Front and to publish a magazine. Cautious authorization arrived in May 1986 to form the Ho Chi Minh City Club of Former Resistance Fighters, but it was not until two years later that the club's chairman, Nguyen Ho, moved into high gear, setting up district-level branches, initiating several business ventures, arranging public historical commemorations, and publishing the journal

Truyen Thong Khang Chien (Resistance Tradition). Meetings on political reform issues attracted larger and larger audiences, with the proceedings then being reprinted in the journal. Club branches emerged in the Mekong delta without official permission. In November 1989 the authorities moved to cut back club activities, and in December they confiscated the printing plates of an imminent issue of the journal. Nguyen Ho nonetheless managed to get the journal typeset anew in Hau Giang province and printed to the tune of 20,000 copies. After that, a stern warning arrived from Hanoi that anyone participating in further publication of the journal risked arrest. No printing press operators were prepared to test this threat, so Nguyen Ho shifted to the use of several mimeograph machines to produce hard-hitting open letters addressed to the Politburo and reports of public meetings increasingly critical of the party. This situation persisted until January 1990, when the Politburo banned a range of club activities and reduced Nguyen Ho to reliance on one illegal mimeograph machine hidden in the countryside. In March, he was accused of trying to foment opposition throughout the country and stripped of his club chairmanship. Still refusing to be silenced, Nguyen Ho was detained in September (Heng 1999: 227–56).

From August 1989 onward, it was apparent that Politburo members opposed to open debate of political issues had the upper hand, yet many writers and editors continued to take risks, to probe the parameters of possible action. Some older intellectuals who had experienced the draconian party crackdowns of the late 1950s and 1960s may have persisted out of desperation, acutely aware of what the authorities could do once groups were broken up and punishments meted out individually. The political climate tightened further in 1990–1991, yet very few intellectuals were imprisoned, and those fired found that the market now offered other work opportunities. Writers refused publication in one city often located a sympathetic editor elsewhere, providing the topic was not overtly political. The dream of intellectuals and the media combining to transform reality would have to be pursued in different ways.

While the political debates were underway, the nature of publishing operations had been changing for other reasons. Rampant inflation made a mockery of the entire state allocation system, compelling writers, editors, printers, and distributors to find new ways to support their families. Economic initiatives required lots of brochures, guides, manuals, and advertisements. A new spirit of competition swept the print media, with provincial publishers often setting the pace. Between 1986 and 1989, local publishing enterprises printed an impressive average of 704 book titles and 8.6 million copies per year, compared to only 300 titles and 900,000 copies in 1980 (Vietnam, General Statistical Office 1991, 145). Up to one-third of all book titles published in the late 1980s were probably translations of popular fiction and nonfiction from English, French, and Spanish into Vietnamese, meeting the pent-up demand among readers who had been fed translations from the Russian for decades. Done quickly for payment by the word, many of these translations were mediocre (Marr and Sidel 1998). Provincial police bureaus discovered another moneymaking formula: the tabloid. While waiting for the Can Tho ferry in March 1988, I came upon *Cong An Cuu Long* (Mekong Police), filled with stories about killings, accidents, crime rings broken up, human foibles, grotesque babies—all material previously excluded from publication. Playing upon human emotions, combining the expected and unexpected, often possessing a simple moral punchline, the tabloid was being purchased and consumed avidly by a dozen or more people around me.

Publishing in the 1990s

From the dowdy, hand typeset, gray paper productions of the 1980s, newspapers and magazines underwent a complete facelift in the 1990s, to become computer designed, multicolored, and as lavishly illustrated as periodicals elsewhere in Southeast Asia. Primitive newsprint was banished after the Swedish-financed Bai Bang pulp and paper mill came on line. Journalists took up computer word processing, and young graphic artists experimented with state-of-the-art displays. Color ads took over whole pages, much to the irritation of party purists. Reporters were permitted to access a variety of foreign news sources, rather than having to depend entirely on Vietnam News Agency as in the past. Photos of scantily clad young women became standard fare. Ho Chi Minh City's police tabloid boasted the largest circulation in the country, while *Nhan Dan* limped along at sixth or seventh place, still heavily subsidized, occasionally making a grudging concession to current tastes.

Journalism has become a popular career choice among young educated Vietnamese. In 1999, more than two thousand journalism students were enrolled at three tertiary institutions, with five different party and state bodies asserting rights of supervision. Almost nine thousand persons possessed official journalist accreditation and worked for 712 different media units (including television and radio) (Dao Quoc Tuan and Ho Bat Khuat 1999: 7–9, 104).[8] Senior journalists from the 1960s and 1970s benefited from property sales and investments by the units to which they belonged. Salaries remained low, yet even the most junior reporters learned quickly how to use their accreditation and contacts to generate additional earnings in business promotion, advertising, and consulting, not to mention publishing under pseudonyms. It became common for journalists to receive payments from enterprises in exchange for favorable coverage. A few journalists went further, systematically promoting projects in exchange for a retainer, or blackmailing companies with threats of bad publicity. While the worst offenders became the object of oral disparagement, the professional Association of Journalists proved unable or unwilling to enforce better standards. The government weighed in with a series of laws designed to regulate press behavior, but their impact has been more cautionary than prescriptive (Heng 2001).

Within subject constraints constantly monitored by the party, today's reporters ferret out news stories assiduously and push them to the hilt, even if it sometimes means fudging the line between fact and fiction. Journalists covering big construction projects expose illegal designs, shoddy workmanship, bureaucratic delays, and financial kickbacks. As street traffic becomes ever more congested, reports of fatal accidents, overflowing sidewalk markets, and ward-level bribery multiply, although newspapers seldom address the broader issues of city planning (Koh 2000). Coverage of disputes between employers and employees tends to focus on foreign enterprises. Legal reporters enjoy new room to question police behavior and court procedures. Newspapers lead public campaigns for justice in specific criminal cases, often embarrassing some party and state officials in the process. Probably the most celebrated case involved a policeman who killed a motorcyclist money-courier crossing a Hanoi bridge in 1993. When prosecutors first treated it as a minor offence, two newspapers mounted a long campaign that ended with the policeman's execution in 1996 (Sidel 1998). On many occasions the press also has targeted corrupt officials, although this is risky unless political clearance is secured in advance. The structural roots of corruption are not yet subject to investigation and analysis. Economic reporting has improved considerably in recent years, with writers using statistics more carefully, presenting bad news as well as good, and canvassing a variety of policy options.

Press coverage of Vietnam's National Assembly has become more important, partly because representatives are making the assembly a more lively, contentious institution than at any time since the late 1980s, and partly due to the current party general secretary, Nong Duc Manh, having good connections with committee chairs and administrative staff. During the November–December 2001 session, newspapers devoted full pages to assembly proceedings. Representatives criticized government performance on a wide front, from the glacial pace of administrative reform to persistent financial losses among state-owned enterprises, from local party and police officials wasting money on Toyota Crowns for themselves to the nationwide inability to enforce traffic laws or motorbike helmet requirements. News articles featured those representatives who put government ministers on the spot at Question Time and chided ministers who read from a prepared statement rather than replying to specific queries. Representatives possessing academic credentials and professional experience in key fields (e.g., economics, agronomy, education) were quoted approvingly (my fieldnotes, Nov.–Dec. 2001). However, the continuing absence of any Vietnamese equivalent of the *Congressional Record* or *Hansard* meant that no one was able to consult a full transcription of proceedings.

The growth of a modest English-language press since the late 1980s is a reflection of the party's perceived need to influence foreign residents and to attract foreign investments, aid, and trade. Most of the content is culled from Vietnamese periodicals and overseas news services, with economic coverage predominating. Editorials are occasionally more revealing than their Vietnamese-language counterparts. Sometimes prominent Vietnamese intellectuals are commissioned to contribute articles. An increasing number of educated Vietnamese readers sample the English papers, looking for different perspectives and improving their language skills.

Newspapers routinely present themselves as defenders of truth and justice, yet many readers remain skeptical and can cite numerous examples of papers being less than disinterested parties. Readers know that each publication still functions under a particular party, state, military, or Fatherland Front supervisory organ. They know that some newspapers have substantial property investments and financial connections with big business enterprises, domestic or foreign. They are aware that it is common practice for journalists and editors to receive gratuities for favorable reporting. Even so, readers have come to identify with specific papers, buying copies regularly, enjoying certain columns or features and appreciating the style of one writer, the investigative skills of another. Editors have built on this reader affiliation by sponsoring scholarships, musical performances, public seminars, and a wide variety of contests. Readers routinely send letters to the editor complaining about local government issues, some of which are printed, some given to reporters to check out, and some dispatched to officials for comment or action. Most major papers also contain "Dien Dan" (Forum) columns in the tradition of the 1930s. Newspapers are seen as useful intermediaries, even the "people's friend" on certain occasions, but few readers believe that editors can or will stand up to sustained pressure from above.

Books

Major bookstores in Hanoi, Ho Chi Minh City, Da Nang, and other cities are often crowded with customers of all ages. Book prices are quite high for the average consumer, yet titles often sell out within a few months of release, partly because publishers keep print runs much smaller than during the era of state subsidies. The variety of books on offer has increased dramatically during the past decade, reflecting not only relaxed state censorship but also the reemergence of a middle class looking for diversion and edification. Intellectuals are making more money as authors, editors, and translators, although only a few can prosper this way.

A visit to the largest bookstore in Ho Chi Minh City in late 2001 revealed at least 1,100 Vietnamese literature titles on sale, together with 310 computer manuals, more than one hundred different dictionaries, 85 English language study and examination primers, 22 chess manuals, and 17 sheet music compilations. There were several hundred translations of foreign novels into Vietnamese, the largest number from English and Chinese, followed by French, Russian, German, Japanese, and Spanish. Nine of Pearl Buck's novels were available in translation, together with multiple offerings from Agatha Christie, Danielle Steel, and Sidney Sheldon. Translations from Chinese were especially diverse, from classical stories like *Water Margin* or *Dream of the Red Chamber* to the latest Hong Kong pulp fiction, from Si Ma-Qian's *History* to a biography of Lee Kwan Yew. Among social science translations, the disciplines of economics and history were well represented, whereas political science, sociology, anthropology, linguistics, ecology, and psychology had only a smattering of titles (see also Marr and Sidel 1998). In the realm of religion, the Confucian classics were all available in translation, as well as several Buddhist, Taoist, and Hindu texts, but there was nothing for Christianity or Islam. However, Catholic publications were available at local churches, and additional Buddhist publications could be acquired at major temples.

Academic publishing has slowly recovered from the doldrums of the 1980s and early 1990s, when financial stringencies forced most scholars to abandon long-term research ambitions and compelled publishers to ignore manuscripts unlikely to make money. Eventually some researchers became adept at securing short-term contracts from local government bureaus, factories, businesses, and UN agencies, but their reports were seldom published. A number of research institutes initiated periodicals aimed at the general public, hoping to profit as well as to demonstrate practical relevance. In 1994, the Vietnam Scientific History Association launched *Xua & Nay* (Past and Present), a popular monthly. Reader response was enthusiastic, partly due to the attractive format and brevity of each article, but also because the editors dared to take on certain topics long regarded as taboo (Marr 2000). The late 1990s saw the state increase substantially its funding of research, according to a well-publicized list of strategic priorities. Those scholars unable or unwilling to join such big research projects often relied on sideline income or the support of their spouses to pursue favorite topics, eventually paying a publisher to print perhaps five hundred copies of the resulting monograph. No longer was the party able to control the day-to-day behavior of researchers by means of criticism and self-criticism sessions, meticulous screening of manuscripts, or allocation of scarce printing paper.

During the 1990s, the Ministry of Education established teams to draft replacements for many of the primary and secondary school textbooks that had been in use for two or three decades already. Anti-imperialist and antibourgeois rhetoric was toned down greatly, yet the party's ideological assumptions remained intact, and no new information was incorporated that might provoke pupils to consider alternatives. Some teachers did employ material from current local newspapers and TV documentaries that implicitly contradicted old textbooks. In the few cases where new topics were being introduced into the school curriculum, textbook writers enjoyed more leeway. Thus, following Vietnam's admission to the Association of Southeast Asian Nations (ASEAN) in 1995, the study of Southeast Asia was incorporated into geography and history textbooks, to include lessons on population, topography, climate, natural resources, economic production, the colonial experience, national liberation movements, and a few muted references to Cold War involvements and capitalism. No attention was given to literature, culture, or ethnicity, except occasionally when treating Vietnam's immediate neighbors, Cambodia and Laos. No comparisons were made with Vietnam. Textbook authors relied almost entirely on Western and Russian sources, apparently unable to access publications by Thai, Indonesian, Filipino, or other Southeast Asian writers (Nguyen Van Chinh 2000). Teachers might try to locate and read books produced by the Institute for Southeast Asia Research in Hanoi, yet these too remained ideologically driven and lacking in comparative analysis.

Film and Television

Vietnam has failed so far to develop a viable film industry, although not for want of trying. The DRV's first motion picture was produced in 1959, titled *We Share the Same [Ben Hai] River*; henceforth the medium of film was used extensively to promote the principal party slogans of "Liberate the South" and "Build Socialism in the North." Mobile projection teams reached even the most distant villages, screening feature films, news, and documentaries to transfixed audiences. City theaters offered a steady diet of Soviet, Eastern European, and Chinese films, the latter dropping away with the advent of the Cultural Revolution in 1966. As of 1974, 60 percent of domestically produced films dealt with the two Resistance wars, 30 percent with economic production, and 10 percent with historical themes.[9] Despite mounting financial stringencies, the state continued to allocate significant resources to domestic filmmaking. In 1980, ninety-five newsreels and documentaries and sixteen feature films were released, but by 1989 priorities had been reversed, with the former category falling to twenty-four and the latter rising to thirty-three. Reflecting the high cost of imported film stock, only three or four copies of each production were made and then circulated at length to Vietnam's 345 movie theaters, 101 "open air" cinemas, and 998 mobile projection teams (Vietnam, General Statistical Office 1991: 146–49).

From the early 1980s, Vietnamese cinematographers started to expand the envelope of permissible topics and to experiment with new techniques. Most provocatively, a series of films asked: who rightfully possesses the memory of fallen soldiers, which wartime sacrifices deserve ongoing commemoration, and what are the real legacies of war? In the process, these films undermined official stereotypes, reopened long taboo social issues, and criticized the crass material direction in which Vietnam appeared to be heading (Bradley 2001). Screenwriters, directors, and actors also managed to break away from "socialist realism" rules in filmmaking, developing complex characters, introducing sex scenes, and often avoiding upbeat endings. Audiences seemed to react positively to these innovations, but no figures are available for attendance or box office income.

As government funding for the Vietnamese film industry continued to be cut back, fewer and fewer quality feature films were released. On the other hand, a few creative artists who managed to acquire video cameras and associated audio equipment chose to concentrate on whatever could be accomplished cheaply and sold on the open market. Popular singers, cai luong groups, dramatic troupes, and musical ensembles soon cut back on face-to-face performances in favor of making video (and audio) cassettes commercially. However, they all quickly faced intense competition from foreign and Viet Kieu tapes, mostly smuggled into the country as single copies and then reproduced by private entrepreneurs. In recent years, the three remaining state film production companies have lobbied the party and government vigorously for increased financial subsidies, pointing out that the total 1997 allocation amounted to only 0.3 percent of the amount spent by Hollywood on just one film—*Titanic*. It appears that one-quarter of that 1997 allocation was earmarked for one film about Ho Chi Minh, which drew lukewarm reviews and limited theater audiences. The party has floated the idea of consolidating all film production and distribution, and possibly television as well, into one big state company, citing China as precedent. Some cinematographers instead urge equitization of relevant enterprises, which would take the bureaucrats out of the decision-making process, leaving producers, screenwriters, directors, actors, and other professionals to sink or swim in the marketplace (*Tuoi Tre* 2 Oct. 1997, 7 March 1998, 6 July 2000; *Sai Gon Giai Phong* 22 March 1998). More and more foreign cinematographers are coming to Vietnam to film on location, and there have been some modest joint ventures with Hong Kong and South Korean film companies, but the party appears reluctant to permit substantial foreign involvements in domestic filmmaking.

Television came to Hanoi in 1968, but the public impact remained minimal for two decades. Equipment captured in Saigon in 1975 helped to enable daily TV transmissions to begin the next year to a few hundred officially designated sites around the capital. Programming improved following the 1984 separation of the Giang Vo TV station in Hanoi from the *Voice of Vietnam* radio establishment, with local writers, artists, and musicians trying their hand at this new medium. Private TV receivers were still rare. In the late 1980s, consequent to the more general loosening of government controls, a few western movies began to supplement the standard diet of Soviet and Eastern European films on TV, news programs became more interesting, and reporters greatly expanded their interviewing of ordinary citizens on the street, in the marketplace, and in private homes. More spectacular, as it turned out, were the daily news feeds from a Soviet satellite, which increasingly offered scenes of parliamentary confrontation in the Duma, large antigovernment demonstrations, and the eventual demise of communist regimes in a whole series of capital cities. By 1990, farmers in villages surrounding Hanoi and families in Ho Chi Minh City with remittance income from overseas relatives were buying up foreign color TV sets newly available in state stores. Even more than radio receivers during the 1930s, TV sets acquired by relatively affluent Vietnamese families more than half a century later became magnets that attracted scores of fascinated neighbors during prime time in the evening. Soon locally fabricated TV sets were being marketed at lower prices in small private shopfronts in every city and town within range of a TV transmitter.

During the early 1990s, western embassies and private corporations provided Vietnam Television (VTV) with scores of free-to-air programs, in hopes of gaining an early edge over their foreign competitors. Mexican, Brazilian, and Australian soap operas were extremely popular. The need to dub the Vietnamese language over foreign soundtracks quickly expanded, providing employment for translators, narrators, and technicians alike. VTV began to earn considerable revenue from advertising. The expensively produced, artistically slick, technically advanced foreign TV ads for soft drinks, cosmetics, condoms, motorbikes, and CD players captivated Vietnamese viewers, especially adolescents and children. Beginning to worry that it was losing control of television, the party proceeded to rein in local stations, to redirect advertising revenues, and to scrutinize foreign program content and ads more vigorously. Losing patience with the glacial pace of contract negotiations, foreign program providers began to terminate their free-to-air "donations." At another level, the party instructed local officials to enforce restrictions on satellite dishes being used by tens of thousands of people to access foreign TV transmissions directly.

In the face of all this foreign programming, domestic television production has not been standing still. For many years local TV dramas had been compared with the inedible soup sold at state shops ("Pho mau dich, kich TV"), but in 1995 VTV3 launched a weekly *Sunday Arts* program featuring dramatic serials that managed to gain a large, devoted audience. Drawing on Vietnamese melodrama traditions as well as foreign soap operas, each serial tried to explore current social or family issues in an entertaining as well as educational manner. Besides generating sacks of letters from viewers, certain serials or episodes provoked lively newspaper comment (Drummond forthcoming). On the eve of Tet 1996, VTV organized its first simultaneous live coverage emanating from multiple locations inside the country, including a mobile station positioned for the occasion in the Spratly islands, a transparent diplomatic gambit and appeal to Vietnamese patriotism. The first TV game show also appeared in 1996, followed by a TV quiz show that pitted high school teams against each other.

Television daily news and current affairs programs remain subject to particular party surveillance, yet they have come a long way since the days of talking heads merely reading newspaper articles or quoting provincial hog statistics. In frank imitation of CNN, an increasing proportion of human interest stories are being presented live, which puts greater responsibility on individual reporters, some of whom clearly aspire to status as nationally recognized media personalities. Aside from this "fire engine chasing" tradition of journalism, TV reporters are also being assigned to investigate stories in depth and pursue them over periods of weeks or months if necessary. TV panel discussions that pit different interest groups and viewpoints against each other are increasingly acceptable. More air time is being given to National Assembly proceedings, enabling some representatives to gain reputations for impromptu eloquence, while others manage on TV to demonstrate by facial expression or body language far more than they dare to put in words. The power of television as an education medium is understood by party leaders in principle, but development of a TV curriculum aimed at different age groups has moved slowly (Marr 1998: 14–19; Forrester 1998).

Viet Kieu Intellectuals

Overseas Vietnamese intellectuals (Viet Kieu) have returned to Vietnam increasingly in the past decade, not only to visit relatives for a few weeks, but also to seek spouses, explore business and professional opportunities, exchange ideas with colleagues, obtain publications, and build longer-term relationships. The domestic press looks for Viet Kieu to interview or to contribute articles, of course treading lightly on political topics. Viet Kieu intellectuals are involved in a number of tertiary education initiatives inside Vietnam. Overseas, most Vietnamese language news-papers remain antagonistic to Communist Party rule, but coverage has gradually become more substantive and less rhetorical. Domestic dissidents can easily dis-seminate copies of their complaints or critical analyses in periodicals based in North America, France, or Australia. One of the most interesting examples was written by "Nguoi Sai Gon" (The Saigonese), in the form of twenty-nine issues of a spicy po-litical newsletter disseminated mainly by fax and email during 1996–1997. The author, apparently a retired party member, presented his biting anecdotes in the tra-dition of the "Rue Catinat telegram," when intellectuals exchanged the latest politi-cal gossip, jokes, and interpretations over endless cups of coffee or tea. That he was able to succeed for seven months, despite energetic police efforts to track him down, revealed how much had changed since the early 1980s.

A different kind of Viet Kieu interaction can be found in the Vietnamese music industry. In the early 1990s, videotapes of Viet Kieu popular music shows pro-duced in America and France inundated the domestic market, making it difficult for local composers and singers to find a creative niche for themselves. *Cai luong* (reform opera) videos produced in Saigon found eager listeners overseas, but be-cause most of the tapes were pirated copies the financial return was minimal. In recent years Viet Kieu entrepreneurs have joined with domestic musical talent and producers to reverse the flow of Vietnamese pop videos and CDs, causing some overseas production companies to go out of business. In the interests of foreign currency generation, party censors appear to look the other way when it comes to local composers and singers reaching the young overseas Vietnamese audience.

The Information and Communications Revolution

During the 1990s, Vietnam experienced a revolution in communications technol-ogy, which made it possible for intellectuals and others to exchange information as never before. Previously, almost all international communication had been con-ducted by post or telex, the latter restricted to a few state bureaus. By 1991, six satel-lite ground stations carried an ever-increasing load of international telephone calls and electronic data transfers. Fax machines and modems began to appear in of-fices, the high price of transmission limiting use more than the plethora of gov-ernment regulations that accompanied them. The domestic telephone system took longer to grow, first by means of microwave links between cities, then by mobile phone networks and local cable installations. People were amazed to be able to direct-dial anywhere in the country or the world. As of June 2000, the state telecommunications monopoly reported 2.7 million telephone subscribers among a population approaching 80 million (Vietnam News Agency 10 July 2000). Uni-versity and high school students often exchanged brief written messages on cell phones for fear of running up big monthly bills that would anger their parents.

The first photocopy machines in Vietnam required special imported paper that was seldom available. When subsequent models were able to employ ordinary domestic paper, the government ordered owners to keep a list of all material being copied, for police perusal, but this procedure soon fell by the wayside. By the mid-1990s, photocopy shops could be found in most urban neighborhoods and district towns, with a page costing 200 dong, or less than two cents each. For intellectuals, the era of circulating typescripts by carbon copy or mimeograph machine was over. Indeed, thanks to the photocopier and fax machine together, intellectuals now exchanged unpublished texts at a quantity and speed previously unimaginable. Already in the early 1990s, this new communications combination was used to circulate critiques of party policies by prominent intellectuals, for example the novelist Duong Thu Huong, the essayist Nguyen Khac Vien, and the scientist Phan Dinh Dieu. Overseas Vietnamese journals were quick to reprint these texts, which sometimes led the government to retaliate against the original authors. Photocopies of internal party documents also circulated on occasion. In late 1999, Tran Quynh, a former deputy prime minister, used the photocopier to disseminate an homage to his late mentor, Le Duan (general secretary, 1960–1986), apparently after his manuscript had been rejected by domestic publishing houses (all state owned) (Tran Quynh, n.d.).[10] It seems only a matter of time before different groups within the party Politburo and Central Committee will be using photocopiers and fax machines to criticize their opponents.

Computers attracted the attention of Vietnamese scientists from the 1960s, and the press was already linking national computer literacy to modernity in the 1980s, yet it was not until the 1990s that more than a handful of people gained hands-on experience. Bookshops featured pirated IT textbooks, private computer courses proliferated, and work units invested in their first IBM clones from Taiwan or Singapore. In only two or three years, an eager, mostly young generation of computer-savvy Vietnamese emerged, able to program in several computer languages, using a variety of pirated word processing, spreadsheet, and database packages, and soon finding well-paid jobs in foreign companies, international agencies, and the more outward-looking state-owned enterprises (banks, export-import, airlines, tourism). As of 1995, however, no more than three hundred locations in Vietnam possessed email capacity, and perhaps half of those were foreign organizations. An ambitious project to develop a Vietnam Academic Research and Education Network (VARENET) faltered for lack of high-level leadership as well as negative vibrations emanating from the Ministry of Interior. As before, social scientists came under more suspicion than natural scientists. Until 1996, the government refused to permit a twenty-four-hour dedicated telephone line to carry the ever-expanding quantity of email traffic into and out of Vietnam. After this restriction was lifted, it became possible to interrogate databases and websites, and the number of email users exploded as well. By early 2000, Vietnam was said to possess 60,000 computer sites linked to five state-owned Internet service providers (ISPs). As of late 2001 that number had climbed to 205,000 sites (*Nguoi Lao Dong*, 9 Dec. 2001).

Young, educated Vietnamese have been quickest to take advantage of the Internet, whether simply as consumers constantly looking for new uses, as instructors to the uninitiated, or as entrepreneurs setting up small service companies. Thanks to global access, ICT groups are improving the use of Vietnamese diacritics on computer, developing websites for hundreds of local customers (including media outlets), experimenting with e-commerce, and even programming video and CD games for big foreign game publishers. Older Vietnamese officials meekly accept ICT tutoring from young men and women in hopes of not falling behind irretrievably. Internet cafes and shops, in 1997–2000 the domain of foreign tourists, have now multiplied and become the haunt of university and high school students participating in Yahoo chat rooms, typing out class papers, or exploring websites (my field notes, 1998, 1999, 2001).

The party repeatedly declares a policy of fostering investment in a domestic ICT industry and promoting a computer-literate society, while simultaneously attempting to control the flow of electronic information to a degree that may prove self-defeating. An array of poorly designed Internet firewalls aimed at pornography, violence, and anticommunist Viet Kieu sites also blocks out other information. Clever citizens find ways of evading the controls, just as they have previously with fax machines, photocopiers, satellite dishes, foreign radio broadcasts, and print media censorship, yet not everyone is in a position to do this. High prices set by the telecommunications monopoly also do nothing to foster Vietnam's competitive position in the information age. Many intellectuals use computer sites belonging to their work units for personal purposes, as a way of finessing both red tape and costs. Ironically, the socialist "supply system" (*che do cung cap*) lingering from the 1980s continues to offer a few such benefits to work unit members, even when income is being earned from other sources entirely.

The media has been remarkably blunt in its criticism of state behavior vis-à-vis the Internet. For example, when the Ministry of Culture announced its intention to compel all creators of websites to register with the ministry, one editorial sourly equated this with trying to regulate the content of ads in the classified section of the newspaper. Already, the paper complained, "Most educators, physicians, scientists and businessmen have their hands tied when it comes to using this technology to exploit new reservoirs of knowledge." Instead, the state should adopt the principle that "Citizens have the right to do anything not forbidden by law"—leaving unsaid the opposite principle, long preferred by Vietnamese rulers, of allowing citizens to do only what was specified in law (*Thoi Bao Kinh Te Sai Gon*, 12 May 2000). A punchy TV documentary featured a series of ICT professionals emphasizing how Vietnam was falling even further behind Thailand and other neighbors for lack of government policies to encourage Internet usage (VTV broadcast, 21 Nov. 2001). Scores of articles have called for the state telecommunications monopoly to be abandoned, the number of Internet ports to the outside world multiplied, and computer education in the schools greatly enhanced. A few writers admit that even with the best of government intentions most Vietnamese villagers will remain out of contact with the Internet for decades to come, due to lack of money, local infrastructure, technical services, literacy, or perceived relevance to their daily lives.

Recent media transformations have tended to exacerbate the rural/urban gap discussed elsewhere in this volume. Newspapers still reach villagers, but the content is more explicitly urban than before, often targeting the upwardly mobile middle class. Although journalists do roam the countryside, and some editors are quite willing to print exposés of local land disputes, administrative bungling, environmental degradation, or the destruction of historical sites, such articles tend to get lost amid the glitzy youth culture, foreign fashion, IT features, or elite educational opportunities. Meanwhile, libraries at the district or village level have degenerated or disappeared. Local radio stations do retain content of value to farmers, but most provincial television stations depend heavily on feeds from Hanoi or Ho Chi Minh City. With telephones still only available in a handful of houses in any given village, the idea of farmers hooking up a computer modem and communicating with the world is only a chimera. While young Vietnamese have been exiting the countryside for over a century, the intensification of urban media cues during the past decade must be an additional pull factor.

CONCLUSION

We have seen how modern Vietnamese intellectuals and the print media grew up together, each dependent on the other for advancement. In the early days, intellectuals were the principal consumers as well as producers of books and periodicals. As literacy increased, readers who did not necessarily think of themselves as intellectuals contributed letters to the editor, "forum" comments, and unsolicited manuscripts. They built up several shelves of books at home, sharing their holdings with family members and friends. From the 1980s, tens of thousands of intellectuals returned from overseas study with a less polymath, more professional outlook. Specialized journals emerged to cater to these constituencies. Nonetheless, many of these scientists, engineers, military officers, university teachers, and state officials continued to read literary and cultural journals, express opinions about specific creative writers, and occasionally submit contributions of their own. This sense of involvement in the print media continues today for several million Vietnamese, not counting those people who simply read a periodical or two for news or entertainment. By contrast, when sitting in front of the radio or television set, few Vietnamese consider themselves as more than passive listeners or viewers, although they do voice strong preferences for particular programs or performers.

Throughout the past eighty years in Vietnam, the state has closely monitored intellectual activities and exercised various forms of censorship over the media. However, state controls have never been absolute, and writers, editors, artists, and musicians have often found ways to pursue their own agendas within state-owned media organizations. During the past fifteen years or so, there has been an unmistakable diminution in the capacity of the state to compel compliance. The state continues to employ the media extensively to instruct, exhort, overawe, or threaten, but citizens have come to read, view, or listen with less credulity than before, partly because they have unprecedented access to overseas sources of information by way of comparison. Quoting from a 1959 speech by Ho Chi Minh, the party still insists that "Politics must be in charge" (*Chinh tri phai lam chu*) when it comes to media content (*Nhan Dan* 22 June 2000). It also warns of the risks inherent in media globalization, and even foreshadows "planification" of the entire media system. Nevertheless, repeated official statements of this kind fail to correspond with ongoing media practice, and there is reason to doubt that the party intends to mount a major media crackdown. Even if it did, the results would not likely meet the expectations of hardline instigators. Meanwhile, media practitioners continue "to negotiate the Vietnamese state as a multi-segmented reality, of which the media itself is a part" (Heng 2001: 230).

Media history worldwide since the 1960s may lead one to predict that television in Vietnam will soon overshadow newspapers, books, radio, stereo music, and the cinema completely. On the other hand, Vietnamese circulation figures for the print media continue to rise, new local FM radio stations are proving popular with listeners, and music of domestic origin is enjoying a revival after being inundated by foreign products in the early 1990s. Film productions require large investments, which the state now provides only infrequently, while still disinclined to allow foreigners to move in. Vietnam Television is starting to face the same dilemma: viewers are demanding higher quality programming, beyond the means of domestic investors, yet the government continues to reject overtures from foreign media magnates. As the party sees it, "It will be completely disastrous if [Vietnam's] mass media receives assistance from a giant corporation in the hands of a reactionary political apparatus" (*Nhan Dan* 22 June 2000).

Global trends suggest that even countries like Vietnam, which insist on keeping the media under state ownership, are compelled to commercialize operations, permit some degree of competition, and seek out foreign advertising if not investment. Vietnam has in fact taken this route since the early 1990s, although both party leaders and older intellectuals are shocked by some of the consequences, to include checkbook journalism, tabloid sensationalism, softcore pornography, and the fostering of middle-class consumer tastes. More fundamentally, some intellectuals worry that new media technologies combined with commercial imperatives possess the power to manipulate both individuals and society as a whole, to replace actual reality with representations of reality. Others reply that intellectuals have always been in the business of symbolizing reality. Besides, a television transmitter is qualitatively no different from a printing press, except that it takes more money to generate content, and there is no need for consumers to be literate. These two differences remain significant to most Vietnamese intellectuals, who seldom get close to big money and equate reading with civilization.

Commercialization may shove Vietnamese intellectuals to the fringes of media decision-making, yet no more so than Marxism-Leninism pushed earlier generations into self-censorship or rhetorical bombast. Most media managers today retain intellectual pretensions, even as they try to make a better profit for their organization. Most newspaper editors and TV producers belong to intellectual circles and follow wider intellectual issues as a matter of course. Below the big media outlets, a variety of niche publications are doing well, often with intellectuals at the forefront. Small-scale video production companies are flourishing, drawing on the talents of writers, artists, actors, singers, and musicians. Community radio stations rely on volunteer help from local intellectuals and retired cadres.

Within a few years, the Internet is likely to provoke the most significant media transformation in Vietnam since the advent of the printing press, making it possible for individuals and groups to receive and generate information to a degree never imagined before. Already perhaps half a million persons are communicating overseas and domestically by email. Office workers, university students, and researchers are setting up websites, announcing themselves to the world, and experimenting with multimedia presentations. A number of mass media outlets have opened websites, and major newspapers are publishing online editions. The party will soon have to decide whether it is more important to maintain current security restrictions on Internet access or pursue its oft-stated objective of making Vietnam a full-fledged, vibrant participant in the information and communications revolution. Even if it attempts to do both simultaneously, which is likely, a new generation of computer-literate citizens will find ways of evading controls and advancing their own agendas.

The Internet offers Vietnamese intellectuals an opportunity to make their mark in ways reminiscent of the extraordinary generation of the 1920s and 1930s, assimilating new ideas, testing received wisdom, experimenting, debating, and disseminating the results to an expanding constituency. It is no accident that writers of the 1920s and 1930s have been republished in recent years, including some of those denounced by the party as reactionaries during the intervening decades. By contrast, much of the published output of the 1946–1986 period is now ignored. It will be interesting to see if current writers of fiction, mindful of the proven capacity of that genre to break new political as well as cultural ground, will use the Internet to disseminate their creations widely.

When discussing state-society relations in Vietnam, can we say that intellectuals as a social group have been able to conduct a dialogue with the authorities? Certainly intellectuals have aimed messages at the authorities very often, and expected or hoped to be taken seriously. However, the state has never accepted intellectuals as equal partners in a public exchange of views on issues of national importance, although it has sometimes gone to great lengths to incorporate intellectuals into its projects. The state has set unequal rules of engagement, prevented intellectuals from organizing autonomously, and punished those who dared to ignore restrictions. On two historic occasions, in 1956–1957 and 1986–1989, the state's rules of engagement became confused, allowing some intellectuals to disseminate heterodox ideas, even to start organizing groups free from party control. Those opportunities proved short-lived, and participants paid a heavy personal price.

Today's intellectuals know that history can repeat itself. More likely, intellectuals and the party will talk past each other more frequently, making dialogue even less meaningful. With Vietnam's media expanding and mutating at a frantic pace, both intellectuals and the state will be hard pressed to keep up, and no on can predict the consequences for Vietnamese society.

NOTES

I would like to thank colleagues for commenting on earlier drafts of this essay, in particular Kim Ninh, Russell Heng, and Hy Van Luong.

1. This is twice the number I estimated in Marr 1981: 51, thanks to new evidence contained in Nguyen Van Ky 1995: 56–57.

2. The National Library of Vietnam contains a collection of more than 4,000 books and pamphlets, as well as scores of periodicals, printed during 1946–1954 in Viet Minh–held areas.

3. Thanks to Kim Ninh for bringing this source to my attention.

4. For a recent biography of one journalist-editor who nurtured this tradition until 1975, see Thien Moc Lan 2000.

5. Interview with Tran Minh Tuoc, Hanoi, 1 January 1975. Tuoc had published poetry during the Popular Front period (1936–1938), shifting to writing short dramas during the anti-French Resistance.

6. Interview with Hoang Tung, Hanoi, 29 December 1974. Earlier I had observed a western music performance in front of the National Bank of Vietnam (topped by a huge picture of Ho Chi Minh) that attracted about 10,000 people.

7. Discussions with Professor Nguyen Van Trung, Ho Chi Minh City, 12 and 18 February 1990, 20 January 1992. Highly respected as researcher, writer, and teacher at the Saigon University before 1975, Prof. Trung had been jailed for six months in 1978 and prevented from teaching throughout the 1980s. In 1994, he migrated to Canada.

8. The state-owned publications exporter, Xunhasaba, lists 366 serials for sale in its 2002 Catalog, but most provincial-level periodicals are ignored.

9. Interview with Ha Xuan Truong, vice minister of culture and president of the Vietnam Film Association, Hanoi, 2 January 1975.

10. It seems Tran Quynh felt compelled to counter criticisms (mostly unpublished) of Le Duan which have circulated since the latter's death in 1986. He is especially scathing in his characterizations of Vo Nguyen Giap and Truong Chinh.

References

Adger, Neil W. 1999. "Exploring Income Inequality in Rural Coastal Vietnam." *Journal of Development Studies* 35, no. 5 (June): 96–119.

Agrawa, Arun, and Clark C. Gibson. 1999. "Enchantment and Disenchantment: The Role of Community in Natural Resource Conservation." *World Development* 27, no. 4: 629–49.

Alley, Rewi. *Refugees from Vietnam in China.* Beijing: New World Press, 1980.

Amer, Ramses. 1991. *The Ethnic Chinese in Vietnam and Sino-Vietnamese Relations.* Kuala Lumpur: Forum.

———. 1996. "Vietnam's Policies and the Ethnic Chinese since 1976." *Sojourn* 1, no. 11: 76–104.

Amor, Abdelfattah. 1998. *Civil and Political Rights, Including the Question of Religious Intolerance: Addendum, Visit to Vietnam.* Geneva: Office of the United Nations High Commissioner for Human Rights.

Banister, Judith. 1993. *Vietnam Population Dynamics and Prospects.* Berkeley: University of California-Berkeley, Institute of East Asian Studies.

Barrow, John. 1975 (1806). *A Voyage to Cochinchina.* Oxford: Oxford University Press.

Beaulieu, Carole. 1994. Is it an NGO? Is it a Civil Society? Is it Pluralism Wriggling Along? Letter no. CB-26 to the Institute of Current World Affairs. New Hampshire, 6 October.

Belanger, Daniele. 1997. Rapport intergenerationnel et rapport hommes-femmes dans la transition demographique au Vietnam, de 1930 a 1990. Ph.D. dissertation, Universite de Montreal.

Beresford, Melanie. 1988. *Vietnam: Politics, Economics and Society.* London: Pinter.

———. 1989. *National Unification and Economic Development in Vietnam.* London: Macmillan.

———. 1995a. "Political economy of primary health care in Vietnam." In *Health and Development in Southeast Asia,* edited by Paul Cohen and John Purcal. Canberra: Australian Development Studies Network.

———. 1995b. "Interpretation of the Vietnamese economic reforms, 1979–85." Pp.1–16 in *Researching the Vietnamese Economic Reforms, 1979–86*, edited by Adam Fforde. Sydney: School of Economic and Financial Studies, Australia-Vietnam Research Project.

Beresford, Melanie, and Dang Phong. 2000. *Economic Transition in Vietnam: Foreign Aid and Trade in the Demise of a Centrally-Planned Economy*. Cheltenham, UK: Edward Elgar.

Beresford, Melanie, and Adam Fforde. 1997. "A Methodology for Understanding the Process of Economic Reform in Vietnam: The Case of Domestic Trade." *Journal of Communist Studies and Transition Politics* 13, no. 4: 99–128.

Beresford, Melanie, and Bruce McFarlane. 1995. "Regional Inequality and Regionalism in Vietnam and China." *Journal of Contemporary Asia* 25, no. 1: 50–72.

Bond, Tim. 1999. *Poverty in Ho Chi Minh City*. Hanoi: Save the Children Fund.

Boudarel, Georges. 1990. "The Nhan Van Giai Pham Affair: Intellectual Dissidence in the 1950s." *Vietnam Forum* 13: 154–74.

———. 1991. *Cent Fleurs Ecloses dans la Nuit du Vietnam: Communisme et Dissidence 1954–1956*. Paris: Jacques Bertoin.

———. 1997. "1954: les dilemmas de l'independence." Pp. 128–48 in *Hanoi 1936–1996, Du drapeau rouge au billet vert*, edited by Georges Boudarel and Nguyen Van Ky. Paris: Autrement.

———. 2002. "1965–1975: War or peace." Pp. 133–52 in *Hanoi: City of the Rising Dragon*, by Georges Boudarel and Nguyen van Ky, translated by Claire Duiker. Boulder: Rowman & Littlefield.

Bradley, Mark Philip. 2001. "Contests of Memory: Remembering and Forgetting War in the Contemporary Vietnamese Cinema." Pp. 196–226 in *The Country of Memory: Remaking the Past in Late Socialist Vietnam*, edited by Hue-Tam Ho Tai. Berkeley and Los Angeles: University of California Press.

Brockerhoff, M. 1998. Internal migration patterns and policies in countries of Southeast Asia. Paper presented at the International Conference on Migration. Hanoi: The Population Council.

Brook, Timothy. 1997. "Auto-organization in Chinese society." Pp. 19–45 in *Civil Society in China*, edited by T. Brook and B. Michael Frolic. Armonk, N.Y.: M. E. Sharpe.

Burchett, Wilfred. 1980. *On the Barricades*. London: Quartet Books.

Cadiere, Leopold. 1992. *Croyances et pratiques religieuses des vietnamiens*. Paris: Ecole Francaise D'Extreme-Orient.

Chan, Anita, Benedict Tria Kerkvliet, and Jonathan Unger. 1999. "Comparing Vietnam and China: An Introduction." Pp. 1–14 in *Transforming Asian Socialism: China and Vietnam Compared*, edited by Anita Chan, B. Kerkvliet, and J. Unger. St. Leonards, Australia: Allen and Unwin.

Chan, Anita, and Irene Norlund. 1999. "Vietnamese and Chinese Labour Regimes: On the Road to Divergence." Pp. 204–28 in *Transforming Asian Socialism: China and Vietnam Compared*, edited by Anita Chan, B. Kerkvliet, and J. Unger. St. Leonards, Australia: Allen and Unwin.

Chanda, Nayan. 1986. *Brother Enemy: The War after the War*. San Diego: Harcourt Brace Jovanovich.

Chanoff, David, and Doan Van Toai. 1996. *Vietnam, A Portrait of Its People at War.* London and New York: I. B. Taurus.

Chayanov, Alexander V. 1986 (1924–1925). *The Theory of Peasant Economy,* translated from Russian by C. Lane and R. Smith, edited by D. Thorner, B. Kerblay, and R. Smith. Madison: University of Wisconsin Press.

Chu Huu Quy. 2001. "Trang trai gia dinh: mot hien tuong kinh te xa hoi moi xuat hien tren mot so vung nong thon Viet Nam" [Family farms: An emerging social and economic phenomenon in some rural regions of Vietnam]. Pp. 374–83 in *Viet nam hoc: Ky yeu hoi thao quoc te lan thu nhat, Ha Noi 15–17.7.1998* [Vietnamese Studies: Proceedings of the First International Conference, Hanoi, July 15–17, 1998], edited by Dai hoc Quoc gia Ha Noi and Trung tam Khoa hoc Xa hoi va Nhan van Quoc gia, vol. 4. Hanoi: Nha xuat ban The gioi.

Chu van Lam. 1990. "45 nam nong nghiep Viet Nam" [Forty five years of Vietnamese agriculture]. Pp. 95–115 in *45 nam kinh te Viet Nam* [Forty five years of Vietnamese economy], edited by Dao van Tap. Hanoi: Nha xuat ban Khoa hoc Xa hoi.

Chu van Lam et al. 1992. *Hop tac hoa nong nghiep Viet Nam: Lich su-van de-trien vong* [Agricultural cooperativization in Vietnam: History, problems, and prospects]. Hanoi: Nha xuat ban Su that.

Cleary, J. C. 1991. "Buddhism and Popular Religion in Medieval Vietnam." *Journal of the American Academy of Religion* 59, no. 1: 93–119.

Condominas, Georges, and Richard Pottier. 1982. *Les refugiés originaires de l'Asie du Sud-Est.* Paris: La Documentation Française.

Crawfurd, John. 1970a (1822). "Narrative of the Crawfurd Mission to Hue, 1822." Pp. 242–54 in *The Mandarin Road to Old Hue: Narratives of Anglo-Vietnamese Diplomacy from the 17th Century to the Eve of the French Conquest,* edited by A. Lamb. London: Chatto and Windus.

———. 1970b (1823). "Report on the State of the Annamese Empire." Pp. 255–77 in *The Mandarin Road to Old Hue: Narratives of Anglo-Vietnamese Diplomacy from the 17th Century to the Eve of the French Conquest,* edited by A. Lamb. London: Chatto and Windus.

Dampier, William. 1906. *Dampier's Voyages,* ed. John Masefield. London: E. Grant Richards.

Dang Canh Khanh. 1991. "Ve su phan tang xa hoi o nong thon hien nay" [On social stratification in the countryside at present]. Pp. 319–66 in *Kinh te - xa hoi nong thon Viet Nam ngay nay* [Vietnamese Rural Economy and Society at Present], vol. 2. Hanoi: Nha xuat ban Tu tuong van hoa.

Dang Nghiem Van. 1989. "Nhung van de xa hoi hien nay o Tay Nguyen" [Contemporary social problems in Tay Nguyen]. Pp. 67–151 in *Tay Nguyen tren duong phat trien* [Tay Nguyen on the path to development]. Hanoi: Vietnam Committee for the Social Sciences.

Dang Nguyen Anh. 1998. "Vai tro cua mang luoi xa hoi trong qua trinh di cu" [The role of social networks in the process of migration]. *Xa Hoi Hoc* no. 2: 16–23.

Dang Nguyen Anh and Nguyen Binh Minh. 1998. "Dam bao cung cap dich vu xa hoi cho nguoi lao dong nhap cu o thanh pho" [Ensuring the social services provision for labor who migrate into cities]. *Xa Hoi Hoc* no. 4: 31–36.

Dang Phong. 1995. "Aspects of Agricultural Economy and Rural Life in 1993." Pp. 165–84 in *Vietnam's Rural Transformation,* edited by Benedict J. Tria Kerkvliet and Doug Porter. Boulder: Westview; and Singapore: ISEAS.

———. History and Significance of Commercial Links with the Soviet Union and Eastern Europe. Hanoi: unpublished manuscript.

———. 1998. Opening the Door: Two Centuries of Markets in Vietnam. Hanoi: unpublished manuscript.

———. 1999. A History of the Vietnamese Diaspora: Its Approaches to Returning and Integrating into Vietnam. Hanoi: unpublished manuscript.

Dang Phong and Melanie Beresford. 1998. *Authority Relations and Economic Decision-Making in Vietnam, A Historical Perspective.* Copenhagen: Nordic Institute of Asian Studies.

Dang Thi Sy. 1998. "A Bio-remediation Solution for Tay Lake." Pp. 161–72 in *Waste management and remediation of polluted sites for sustainable development,* edited by Le Trong Cuc and Michael DiGregorio. Hanoi: Center for Natural Resources and Environmental Studies.

Dang Van Sinh. 1964. "Kinh nghiem cua Truc Tam da giup cho Dong Xuan chung toi loi thoat" [Truc Tam's experience has already helped our Dong Xuan find a way out]. *Tien Len* (30 March): 2.

Dao Quoc Toan and Ho Bat Khuat. 1999. "Dao tao phong vien bao chi - nghe va nghiep" [Training news reporters—craft and profession]. *The Gioi Moi,* no. 341 (21 June): 7–9, 104.

Dao The Tuan. 1993. "Kinh te ho gia dinh cua nong dan va su thay doi xa hoi o Viet Nam" [The peasant household economy and social change in Vietnam]. *Xa Hoi Hoc* [Sociology] no. 44: 5–16.

———. 1997. *The Diversification of Agriculture in Different Regions of Vietnam, Interim Report.* Hanoi: Vietnam Agricultural Science Institute.

Dao Tri Uc. 1997. "Tham nhung: nhan dien tu cac khia canh phap ly va co so phap ly moi" [Corruption: Recognizing it from new legal perspectives and bases]. *Tap chi Cong San* (February): 24–28.

Dau Tu. 2001.

Davies, Susanna. 1996. *Adaptable Livelihoods: Coping with Food Insecurity in the Malian Sahel.* London: Macmillan.

De Koninck, Rodolphe. 1996. "The Peasantry as the Territorial Spearhead of the State in Southeast Asia: The Case of Vietnam." *Sojourn* 2, no. 11: 231–58.

———. 1999. *Deforestation in Viet Nam.* Ottawa: International Development Research Centre.

De Vylder, Stefan, and Adam Fforde. 1988. *Vietnam: An Economy in Transition.* Stockholm: Swedish International Development Authority.

Denny, Stephen. 1992. "Religious Repression in Vietnam: The Protest of Thich Huyen Quang." *Vietnam Journal* 1: 3–7.

Desbarats, Jacqueline. 1987. "Population redistribution in the Socialist Republic of Vietnam." *Population and Development Review* 13, no. 1: 43–76.

Didier, Bertrand. 1996. "Renaissance du *Len Dong* a Hue (Viet Nam): Premiers Elements d'une Recherche." *Bulletin de l'Ecole Francais d'Extreme-Orient* 83: 271–85.

———. 1997. "The Thay: Masters in Hue." *Asian Folklore Studies* 55, no. 2: 271–86.

DiGregorio, Michael R. 1994. *Urban Harvest: Recycling as a Peasant Industry in Northern Vietnam.* Honolulu: East-West Center.

———. 1999. *Report on the Environment of Development in Industrializing Craft Villages.* Hanoi: Center for Natural Resources and Environmental Studies.

DiGregorio, Michael et al. 1995. *Recent Urbanization and Environmental Change in Viet Tri City, Vietnam.* Working paper no. 3. Berkeley: Institute of International Studies.

Dinh Thu Cuc. 1977. "Tim hieu qua trinh tung buoc cung co va hoan thien quan he san xuat xa hoi chu nghia trong cac hop tac xa san xuat nong nghiep o mien Bac nuoc ta" [The process of step-by-step consolidation and strengthening of socialist relations production in agricultural cooperatives in the northern region of our country]. *Nghien Cuu Lich Su* 4/145 (July and August): 37–50, 76.

Do Long. 1985. "Tam ly xa hoi truyen thong va ke hoach dan so Viet Nam" [Traditional mentality and demographic planning in Vietnam]. *Tap chi Xa Hoi Hoc* no. 12: 32–33, 41.

Do Hoai Nam. 1994. "Industry in the Process of Economic Restructuring." In *Vietnam's Economic Reform: Results and Problems.* Hanoi: Social Science Publishing House.

Do, Thien. 1997. "Popular Religion in Contemporary Southern Vietnam: A Personal Approach." *Sojourn* 12, no. 1: 64–91.

———. 1995. The Mountain's Shadow and Reflection in the River: Vietnamese Supernaturalism in the Mekong River. Ph.D. dissertation, Australian National University, Canberra.

———. 1998. "Charity and Charisma: The Dual Path of the Tinh Do Cu Si, a Popular Buddhist Group in Southern Vietnam." ISEAS Working Papers, Social and Cultural Issues no. 2. Singapore: Institute of Southeast Asian Studies.

Doan Mau Diep et al. 1998. "Forms of Rural-urban Migration and Solutions to the Problem: A Case Study of Ha Noi." *International Conference on Migration.* Hanoi: The Population Council.

Doan Trung Tue. 1997. "Chat Luong Hoc Sinh Vung Cao" [Quality of Highland students]. *Nhan Dan,* 23 October: 4.

Dollar, David, Paul Glewwe, and Jennie Litvack, eds. 1998. *Household Welfare and Vietnam's Transition.* Washington, D.C.: World Bank.

Donovan, D. G. 1999. "Strapped for Cash, Asians Plunder Their Forests and Endanger Their Future." *Asia Pacific Issues* no. 39. Honolulu: East-West Center.

Donovan, Deanna, ed. 1998. *Policy Issues of Transboundary Trade in Forest Products in Northern Vietnam, Lao PDR and Yunnan PRC.* Washington, D.C.: World Resources Institute.

Drummond, Lisa. Forthcoming. "Popular Television and Images of Urban Life." In *Consuming Urban Culture in Contemporary Vietnam,* edited by Lisa Drummond and Mandy Thomas. New York and London: Routledge.

Duong Hong Dat. 1994. *Lich su nong nghiep Viet Nam* [The history of agriculture in Vietnam]. Ho Chi Minh City: Hoc vien Chinh tri Quoc gia Ho Chi Minh.

Duong thi Thanh Mai. 1985. "Van de hon nhan qua khao sat thuc te o mot so noi" [The question of marriage: empirical research in a number of localities]. Pp. 64–68 in *Tinh yeu, hon nhan, gia dinh trong xa hoi ta* [Love, marriage, and the family in our society], edited by Vien Xa hoi hoc. Hanoi: Nha xuat ban Khoa hoc Xa hoi.

Durand, Maurice. 1989. *Technique et Pantheon des Mediums Vietnamiens*. Paris: Ecole Francaise D'Extreme-Orient.

Ebbesen, Niels Funk. 1997. Music in a Changing City: Hanoi, Vietnam: A Preliminary Examination of the History of Modern Vietnamese Music, 1938–1996. Unpublished manuscript.

Elliott, Duong Van Mai. 1999. *The Sacred Willow: Four Generations in the Life of a Vietnamese Family*. New York and Oxford: Oxford University Press.

Endres, Kirsten W. 1999. "Culturalizing Politics: *doi moi* and the Restructuring of Ritual in Contemporary Rural Vietnam." Pp. 197–221 in *Vietnamese Villages in Transition. Background and Consequences of Reform Policies in Rural Vietnam*, edited by Bernhard Dahm and Vincent Houben. Passau: Passau Contributions to Southeast Asian Studies.

———. 2001. "Local Dynamics of Renegotiating Ritual Space in North Vietnam: The Case of the *Dinh*." *Sojourn* 16, no. 1: 71–103.

Evans, Grant. 1992. "Internal Colonialism in the Central Highlands of Vietnam." *Sojourn* 2, no. 7: 274–304.

Evans, Grant, and Kelvin Rowley. 1990. *Red Brotherhood at War: Vietnam, Cambodia and Laos since 1975*. London and New York: Verso.

Fforde, Adam. 1989. *The Agrarian Question in North Vietnam 1974–78: A Study of Cooperator Resistance to State Policy*. Armonk, N.Y.: M. E. Sharpe.

———. 1999. "From Plan to Market: The Economic Transition in Vietnam and China Compared." Pp. 43–72 in *Transforming Asian Socialism: China and Vietnam Compared*, edited by Anita Chan, B. Kerkvliet, and J. Unger. St. Leonards, Australia: Allen and Unwin.

Fforde, Adam, and Stefan de Vylder. 1996. *From Plan to Market: The Economic Transition in Vietnam*. Boulder: Westview.

Fforde, Adam, and S. H. Paine. 1987. *The Limits to National Liberation*. London: Croom Helm.

Fforde, Adam, and Doug Porter. 1994. Public Goods, the State, Civil Society and Development Assistance in Vietnam: Opportunities and Prospects. Paper presented to Vietnam Update Conference, The Australian National University, Canberra, November.

Fitzgerald, Frances. 1972. *Fire in the Lake: The Vietnamese and the Americans in Vietnam*. New York: Vintage Books.

Fitzpatrick, Sheila. 1999. *Everyday Stalinism: Ordinary Life in Extraordinary Times, Soviet Russia in the 1930s*. Oxford and New York: Oxford University Press.

Fjelstad, Karen. 1995. Tu Phu Cong Dong: Vietnamese Women and Spirit Possession in the San Francisco Bay Area. Ph.D. dissertation, University of Hawaii.

Forbes, Dean, and Nigel Thrift. 1987. "Territorial Organization, Regional Development and the City in Vietnam." Pp. 98–128 in *The Socialist Third World*, edited by Dean Forbes and N. Thrift. London: Basil Blackwell.

Ford Foundation. 1997. *Forestry for Sustainable Rural Development: A Review of Ford Foundation Supported Community Forestry Programs in Asia*. New York: Ford Foundation.

Forrester, Jan. 1998. "Instant Noodle Propaganda: Vietnam Television in the Late 1990s." Pp. 78–90 in *The Mass Media in Vietnam*, edited by David Marr. Canberra: Department of Social and Political Change, National Australian University.

Fox, Jefferson, Dao Minh Truong, A. Terry Rambo, Nghiem Phuong Tuyen, Le Trong Cuc, and Stephen Leisz. 2000. "Shifting Cultivation: A New Paradigm for Managing Tropical Forests." *BioScience* 50, no. 6: 521–28.

Frolic, B. Michael. 1997. "State-Led Civil Society." Pp. 46–67 in *Civil Society in China*, edited by T. Brook and B. Michael Frolic. Armonk, N.Y.: M. E. Sharpe.

Gammeltoft, Tine. 1999. *Women's Bodies, Women's Worries: Health and Family Planning in a Vietnamese Rural Community*. Richmond, Surrey: Curzon.

———. 2002. "The Irony of Sexual Agency: Pre-Marital Sex in Urban Northern Viet Nam." Pp. 111–28 in *Gender, Household, State: Doi Moi in Viet Nam*, edited by Jayne Werner and Daniele Belanger. Ithaca: Cornell University Southeast Asia Program.

Gheddo, Piero. 1970. *The Cross and the Bo-Tree: Catholics and Buddhists in Vietnam*. Trans. Charles Quinn. New York: Sheed and Ward.

Giebel, Christoph. 2001. "Museum-Shrine: Revolution and its Tutelary Spirit in the Village of My Hoa Hung." Pp. 77–105 in *The Country of Memory: Remaking the Past in Late Socialist Vietnam*, edited by Hue-Tam Ho Tai. Berkeley: University of California Press.

Goodkind, Daniel. 1995. "Rising Gender Inequality in Vietnam since Reunification." *Pacific Affairs* 48, no. 3: 342–59.

———. 1996. "State Agendas, Local Sentiments: Vietnamese Wedding Practices Amidst Socialist Transformations." *Social Forces* 75, no. 2: 717–42.

Gordon, Alec. 1981. "North Vietnam's Collectivisation Campaigns: Class Struggle, Production and the 'Middle Peasant' Problem." *Journal of Contemporary Asia* 11, no. 1: 19–43.

Gough, Kathleen. 1990. *Political Economy in Vietnam*. Berkeley: Folklore Institute.

Gourou, Pierre. 1936. *Les paysans du delta tonkinois*. Paris: Les Editions de l'Art et de l'Histoire.

———. 1940. *L'utilisation du sol en Indochine francaise*. Paris: Centre d'Etude de Politique Etrangere.

Gray, Michael. 1997. Creating Civil Society? The Emergence of NGOs in Vietnam. Master's thesis, School of Oriental and African Studies, University of London.

Greenfield, Gerard. 1994. "The Development of Capitalism in Vietnam." Pp. 203–34 in *Between Globalism and Nationalism: Socialist Register 1994*, edited by Ralph Miliband and Leo Panitch. London: Merlin Press.

Ha Nam Ninh, Cultural Service. 1976. *Day! Thuc Chat Hoi Phu Giay* [Here: The Reality of Phu Giay Festival]. Ha Nam Ninh: Ha Nam Ninh Cultural Service.

Ha thi Phuong Tien and Ha Quang Ngoc. 2001. *Female Labour Migration*. Hanoi: Women's Publishing House.

Hainesworth, Geoffrey. 2000. Human Development in Vietnam. Hanoi: UNDP, unpublished report.

Hardy, Andrew. 2000. "Strategies of Migration to Upland Areas in Contemporary Vietnam." *Asia Pacific Viewpoint* 41, no. 1 (April): 23–34.

———. 2001. "Rules and Resources: Negotiating the Household Registration System in Vietnam under Reform." *Sojourn* 16, no. 2: 187–212.

Harrison, James P. 1982. *The Endless War: Fifty Years of Struggle in Vietnam.* New York: Free Press.

Haughton, Dominique, Jonathan Haughton, Sarah Bales, Truong thi Kim Chuyen, and Nguyen Nguyet Nga, eds. 1999. *Health and Wealth in Vietnam: An Analysis of Household Living Standards.* Singapore: Institute of Southeast Asian Studies.

Hawthorne, Lesleyanne, ed. 1982. *Refugee, The Vietnamese Experience.* Oxford, Auckland, and New York: Oxford University Press.

Heng, Russell Hianh-Khng. 1998. "Media in Vietnam and the Structure of its Management." Pp. 27–53 in *The Mass Media in Vietnam*, edited by David Marr. Canberra: Dept. of Political and Social Change, Australian National University.

———. 1999. Of the State, For the State, Yet Against the State: The Struggle Paradigm in Vietnam's Media Politics. Ph.D. dissertation, Australian National University, Canberra.

———. 2001. "Media Negotiating the State: In the Name of the Law in Anticipation." *Sojourn* 16, 2: 213–37.

Henry, Yves. 1932. *L'economie agricole de l'Indochine francaise.* Hanoi: Extreme-Orient.

Hickey, Gerald. 1958. "Problems of Social Change in Vietnam." *Bulletin de la Societe des Etudes Indochinoises* 33 (new series), no. 4.

———. 1964. *Village in Vietnam.* New Haven: Yale University Press.

———. 1982. *Free in the Forest: Ethnohistory of the Vietnamese Central Highlands, 1954–1976.* New Haven: Yale University Press.

———. 1993. *Shattered World: Adaptation and Survival among Vietnam's Highland Peoples during the Vietnam War.* Philadelphia: University of Pennsylvania Press.

Hirschman, Charles, Samuel Preston, and Vu Manh Loi. 1995. "Vietnamese Casualties during the American War." *Population and Development Review* 21: 783–812.

Hitchcox, Linda. 1990. *Vietnamese Refugees in Southeast Asian Camps.* Basingstoke and London: Macmillan.

Ho Chi Minh City, Institute for Economic Research. 1996. *Migration, Human Resources, Employment and Urbanization in Ho Chi Minh City.* Hanoi: The National Political Publishing House.

———. 1997. "Bao cao ket qua dieu tra di dan tu do vao TP Ho Chi Minh" [Report on the results of a survey into free migration to Ho Chi Minh City]. Ho Chi Minh City: Institute of Economic Research.

———. 1998. "Survey of Spontaneous Migration to Ho Chi Minh City." Ho Chi Minh City: Ministry of Agriculture and UNDP.

Hoang Thi Thu Ha. 1999. The System of Rationing by Stamps and Tickets in North Vietnam, 1955–1975. Paper presented at the conference on *The Economic History of Vietnam in the Context of Southeast Asia.* Singapore: National University of Singapore, October.

Hoang Uoc. 1968. "Cach mang ruong dat o Viet Nam, phan 1 va phan 2" [The land revolution in Vietnam, parts 1 and 2]. Pp. 1–217 in *Cach mang ruong dat o Viet Nam* [The land revolution in Vietnam], edited by Tran Phuong. Hanoi: Nha xuat ban Khoa hoc xa hoi.

Hoang Van Quang. 2000. "Mot Quan Tai: Truong Gia Hoc Lam Sang" [A coffin: when the new rich learn how to put on a cultivated appearance]. *An Ninh Thu Do* (20 February).

Houtart, Francois, and Genevieve Lemercinier. 1981. *La sociologie d'une commune vietnamienne.* Louvain La Neuve: Catholic University of Louvain.

———. 1984. *Hai Van: Life in a Vietnamese Commune.* London: Zed Books.

Human Rights Watch/Asia. 1995. *Vietnam: The Suppression of the Unified Buddhist Church.* New York: Human Rights Watch.

Indochine, Gouvernement General de l'. 1931. *Indochine scholaire.* Hanoi: Extreme-Orient.

Indra, Doreen Marie. 1987. "Introduction." Pp. 1–4 in *Uprooting, Loss and Adaptation: The Resettlement of Indochinese Refugees in Canada,* edited by Kwok B. Chan and Doreen Marie Indra. Ottawa: Canadian Public Health Association.

Jamieson, Neil. 1991. *Culture and Development in Vietnam.* Honolulu: East-West Center, Indochina Initiative Working Paper no. 1.

———. 1993. *Understanding Vietnam.* Berkeley: University of California Press.

Jamieson, Neil L., Le Trong Cuc, and A. Terry Rambo. 1998. *The Development Crisis in Vietnam's Mountains.* Honolulu: East-West Center Special Report No. 6.

Jeong, Yeonsik. 1997. "The Rise of State Corporatism in Vietnam." *Contemporary Southeast Asia* 19 (September): 152–71.

Keane, John. 1988. "Despotism and Democracy." Pp. 55–62 in *Civil Society and the State,* edited by John Keane. London: Verso.

Kerkvliet, Benedict J. Tria. 1995a. "Politics of Society in the mid 1990s." Pp. 5–44 in *Dilemmas of Development: Vietnam Update 1994,* edited by Benedict Kerkvliet. Canberra: Dept. of Political and Social Change, Australian National University.

———. 1995b. "Rural Society and State Relations." Pp. 65–96 in *Vietnam's Rural Transformation,* edited by Benedict Kerkvliet and Doug Porter. Boulder and Singapore: Westview Press and Institute of Southeast Asian Studies.

———. 1995c. "Village-State Relations in Vietnam: The Effect of Everyday Politics on Decollectivization." *Journal of Asian Studies* 54, no. 2: 396–418.

———. 1998. "Wobbly Foundations: Building Cooperatives in Rural Vietnam." *South East Asia Research* 6 (November): 193–251.

———. 1999. "Dialogical Law Making and Implementation in Vietnam." Pp. 372–400 in *East Asia—Human Rights, Nation-Building, Trade,* edited by Alice Tay. Baden-Baden: Nomos Verlagsgesellschaft.

———. 2001. "An Approach for Analysing State–Society Relations in Vietnam." *Sojourn: Journal of Social Issues in Southeast Asia* 16 (October): 238–78.

Kerkvliet, Benedict, and Mark Selden. 1999. "Agrarian Transformation in China and Vietnam." Pp. 98–119 in *Transforming Asian Socialism: China and Vietnam Compared,* edited by Anita Chan, B. Kerkvliet, and J. Unger. St. Leonards, Australia: Allen and Unwin.

Khanh Duyen. 1994. *Tin nguong ba Chua Kho* [Beliefs regarding the Goddess of the Treasury]. Ha Bac: So Van hoa Thong tin va The thao Ha Bac.

Khong Dien. 1995. *Dan so va dan so toc nguoi o Viet Nam* [Population and Ethnic Population in Vietnam]. Hanoi: Nha xuat ban Khoa hoc Xa hoi.

Kim Ngoc Bao Ninh. 1996. Revolution, Politics and Culture. Ph.D. dissertation, Yale University.

Kleinen, John. 1999. *Facing the Future, Reviving the Past: A Study of Social Change in a Northern Vietnamese Village.* Singapore: Institute of Southeast Asian Studies.

Koh, David. 2000. Wards of Hanoi and State-Society Relations in the Socialist Republic of Vietnam. Ph.D. dissertation, Australian National University, Canberra.

Kohli, Atul, and Vivienne Shue. 1994. "State Power and Social Forces: On Political Contention and Accommodation in the Third World." Pp. 293–326 in *State Power and Social Forces: Domination and Transformation in the Third World,* edited by Joel Migdal, Atul Kohli, and Vivienne Shue. Cambridge: Cambridge University Press.

Kolko, Gabriel. 1997. *Vietnam: Anatomy of a Peace.* London: Routledge.

Krowolski, Nellie. 2002. "Village Households in the Red River Delta: The Case of Ta Thanh Oai, On the Outskirts of the Capital City, Ha Noi." Pp. 73–88 in *Gender, Household, State: Doi Moi in Viet Nam,* ed. Jayne Werner and Daniele Belanger. Ithaca: Cornell University Southeast Asia Program.

Krygier, Martin. 1996. "The Sources of Civil Society," The Second Richard Krygier Memorial Lecture. Melbourne: Radio National, 29 August.

Kumar, Krisha. 1993. "Civil Society: An Inquiry into the Usefulness of an Historical Term." *British Journal of Sociology* 44 (September): 375–401.

Lam Du. 2000. "Di Tra Tien Cho Ba Chua Kho" [To Make Payments to the Goddess of Treasury]. *Phap Luat* (26 January).

Lam Quang Huyen. 1985. *Cach mang ruong dat o mien Nam Viet Nam* [The Agricultural Land Revolution in South Vietnam]. Hanoi: Nha xuat ban Khoa hoc Xa hoi.

Lam Thanh Liem. 1995. *Chinh sach cai cach ruong dat Viet Nam (1954–1994)* [Land reform policies in Vietnam (1954–1994)]. Paris: Nam A.

Lam Thanh Liem and Gustave D. Meillon. 1990. *Tu Saigon toi thanh pho Ho Chi Minh* [From Saigon to Ho Chi Minh City]. Paris: Nam A.

Le Anh Ba. 1998. "Do thi phat trien nhung quan ly chua tot" [Urban areas developing but management not yet good]. *Nhan Dan* (22 November).

Le Bach Duong. 1998a. State, Economic Development, and Internal Migration in Vietnam. Ph.D. dissertation, Binghamton University, New York.

———. 1998b. "Nha nuoc, kinh te thi truong va di dan noi dia o Viet Nam" [The state, market economy and internal migration in Vietnam]. *Xa Hoi Hoc* 2, no. 63: 38–45.

Le Duan. 1960. "Bao cao chinh tri cua Ban Chap hanh Trung uong Dang o Dai hoi toan quoc lan thu ba" [Political report of the Central Party Committee at the Third National Congress of Delegates]. *Nhan Dan,* 6 September.

———. 1974. "Role and Tasks of the Vietnamese Woman in the New Revolutionary Stage." Pp. 48–84 in *Some Present Tasks,* ed. Le Duan. Hanoi: Foreign Language Publishing House.

———. 1977. *Bao cao chinh tri cua Ban Chap hanh Trung uong Dang tai dai hoi dai bieu toan quoc lan thu IV (do dong chi Le Duan, tong bi thu Ban Chap hanh Trung uong Dang, trinh bay)* [Political report of the Central Party Committee to the Fourth National Congress of Delegates presented by Comrade Le Duan, General Secretary of the Central Party Committee]. Hanoi: Nha xuat ban Su that.

Le Huy. 1998. "Dan so va moi truong do thi Ha Noi" [Population and Hanoi's urban environment]. *Nhan Dan* (10 July): 4.

Le Khanh. 1983. *Que moi nguoi Ha Noi o Lam Dong* [New Home for Hanoi People in Lam Dong]. Hanoi: Nha xuat ban Nong nghiep.

Le Minh Ngoc. 1992. "Thu nhin lai qua trinh hop tac hoa nong nghiep o Nam Bo" [A retrospective view on the process of agricultural cooperativization in South Vietnam]. Pp. 29–38 in *Nhung van de xa hoi hoc o mien Nam* [Sociological issues in the south], edited by Nguyen Quang Vinh et al. Hanoi: Nha xuat ban Khoa hoc Xa hoi.

Le Ngoc Luan. 1995. "Di dan xay dung kinh te moi – tai dinh cu, gop phan xoa doi giam ngheo" [Migration to build the new economy and sedentarisation, contributions to the elimination of hunger and alleviation of poverty]. *Lao Dong va Xa Hoi* (April): 19–21.

Le Thanh Nghi. 1979. *Xay dung huyen thanh don vi kinh te nong cong nghiep* [Building districts to become agricultural and industrial economic units]. Hanoi: Nha xuat ban Su that.

Le thi My Dung. 2001. "Tac dong cua do thi hua doi voi vung dan cu ngoai thanh" [The impact of urbanization on population on the city outskirts]. Pp. 332–75 in *Van de giam ngheo trong qua trinh do thi hoa o thanh pho Ho Chi Minh* [The issue of poverty alleviation in the urbanization process in Ho Chi Minh City], edited by Nguyen The Nghia et al. Hanoi: Nha xuat ban Khoa hoc Xa hoi.

Le thi Nham Tuyet. 1975. *Phu nu Viet Nam qua cac thoi dai* [Vietnamese women through different eras]. Hanoi: Nha xuat ban Khoa hoc Xa hoi.

Le Trong Cuc. 1999. "Vietnam: Traditional Concepts of Human Relations with the Environment." *Asian Geographer* 18: 67–74.

Le Trong Cuc and A. Terry Rambo, eds. 1993. *Too Many People, Too Little Land: The Human Ecology of a Wet Rice-growing Village in the Red River Delta of Vietnam.* Honolulu: East-West Center, Occasional Papers of the Program on Environment No. 15.

———. 2001. *Bright Peaks, Dark Valleys: A Comparative Analysis of Environmental and Social Conditions and Development Trends in Five Communities in Vietnam's Northern Mountain Region.* Hanoi: National Political Publishing House.

Le Trong Cuc, A. T. Rambo, K. Fahrney, Tran Duc Vien, J. Romm, and Dang Thi Sy, eds. 1996. *Red Books, Green Hills: The Impact of Economic Reform on Restoration Ecology in the Midlands of Northern Vietnam.* Honolulu: Program on Environment, East-West Center.

Le Trung Vu and Nguyen Hong Duong. 1997. *Lich Le Hoi* [Calendar of festivals]. Hanoi: Nha xuat ban Van hoa-Thong tin.

Le Van Thanh. 1998. Migrants and Development in a Large City like Ho Chi Minh City. *International Conference on Migration.* Hanoi: The Population Council.

Lee, Ching Kwan. 1999. "Pathways of Labor Insurgency." Pp. 41–61 in *Chinese Society: Change, Conflict, and Resistance,* edited by Elizabeth Perry and Mark Selden. London and New York: Routledge.

Lee, Y. S. 1997. "The Privatisation of Solid Waste Infrastructure and Services in Asia." *Third World Planning Review* 19: 139–62.

Lee, Y. S., and A. Y. So, eds. 1999. *Asia's Environmental Movements: Comparative Perspectives.* Armonk, N.Y.: M. E. Sharpe.

Lewallen, John. 1971. *Ecology of Devastation: Indochina.* Baltimore: Penguin.

Lewy, Guenter. 1978. *America in Vietnam.* New York: Oxford University Press.

Li, Tania M. 1999. "Compromising Power: Development, Culture, and Rule in Indonesia." *Cultural Anthropology* 14, no. 3: 295–322.

Li, Tana. 1996. *Peasants on the Move, Rural-Urban Migration in the Hanoi Region.* Singapore: Institute of Southeast Asian Studies.

Liljestrom, Rita, Eva Lindskog, Nguyen Van Ang, and Vuong Xuan Tinh. 1998. *Profit and Poverty in Rural Vietnam, Winners and Losers of a Dismantled Revolution.* Richmond: Curzon Press.

Ljunggren, Borje. 1993. "Market Economies under Communist Regimes: Reform in Vietnam, Laos, and Cambodia." Pp. 38–121 in *The Challenge of Reform in Indochina,* edited by B. Ljunggren. Cambridge: Harvard Institute for International Development.

———. 1994. Challenge of Development and Democracy: The Case of Vietnam. Paper presented at University of Louvain, Center for Asian Studies.

Luong, Hy Van. 1989. "Vietnamese Kinship: Structural Principles and the Socialist Transformation in Twentieth-Century Vietnam." *Journal of Asian Studies* 48 (1989): 741–56.

———. 1992. *Revolution in the Village: Tradition and Transformation in North Vietnam, 1925–1988.* Honolulu: University of Hawaii Press.

———. 1993a. "The Political Economy of Vietnamese Reforms: A Microscopic Perspective from Two Ceramics Manufacturing Centers." Pp. 119–48 in *Reinventing Vietnamese Socialism: Doi Moi in Comparative Perspective,* edited by William Turley and Mark Selden. Boulder: Westview.

———. 1993b. "Economic Reform and the Intensification of Rituals in Two Northern Vietnamese Villages, 1980–90." Pp. 259–92 in *The Challenge of Reform in Indochina,* edited by Borje Ljunggren. Cambridge: Harvard Institute for International Development.

———. 1994. "The Marxist State and the Dialogic Restructuration of Culture in Rural Vietnam." Pp. 79–117 in *Indochina: Social and Cultural Change,* by David Elliott H. V. Luong, B. Kiernan, and T. Mahoney. Claremont: Claremont-McKenna College.

———. 1998. "Engendered Entrepreneurship: Ideologies and Political Economic Transformation in a Northern Vietnamese Centre of Ceramics Production." Pp. 290–314 in *Market Cultures: Society and Morality in the New Asian Capitalisms,* edited Robert Hefner. Boulder: Westview.

———. 2000. The Dynamics of Agrarian Transformation in Rural Northern Vietnam. Paper presented at the annual meetings of the Association for Asian Studies, San Diego, March.

———. 2001a. "Thanh pho Ho Chi Minh: Van de tang truong kinh te, di dan, va do thi hoa" [Ho Chi Minh City: Economic growth, migration, and urbanization]. Pp. 224–39 in *Van de giam ngheo trong qua trinh do thi hoa o thanh pho Ho Chi Minh* [The issue of poverty reduction in the process of urbanization in Ho Chi Minh City], edited by Nguyen The Nghia et al. Hanoi: Nha xuat ban Khoa hoc Xa hoi.

———. 2001b. "Ngheo kho, cau truc va dac diem nhan khau hoc cua ho gia dinh tai TP. Ho Chi Minh: phan tich khia canh van hoa xa hoi" [Poverty, household structure and demography, and their sociocultural dimension in Ho Chi Minh City]. Pp. 307–31 in *Van de giam ngheo trong qua dinh do thi hoa o thanh pho Ho Chi Minh* [The issue of poverty reduction in the process of urbanization in Ho Chi Minh City], edited by Nguyen The Nghia et al. Hanoi: Nha xuat ban Khoa hoc Xa hoi.

Luong, Hy V., and Diep Dinh Hoa. 2000. "Bon cong dong nong thon va thanh thi Viet Nam: Canh quan kinh te, xa hoi, va van hoa" [Four rural and urban communities in Vietnam: economic, social and cultural landscapes]. Pp. 39–97 in *Ngon tu, gioi va nhom xa hoi tu thuc tien tieng Viet* [Discourse, gender, and society: The Vietnamese reality], edited by H. V. Luong. Hanoi: Nha xuat ban Khoa hoc Xa hoi.

Luong, Hy V., and Jonathan Unger. 1999. "Wealth, Power, and Poverty in the Transition to Market Economies: The Process of Socio-Economic Differentiation in Rural China and Northern Vietnam." Pp. 120–52 in *Transforming Asian Socialism: China and Vietnam Compared*, edited by Anita Chan, B. Kerkvliet, and J. Unger. St. Leonards, Australia: Allen and Unwin.

Luong Hong Quang. 1997. *Van hoa cong dong lang: Vung Dong bang song Cuu Long thap ky 80–90* [Village community culture in the Mekong Delta in the 1980–90 decade]. Hanoi: Nha xuat ban Van hoa-Thong tin.

Luong Hong Quang and Pham Nam Thanh. 2000. "Su bien doi trong van hoa lang xa" [The transformation of village and commune cultures]. Pp. 111–68 in *Su bien doi cua lang xa Viet Nam ngay nay o dong bang song Hong* [The changes in Vietnamese villages and communes in the Red River Delta at present], edited by To Duy Hop. Hanoi: Nha xuat ban Khoa hoc Xa hoi.

Luong Hong Quang et al. 2001. *Van hoa cua nhom ngheo o Viet Nam; thuc trang va giai phap* [The culture of poor groups: Current situation and solutions]. Hanoi: Vien Van hoa and Nha xuat ban Van hoa Thong tin.

Luu Dinh Nhan. 1991. The Migration Issue in Vietnam: A Case Study of Rural Migration from North to South. Hanoi: unpublished manuscript.

McHale, Shaun F. 1995. Printing, Power, and the Transformation of Vietnamese Culture, 1920–1945. Ph.D. dissertation, Cornell University.

Mai Huy Bich. 2000. "Noi cu tru sau hon nhan o dong bang song Hong" [Post-marital residence in the Red River Delta]. *Xa Hoi Hoc* no. 4: 33–43.

Mai Thanh Hai. 2000. "Niem tin dat o dau?" [Where to put our beliefs?] *Tap Chi Cong San* no. 5 (May): 58–59.

Mai van Hai and Nguyen Phan Lam. 2001. "Luat dat dai va tac dong ban dau toi co cau gia dinh o mot lang chau tho song Hong" [The land law and its initial impact on family structure in a Red River Delta village]. *Xa Hoi Hoc* no. 1/2001: 40–45.

Malarney, Shaun Kingsley. 1933. Ritual and Revolution in Viet Nam. Ph.D. dissertation, University of Michigan.

———. 1996a. "The Emerging Cult of Ho Chi Minh? A Report on Religious Innovation in Contemporary Northern Viet Nam." *Asian Cultural Studies* 22: 121–31.

———. 1996b. "The Limits of 'State Functionalism' and the Reconstruction of Funerary Ritual in Contemporary Northern Viet Nam." *American Ethnologist* 23, no. 3: 540–60.

———. 1997. "Culture, Virtue, and Political Transformation in Contemporary Northern Vietnam. *Journal of Asian Studies* 56 (November): 899–920.

———. 1998. "The Consequences of the Revolutionary Reform of Marriage and the Wedding Ceremony in Northern Vietnamese Village Life." *Asian Cultural Studies* 24: 127–42.

———. 2001. "'The Fatherland Remembers Your Sacrifice': Commemorating War Dead in North Vietnam." Pp. 46–76 in *The Country of Memory: Remaking the Past in Late Socialist Vietnam*, edited by Hue-Tam Ho Tai. Berkeley: University of California Press.

———. 2002. *Culture, Ritual and Revolution in Vietnam*. London: Routledge Curzon.

Marr, David. 1981. *Vietnamese Tradition on Trial, 1920–1945*. Berkeley: University of California Press.

———. 1988. "Tertiary Education, Research, and the Information Sciences in Vietnam." Pp. 15–44 in *Postwar Vietnam: Dilemmas of Socialist Development*, edited by David Marr and Christine White. Ithaca: Cornell University Southeast Asia Program.

———. 1995. *1945: The Quest for Power*. Berkeley: University of California Press.

———. 1996. *Vietnamese Youth in the 1990s*. Sydney: Macquarie University, Australian-Vietnam Research Project Working paper #3.

———. 1998. "Introduction." Pp. 14–19 in *The Mass Media in Vietnam*, edited by David Marr. Canberra: Dept. of Political and Social Change, Australian National University.

———. 2000. "History and Memory in Vietnam Today: The Journal *Xua va Nay*." *Journal of Southeast Asian Studies* 31, no. 1 (March): 1–25.

Marr, David, and Mark Sidel. 1998. "Understanding the World Outside: Vietnamese Translations of Foreign Social Science Publications." Pp. 120–45 in *The Mass Media in Vietnam*, edited by David Marr. Canberra: Department of Political and Social Change, The Australian National University.

Migdal, Joel S. 1994. "The State in Society: An Approach to Struggles for Domination." Pp. 7–34 in *State Power and Social Forces: Domination and Transformation in the Third World*, edited by J. Migdal, Atul Kohli, and Vivienne Shue. Cambridge: Cambridge University Press.

Minh Anh. 2000. "Ta dao Long Hoa Di Lac—Nguy hai khon luong" [The cult Long Hoa Di Lac: Unfathomable dangers]. *Vinh Phuc* (22 March).

Minh Chi, Ha Van Tan, and Nguyen Tai Thu. 1993. *Buddhism in Vietnam: From Its Origins to the 19th Century*. Hanoi: The gioi Publishers.

Minh Quang. 1999. "Dua lao dong Viet Nam ra nuoc ngoai lam viec. Nam 2000: Nhieu thi truong moi" [Sending Vietnamese labor abroad for work. The year 2000: many new markets]. *Lao Dong* (29 December): 1, 7.

Miribel, A. de. 1904. "Les provinces du Tonkin: Hung Yen." *Revue Indochinoise*: 509–21, 578–87, 671–82, 751–59.

Mitchell, Timothy. 1991. "The Limits of the State: Beyond Statist Approaches and their Critics." *American Political Science Review* 85 (March): 77–96.

Montinola, G., Yingyi Qian, and B. R. Weingast. 1995. "Federalism, Chinese Style: The Political Basis for Economic Success in China." *World Politics* 48, no. 1: 50–81.

Mydans, Seth. 1996. "Vietnam, a Convert, Pursues Capitalism Devoutly." *The New York Times*, 5 April.

Nam Ha, Cultural Service. 1971. *Chi thi ve hoi he va quy uoc ve to chuc dam cuoi, dam ma, ngay gio, ngay Tet va ngay ky niem lon* [Directive on festivals and regulations on the organization of weddings, funerals, death anniversaries, and big anniversaries]. Nam Ha: Ty Van hoa Nam Ha.

Nga My. 1997 "Di dan nong thon–do thi voi nha o, mot van de xa hoi" [Rural-urban migration and housing, a social problem]. *Xa Hoi Hoc* 2, no. 58: 56–59.

Ngo Duc Thinh, ed. 1996. *Dao mau o Viet Nam* [Female deity cults in Vietnam], vols. 1 and 2. Hanoi: Nha xuat ban Van hoa Thong tin.

Ngo thi Chinh. 1977. "Vai net ve nguoi phu nu nong dan trong san xuat nong nghiep va trong moi quan he hon nhan gia dinh moi" [A Sketch of woman cultivators in agricultural production and in new marital relations]. *Tap chi Dan Toc Hoc* no. 3/1977: 61–70.

Ngo thi Ngan Binh. 2001. Sociocultural Aspects of the Mother- and Daughter-in-law Tension in the Southern Vietnamese Family. M.A. thesis, National University of Singapore.

Ngo Van Ly and Nguyen Van Dieu. 1992. *Tay Nguyen tiem nang va trien vong* [The Central Highlands, potential and prospects]. Ho Chi Minh City: Nha xuat ban Thanh pho Ho Chi Minh.

Ngo Vinh Long. 1988. "Some Aspects of Cooperativization in the Mekong Delta." Pp. 163–76 in *Postwar Vietnam: Dilemmas in Socialist Development*, edited by David Marr and Christine P. White. Ithaca: Cornell University Southeast Asia Program.

———. 1993. "Reform and Rural Development: Impact on Class, Sectoral, and Regional Inequalities." Pp. 165–208 in *Reinventing Vietnamese Socialism: Doi Moi in Comparative Perspectives*, edited by William Turley and Mark Selden. Boulder: Westview.

Nguoi Lao Dong. 2000–2001.

Nguyen, Cuong Tu. 1997. *Zen in Medieval Vietnam: A Study and Translation of the Thien Uyen Tap Anh*. Honolulu: University of Hawaii Press.

Nguyen Dang Manh, ed. 1999. *Nguyen Tuan ban ve van hoc nghe thuat* [Nguyen Tuan discusses literature and the arts]. Hanoi: Hoi Nha Van.

Nguyen Dinh Dau. 1994. *Tong ket nghien cuu dia ba Nam Ky luc tinh* [Research on land registers in the the six southern provinces]. Ho Chi Minh City: Nha xuat ban Thanh pho Ho Chi Minh.

Nguyen Dinh Huong. 1999. *San xuat va doi song cua cac ho nong dan khong co dat hoac thieu dat o dong bang song Cuu Long: Thuc trang va giai phap* [Production and livelihoods of peasant households without land or short of land in the Mekong Delta: Reality and solution]. Hanoi: Nha xuat ban Chinh tri Quoc gia.

Nguyen Duc Truyen. 1997. "Van hoa va su ke thua van hoa trong viec chia thua ke o dong bang song Hong hien nay" [Culture and cultural heritage in inheritance in the Red River Delta at present]. *Xa Hoi Hoc* 3 (1997): 48–54.

Nguyen Duy Hinh. 1996. *Tin nguong thanh hoang Viet Nam* [The beliefs and worship of tutelary deities in Vietnam]. Hanoi: Nha xuat ban Khoa hoc Xa hoi.

Nguyen Hong Minh. 1993. *Di dan tu do, tong luan khoa hoc* [Free migration, a general scientific conclusion]. Hanoi: Bo Lao dong Thuong binh va Xa hoi.

Nguyen Hong Thanh. 1998. "Ha Noi's Housing Shortage Leads to Growing Slums and Social Problems." *Vietnam News* (14 Feb.): 2.

Nguyen Hung Quoc. 1991. *Van hoc Viet Nam duoi che do Cong San, 1945–1990* [Vietnamese literature under the Communist regime, 1945–1990]. Westminster, Calif.: Van Nghe.

Nguyen Huu Minh. 1998. Tradition and Change in the Vietnamese Marriage Patterns in the Red River Delta. Ph.D. thesis, University of Washington, Seattle.

Nguyen Huu Minh and Charles Hirschman. 2000. "Mo hinh song chung voi gia dinh chong sau khi ket hon o dong bang Bac Bo va cac nguyen nhan tac dong" [Patrilocal residence model after marriage in the Red River Delta and the factors at work]. *Xa hoi hoc* no. 1/2000: 41–54.

Nguyen Huy Thiep. 1992. *The General Retires and Other Stories*, translated with an introduction by Greg Lockhart. Singapore: Oxford University Press.

———. 1999. *Nhung nguoi tho xe* [The sawyers]. Pp. 245–89 in Nguyen Huy Thiep, *Nhu nhung ngon gio* [Like gusts of wind]. Hanoi: Nha xuat ban Van hoc.

Nguyen Lang. 1977. *Viet Nam Phat giao su luan* [A discussion of Vietnamese Buddhist history]. San Jose: La Boi.

Nguyen Linh Khieu. 2001. *Gia dinh and phu nu trong bien doi van hoa-xa hoi nong thon* [Family and women in the transformation of rural culture and society]. Hanoi: Nha xuat ban Khoa hoc Xa hoi.

Nguyen Manh Tuan. 1982. *Dung truoc bien* [Facing the sea]. Ho Chi Minh City: Nha xuat ban Van nghe Thanh pho Ho Chi Minh.

Nguyen Sinh Cuc. 1990. "Sau 30 nam hop tac hoa nong nghiep: Doi song nong dan va van de quan ly san xuat nong nghiep hien nay" [After thirty years of agricultural co-operatization: peasant life and the problem of agricultural production management at present]. Pp. 27–60 in *Thuc trang kinh te - xa hoi Viet Nam giai doan 1986–1990* [The reality of Vietnamese economy and society in the 1986–1990 period], edited by Nguyen Luc. Hanoi: Nha xuat ban Thong ke.

Nguyen Thanh. 1984. *Bao chi cach mang Viet Nam, 1925–1945* [The Vietnamese Revolutionary Press, 1925–1945]. Hanoi: Nha xuat ban Khoa hoc Xa hoi.

Nguyen Thanh Liem. 1998. "Nguoi di chuyen tam thoi song tai cac nha tro trong qua trinh hien dai hoa va do thi hoa" [Temporary migrants living in boarding houses in the modernisation and urbanisation process]. Hanoi: Institute of Sociology and UNFPA.

Nguyen thi Hoa. 2001. "Vai tro cua phu nu trong cac ho ngheo" [The role of women in poor households]. Pp. 376–89 in *Van de giam ngheo trong qua trinh do thi hoa o thanh pho Ho Chi Minh* [The issue of poverty alleviation in the urbanization process in Ho Chi Minh City], edited by Nguyen The Nghia et al. Hanoi: Nha xuat ban Khoa hoc Xa hoi.

Nguyen Thi Thanh Binh. 1998. *Tac dong cua di chuyen lao dong theo mua vu len cac moi quan he lang xa o mot lang dong bang chau tho song Hong* [The effects of seasonal labor migration on village relations in a Red River Delta village]. Hanoi: Luan van tap su, Vien Dan Toc Hoc.

Nguyen thi Van Anh. 1993. "So thich ve sinh de o mot so vung nong thon Viet Nam" [Reproductive preferences in a few rural areas of Vietnam]. *Xa Hoi Hoc* no. 2/1993: 35–47.

Nguyen Thu Sa. 1990. "Van de ruong dat o dong bang song Cuu Long" [The land problem in the Mekong Delta]. Pp. 141–54 in *Mien Nam trong su nghiep doi moi cua ca nuoc* [The south in the renovation task of the country], edited by Nguyen Quang Vinh et al. Hanoi: Nha xuat ban Khoa hoc Xa hoi.

———. 1992. "Suy nghi tu nhung khao sat moi ve van de ruong dat o dong bang song Cuu Long" [Ideas from the new studies on the land problem in the Mekong Delta]. Pp. 39–48 in *Nhung van de xa hoi hoc o mien Nam* [Sociological issues in the south], edited by Nguyen Quang Vinh et al. Hanoi: Nha xuat ban Khoa hoc Xa hoi.

Nguyen Van Chinh. 1997. "Bien doi kinh te-xa hoi va van de di chuyen lao dong nong thon-do thi o mien Bac Viet Nam" [Social-economic change and the rural-urban migration of labor in the north of Vietnam]. *Xa Hoi Hoc* 2, no. 58: 25–38.

———. 2000. Representations of Southeast Asia in Vietnamese pre-university textbooks. Hanoi: unpublished paper, April.

Nguyen Van Khoan. 1930. "Essai sur le *dinh* et le culte du genie tutelaire des villages au Tonkin." *Bulletin de l'Ecole Francaise d'Extreme-Orient* 30, no. 1–2: 107–39.

Nguyen Van Ky. 1995. *La societe vietnamienne face a la modernite*. Paris: L'Harmattan.

Nguyen van Tiem, ed. 1993. *Giau ngheo trong nong thon hien nay* [Wealth and poverty in the countryside at present]. Hanoi: Nha xuat ban Nong nghiep.

Nguyen Vo Thu Huong. 2002. "Governing Sex: Medicine and Governmental Intervention in Prostitution." Pp. 129–52 in *Gender, Household, State: Doi Moi in Viet Nam*, edited by Jayne Werner and Daniele Belanger. Ithaca: Cornell University Southeast Asia Program.

Nguyen Xuan Hung. 1998. "West Lake Bears Scars of Modernization." *Vietnam News* (23 Aug.) 5.

Nhan Dan. 1961–2001.

Nhi Le. 1994. "Viec giai quyet 'diem nong' o Thanh Hoa" [Resolving 'hot spots' in Thanh Hoa]. *Tap Chi Cong San* (March): 49–52.

Ninh, Kim Ngoc Bao. 1996. Revolution, Politics and Culture. Ph.D. dissertation, Yale University.

———. 2002. *A World Transformed: The Politics of Culture in Revolutionary Vietnam, 1945–1965*. Ann Arbor: University of Michigan Press.

Ninh Binh, Cultural Service. 1968. *Chi thi ve hoi he va quy uoc ve to chuc dam cuoi, dam ma, ngay gio, ngay Tet va ngay ky niem lon* [Directive on festivals and regulations on the organization of weddings, funerals, death anniversaries, and big anniversaries]. Ninh Binh: Ninh Binh Cultural Service.

Nong Thon Ngay Nay, To Phong vien Chinh tri Xa hoi. 1999. "Vi sao Ha Noi van chua co cho do rac?" [Why does Hanoi still have no place to dispose of rubbish?] *Nong Thon Ngay Nay* (17 September): 3.

Norton, Barley. 1999. Music and Possession in Vietnam. Ph.D. dissertation, University of London.

———. "'Effeminate' Men and 'Hot-Tempered' Women: Vietnamese Mediumship and the Negotiation of Gender Identity." London: unpublished manuscript, n.d.

Oliver, Victor L. 1976. *Cao Dai Spiritism: A Study of Religion in Vietnamese Society*. Leiden: E. J. Brill.

O'Rourke, D. 2001. "Community-driven Regulation: Towards an Improved Model of Environmental Regulation in Vietnam." Pp. 115–59 in *Livable Cities: Urban Struggles for Livelihood and Sustainability,* edited by Peter B. Evans. Berkeley: University of California Press.

Papin, Philippe. 1999. *Viet-Nam, Parcours d'une nation.* Paris: La Documentation Française.

Pelzer, Kristin. 1993. "Socio-Cultural Dimensions of Renovation in Vietnam: *Doi Moi* as Dialogue and Transformation in Gender Relations." Pp. 309–36 in *Reinventing Vietnamese Socialism,* edited by William Turley and Mark Selden. Boulder: Westview.

Perry, Elizabeth, and Christine Wong. 1985. "Introduction: The Political Economy of Reform in Post-Mao China: Causes, Content, and Consequences." Pp. 1–27 in *The Political Economy of Reform in Post-Mao China,* edited by Elizabeth Perry and Christine Wong. Cambridge: Harvard University Council on East Asian Studies.

Perry, Elizabeth, and Mark Selden, eds. 2000. *Chinese Society: Change, Conflict, and Resistance.* London and New York: Routledge.

Pham Do Nhat Tan. 1992. Hoan thien hon nua viec di dan nong nghiep co to chuc di xay dung cac vung kinh te moi [Further improving organised agricultural migration to go and build new economic zones]. Doctoral thesis, University of Economics, Hanoi.

Pham Ngoc Dang. 1998. "Urban Environment and Industrialization in Vietnam." *Vietnam Studies* 3: 80–95.

Pham Thanh Binh. 1997. *Nhung dieu can biet ve quan ly va dang ky ho khau (nhung qui dinh moi nhat)* [Things necessary to know about the administration and registration of household residence (the newest regulations)]. Hanoi: Nha xuat ban Chinh tri Quoc gia.

Pham van Bich. 1999. *The Vietnamese Family in Change: The Case of the Red River Delta.* Richmond, Surrey: Curzon.

Pham Van Dong. 1975. *To chuc lai san xuat va cai tien quan ly nong nghiep va lam nghiep trung du va mien nui* [Reorganisation of production and improvement in agricultural and forestry management in the midlands and highlands]. Hanoi: Nha xuat ban Su that.

———. 1978. Che do doi voi lao dong di xay dung vung kinh te moi [The system for labor going to build new economic zones]. Hanoi: Nha xuat ban Lao dong.

———. 1994. *Van hoa va Doi Moi* [Culture and Doi Moi]. Hanoi: Nha xuat ban Chinh tri Quoc gia.

Pham Viet Dao. 1996. *Mat trai cua co che thi truong* [The underside of the market system]. Hanoi: Nha xuat ban Van hoa Thong tin.

Phan Chanh Cong. 1993. "The Vietnamese Concept of the Human Soul and the Rituals of Birth and Death." *Southeast Asian Journal of Social Science* 21, no. 2: 159–98.

Phan Dai Doan. 2001. *Lang xa Viet Nam: Mot so van de kinh te-van hoa-xa hoi* [Vietnamese villages and communes: A number of economic, cultural, and social issues]. Hanoi: Nha xuat ban Chinh tri Quoc gia.

Phan Huu Dat. 1973. *Co so dan toc hoc* [Fundamentals of ethnology]. Hanoi: Nha xuat ban Dai hoc va Trung hoc Chuyen nghiep.

Phan Huy Le et al. 1995. *Dia ba Ha Dong* [Land registers in Ha Dong]. Hanoi: Nha xuat ban The gioi.

————. 1997. *Dia ba Thai Binh* [Land registers in Thai Binh]. Hanoi: Nha xuat ban The gioi.

Phan Ke Binh. 1990. *Viet Nam phong tuc* [Vietnamese customs]. Saigon: Nha xuat ban Thanh pho Ho Chi Minh.

Phan Khanh. 1992. *Bao tang di tich le hoi* [Museum of festival artefacts]. Hanoi: Nha xuat ban Thong tin.

Phap Luat Thanh Pho Ho Chi Minh. 2000. "Hai Duong: No Dress for the Brides." *Phap Luat Thanh Pho Ho Chi Minh* (19 January).

Porter, Doug J. 1995. "Economic Liberalization, Marginality, and the Local State." Pp. 215–46 in *Vietnam's Rural Transformation*, edited by Benedict J. Tria Kerkvliet and Doug J. Porter. Boulder: Westview; and Singapore: ISEAS.

Porter, Gareth. 1993. *Vietnam: The Politics of Bureaucratic Socialism*. Ithaca: Cornell University Press.

Post, Ken. 1989. *Revolution, Socialism and Nationalism in Vietnam*, vol. 3. Hants, England: Dartmouth Publishing.

Putnam, Robert. 1993. *Making Democracy Work: Civic Traditions in Modern Italy*. Princeton: Princeton University Press.

Quach Thu Cuc. 1997. "Cong dong Quang Nam o Sai Gon, Thanh pho Ho Chi Minh" [The Quang Nam Community in Saigon, Ho Chi Minh City]. Pp. 361–71 in *Moi truong nhan van va do thi hoa tai Viet Nam, Dong Nam A va Nhat Ban* [The human environment and urbanization in Vietnam, Southeast Asia, and Japan], edited by Trung tam nghien cuu Dong Nam A, Vien Khoa hoc Xa hoi tai Thanh pho Ho Chi Minh. Ho Chi Minh City: Nha xuat ban Thanh pho Ho Chi Minh.

Quach-Langlet, Tam. 1991. "Saigon: capitale de la Republique du Sud Vietnam (1954–1975) ou une urbanisation sauvage." Pp. 185–206 in *Peninsule Indochinoise, Etudes urbaines*, ed. P. B. Lafont. Paris: Harmattan.

Quang Truong. 1987. *Agricultural Collectivization and Rural Development in Vietnam: A North/South Study, 1955–1985*. Amsterdam: Vrije Universiteit te Amsterdam.

Quang Vu and Nguyen Pho. 1997. "Flushed Away." *Vietnam Economic Times* (June): 34–35.

Raiser, Martin. 1998. "Subsidising Inequality: Economic Reforms, Fiscal Transfers and Convergence across Chinese Provinces." *Journal of Development Studies* 34, no. 3: 1–26.

Rambo, A. T. 1973. *A Comparison of Peasant Social Systems of Northern and Southern Vietnam*. Carbondale: Southern Illinois University Center for Vietnamese Studies, Monograph Series 3.

————. 1997. "Development Trends in Vietnam's Northern Mountain Region." Pp. 5–52 in *Development Trends in Vietnam's Northern Region*, edited by Deanna A. Donovan, A. Terry Rambo, Jefferson Fox, Le Trong Cuc, and Tran Duc Vien, vol. 1. Hanoi: National Political Publishing House.

————. 1998. "The Composite Swiddening Agroecosystem of the Tay Ethnic Minority of the Northwestern Mountains of Vietnam." Pp. 43–64 in *Land Degradation and Agricultural Sustainability: Case Studies from Southeast and East Asia*, edited by Aran Patanothai. Khon Kaen: Suan Regional Secretariat.

Rambo, A. Terry, Robert R. Reed, Le Trong Cuc, and Michael Digregorio. 1995. *The Challenges of Highland Development in Vietnam.* Honolulu: East-West Center.

Rambo, A. Terry, and Tran Duc Vien. 2001. "Social Organization and the Management of Natural Resources: A Case Study of Tat Hamlet, a Da Bac Tay Ethnic Minority Settlement in Vietnam's Northern Mountain Region." *Southeast Asian Studies (Kyoto)* 39, no. 3: 299–324.

Rao, M. Govinda, Richard M. Bird, and Jenny I. Litvack. 1998. "Fiscal Decentralization and Poverty Alleviation in a Transitional Economy: The Case of Vietnam." *Asian Economic Journal* 12, no. 4: 353–78.

Robinson, W. Courtland. 1998. *Terms of Refuge: The Indochinese Exodus and the International Response.* London and New York: Zed Books.

Rondinelli, Dennis, and Jennie Litvack, eds. 1999. *Market Reform in Vietnam: Building Institutions for Development.* Westport, Conn.: Quorum Books.

Rydstrom, Helle. 1998. *Embodying Morality: Girls' Socialization in a North Vietnamese Commune.* Linkoping, Sweden: Linkoping University.

Saigon Giai Phong. 1998–2002.

Salemink, Oscar. 1997. "The King of Fire and Vietnamese Ethnic Policy in the Central Highlands." Pp. 488–535 in *Development or Domestication? Indigenous Peoples of Southeast Asia,* edited by Don McCaskill and Ken Kampe. Chiang Mai: Silkworm Books.

Scott, Steffanie. 2000. "Changing Rules of the Game: Local Responses to Decollectivisation in Thai Nguyen, Vietnam." *Asia Pacific Viewpoint* 41 (April): 77–78.

———. 2001. Vietnam Decollectivizes: Land, Property, and Institutional Change at the Interface. Ph.D. dissertation, University of British Columbia, Vancouver.

Sidel, Mark. 1998. "Law, the Press, and Police Murder in Vietnam." Pp. 97–119 in *The Mass Media in Vietnam,* edited by David Marr. Canberra: Dept. of Political and Social Change, The Australian National University.

Sikor, Thomas. 1999. The Political Economy of Decollectivization: A Study of Differentiation in and among Black Thai Villages of Northern Vietnam. Ph.D. dissertation, University of California at Berkeley.

Sikor, Thomas, and Dao Minh Truong. 2000. *Sticky Rice, Collective Fields: Community-based Development among the Black Thai.* Hanoi: Agricultural Publishing House.

Simon, Pierre J., and Ida Simon-Barouh. 1973. *Hau Bong: un culte vietnamien de possession transplante en France.* Paris: Mouton.

Smith, K. R. 1997. "Development, Health, and the Environmental Risk Transition." Pp. 51–62 in *International Perspectives in Environment, Development, and Health,* edited by G. Shahi et al. New York: Springer.

Spoor, Max 1988. "State Finance in the Socialist Republic of Vietnam: The Difficult Transition from 'State Bureaucratic Finance' to 'Socialist Economic Accounting.'" Pp. 111–31 in *Postwar Vietnam: Dilemmas in Socialist Development,* edited by David G. Marr and Christine P. White. Ithaca: Cornell University, Southeast Asia Program.

Stern, Lewis. 1993. *Renovating the Vietnamese Communist Party.* New York: St. Martin's Press.

Stromseth, Jonathan R. 1998. Reform and Response in Vietnam: State-Society Relations and the Changing Political Economy. Ph.D. dissertation, Columbia University.

Szelenyi, Ivan. 1998. *Socialist Entrepreneurs: Embourgeoisement in Rural Hungary.* Madison: University of Wisconsin Press.

Tai, Hue Tam Ho. 1983. *Millenarianism and Peasant Politics in Vietnam.* Cambridge: Harvard University Press.

———. 1992. *Radicalism and the Origins of the Vietnamese Revolution.* Cambridge: Harvard University Press.

Tan, B.-H. Stan. 2000. "Coffee Frontiers in the Central Highlands of Vietnam: Networks of Connectivity between New Productive Spaces and Global Markets." *Asia Pacific Viewpoint* 41, no. 1 (April): 51–67.

Taylor, Keith Weller. 1983. *The Birth of Vietnam.* Berkeley: University of California Press.

Thai Binh, So Cong an [Department of Public Security]. 1972. *Tai lieu hoc tap ve cong tac kiem tra doi so ho khau va cap giay chung nhan can cuoc cho cac khu pho, xa, ho tap the* [Study document concerning the verification of changes to household registration booklets and the issue of identification papers to zones, streets, villages and collective households]. Thai Binh: Xi nghiep in Thai Binh.

Thai Quang Truong. 1985. *Collective Leadership and Factionalism.* Singapore: Institute of Southeast Asian Studies.

Thanh Ha. 1998. "Tranquil and Picturesque West Lake is Being Ravaged by Development." *Vietnam News* (1 March): 1, 4.

Thanh The Vy. 1961. *Ngoai thuong Viet Nam hoi the ky XVII, XVII va dau XIX* [The external trade of Vietnam in the seventeenth, eighteenth, and early nineteenth century]. Hanoi: Nha xuat ban Su hoc.

Thanh Tin. 1991. *Hoa xuyen tuyet* [Flowering through the snow]. Paris: Nhan quyen.

———. 1994. *Mat that* [Real faces]. Irvine: Saigon-Turpin Press.

Thayer, Carlyle A. 1992a. "Political Reform in Vietnam: *Doi Moi* and the Emergence of Civil Society." Pp. 110–29 in *The Developments of Civil Society in Communist Systems,* edited by Robert F. Miller. Sydney: Allen and Unwin.

———. 1992b. "The Challenges Facing Vietnamese Communism." Pp. 349–64 in *Southeast Asian Affairs 1992,* edited by Daljit Singh. Singapore: Institute of Southeast Asian Studies.

———. 1993. "Recent Political Development: Constitutional Change and the 1992 Elections." Pp. 50–80 in *Vietnam and the Rule of Law,* edited by C. Thayer and David Marr. Canberra: Dept. of Political and Social Change, Australian National University.

Thich Nhat Hanh. 1967. *Vietnam: Lotus in a Sea of Fire.* New York: Hill and Wang.

Thich Quang Do. 1995. *Nhan dinh ve nhung sai lam tai hai cua Dang Cong San Viet Nam doi voi dan toc va Phat Giao* [An evaluation of the grave mistakes of the Vietnam Communist Party against the people and Buddhism]. Paris: Phong Thong tin Phat giao Quoc te; Que Me.

Thien Moc Lan. 2000. *Tran Tan Quoc: Bon muoi nam lam bao* [Tran Tan Quoc: Forty years making a newspaper]. Ho Chi Minh City: Nha xuat ban Tre.

Thoi Bao. 1998.

Thoi Bao Kinh te Viet Nam. 1996–2002.

———. 1996. *Kinh te 95–96.* Hanoi: Thoi Bao Kinh te Viet Nam.

———. 2001. *Kinh te 2000–2001*. Hanoi: Thoi Bao Kinh te Viet Nam.

———. 2002. *Kinh te 2001–2002*. Hanoi: Thoi Bao Kinh te Viet Nam.

Thrift, Nigel, and Dean Forbes. 1986. *The Price of War: Urbanisation in Vietnam, 1954–1985*. London: Allen and Unwin.

Toan Anh. 1968. *Nep cu: Lang xom Viet Nam* [Old customs: Vietnamese villages]. Saigon: Nam Chi Tung thu.

———. 1969. *Nep cu: Hoi he dinh dam, Quyen thuong va ha* [Old customs: Festivals, vol. 1 and 2]. Saigon: Nam Chi Tung thu.

Ton Nu Quynh Tran. 1999. *Van hoa lang xa truoc su thach thuc cua do thi hoa tai thanh pho Ho Chi Minh* [Village culture in face of the challenge of urbanization in Ho Chi Minh City]. Ho Chi Minh City: Nha xuat ban Tre.

Tran, Angie Ngoc. 2002. "Gender Expectations of Vietnamese Garment Workers: Vietnam's Re-integration into the World Economy." Pp. 49–71 in *Gender, Household, State: Doi Moi in Vietnam*, edited by J. Werner and D. Belanger. Ithaca: Cornell University Southeast Asia Program.

Tran An Phong. 1996. *Nghien cuu xay dung luan cu khoa hoc cho dinh huong phat trien kinh te-xa hoi cac tinh Tay Nguyen* [Research towards the construction of a scientific project guiding the socio-economic development of the provinces of the Central Highlands]. Hanoi: Nha xuat ban Nong nghiep.

Tran Anh Dung. 1992. *So thao thu muc Cong Giao Viet Nam* [A bibliographical sketch on Vietnamese Catholicism]. Paris: Tran Anh Dung.

Tran Duc. 1991. *Hop tac xa va thoi vang son cua kinh te gia dinh* [Cooperatives and the resplendent period of the family economy]. Hanoi: Nha xuat ban Tu tuong-Van hoa.

Tran Duc Vien. 1998. "Soil Erosion and Nutrient Balance in Swidden Fields of the Composite Swiddening Agroecosystem in the Northwestern Mountains of Vietnam." Pp. 65–86 in *Land Degradation and Agricultural Sustainability: Case Studies from Southeast and East Asia*, edited by Aran Patanothai. Khon Kaen: SUAN Regional Secretariat, Khon Kaen University.

Tran Hoang Kim and Le Thu. 1992. *Cac thanh phan kinh te Viet Nam: thuc trang, xu the, va giai phap* [Economic sectors in Vietnam: situation, tendency, and solutions]. Hanoi: Nha xuat ban Thong ke.

Tran Quynh. n.d. Nhung ky niem ve Le Duan (Trich) [Souvenirs concerning Le Duan (excerpts)]. Hanoi: unpublished manuscript, 59 pp.

Tran thi Van Anh and Le ngoc Hung. 1996. *Phu nu, gioi, va phat trien* [Women, gender, and development]. Hanoi: Nha xuat ban Phu nu.

Tran Trac. 1999. "Tim hieu them ve kinh te trang trai" [To understand better the farm economy]. *Nghien Cuu Kinh Te* 258: 40–47.

Tran Trong Kim. 1954. *Viet Nam su luoc* [A summary history of Vietnam]. Saigon: Tan Viet.

Tran van Tho et al. 2000. *Kinh te Viet Nam 1955–2000* [Vietnamese economy 1955–2000]. Hanoi: Nha xuat ban Thong ke.

Treglode, Benoit de. 2001. *Heros et Revolution au Viet Nam: 1948–1964*. Paris: L'Harmattan.

Trinh Hai. 1997. "Ho Chi Minh City's Garbage Raises a Stink." *Vietnam News* (9 December): 9.

Trinh thi Quang. 1984. "May van de ve quan he than toc o nong thon" [Certain questions regarding kinship relations in the countryside]. *Tap chi Xa Hoi Hoc* no. 6: 47–52.

Trinh van Thao. 1990. *Vietnam du Confucianisme au Communisme*. Paris: L'Harmattan.

Truong Huyen Chi. 2001. Changing Processes of Social Reproduction in the Northern Vietnamese Countryside: An Ethnographic Study of Dong Vang Village (Ha Tay Province, Vietnam). Ph.D. dissertation, University of Toronto.

Truong Si Anh, Patrick Gubry, Vu Thi Hong, Jerrold W. Huguet. 1996. *Ho Chi Minh Ville: de la migration a l'emploi*. Paris: Centre Français sur la Population et le Développement.

Tuoi Tre. 2000.

Tuong Lai. 1998. "Ve di dan o Viet Nam trong qua khu va hien nay" [Migration in Vietnam in the past and at present]. *Xa Hoi Hoc* no. 2, 3–15.

Turley, William S. 1993a. "Party, State, and People: Political Structure and Economic Prospects." Pp. 257–76 in William Turley and Mark Selden, eds., *Reinventing Vietnamese Socialism*. Boulder: Westview.

———. 1993b. "Political Renovation in Vietnam: Renewal and Adaptation." Pp. 327–47 in Borje Ljunggren, ed., *The Challenge of Reform in Indochina*. Cambridge: Harvard Institute for International Development.

United Nations Commission on Human Rights. 1998. *Civil and Political Rights, Including the Question of Religious Intolerance: Visit to Vietnam*. Geneva: UNCHR.

United Nations Development Program. 1996. *Vietnam: Public Expenditure Review*, vol. 1. Hanoi: UNDP, April.

United Nations High Commission on Refugees. 1998. *Insight into the Return of the "Boat People": UNHCR's Monitoring Experience in Vietnam, 1989–1998*. Hanoi: UNHCR.

United States Department of State. 1999. *Annual Report on International Religious Freedom for 1999: Vietnam*. Washington, D.C.: Bureau for Democracy, Human Rights, and Labor.

Van de Walle, Dominique. 1999. "Protecting the Poor in an Emerging Market Economy." Pp. 113–32 in *Market Reform in Vietnam: Building Institutions for Development*, edited by Dennis Rondinelli and Jennie Litvack. Westport: Quorum Books.

Vasavakul, Thaveeporn. 1996. "Politics of the Reform of State Institutions in the Postsocialist Era." Pp. 42–67 in *Vietnam Assessment: Creating a Social Investment Climate*, edited by Suiwah Leung. Singapore: Institute of Southeast Asian Studies.

———. 1998. "Vietnam's One-Party Rule and Socialist Democracy." Pp. 309–27 in *Southeast Asian Affairs 1998*. Singapore: Institute of Southeast Asian Studies.

———. 1999. "Rethinking the Philosophy of Central-Local Relations in Post-Central-Planning Vietnam." Pp. 166–95 in *Central-Local Relations in Asia-Pacific*, edited by Mark Turner. London: Macmillan.

Vickerman, Andrew. 1986. *The Fate of the Peasantry: Premature "Transition to Socialism" in the Democratic Republic of Vietnam*. Monograph. New Haven: Yale University Southeast Asian Studies.

Vietnam, Communist Party of. 1996. *VIIIth National Congress Documents*. Hanoi: The gioi Publishers.

Vietnam, General Statistical Office. 1973. *12 nam phat trien nen nong nghiep nuoc Viet Nam Dan Chu Cong Hoa, 1960–1971* [12 years of agricultural development in the Democratic Republic of Vietnam, 1960–1971]. Hanoi: Tong cuc Thong ke.

———. 1976. *Nien giam thong ke 1975* [Statistical Yearbook 1975]. Hanoi: Tong cuc Thong ke.

———. 1982. *Nien giam thong ke 1981* [Statistical Yearbook 1981]. Hanoi: Tong cuc Thong ke.

———. 1989. *Nien giam thong ke 1987* [Statistical Yearbook 1987]. Hanoi: Tong cuc Thong ke.

———. 1991. *So lieu thong ke Cong hoa xa hoi chu nghia Viet Nam* [Statistical data of the Socialist Republic of Vietnam]. Hanoi: Tong cuc Thong ke.

———. 1992. *So lieu thong ke cong nghiep Viet Nam (1985–1991)* [Vietnam's industrial statistics (1986–1991)]. Hanoi: Nha xuat ban Thong ke.

———. 1994. *Khao sat muc song dan cu Viet Nam* [Vietnam Living Standards Survey, 1992–1993]. Hanoi: Nha xuat ban Thong ke.

———. 1995. *Niem giam thong ke 1994* [Statistical Yearbook 1994]. Hanoi: Nha xuat ban Thong ke.

———. 1996a. *Dong thai va thuc trang kinh te xa hoi Viet Nam 10 nam doi moi (1986–1996)* [Impetus and present situation of Vietnam(ese) society and economy after 10 years of doi moi]. Hanoi: Nha xuat ban Thong ke.

———. 1996b. *Nien giam thong ke 1995* [Statistical Yearbook 1995]. Hanoi: Nha xuat ban Thong ke.

———. 1998. *Niem giam thong ke 1997* [Statistical Yearbook 1997]. Hanoi: Nha xuat ban Thong ke.

———. 1999a. *Results of the Socio-economic Survey of Households 1994–1997*. Hanoi: Statistical Publishing House.

———. 1999b. *Ket qua dieu tra toan bo cong nghiep nam 1998* [Results of survey on industry 1998]. Hanoi: Nha xuat ban Thong ke.

———. 1999c. *Tu lieu kinh te-xa hoi 61 tinh va thanh pho* [Socio-economic data on 61 provinces and cities]. Hanoi: Statistical Publishing House.

———. 2000a. *Nu gioi va nam gioi o Viet Nam thap ky 90* [Female and male in Vietnam in the 1990s]. Hanoi: Nha xuat ban Thong ke.

———. 2000b. *Dieu tra muc song dan cu Viet Nam* [Vietnam Living Standards Survey] 1997–1998. Hanoi: Nha xuat ban Thong ke.

———. 2001a. *Tinh hinh kinh te xa hoi Viet Nam 10 nam 1991–2000* [The economic and social conditions in Vietnam in the ten years 1991–2000]. Hanoi: Nha xuat ban Thong ke.

———. 2001b. *Population and Housing Census Vietnam 1999: Completed Census Results*. Hanoi: Statistical Publishing House.

———. 2001c. *Niem giam thong ke 2000* [Statistical Yearbook 2000]. Hanoi: Nha xuat ban Thong ke.

———. 2002. *Niem giam thong ke 2001* [Statistical Yearbook 2001]. Hanoi: Nha xuat ban Thong ke.

Vietnam, General Statistical Office, and the Ministry of Agriculture and Food Industries. 1991. *So lieu nong nghiep Viet Nam 35 nam, 1956–1990* [35 years of agricultural statistics for Vietnam, 1956–1990]. Hanoi: Nha xuat ban Tong Cuc Thong ke.

Vietnam, Government of. 1962. *Dau tranh chong doi phong bai tuc cai tao thoi quen cu xay dung nep song moi* [Struggle against bad tradition and customs, reform old habits and build a new way of life].

———. 1999. *Nhung van ban phap luat ve dan chu va quy dinh dam bao thuc hien* [Legal documents on democracy and implementation regulations]. Hanoi: Nha xuat ban Lao dong.

———. 2001. *Luat hon nhan va gia dinh* [Marriage and family law]. Hanoi: Nha xuat ban Chinh tri Quoc gia.

Vietnam, Ministry of Agriculture. 1981. "Cung co hop tac xa san xuat nong nghiep, day manh cong tac khoan" [Reinforce agriculture producer cooperatives, speed up contract work]. Pp. 32–78 in Le Thanh Nghi, *Cai tien cong tac khoan mo rong khoan san pham de thuc day san xuat cung co hop tac xa nong nghiep.* Hanoi: Nha xuat ban Su that.

Vietnam, Ministry of Interior. 1988. Mot so tinh hinh ve nguoi Viet Nam di cu ra nuoc ngoai va nguoi nuoc ngoai di cu vao Viet Nam [Some circumstances regarding the emigration of Vietnamese people and the immigration to Vietnam of foreigners]. Hanoi: Paper presented at the conference on migration, Ministry of Labor, Invalids, and Social Affairs, August.

Vietnam, Ministry of Labor, Invalids and Social Affairs. 1997. "Report on the Result of the Survey on Rural Migration in Dak Lak Province." Hanoi.

Vietnam, Ministry of Planning and Investment. 1996. *Public Investment Program 1996–2000.* Hanoi.

Vietnam, National Census Steering Committee. 1991. *Ket qua dieu tra toan dien—Completed Census Results,* vol. 2. Hanoi: Central Census Steering Committee.

———. 2000. *Tong dieu tra dan so va nha o Viet Nam 1999: ket qua dieu tra mau.* Hanoi: Nha xuat ban. The Gioi.

Vietnam, Phu Tong uy Di cu Ti nan. c1958. *Cuoc di cu lich su tai Viet Nam* [The historic migration in Vietnam]. Saigon: Phu Tong uy Di cu Ti nan.

Viet Nam Thong Tan Xa. 1995. *Nua the ky Tieng Noi Viet Nam* [A half century of the Voice of Vietnam]. Hanoi: Viet Nam Thong Tan Xa.

Vietnam, Uy ban Dan toc mien nui [Committee on Ethnic Peoples and Mountainous Regions]. 1996. *Bao cao ve di dan tu do o mien nui Viet Nam* [Report on free migration in the Vietnamese highlands]. Hanoi: Trung tam Dan so Lao dong va Xa hoi.

Vietnam, Uy ban Khoa hoc Xa hoi Viet Nam and Tinh Uy Uy ban Nhan dan Dac Lac [State Committee for Social Sciences, Party Executive Committee and People's Committee of Dac Lac]. 1990. *Van de phat trien kinh te xa hoi cac dan toc thieu so o Dac Lac* [The problem of socioeconomic development of ethnic minorities in Dac Lac Province]. Hanoi: Social Science Publishing House.

Vietnam, Vien Thong tin Khoa hoc Xa hoi. 1995. *Phap luat dan so Viet Nam, gioi thieu va binh luan* [Vietnam's population law: introduction and discussion]. Hanoi: Trung tam Khoa hoc Xa hoi va Nhan van Quoc gia.

Vietnam and International Donor Group. 2000. *Vietnam: Managing Public Resources Better,* 2 volumes. Hanoi: Vietnam Development Information Center.

Vietnam and World Bank. 1999. *Attacking Poverty.* Hanoi: World Bank-Vietnam.

Vietnam Economic Times. 2000.

Vietnam News. 1997–2001.

Vo Nhan Tri. 1990. *Vietnam's Economic Policy since 1975.* Singapore: Institute of Southeast Asian Studies.

Vo Quy. 1998. "An Overview of Environmental Problems in Vietnam." *Vietnam Studies* 3: 7–32.

Vu Dinh Loi, Bui Minh Dao, and Vu thi Hong. 2000. *So huu va su dung dat dai o cac tinh Tay nguyen* [Land ownership and land use in the Central Highlands provinces]. Hanoi: Nha xuat ban Khoa hoc xa Hoi.

Vu Quang. 1978. "Trung doan II (thanh nien Thai Binh) ra quan dau nam, khai hoang xay dung vung kinh te moi Ea Sup" [Regiment II (young people of Thai Binh) left the army at the beginning of the year, to clear land and build Ea Sup New Economic Zone]. *Dak Lak,* 12 January: 1.

Vu Tuan Anh and Tran thi Van Anh. 1997. *Kinh te ho: lich su va trien vong phat trien* [The household economy: history and development potential]. Hanoi: Nha xuat ban Khoa hoc Xa hoi.

Vu Thu Hien. 1997. *Dem giua ban ngay* [Darkness during daytime]. Westminster, Calif.: Van Nghe.

Weber. 1978. *Economy and Society.* Vol. 1. Berkeley: University of California Press.

Weller, Robert. 1999. *Alternate Civilities: Democracy and Culture in China and Taiwan.* Boulder: Westview.

Werner, Jayne. 1981a. *Peasant Politics and Religious Sectarianism: Peasant and Priest in the Cao Dai in Vietnam.* New Haven: Yale University Southeast Asian Studies.

———. 1981b. "Women, Socialism, and the Economy of Wartime Vietnam, 1960–1975." *Studies in Comparative Communism* 14: 165–90.

———. 1988. "The Problem of the District in Vietnam's Development Policy." Pp. 147–62 in *Postwar Vietnam: Dilemmas in Socialist Development,* edited by David Marr and Christine P. White. Ithaca: Cornell University Southeast Asia Program.

———. 2002. "Gender, Household, and State: Renovation (*Doi Moi*) as Social Process in Viet Nam." Pp. 29–47 in *Gender, Household, State: Doi Moi in Vietnam,* edited by J. Werner and D. Belanger. Ithaca: Cornell University Southeast Asia Program.

Werner, Jayne, and Daniele Belanger, eds. 2002. *Gender, Household, State: Doi Moi in Vietnam.* Ithaca: Cornell University Southeast Asia Program.

White, Christine Pelzer. 1985. "Agricultural Planning, Pricing Policy and Co-operatives in Vietnam." *World Development* 13 (January): 97–114.

Whitmore, John. n.d. Administrative Control of the Spirits. Ann Arbor: unpublished manuscript.

Womack, Brantly. 1992. "Reform in Vietnam: Backwards Toward the Future." *Government and Opposition* 27: 179–89.

Wong, Christine P. W. 1991. "Central-Local Relations in the Era of Fiscal Decline: The Paradox of Fiscal Decentralization in Post-Mao China." *China Quarterly* no. 128 (December).

Wong, Monica. 1993. "Gender and Poverty in Vietnam." Washington, D.C.: Education and Social Policy Discussion Paper, the World Bank.

———. 1994. "Poverty and Ethnic Minorities in Vietnam." Washington, D.C.: Education and Social Policy Discussion Paper, the World Bank.

Woodside, Alexander. 1971. *Vietnam and the Chinese Model*. Cambridge: Harvard University Press.

———. 1976. *Community and Revolution in Modern Vietnam*. Boston: Houghton Mifflin.

———. 1979. "Nationalism and Poverty in the Breakdown of Sino-Vietnamese Relations." *Pacific Affairs* 52 (fall): 318–401.

World Bank. 1994. *Vietnam: Public Sector Management and Private Sector Incentives Economic Report*. Hanoi: The World Bank.

———. 1995. *Vietnam: Poverty Assessment and Analysis*. Washington, D.C.: World Bank.

———. 1996. *Vietnam: Fiscal Decentralization and the Delivery of Rural Services: An Economic Report*, no. 15745-VN. Washington, D.C.: Country Operations Division, East Asia and Pacific Region.

World Bank, Asian Development Bank, and United Nations Development Program. 2000. *Vietnam 2010: Entering the 21st Century*. Vietnam Development Report 2001. Hanoi: World Bank.

World Bank and UK Department for International Development. 1999. *Vietnam: Voices of the Poor*. Hanoi: World Bank-Vietnam.

Xuan Binh. 1999. "Ha Noi kho vi rac" [Hanoi is suffering because of the rubbish]. *Saigon Tiep Thi* (18 September): 4.

Yan, Yunxiang. 1996. *The Flow of Gifts: Reciprocity and Social Networks in a Chinese Village*. Palo Alto, Calif.: Stanford University Press.

Yang, Mayfair Mei-hui. 1994. *Gifts, Favors, and Banquets: The Art of Social Relationships in China*. Ithaca: Cornell University Press.

Index

academic: research, 225, 273, 277, 285; researchers, 285. *See also* intellectuals

agriculture: collective, 1–2, 6–8, 9, 13, 25n7, 40–45, 57–59, 60–61, 83–84, 109, 112–13, 120, 124; during American-Vietnamese war, 6, 32; environmental issues in, 183, 191; household contract system in, 8–9, 43–44, 57–58, 60, 62–63; military plantations in, 112; policy reform in, 10, 66, 124; price support by government in, 21, 94; procurement prices in, 7–8, 58, 62; rice yield in, 25n6, 144, 148, 151, 178; shifting, 148, 174–75, 178, 191, 200n8; state and non-state sectors in, 114; state plantations in, 19, 112–13, 154, 159, 163, 174; swidden, 148, 174–75, 178, 191, 200n8; urban, 8, 119. *See also* export; household economy; water control

ancestor worship, 208, 227, 230

Annam. *See* Trung bo

aquaculture, 183

arts, 272–73. *See also* media

association: state-controlled, 268, 271, 273, 276–79, 282, 285; voluntary, 23, 35, 100, 216, 227–28, 232–33, 235–36, 280–81. *See also* civil society; mass organization; nongovernmental organization

Bac bo (Northern Vietnam): community structure in, 192–93; environmental risk in, 192–93; equality and inequality in, 4–5, 58, 64, 70, 75, 82, 84–85, 86–87, 99–100, 104; foreign direct investment in, 71–72, 89; household structure, 223n7; land distribution in, 99–100; marriage pattern, 100; population pressure in, 83, 188–89; post-marital residence in, 201, 209, 217, 222n6; poverty in, 97–98, 100. *See also* Hanoi; northern highlands; Quang Ninh; regional development; unrest; water control

banking system, 63, 64

biodiversity, 142, 148–49, 175, 176, 177–78; impact of foreign trade on, 149, 177, 188. *See also* environment

bureaucracy: corruption in, 20, 40, 45–50, 52n32, 57, 94–97, 121, 188, 196; ethnic dimension of, 155, 157–59; expertise in bureaucracy, 273; government's solutions to corruption in, 46, 48; ideology in, 273; privileges of members of, 64, 85, 273; role of the press in exposing corruption in, 282–83. *See also* law and regulations; mass organization; state; state and society

68. *See also* agriculture; banking system; capital; economic reform; economic renovation; employment; environment; export; fiscal issues; foreign aid; foreign debt; foreign direct investment; gross domestic product; household economy; industry; inflation; informal economy; investment; labor; land market; land reform; living standard; price reform; regional development; remittance; trade reform

education: contribution of overseas Vietnamese to, 289; expense coverage, 19, 97; fee exemptions for the poor, 95; gender gap in, 20, 259; media in, 288; overseas, 81, 274, 292; in precolonial period, 258–59; role of wealth in, 81; state expenditures on, 64, 95; as a strategy for upward mobility, 103; textbooks in, 285. *See also* literacy

election: 32, 36

employment, 10–11, 62–63, 101–4, 120. *See also* labor

environment: community solutions on, regional variation in, 192–93; degradation of, 142, 147–49; and development, 149, 172, 176–91, 193, 198–99; and health,172; impact of American-Vietnamese war on, 3, 174, 186–87; impact of economic growth on, 15–16; law enforcement on, 21, 188, 195–97; law on, 20–21, 152, 195, 196–97, 200n8; management of, private sector in, 197–8; policy on, 187, 194–96, 198–99; protection of, 145, 168, 177–78, 194–96, 198–99; solid waste in, 178–81, 188–90; in urbanization, 182–90; worldview on, 187. *See also* agriculture; Bac bo; deforestation; degradation; development; health; industry; inequality; land; migration; pollution; reforestation; water control

ethnic: community, social stratification in, 142, 160; diversity, 139–41; policy, 76, 114, 141; stereotypes, 154–56. *See also* bureaucracy; Central Highlands; Chinese; development; ethnic minorities; inequality; migration; northern highlands; poverty

ethnic minorities: economic changes among, 19–20, 141, 142, 143–47, 150–52, 162–65; education among, 154–55; lack of power among, 155, 157–59; law and its unintended consequences among, 200n8; migration of, 126, 142, 153–54; poverty among, 20, 26n15, 99, 142, 147, 149–51, 168; relation of, to national culture, 152–57; relation of, to the state, 151–52; religious conversion among, 142; sedentarization of, by the state, 114; social capital among, 161–62; stress among, 142. *See also* Central Highlands; Chinese; ethnic; inequality; migration; northern highlands; poverty

export, 11, *14–5*, 64; of agricultural commodities, 62, 68, 89, 126, 163; price fluctuation, 16, 90, 163

family relation, 218–20. *See also* gender, socialization; household; kinship

festival, 233, 239–40; state's perspective on, 240

film, 264–65, 269, 273, 286–87. *See also* media

fiscal issues, 59, 62, 63–64, 67, 69, 73

foreign aid: in 1975–90 period, 60, 62, 79n4, 282; in the 1990s, 12, 62, 64; to North Vietnam during American-Vietnamese war, 6, 10, 59–60

foreign debt, 120

foreign direct investment: 1987 law on, 10, 12, 62; dispersal, 89; and environmental issues, 196; importance of, 12, *15*, 62; regional differences in, 89, 68; tax incentives for, 94. *See also* investment

foreign relation: with ASEAN, 12; with Cambodia, 2, 111; with China, 1, 2, 25n9, 79n4, 111, 118, 268–69; response to Sino-Soviet split, 5; with the United States, 2, 10, 12. *See also* China; foreign aid; foreign debt; nationalism; political purge; Soviet Union; United States of America; war

funeral, 229–30; resistance to state control of, 231–33; revitalization of, 235, 253

gender: gap in education, 20, 202–4, 211, 259; inequality, 64, 221; in labor force, 202, 203 205, 207–8, 210–11, 219–20, 222; in media, 219; in religion, 203, 220, 229, 235–36; in ritual, 240; socialization, 218–19; wage gap, 211. *See also* gender relation; household; inheritance; kinship; marriage; mental illness; National Assembly; patrilineage; politics; spirit medium; women

gender relation: double moral standard in, 211–12; impact of American-Vietnamese war on, 5; impact of household structure on, 209; power and authority in, 202, 203, 205, 221, 235–36; in renovation period, 20, 23, 63, 201ff.; state influence on, 24, 207; state policy on, 209–12. *See also* gender; household; inheritance; kinship; marriage; National Assembly; patrilineage; politics; women

government: levels of, 32; local, 23–24, 190, 200n11; relation of central and local, 61, 63, 67, 73, 77–78, 159, 187–88. *See also* bureaucracy; development; economic reform; economic renovation; economy; education; health; law and regulations; regional development; state; state and society; unrest

gross domestic product (GDP), 1, 12, 11, 14, 63. *See also* living standard

Hanoi: during American-Vietnamese war, 4, 8; economy, 66, 68, 71–72; environment, 179–81, 183–85, 197, 200n11; housing in, 190; industrial concentration in, 64; land price, 91; migration to and from, 108, 125, 128, 133, 189; population, 108, 189–90; settlement pattern in, 104–5; urban regulations in, 200n2; wealth in, 81

health: environmental impact on, 183, 193; expenditures, 64, 95; expense coverage, 18, 19, 97; impact of, on poverty, 19; insurance for the poor, 21, 85, 95. *See also* environment

Ho Chi Minh city: anti-colonial activities in, 267; economy, 17–18, 66, 68, 71–72, 86; environment, 16, 179–80, 184–85; household structure, 101–4, 106n12; housing in, 4, 190; inequality in, 85, 101–4; land price, 91; migration to, 125, 129–30, 133, 137n58, 189; population, 4, 18, 83, 189–90; poverty in, 4, 83, 101–4; settlement pattern, 104–5; wealth in, 81, 83

ho khau. *See* household, registration system

homosexuality, 246

household: developmental cycle and poverty, 84, 101–4; division of labor, 204, 207–9, 217–19; head, gender of, 221–22; registration system (ho khau), 109, 116–17, 124, 130, 200n2; in relation to the state, 212; structure, 106n12, 209, 221–22. *See also* agriculture, family relation; kinship, inheritance

household economy: during command economy period, 6, 25n7, 42–43, 57–58, 61, 84. *See also* agriculture, household contract system in; industry, household sector in

industrial zones, 181–82

industry: collectivization of, 9; concentration of, 65, 68; employment trends in, 10–11, 63; firms in, 10–11, 60, 67, 68; household sector in, 7–8, 68; impact of war on, 6, 59; local, 68–69, 72; output in, 8, 60, 68; policy, 58; pollution in, 180–82, 183, 191; productivity in, 62, 63, 64; reform in, 9–10, 60, 63, 64, 68; rural, 18; state sector in, 7, 58, 59, 60, 63, 67, 68. *See also* economy; industrial zones

inequality (socioeconomic): and differential environmental risks, 192,

About the Contributors

Melanie Beresford is associate professor of economics at Macquarie University, Sydney. She is the author of *Vietnam: Politics, Economics, and Society* (1988), *National Unification and Economic Development in Vietnam* (1989), and coauthor, with Dang Phong, of *Authority Relations and Economic Decision-Making in Vietnam* (1998) and *Economic Transition in Vietnam: Foreign Aid and Trade in the Demise of a Centrally Planned Economy* (2000).

Michael DiGregorio is the Ford Foundation's program officer for education, media, arts and culture in Vietnam and Thailand. His research has followed the fortunes of village industries in the Red River delta. He is the author of *Urban Harvest: Recycling as a Peasant Industry in Northern Vietnam* (1994). His most recent work, together with Dr. C. Michael Douglass at the University of Hawaii, analyzes the urban transition now underway in Vietnam.

Andrew Hardy is a member of the Ecole Francaise d'Extreme-Orient, based in Hanoi. His research focuses on the history of Vietnamese migration, both within Vietnam and overseas. He has written two books on the Vietnamese highlands: *Red Hills: Migrants and the State in the Highlands of Vietnam*, and *Civilisations de la forêt et états modernes. L'intégration nationale des montagnards des hautes terres du Vietnam et du Cambodge* (coauthored with Mathieu Guérin, Nguyen Van Chinh, and Stan Tan Boon Hwee).

Neil Jamieson is a cultural anthropologist who is currently a visiting scholar at the Center for Southeast Asian Studies, Kyoto University. He is coauthor of "The Development Crisis in Vietnam's Mountains" (1998) and author of *Understanding Vietnam* (1993) and many articles on the process of change in twentieth-century Vietnamese culture and society.

Benedict J. Tria Kerkvliet is professor and head of the department of political and social change in the Research School of Pacific and Asian Studies, The Australian National University. His publications include *The Huk Rebellion* (1977), *Everyday Politics in the Philippines* (1990), *Vietnam's Rural Transformation* (coedited with D. Porter, 1995), and other books, articles, and book chapters on agrarian politics in Asia.

Hy V. Luong is professor and chair of the department of anthropology at the University of Toronto. His major publications include *Discursive Practices and Linguistic Meanings: The Vietnamese System of Person Reference* (1990), *Revolution in the Village: Tradition and Transformation in North Vietnam* (1992), *Ngon tu, gioi, va nhom xa hoi tu thuc tien tieng Viet* (Discourse, Gender, and Social Groups: The Vietnamese Reality) (2000, senior author), and numerous articles and book chapters on discourse, gender, sociocultural change, and political economy in Vietnam.

Shaun Kingsley Malarney is associate professor of cultural anthropology at International Christian University in Tokyo. He has conducted research in northern Vietnam since 1990 and has published articles on such topics as the transformation of funerary rites, the commemoration of war dead, and the cultural dimensions of local politics in northern Vietnam. He is also the author of *Culture, Ritual and Revolution in Vietnam* (2002). He is presently conducting research on topics related to medicine and ecology in twentieth-century northern Vietnam.

David G. Marr is professor in the Pacific and Asian history division, Australian National University. He is the author of *Vietnamese Anticolonialism, 1885–1925* (1971), *Vietnamese Tradition on Trial, 1920–1945* (1981), and *Vietnam 1945: The Quest for Power* (1995). He is the compiler of a book-length annotated bibliography of Vietnam and editor of many volumes on twentieth-century Vietnam. He is presently conducting research on state formation and political culture in twentieth-century Vietnam.

A. Terry Rambo is professor of human environment at the Center of Southeast Asian Studies, Kyoto University. A specialist on the human ecology of Southeast Asia, he has edited several volumes on the problems of development in Vietnam's uplands including "The Challenges of Development in Vietnam's Highlands" and *Bright Peaks, Dark Valleys: A Comparative Analysis of Environmental and Social Conditions in Five Communities in Vietnam's Northern Mountain Region*.

Masayuki Yanagisawa is research associate in tropical agro-ecology at the Center for Southeast Asian Studies at Kyoto University. He has conducted fieldwork in Vietnam and Thailand and published on natural resource management in Southeast Asia.

8674